THE PRAYER OF THE CHURCH

THE PRAYER OF THE CHURCH

Interim Version of the new Roman Breviary

GEOFFREY CHAPMAN

LONDON DUBLIN MELBOURNE 1970

Geoffrey Chapman Ltd
18 High Street, Wimbledon, London SW19

Geoffrey Chapman (Ireland) Ltd
5–7 Main Street, Blackrock, County Dublin

First published, English edition, 1970
ISBN 0 225 65814 3
© compilation Geoffrey Chapman Ltd

Authorised for optional use in Ireland; confirmed by
the Holy See, December 1969, (Prot. no 2905 69).

Nihil obstat: Peter Coughlan STL
Imprimatur: ✠ John Cardinal Heenan
                          Archbishop of Westminster
Westminster, 30.4.70
Made and printed in Great Britain by
C. Nicholls & Company Ltd.,
The Philips Park Press, Manchester 11.

Bound in Ireland.

Contents

Acknowledgements

Scripture passages (apart from psalms) are from the Revised Standard Version, Catholic Edition, of the complete Bible, incorporating Old Testament, New Testament and Apocrypha © 1966 by the Division of Christian Education of the National Council of the Churches of Christ in the United States of America, and used by permission.

The Psalms are translated from the Hebrew by the Grail, © The Grail (England) 1963, and published by Collins in Fontana Books, London, 1963. Used by permission.
Canticles from Luke, Exodus; Deuteronomy; 1 Samuel; 1 Chronicles; Isaiah 12;38;45; Jeremiah; Daniel; Habakkuk; Tobit; Judith; Sirach are © The Grail (England) 1963. Used by permission.

The hymns used at Midday and Night Prayer, and in the Commons, and the Hymn of Praise (Te Deum) are from Rev Joseph Connelly, *Hymns of the Roman Breviary*, published by Longman Green & Co, London, and Newman Press, Westminster, Maryland. Used by permission.

The hymns used at Sunday Morning Prayer; Monday Morning and Evening Prayer; Tuesday Readings and Morning Prayer; Wednesday Readings, Morning and Evening Prayer; Thursday Readings, Morning and Evening Prayer; Friday Readings; Saturday Readings; Office of Dead, Readings; are from James Quinn SJ, *New Hymns for All Seasons*, © James Quinn SJ, published by Geoffrey Chapman Ltd., London, 1969. Used by permission.

The prayer endings, and the Acclamation used as Refrain for the hymn at Sunday Evening Prayer I, are copyright © 1969, International Committee on English in the Liturgy, Inc. All rights reserved. Used by permission.

ACKNOWLEDGEMENTS

The Prayers (except those in the Commons) are newly translated for this publication. © 1970 Geoffrey Chapman Ltd.

The Prayers in the Commons and some of the Marian Antiphons at Night Prayer are taken from the St Andrew Bible Missal © copyright Abbaye de St André, 1966, and used by permission.

The publishers would like to express their thanks to the Benedictine Nuns of Stanbrook Abbey, England, for their invaluable assistance in compiling this volume.

Preface

The publication of this book is the result of an application to the Holy See made by the Irish Hierarchy last November. As is well known, the Breviary of the Divine Office is being radically revised by the Sacred Congregation for Divine Worship and the definitive version of this new breviary is already far advanced. It is likely to be a few years, however, before definitive vernacular versions are ready and approved.

Meanwhile sub-deacons, requiring a new breviary, will be ordained and, moreover, some priests will be anxious to avail of a new breviary as soon as possible.

The present publication has been issued to meet these pastoral needs. Authority to produce it, for use in Ireland, was given by the Holy See to the Irish Hierarchy in December last year (Prot. No. 2905/69). In virtue of this authority clerics in sacred orders in Ireland may satisfy their canonical obligation by reciting the Divine Office according to this interim breviary.

Two points need to be stressed.

Firstly, this is an *interim* breviary. It will be withdrawn from sale some time before the publication in the vernacular of the definitive breviary, probably in a few years time, and sometime after that the use of the definitive breviary of the universal Church will become obligatory.

It should be noted, of course – as the Introduction to the present volume points out – that this volume is based on the revision, not yet complete, of the Latin *editio typica* and on material prepared by the Sacred Congregation for Divine Worship and released to those hierarchies that have requested its use. The use of this breviary, therefore, will prepare the way for the use of the new Divine Office for the universal Church.

PREFACE

Secondly, the use of this particular breviary in Ireland during the interim period is *optional*. Those in sacred orders who wish to continue using the existing Roman Breviary may, of course, continue to do so.

The Divine Office is the official prayer of the Church and also a rich source of personal prayer for the individual who uses it. There is no doubt that the worthy and attentive recitation of the divine office can add a new dimension of prayer to the priest's day and there is wide agreement that this was never more necessary than at the present time. I pray that this new breviary may help to fill this great need at the present time.

✠ W. Cardinal Conway
Archbishop of Armagh
24 April 1970   Primate of all Ireland.

General Roman Calendar [1]

January

1	Octave of Christmas	
	Solemnity of Mary Mother of God	Solemnity
2	Ss Basil the Great and Gregory Nazianzen	
	Bishops and doctors of the Church	Memorial
6	Epiphany	Solemnity
7	St Raymond of Penafort, priest*	
13	St Hilary, bishop and doctor of the Church*	
17	St Anthony, abbot	Memorial
20	St Fabian, pope and martyr*	
	St Sebastian, martyr*	
21	St Agnes, virgin and martyr	Memorial
22	St Vincent, deacon and martyr*	
24	St Francis of Sales, bishop and doctor of the Church	Memorial
25	The Conversion of St Paul	Feast
26	Ss Timothy and Titus, bishops	Memorial
27	St Angela Merici, virgin*	
28	St Thomas Aquinas, priest and doctor of the Church	Memorial
31	St John Bosco, priest	Memorial
	Sunday after 6 January, Baptism of the Lord	Feast

February

2	The Presentation of the Lord	Feast
3	St Blaise, bishop and martyr*	
	St Ansgar, bishop*	
5	St Agatha, virgin and martyr	Memorial
6	Ss Paul Miki, priest, and companions, martyrs	Memorial
8	St Jerome Emilian, priest*	
10	St Scholastica, virgin	Memorial
11	Blessed Virgin Mary of Lourdes*	
14	Ss Cyril, monk, and Methodius, bishop	Memorial
17	The Seven Holy Founders of the Servite Order*	
21	St Peter Damian, bishop and doctor of the Church*	
22	The Chair of St Peter, apostle	Feast
23	St Polycarp, bishop and martyr	Memorial

March

4	St Casimir*	
7	Ss Perpetua and Felicity, martyrs	Memorial

[1]Dates not given are ferias (if they do not fall on a Sunday).

The precise date when this Calendar will go into effect will depend on the promulgation and publication of the revised Missal and Breviary. Until that time, the interim Calendar given in the supplements should be followed.

*indicates an optional Memorial.

8	St John of God, religious*	
9	St Frances of Rome, religious*	
17	St Patrick, bishop*	
18	St Cyril of Jerusalem, bishop and doctor of the Church*	
19	St Joseph, husband of the BVM	Solemnity
23	St Turibius of Mongrovejo, bishop*	
25	The Annunciation of the Lord	Solemnity

April

2	St Francis of Paola, hermit*	
4	St Isidore, bishop and doctor of the Church*	
5	St Vincent Ferrer, priest*	
7	St John Baptist de la Salle	Memorial
11	St Stanislaus, bishop and martyr*	
13	St Martin I, pope and martyr*	
21	St Anselm, bishop and doctor of the Church*	
23	St George, martyr*	
24	St Fidelis of Sigmaringen, priest and martyr*	
25	St Mark, evangelist	Feast
28	St Peter Chanel, priest and martyr*	
29	St Catherine of Siena, virgin	Memorial
30	St Pius V, pope*	

May

1	St Joseph the Worker*	
2	St Athanasius, bishop and doctor of the Church	Memorial
3	Ss Philip and James, apostles	Feast
12	Ss Nereus and Achilleus, martyrs*	
	St Pancras, martyr*	
14	St Matthias, apostle	Feast
18	St John I, pope and martyr*	
20	St Bernadine of Siena, priest*	
25	St Bede the Venerable, priest and doctor of the Church	
	St Gregory VII, pope*	
	St Mary Magdalen of Pazzi, virgin*	
26	St Philip Neri, priest	Memorial
27	St Augustine of Canterbury, bishop*	
31	Visitation of the BVM	Feast
First Sunday after Pentecost: Holy Trinity		Solemnity
Thursday after Trinity Sunday: Corpus Christi		Solemnity
Friday after Second Sunday after Pentecost: Sacred Heart		Solemnity
Saturday after Second Sunday after Pentecost:		
Immaculate Heart of the BVM*		

*indicates an optional Memorial.

June

1	St Justin, martyr	Memorial
2	Ss Marcellinus and Peter, martyrs*	
3	Ss Charles Lwanga and companions, martyrs	Memorial
5	St Boniface, bishop and martyr	Memorial
6	St Norbert, bishop*	
9	St Ephrem, deacon and doctor of the Church*	
11	St Barnabus, apostle	Memorial
13	St Anthony of Padua, priest and doctor of the Church	Memorial
19	St Romuald, abbot*	
21	St Aloysius Gonzaga, religious	Memorial
22	St Paulinus of Nola, bishop*	
	St John Fisher, bishop, and St Thomas More, martyr*	
24	Birth of St John the Baptist	Solemnity
27	St Cyril of Alexandria, bishop and doctor of the Church*	
28	St Irenaeus, bishop and martyr	Memorial
29	Ss Peter and Paul, apostles	Solemnity
30	The Protomartyrs of the Church in Rome*	

July

3	St Thomas, apostle	Feast
4	St Elizabeth of Portugal*	
5	St Anthony Mary Zaccaria, priest*	
6	St Maria Goretti, virgin and martyr*	
11	St Benedict, abbot	Memorial
13	St Henry*	
14	St Camillus of Lellis, priest*	
15	St Bonaventure, bishop and doctor of the Church	Memorial
16	Blessed Virgin Mary of Mount Carmel*	
21	St Lawrence of Brindisi, priest and doctor of the Church*	
22	St Mary Magdalene	Memorial
23	St Bridget, religious*	
25	St James, apostle	Feast
26	Ss Joachim and Anne, parents of the BVM	Memorial
29	St Martha	Memorial
30	St Peter Chrysologus, bishop and doctor of the Church*	
31	St Ignatius of Loyola	Memorial

August

1	St Alphonsus Mary de Liguori, bishop and doctor of the Church	Memorial
2	St Eusebius of Vercelli, bishop*	
4	St John Mary Vianney, priest	Memorial
5	The dedication of the basilica of St Mary*	
	Ss Sixtus II, pope, and companions, martyrs*	

*indicates an optional Memorial.

6	The Transfiguration of the Lord	Feast
7	St Dominic, priest	Memorial
8	St Cajetan, priest*	
10	St Lawrence, deacon and martyr	Feast
11	St Clare, virgin	Memorial
13	Ss Pontianus, pope and Hippolytus, priest, martyrs*	
15	The Assumption of the BVM	Solemnity
16	St Stephen of Hungary*	
19	St John Eudes, priest*	
20	St Bernard, abbot and doctor of the Church	Memorial
21	St Pius X, pope	Memorial
22	The Blessed Virgin Mary, Queen	Memorial
23	St Rose of Lima, virgin*	
24	St Bartholomew, apostle	Feast
25	St Louis*	
	St Joseph Calasanctius, priest*	
27	St Monica	Memorial
28	St Augustine, bishop and doctor of the Church	Memorial
29	The passion of St John the Baptist, martyr	Memorial

September

3	St Gregory the Great, pope and doctor of the Church	Memorial
8	The birthday of the BVM	Feast
13	St John Chrysostom, bishop and doctor of the Church	Memorial
14	The exaltation of the holy cross	Feast
15	The Blessed Virgin Mary of Sorrows	Memorial
16	Ss Cornelius, pope, and Cyprian, bishop, martyrs	Memorial
17	St Robert Bellarmine, bishop and doctor of the Church*	
19	St Januarius, bishop and martyr*	
21	St Matthew, apostle and evangelist	Feast
26	Ss Cosmas and Damian, martyrs*	
27	St Vincent de Paul, priest	Memorial
28	St Wenceslaus, martyr*	
29	Ss Michael, Gabriel and Raphael, archangels	Feast
30	St Jerome, priest and doctor of the Church	Memorial

October

1	St Theresa of the Child Jesus, virgin	Memorial
2	The holy guardian angels	Memorial
4	St Francis of Assisi	Memorial
6	St Bruno, priest*	
7	The Blessed Virgin Mary of the Rosary	Memorial
9	St Denis, bishop, and companions, martyrs*	
	St John Leonard, priest*	

*indicates an optional Memorial.

14	St Callistus I, pope and martyr*	
15	St Teresa of Avila, virgin	Memorial
16	St Hedwig, religious*	
	St Margaret Mary Alacoque, virgin*	
17	St Ignatius of Antioch, bishop and martyr	Memorial
18	St Luke, evangelist	Feast
19	Ss Isaac Jogues, priest, and companions, martyrs*	
	St Paul of the Cross, priest*	
23	St John Capistrano, priest*	
24	St Anthony Mary Claret, bishop*	
28	Ss Simon and Jude, apostles	Feast

November

1	All Saints	Solemnity
2	Commemoration of all the faithful departed	Solemnity
3	St Martin of Porres, religious*	
4	St Charles Borromeo, bishop	Memorial
9	The Dedication of the Lateran Basilica	Feast
10	St Leo the Great, pope and doctor of the Church	Memorial
11	St Martin of Tours, bishop	Memorial
12	St Josaphat, bishop and martyr	Memorial
15	St Albert the Great, bishop and doctor of the Church*	
16	St Margaret of Scotland*	
	St Gertrude, virgin*	
17	St Elizabeth of Hungary, religious	Memorial
18	Dedication of the Basilicas of Ss Peter and Paul, apostles*	
21	The Presentation of the BVM	Memorial
22	St Cecilia, virgin and martyr	Memorial
23	St Clement I, pope and martyr*	
	St Columbanus, abbot*	
30	St Andrew, apostle	Feast
	Last Sunday of the Year: Christ Universal King	Solemnity

December

3	St Francis Xavier, priest	Memorial
4	St John Damascene, priest and doctor of the Church*	
6	St Nicholas, bishop*	
7	St Ambrose, bishop and doctor of the Church	Memorial
8	Immaculate Conception of the BVM	Solemnity
11	St Damasus I, pope*	
12	St Jane Frances de Chantal, religious*	
13	St Lucy, virgin and martyr	Memorial
14	St John of the Cross, priest and doctor of the Church	Memorial
21	St Peter Canisius, priest and doctor of the Church*	
23	St John of Kety, priest*	

*indicates an optional Memorial.

25	Christmas	Solemnity
26	St Stephen, protomartyr	Feast
27	St John, apostle and evangelist	Feast
28	The Holy Innocents, martyrs	Feast
29	St Thomas Becket, bishop and martyr*	
31	St Sylvester I, pope*	

Sunday within the octave of Christmas: the Holy Family   Feast

*indicates an optional Memorial.

Introduction

PRAYER OF THE CHURCH

The 'Prayer of the Church' as this interim version of the revised Roman Breviary is called, is intended for use in those countries where it has been approved for use by the Episcopal Conference. It is presented as an alternative to the present Roman Breviary until such time as a definitive translation of the *editio typica* is ready and approved for use by the English-speaking hierarchies, and confirmed by the Holy See.

This is an interim edition, because at the time of writing the preparation of the Latin *editio typica* is not complete. The interim edition, however, is based on the revision and material prepared by the Congregation for Divine Worship for the new Roman Breviary, and released to those hierarchies that have requested its use.

Background to the revision

The discussions in the Second Vatican Council reflected a widespread desire for the reform of the Roman Breviary. It was felt that the Office should not be a burden to priests and religious, but a source of strength and nourishment for their personal life and pastoral work. Reform was also desired to make it easier to pray at least some of the Hours of the Office together with a congregation in Church. At the same time, as it stood, the Roman Breviary had its roots in the monastic choral Office. As the Constitution on the Liturgy shows, the Council was in no mind simply to reject this tradition.

It is against this background that, for five years, more than eighty experts from various parts of the world have been working on the revision of the Roman Breviary. Divided into twelve study groups and basing their work on the guidelines given in the Constitution, they submitted the various stages of the revision to the judgement of the bishops who came to the twice-yearly sessions of the Liturgy Consilium.

The principles of the reform of the Divine Office were submitted to the first Synod of Bishops in 1967, and the Synod expressed its approval. In a further attempt to sound world opinion, in 1969 the Liturgy Consilium sent out to all the bishops of the Latin rite a booklet describing the ideas underlying the revision. Two examples were offered – a feast and a feria – of how it would work out in practice. The reaction was generally favourable, although a number of useful modifications were suggested.

Briefly, we shall now consider the reformed Office as it is found in the present volume.

Meaning of the Office: Christ's prayer, Prayer of the Church

This edition is well named *Prayer of the Church*, for the Divine Office is intended to be the public and common prayer of the People of God. One of the main aims of the new Breviary is that its riches should not be reserved to priests and religious, but that it should also be a prayer book which many of the faithful could use whether in Church or on their own. This holds especially for the Morning and Evening Prayers.

From the earliest times, as the Acts of the Apostles tells us, those who had been baptized 'devoted themselves to the apostles' teaching and fellowship, to the breaking of bread and the prayers' (Acts 2:42). These 'prayers' refer both to prayer in common and to individual prayers. The Christians were doing what Jesus himself repeatedly recommended and personally practised. Certain moments of the day were set aside for prayer, and as time went on the Hours of the Office as we have them today gradually took shape.

Christ's prayer: As the expression of the Prayer of the Church, the Divine Office is a sharing in the intercession which Christ makes before the Father on our behalf. It is through him that we return to the Father, and Christians pray in his name. In this prayer of his spouse, Christ continues, through the action of his Spirit, to embrace the whole Church into his prayer to the Father on behalf of man and his world.

The heart of the Divine Office, as expressed in its psalms and canticles, readings, responses and prayers, is the dialogue between God and man which we find in the scriptures. But what the scriptures give us is not merely something from the past. In the Office, these same psalms, readings and prayers are the instrument by which God continues to speak to us and we respond. The purpose of the Office is to help achieve the union of man with God, in and through Christ. Like our faith, like the Church itself, the Office has its ground and origin in the actions and words of Jesus Christ. We can see how it is intimately linked with the celebration of the Eucharist. Together with the Mass, the Office presents us with the saving mysteries of Jesus Christ as the liturgical year gradually unfolds.

The Breviary and personal prayer

By helping to develop a prayerful and responsive attitude in the presence of God, the Breviary provides inspiration and nourishment for personal prayer, and gives this prayer an objective standard and point of reference. The Breviary in fact contains the essential values of prayer: it includes meditative openness to the Word of God, praise and thanksgiving, intercession and supplication.

Sanctification of the day

A principal purpose of the Divine Office has always been to sanctify the day. That is how the various Hours of the Office appeared in the first place. The Constitution on the Liturgy maintains this emphasis: 'that the day may be truly sanctified and that the hours themselves may be recited with spiritual advantage, it is best that each of them be prayed at a time which most corresponds with its true canonical time' (art.94). The revision of the Breviary has been drawn up with the aim of making the morning and evening prayer genuinely suited to those times of the day. It would be cutting across the whole pattern of the Breviary to celebrate the Morning Prayer in the evening and vice-versa. This brings us to a consideration of the structure of the Office itself.

GENERAL STRUCTURE OF THE OFFICE

The new Office presents us with:

> two major hours: Morning Prayer (Lauds) and Evening Prayer (Vespers);
>
> an Office of Readings (Matins) which may be said at whatever time of the day is found most suitable, or as a Vigil;
>
> a Midday Prayer (Little Hour);
>
> a Night Prayer (Compline).

NEW ARRANGEMENT OF THE BREVIARY

In the new arrangement of the Breviary the day begins with the 'O Lord, open my lips . . .', Ps 94 and its refrain (this refrain may be repeated if desired).

Morning Prayer normally begins the day. If the Office of Readings is used first, however, the introductory verse with Ps 94 and its refrain precedes the Office of Readings. Therefore 'O Lord, open my lips' (*Domine, labia mea aperies*) is not linked to Matins (Office of Readings) as in the previous Breviary, but is linked to Ps 94 which serves as an introduction to the whole of the Divine Office. All the other Hours begin with 'O God, come to my assistance . . .', 'Glory be . . .'.

Both the *Morning and Evening Prayers* have been revised with a view to making their celebration in common more feasible. The revision also seeks to adapt these Hours to the time of day in which they are to be celebrated. In the words of the Constitution on the Liturgy: 'Lauds as morning prayer and Vespers as evening prayer are the two hinges on which the daily Office turns: hence they are to be considered as the chief hours and are to be celebrated as such' (art. 89a)·

The *Office of Readings* takes on the quality of the ancient *lectio divina*. It is intended as a meditative reading of the Word of God, and prayerful reflection upon it. Since the revised patristic texts are not ready at the time of publishing this volume, the patristic readings of the present Roman Breviary will continue to be used until the *editio typica* is available. The 'Glory be to the Father . . . ' is no longer said in the response after the Readings.

In this interim version different texts for Terce, Sext and None are not given, but only a *Midday Prayer*. In the *editio typica* provision will be made both for those who want to say only one Hour and for those who want to say all three of the Little Hours. In the present edition, for those who have the obligation or desire to pray the three Little Hours, indications of the psalms (the so-called Gradual Psalms) are given on p. xxxii.

The *Night Prayer* is intended as the final prayer of the day. It may begin with an examination of conscience, and, if celebrated in common, this examination may be followed by a rite or act of penance. The psalms chosen for this Hour have the purpose of stimulating trust in God. If preferred, the weekday psalms may be replaced by those of the Sunday. This is for the convenience of those who prefer to say this Hour from memory.

MAJOR PARTS

The Psalms

One of the principal changes in the new Office is the re-distribution of the psalms over a four week period. Certain well-known psalms will be said more frequently. The grouping of many psalms of the same type is avoided. Morning, Evening and Night Prayers have psalms which express the character of the Hour.

STRUCTURE OF EACH HOUR

I. MORNING PRAYER	II. EVENING PRAYER
1. **INTRODUCTION**	
Introductory verse and psalm (Psalm 94)	Introductory verse
2. **Hymn**	
3. **Psalms**	
A 'morning' psalm Old Testament song A psalm of praise	2 psalms New Testament song
4. **Word of God** Pause of silence	
5. **Short Response**	
6. **Gospel Song**	
Song of Zechariah	Song of Virgin Mary
7. **Prayers**	
Prayer of offering, praise and work for the day	Prayers of intercession (final prayer for the faithful departed)
Pause of silence Lord's Prayer	
8. **Concluding Prayer**	
9. **Blessing**	
10. —	—

STRUCTURE OF EACH HOUR

III. OFFICE OF READINGS	IV. MIDDAY PRAYER	V. NIGHT PRAYER
1. **Introduction**		
2. **Hymn**		
3. **Psalms**		
3 psalms or sections of psalms	3 psalms or sections of psalms	1 psalm (expressing confidence and trust)
Verse (of transition to the readings)		
4. **Readings** a. Scripture Reading, Response b. Patristic or Hagiographical Reading, Response	**Word of God** Pause of Silence	
5. —	**Short Response**	
6. —	—	**Gospel Song** Song of Simeon
7. **Hymn of Praise** The 'Te Deum'	—	—
8. **Concluding Prayer**		
9. —	—	—
10. —	—	**Conclusion** Marian Antiphon

Three psalms which express salvation history at length (Ps 77, 104 and 105) are reserved to Advent, Christmas, Lent and Easter. Three psalms which do not easily lend themselves to Christian usage have been omitted (Ps 57, 82 and 108). Certain verses of other psalms have been omitted for the same reason.

The reduction in the number of psalms at each Hour, and their division into reasonable lengths is intended to make them more suitable for calm and prayerful recitation. It may well help people to use the psalms as true prayer if there is at times a short pause of silence between psalms. The titles and antiphons are also intended to help in this. A first title indicates the literal sense, while a second helps show us how the psalm may become the prayer of Christ and his Church. In a similar way the antiphons draw our attention to the meaning and content of the psalm. The antiphons are of particular value as refrains when the psalms are sung.

Hymns

In the new Breviary the hymn is always found at the beginning of each Hour. Its role is to lead those present into contemplation of the mystery being celebrated, and to foster a spirit of prayer.

Among the hymns, perhaps more than in any other part of the Office, it is difficult to find texts of universal appeal. In the present edition a selection has been offered. Some are taken from already existing translations, some are new, many of them taken from the Bible itself. An appendix suggests sources for other hymns suitable for singing. When the *editio typica* appears there will be a need for new hymns, written and composed according to the demands of the vernacular and song.

Prayers

The Divine Office celebrates the praises of the Lord. In both Jewish and Christian tradition the prayer of petition accompanied the prayer of praise and thanksgiving. One flowed from the other. St Paul recommends that 'supplications, prayers, intercessions, and thanksgivings be made for all men, for kings and all who are in high positions, that we may lead a quiet and peaceable life, godly and respectful in every way. This is good, and it is acceptable in the sight of God our Saviour, who desires all men to be saved and to come to the knowledge of the truth' (1 Tim 2:1–4).

In the new Breviary, the intercessory aspect is prominent in the prayers at Evening Prayer. In the Morning Prayer the prayers emphasize the consecration of the day and its work to God – formerly an aspect of Prime. Prayer in both these Hours are summed up in a final Our Father. The Concluding Prayer brings the Hour to a close.

The Readings

The cycle of scripture passages in the Office of Readings has been thoroughly revised. The practice of reading particular books at certain seasons is maintained (e.g. Isaiah in Advent, Acts of the Apostles at Eastertide), while in general a much richer selection of texts is offered.

Excepting the major seasons of the Church's year, there is a cycle of readings over a two year period. In this way the whole of the New Testament is read, partly at Mass and partly in the Office, over a period of two years. Through the series of Old Testament books, an overall view of the history of salvation is also provided.

The scripture readings at other Hours – entitled the *Word of God* in the present volume – are considerably shorter than those of the Office of Readings. They can of course always be lengthened. Moreover, whether in individual or community celebration, there is nothing to prevent people selecting different texts. These could be taken from those given for the Office of Readings, from the Lectionary used at Mass. or from other parts of the Sacred Scriptures. Since at Evening Prayer a New Testament Song is used, the reading should also be taken from the New Testament.

A pause of silence is suggested as a way of fostering personal understanding and acceptance of God's Word. The responses have the same purpose; these reponses are particularly effective when sung.

When the patristic or hagiographical reading is required, it will be necessary, if using this interim edition, to refer to the present Roman Breviary.

THE CALENDAR AND THE OFFICE

The new Calendar was drawn up with the aim of making the feasts and seasons of the 'temporal cycle' stand out in clear relief. This is because the 'temporal cycle' presents us directly with the mysteries of salvation. As regards the 'sanctoral cycle', the new Calendar intended to give fuller scope to devotion to particular saints in various regions of the world. The way the celebration of the Office is arranged reflects this dual aim.

In the new Calendar there are three grades of celebration of the saints:

(a) *Solemnities*, either in the universal or in a local Calendar, have precedence over the Sundays 'per annum'. They correspond to former feasts of the first class.

(b) *Feasts*, which correspond to the former feasts of the second class. These do not have precedence over the Sundays unless they are feasts of our Lord.

(c) *Memorial* days of the saints. The Calendar will specify in each case whether the memorials are obligatory or optional.

Arrangement of the Office on Solemnities

Solemnities begin with an Evening Prayer on the day before (equivalent to the former first Vespers). This Hour is referred to as Evening Prayer I.

In both Evening Prayers: the hymns, antiphons, Word of God, Short Responses and the Concluding Prayer are all proper; where no proper text is given, the texts are to be taken from the Common. In *Evening Prayer I*, the psalms are taken from the series of praise psalms (namely psalms 112, 116, 134, 145, 146, 147) in accordance with ancient tradition; the New Testament Song is indicated in the text. In *Evening Prayer II*, the first psalm is always psalm 109, and the prayers are either proper or taken from the Sunday.

Office of Readings: all the texts are proper; the Hour concludes with the Hymn of Praise (*Te Deum*) and the Concluding Prayer is proper.

Morning Prayer: the hymns, antiphons, the Word of God, Short Responses, and Concluding Prayer are all proper; where no proper text is given, the texts are to be taken from the Common. The psalms are taken from the first Sunday of the psalter. The prayers are either proper or taken from the Common.

Midday Prayer: after the hymn of the Hour, the psalms of the Sunday I Midday Prayer are used together with the proper antiphons. The Word of God and Short Response are proper.

Night Prayer: after Evening Prayer I, Night Prayer is taken from the preceding Sunday; after Evening Prayer II, Night Prayer is taken from the following Sunday (or the day itself, if the solemnity falls on a Sunday).

Arrangement of the Office on Feasts

With the exception of feasts of our Lord falling on a Sunday, feasts do not have an Evening Prayer I.

Morning Prayer, Evening Prayer, Office of Readings: everything as in the Office for Solemnities.

Midday Prayer: only the Word of God and the Prayer are proper. The rest as in the psalter.

Night Prayer: as on ferial days.

Arrangement of the Office on Memorials

As the name implies, optional Memorials may or may not be celebrated, as desired. When they are celebrated, the Office is carried out in exactly the same way as on obligatory Memorials.

INTRODUCTION

1. Celebration of Memorials on days 'per annum':

   In the Office of Readings, Morning Prayer, Evening Prayer:

   (a) the psalms and antiphons are taken from the psalter unless otherwise indicated;

   (b) the introductory psalm and refrain, the hymn, the Word of God, antiphons for the Gospel Songs, prayers, are all taken from the proper of the saint if there is one; otherwise they may be taken either from the Common or from the feria;

   (c) the Concluding Prayer is that of the saint;

   (d) in the Office of Readings, the Scripture reading and its response are taken from the cycle of readings; for the patristic or hagiographical reading, cf. the present Roman Breviary. The Hymn of Praise (*Te Deum*) is not said.

2. Celebration of Memorials in major seasons of the year:

   (a) On Sundays, Solemnities, Feasts, Ash Wednesday, Holy Week and Easter Week, Memorials are not celebrated;

   (b) on the ferias from 17 to 24 December, in the Octave of Christmas and on the ferias of Lent, there are no obligatory Memorials even in local Calendars. Memorials falling in Lent are optional Memorials.

3. Celebrations of Memorials of the Blessed Virgin Mary on Saturdays:

   On Saturdays 'per annum' the optional Memorial of the Blessed Virgin Mary may be celebrated in the same way as for the obligatory Memorial of a saint.

Using the Four Week Psalter

The first Week of the Psalter is always used from the first Sunday of Advent, Monday of the First Week of the Year (following the Baptism of the Lord), the first Sunday of Lent, and Easter Sunday.

On particular occasions psalms which seem better suited to the celebration may be chosen.

With the exception of Sundays, Solemnities, Feasts and ferias of Lent, votive Offices can be celebrated for community occasions (e.g. pilgrimages, local feasts).

HOW TO USE 'THE PRAYER OF THE CHURCH'

Organization of the Breviary

For convenience, a selection of the texts most frequently used in the Office is given on a card, which can be inserted wherever required, as well as in the first pages of the book.

The main part of the Breviary then follows, namely the distribution of the psalter over a four-week period, together with the other elements of the Hours. Each week begins with Evening Prayer I of the Sunday and goes up to Midday Prayer of the following Saturday.

This section is followed by the seven different formulas for Night Prayer.

The scripture readings follow: a selection of general responses is given, the table of references to the scripture readings for the two year cycle, and a selection of readings given *in extenso*, for use by those who are travelling.

The Common Offices, and Prayer for the Dead, conclude the main book.

Separate from the book, but able to be carried in the pockets of the wallet binding, are the Supplements, containing the Propers of the seasonal and sanctoral cycles. These indicate which texts should be used for the Solemnity, Feast or Memorial in question.

The General Roman Calendar is contained in the book itself; the Interim Roman Calendar is bound into the Supplement containing the sanctoral cycle.

INTRODUCTION

Introduction

Midday Prayer, Evening Prayer and Night Prayer open with the introductory verse 'O God, come to my assistance . . .', 'Glory be . . .', and 'Alleluia'. During Lent the 'Alleluia' is omitted, and nothing is added.

The first Hour of the day, namely either Morning Prayer or Office of Readings, opens with the introductory verse 'O God, open my lips . . .', with Psalm 94 and its refrain (this refrain may be, but is not necessarily, repeated after each stanza). The refrain will be taken either from the section 'per annum', from the Common, or from the Proper, as indicated in each case.

Conclusion

The final versicles of the different hours remain constant on all occasions.

Hymns

Besides the hymns given for the various Hours, alternative hymns are suggested in the Appendix. If desired, other hymns may be substituted for those given in the Breviary, provided they are suited to the Hour.

The refrains indicated with some of the hymns are intended for celebration of the Office in common.

At Midday Prayer on solemnities or feasts, the hymns are taken from the Psalter.

Psalms

As this book is intended for individual as well as community use, pointing has been kept to a minimum. Groups or communities however, will find no difficulty in using it chorally. In most cases psalm verses fall into couplets which may be recited alternately by each side of the choir, a pause being made between each half of the couplet. However, when the sense extends over three lines, a † has been introduced after the first line. The last syllable of a line thus marked would be slightly prolonged and the recitation proceed unbroken to the usual pause at the end of the first half of the couplet.

The psalms may be said or sung responsorially, the antiphon or refrain being repeated as often as is desired.

After each psalm the 'Glory be to the Father' is said.

Private recitation

In private recitation parts which presuppose celebration of the Office in common may be omitted, for example: refrains in the psalms and canticles, repetition in the responses, the final blessing, the invitation at the beginning of Prayers in the Morning and Evening Hours.

Prayers

In private recitation, the suggested refrain does not have to be said. When celebrated in common there are two ways of saying the Prayers:

a. after the introductory verse, the first part of the petition is said by one person, and the second part (marked with a—) is said by all;

b. or one person may say the entire petition and everyone may repeat the response (indicated by *R*).

Other responses may replace those suggested in the text.

Personal petitions may be added in the place indicated. After the last petition, everyone says the Our Father, and the celebrant or leader says the concluding prayer and final responses.

At the end of the Office of Readings, except on Sundays, solemnities, feasts or obligatory memorials, one or other of the Alternative prayers given on the card, and on p. 2, may be used instead of the Sunday prayer.

The Little Hours

For those who ''are able or wish'' to keep three periods of prayer in the course of the day, a double psalmody is proposed:

(a) the current one (from midday prayer).

(b) a complementary one.

If a single office only is celebrated, the psalmody from midday prayer is used.

If three offices are celebrated, the daily psalmody is used at one, the complementary psalmody at the other two.

The structure followed is that of midday prayer, the texts may be chosen at will.

The psalms suggested are:

in the morning: 119, 120, 121.

at midday: 122, 123, 124.

in the afternoon: 125, 126 127.

Introductory verse and psalm

Introductory verse for first prayer of the day

O Lord, open my lips.
And my mouth shall declare your praise.
Glory be to the Father, and to the Son, and to the Holy
   Spirit.
As it was in the beginning, is now, and ever shall be, world
   without end. Amen. Alleluia!

Psalm 94

This psalm may replace the Hymn *at* Morning Prayer
   Refrain: (may be repeated after each verse)

Come, ring out our joy to the Lord;
hail the rock who saves us.
Let us come before him, giving thanks,
with songs let us hail the Lord. (*R.*)

A mighty God is the Lord,
a great king above all gods.
In his hand are the depths of the earth;
the heights of the mountain are his.
To him belongs the sea, for he made it
and the dry land shaped by his hands. (*R.*)

Come in; let us bow and bend low;
let us kneel before the God who made us
for he is our God and we the people who belong to his
   pasture,
the flock that is led by his hand. (*R.*)

O that today you would listen to his voice!
'Harden not your hearts as at Meribah,
as on that day at Massah in the desert†
when your fathers put me to the test;
when they tried me, though they saw my work. (*R.*)

For forty years I was wearied of these people and I said:†
"Their hearts are astray,
these people do not know my ways."

1

Then I took an oath in my anger:
"Never shall they enter my rest." (*R.*)

Psalm 99

This psalm may replace the Hymn *at* Morning Prayer

Cry out with joy to the Lord, all the earth.†
Serve the Lord with gladness.
Come before him, singing for joy.

Know that he, the Lord, is God.†
He made us, we belong to him,
we are his people, the sheep of his flock.

Go within his gates, giving thanks.†
Enter his courts with songs of praise.
Give thanks to him and bless his name.

Indeed, how good is the Lord,†
eternal his merciful love.
He is faithful from age to age.

Office of Readings: Alternative prayers

Lord, may your words be the food that nourishes us in this life and gives us the strength to attain eternal life. Through Christ our Lord.

Lord, may your Word teach us the true way of salvation, so that when we have moderated our desire for earthly things we may more readily turn our minds to the things of heaven. Through Christ our Lord.

Hymn of Praise

We praise you, O God;
we acclaim you Lord and Master.
Everlasting Father,
all the world bows down before you.
All the angels sing your praise,
the hosts of heaven and all the angelic powers;
all the cherubim and seraphim
call out to you in unending chorus:
Holy, holy, holy

is the Lord God of angel hosts!
The heavens and the earth are filled, Lord,
with your majesty and glory.
Your praises are sung by the renowned apostles;
by all the prophets who themselves deserve our praise;
by that mighty white-robed army
who shed their blood for Christ.
And to the ends of the earth
the holy Church proclaims her faith in you:
Father, whose majesty is boundless;†
your only Son, who is true God, and who is to be adored;
the Holy Ghost, sent to be our advocate.
O Christ, the king of glory!
You alone are the Father's eternal Son.
When you were to become man
so as to save mankind,
you did not shrink back
from the chaste virgin's womb.
When you triumphantly destroyed death's sting,
you opened up to believers the kingdom of heaven.
You are now enthroned at God's right hand, in the
    Father's glory.
We believe that you will come for judgment.
We therefore implore you to grant your servants grace and
    aid,
for you to shed your precious blood for their redemption.
Admit them all to the ranks of your saints
in everlasting glory.

ad lib.

V. Be the Saviour of your faithful people, Lord;
R. Grant them your blessing, for they belong to you.
V. Be their shepherd, Lord,
R. Uphold and exalt them forever and ever.
V. Day by day we praise you, daily we acclaim you.
R. We will confess and glorify your holy name, now and for
    all eternity.

V. In your great mercy, Lord, keep us free from sin throughout this day.

R. Have mercy on us, we humbly pray; Lord, have mercy
on us.

V. May your mercy, Lord, your loving kindness, always
remain with us;

R. For we have placed our confidence in you.

Song of Zechariah   Luke 1:68–79

Blessed be the Lord, the God of Israel!
He has visited his people and redeemed them.

He has raised up for us a mighty saviour
in the house of David his servant,
as he promised by the lips of holy men,
those who were his prophets from of old.

A saviour who would free us from our foes,
from the hands of all who hate us.
So his love for our fathers is fulfilled
and his holy covenant remembered.

He swore to Abraham our father to grant us,
that free from fear, and saved from the hands of our foes,
we might serve him in holiness and justice
all the days of our life in his presence.

As for you, little child,
you shall be called a prophet of God, the Most High.
You shall go ahead of the Lord
to prepare his ways before him.

To make known to his people their salvation
through forgiveness of all their sins,
the loving-kindness of the heart of our God
who visits us like the dawn from on high.

He will give light to those in darkness,†
those who dwell in the shadow of death,
and guide us into the way of peace.

4

Song of the Virgin Mary   Luke 1:46–55

My soul glorifies the Lord,
my spirit rejoices in God, my Saviour.
He looks on his servant in her nothingness;
henceforth all ages will call me blessed.

The Almighty works marvels for me.
Holy his name!
His mercy is from age to age,
on those who fear him.

He puts forth his arm in strength
and scatters the proud-hearted.
He casts the mighty from their thrones
and raises the lowly.

He fills the starving with good things,
sends the rich away empty.

He protects Israel, his servant,
remembering his mercy,
the mercy promised to our fathers,
for Abraham and his sons for ever.

Song of Simeon   Luke 2:29–32

At last, all-powerful Master,†
you give leave to your servant
to go in peace, according to your promise.
For my eyes have seen your salvation
which you have prepared for all nations,
the light to enlighten the Gentiles
and give glory to Israel, your people.

Introduction to the Lord's Prayer
ad lib.

Let us now pray in the words Christ taught us: Our
    Father . . .

(*To Christ*) Remember us, Lord, in your kingdom, and
    teach us to say: Our Father . . .

Now in obedience to our Lord's command, let us say: Our
    Father . . .

5

Prayer endings[1]

We make our prayer (*or* We ask you this) through our Lord Jesus Christ, your Son, who lives and reigns with you and the Holy Spirit, one God, for ever and ever.

Who lives and reigns with you and the Holy Spirit, one God, for ever and ever.

You live and reign with the Father and the Holy Spirit, one God, for ever and ever.

Through Christ our Lord.

Who lives and reigns with you for ever and ever.

You live and reign for ever and ever.

The Psalter

Sunday I

EVENING PRAYER I

O God, come to my assistance.
Lord, make haste to help me.
Glory be to the Father, and to the Son, and to the Holy
Spirit.
As it was in the beginning, is now, and ever shall be, world
without end. Amen. Alleluia!

Hymn   2 Tim 2:11–13

R. Christ has died,
Christ is risen,
Christ will come again.[1]

If we have died with him,
we shall also live with him;
If we endure,
we shall also reign with him. (*R.*)

If we deny him,
he will also deny us;
If we are faithless, he remains faithful—
for he cannot deny himself. Alleluia! (*R.*)

Psalmody

Psalm 140   **Evening prayer for protection**

*The smoke of the incense rose with the prayers of the
saints from the hand of the angel before God* (Rev 8:4).

Ant. Let my prayer come before you like incense,
    the raising of my hands like an evening oblation.

I have called to you, Lord; hasten to help me!
Hear my voice when I cry to you.

Let my prayer come before you like incense,
the raising of my hands like an evening oblation.

Lord, set a guard over my mouth;
keep watch at the door of my lips!
Do not turn my heart to things that are wrong,
to evil deeds with men who are sinners.

Never allow me to share in their feasting.
If a good man strikes or reproves me it is kindness;
but let the oil of the wicked not anoint my head.
Let my prayer be ever against their malice.

Their princes were thrown down by the side of the rock:
then they understood that my words were kind.
As a millstone is shattered to pieces on the ground,
so their bones were strewn at the mouth of the grave.

To you, Lord God, my eyes are turned:
in you I take refuge; spare my soul!
From the trap they have laid for me keep me safe:
keep me from the snares of those who do evil . . .

Ant. Let my prayer come before you like incense,
the raising of my hands like an evening oblation.

Psalm 141   **Prayer of a man deserted by his friends**

*All deserted me . . . but the Lord stood by me and gave me
strength (2 Tim 4:16–17).*

Ant. The Lord is all I have left
in the land of the living.

With all my voice I cry to the Lord,
with all my voice I entreat the Lord.
I pour out my trouble before him;†
I tell him all my distress while my spirit faints within me.
But you, O Lord, know my path.

On the way where I shall walk
they have hidden a snare to entrap me.

Look on my right and see:
there is not one who takes my part.
I have no means of escape,
not one who cares for my soul.

I cry to you, O Lord.†
I have said: 'You are my refuge,
all I have left in the land of the living.'
Listen then to my cry
for I am in the depths of distress.

Rescue me from those who pursue me
for they are stronger than I.
Bring my soul out of this prison
and then I shall praise your name.
Around me the just will assemble
because of your goodness to me.

Ant. The Lord is all I have left
in the land of the living.

Phil 2:6–11   **Song of the Easter mystery**

Ant. Christ died for our sins
and rose that we might live.

Though he was in the form of God,
Jesus did not count equality with God a thing to be grasped.

R. Jesus Christ is Lord
to the glory of God the Father!

He emptied himself,†
taking the form of a servant,
being born in the likeness of men. (*R.*)

And being found in human form,†
he humbled himself and became obedient unto death,
even death on a cross. (*R.*)

Therefore God has highly exalted him
and bestowed on him the name which is above every
name. (*R.*)

That at the name of Jesus every knee should bow,
in heaven and on earth and under the earth. (*R.*)

And every tongue confess that Jesus Christ is Lord,
to the glory of God the Father. (*R.*)

Ant. Christ died for our sins
and rose that we might live.

Word of God   Rom 11:33–36
O the depth of the riches and wisdom and knowledge of
God! How unsearchable are his judgments and how
inscrutable his ways!
'For who has known the mind of the Lord,
or who has been his counsellor?'
'Or who has given a gift to him
that he might be repaid?'
For from him and through him and to him are all things.
To him be glory for ever. Amen.

Short Response
Our Lord is great
and almighty. (*Repeat*)
V. His wisdom can never be measured.
R. Our Lord is great and almighty.
V. Glory be to the Father, and to the Son, and to the Holy
Spirit.
Our Lord is great
and almighty.

Song of the Virgin Mary
Ant. Blessed are you among women,
and blessed is the fruit of your womb.

Prayers
God is the joy of all who hope in him. Let us entreat him
saying:

R. Look upon us, and hear us, O Lord.

O God, the source of all goodness, from whom come all good things,
—make us always mindful of the marvellous deeds you have done. (*R.*)

You have called men to be heralds of the good news of salvation,
—may they give tireless and faithful witness to the mystery of your kingdom. (*R.*)

O King of peace, may your spirit enter into the hearts of those who rule the nations:
—may their eyes turn with compassion towards the poor and afflicted. (*R.*)

May the hungry be fed,
—may the gospel be preached to the poor. (*R.*)

Other prayers may be added

May all who die in your love be sharers of heavenly blessedness,
—with the Virgin Mary and all your saints. (*R.*)

Our Father . . .

Concluding prayer of the Sunday

May the Lord bless us,
may he keep us from all evil
and lead us to life everlasting.
Amen.
Let us bless the Lord.
R. Thanks be to God.

OFFICE OF READINGS

O God, come to my assistance.
Lord, make haste to help me.
Glory be to the Father, and to the Son, and to the Holy Spirit.

As it was in the beginning, is now, and ever shall be, world without end. Amen. Alleluia!

Or, if used as first prayer of the day: O Lord, open my lips . . .

Hymn

R. Alleluia! Christ is risen, alleluia!

R. (*in Lent*) If we have died with him, we shall also live with him.

I will sing to the Lord, glorious his triumph!
Horse and rider he has thrown into the sea.
Lord, you are great, you are glorious,
wonderful in strength, none can conquer you.
God has arisen, and his foes are scattered;
those who hate him have fled before him. (*R.*)

He has burst the gate of bronze
and shattered the iron bars.
This God of ours is a God who saves;
the Lord our God holds the keys of death.
This is the day which the Lord has made;
let us rejoice and be glad. (*R.*)

Awake, O sleeper, and rise from the dead,
and Christ shall give you light.
For he has been raised from the dead,
never to die any more.
God has not left his soul among the dead,
not let his beloved know decay. (*R.*)

The Lord is risen from the tomb
who hung for us upon the tree.
Beasts of the field, do not be afraid;
the pastures of the wilderness are green again.
The tree bears its fruit once more,
vine and fig tree yield abundantly. (*R.*)

Psalmody

Psalm 1   **Two ways of living**

Blessed are those who hear the word of God and keep it (Luke 11:28).

Ant. Your cross, O Lord, is the tree of life, alleluia.

Happy indeed is the man
who follows not the counsel of the wicked;
nor lingers in the way of sinners
nor sits in the company of scorners,
but whose delight is the law of the Lord
and who ponders his law day and night.

He is like a tree that is planted
beside the flowing waters,
that yields its fruit in due season
and whose leaves shall never fade;
and all that he does shall prosper.
Not so are the wicked, not so!

For they like winnowed chaff
shall be driven away by the wind.
When the wicked are judged they shall not stand,
nor find room among those who are just;
for the Lord guards the way of the just
but the way of the wicked leads to doom.

Ant. Your cross, O Lord, is the tree of life, alleluia.

Psalm 2   **The Messianic kingship: warning to rulers and nations**

Truly there were gathered together against your holy servant Jesus, whom you anointed, both Herod and Pontius Pilate, with the Gentiles and the peoples of Israel (Acts 4:27)

Ant. Behold the king whom I have set up on my holy mountain:
he is my well-beloved Son, alleluia.

Why this tumult among nations,
among peoples this useless murmuring?

They arise, the kings of the earth,
princes plot against the Lord and his Anointed.
'Come, let us break their fetters,
come, let us cast off their yoke.'

He who sits in the heavens laughs;
the Lord is laughing them to scorn.
Then he will speak in his anger,
his rage will strike them with terror.
'It is I who have set up my king
on Zion, my holy mountain.'

I will announce the decree of the Lord:†
The Lord said to me: 'You are my Son.
It is I who have begotten you this day.
Ask and I shall bequeath you the nations,
put the ends of the earth in your possession.
With a rod of iron you will break them,
shatter them like a potter's jar.'

Now, O kings, understand,
take warning, rulers of the earth;
serve the Lord with awe
and trembling, pay him your homage
lest he be angry and you perish,
for suddenly his anger will blaze.

All: Blessed are they who put their trust in God.

Ant. Behold the king whom I have set up on my holy
mountain:
he is my well-beloved Son, alleluia.

Psalm 3   **Confidence under persecution**

*Jesus slept and woke from the sleep of death, for the Lord
upheld him* (St Irenaeus).

Ant. You, Lord, are a shield about me,
my glory, who lift up my head.

How many are my foes, O Lord!
How many are rising up against me!

15

How many are saying about me:
'There is no help for him in God.'

But you, Lord, are a shield about me,
my glory, who lift up my head.
I cry aloud to the Lord.
He answers from his holy mountain.

I lie down to rest and I sleep.
I wake, for the Lord upholds me.
I will not fear even thousands of people
who are ranged on every side against me.

Arise, Lord; save me, my God,†
you who strike all my foes on the mouth,
you who break the teeth of the wicked!
O Lord of salvation,
bless your people!

Ant. You, Lord, are a shield about me,
   my glory, who lift up my head.

V. I yearn for your saving help;
R. I hope in your word.

Readings

(Hymn of Praise)
Prayer of the Sunday

MORNING PRAYER

Introductory verse and psalm
O Lord, open my lips.
And my mouth shall declare your praise.
Glory be to the Father, and to the Son, and to the Holy Spirit.
As it was in the beginning, is now, and ever shall be, world without end. Amen. Alleluia!

Psalm 94
Refrain: Come, let us worship the Lord our God.
Or, if not used as first prayer of the day: O God, come to my assistance

Hymn

Sing, all creation, sing to God in gladness!
Joyously serve him, singing hymns of homage!
Chanting his praises, come before his presence!
Praise the Almighty!

Know that our God is Lord of all the ages!
He is our maker; we are all his creatures,
People he fashioned, sheep he leads to pasture!
Praise the Almighty!

Enter his temple, ringing out his praises!
Sing in thanksgiving as you come before him!
Blessing his bounty, glorify his greatness!
Praise the Almighty!

Great in his goodness is the Lord we worship;
Steadfast his kindness, love that knows no ending!
Faithful his word is, changeless, everlasting!
Praise the Almighty!

Psalmody

Psalm 62   **Longing for God**

*The water that I shall give him will become in him a spring
of water welling up to eternal life* (John 4:14).

Ant. I will bless you, O my God,
    in your name I lift up my hands, alleluia.

O God, you are my God, for you I long;
for you my soul is thirsting.
My body pines for you
like a dry, weary land without water.
So I gaze on you in the sanctuary
to see your strength and your glory.

For your love is better than life,
my lips will speak your praise.
So I will bless you all my life,

in your name I will lift up my hands.
My soul shall be filled as with a banquet,
my mouth shall praise you with joy.

On my bed I remember you.
On you I muse through the night
for you have been my help;
in the shadow of your wings I rejoice.
My soul clings to you;
your right hand holds me fast.

Those who seek to destroy my life
shall go down to the depths of the earth.
They shall be put unto the power of the sword
and left as the prey of the jackals.
But the king shall rejoice in God;†
all that swear by him shall be blessed
for the mouth of liars shall be silenced.

Ant. I will bless you, O my God,
in your name I lift up my hands, alleluia.

Dan 3:57–88, 56   **Song of the universe**

*Creation waits with eager longing for God who is blessed
for ever* (Rom 8:19; 1:25)

Ant. You fountains and springs, and all you creatures that
live in the waters, O bless the Lord, alleluia.

O all you works of the Lord, O bless the Lord.
R. To him be highest glory and praise for ever.

And you, angels of the Lord, O bless the Lord.
R. To him be highest glory and praise for ever.

And you, the heavens of the Lord, O bless the Lord.
And you, clouds of the sky, O bless the Lord.
And you, all armies of the Lord, O bless the Lord.
R. To him be highest glory and praise for ever.

And you, sun and moon, O bless the Lord.
And you, the stars of the heav'ns, O bless the Lord.

And you, showers and rain, O bless the Lord.
R. To him be highest glory and praise for ever.

And you, all you breezes and winds, O bless the Lord.
And you, fire and heat, O bless the Lord.
And you, cold and heat, O bless the Lord.
R. To him be highest glory and praise for ever.

And you, showers and dew, O bless the Lord.
And you, frosts and cold, O bless the Lord.
And you, frost and snow, O bless the Lord.
R. To him be highest glory and praise for ever.

And you, night-time and day, O bless the Lord.
And you, darkness and light, O bless the Lord.
And you, lightning and clouds, O bless the Lord.
R. To him be highest glory and praise for ever.

O let the earth bless the Lord.
R. To him be highest glory and praise for ever.

And you, mountains and hills, O bless the Lord.
And you, all plants of the earth, O bless the Lord.
And you, fountains and springs, O bless the Lord.
R. To him be highest glory and praise for ever.

And you, rivers and seas, O bless the Lord.
And you, creatures of the sea, O bless the Lord.
And you, every bird in the sky, O bless the Lord.
And you, wild beasts and tame, O bless the Lord.
R. To him be highest glory and praise for ever.

And you, children of men, O bless the Lord.
R. To him be highest glory and praise for ever.

O Israel, bless the Lord. O bless the Lord.
And you, priests of the Lord, O bless the Lord.
And you, servants of the Lord, O bless the Lord.
R. To him be highest glory and praise for ever.

And you spirits and souls of the just, O bless the Lord,
And you holy and humble of heart, O bless the Lord.

Ananias, Azarias, Mizael, O bless the Lord.
R. To him be highest glory and praise for ever.

May you be blessed, O Lord, in the heavens.
R. To you be highest glory and praise for ever.

Ant. You fountains and springs, and all you creatures that live in the waters, O bless the Lord, alleluia.

Psalm 149   **Praise to the God of victories**

He who conquers and who keeps my works until the end, I will give him power over the nations (Rev 2:26).

Ant. Let the people of God exult in their king.

Sing a new song to the Lord,
his praise in the assembly of the faithful.
Let Israel rejoice in its Maker,
let Zion's sons exult in their king.
Let them praise his name with dancing
and make music with timbrel and harp.

For the Lord takes delight in his people.
He crowns the poor with salvation.
Let the faithful rejoice in their glory,
shout for joy and take their rest.
Let the praise of God be on their lips
and a two-edged sword in their hand,

to deal out vengeance to the nations
and punishment on all the peoples;
to bind their kings in chains
and their nobles in fetters of iron;
to carry out the sentence pre-ordained:
this honour is for all his faithful.

Ant. Let the people of God exult in their king.

Word of God   Rev 7:10, 12
Salvation belongs to our God who sits upon the throne,
and to the Lamb!
Blessing and glory and wisdom

and thanksgiving and honour and power and might
be to our God for ever and ever! Amen.

Short Response

Christ, son of the living God,
have mercy on us.
V. You who are seated at the right hand of the Father,
R. Have mercy on us.
V. Glory be to the Father, and to the Son, and to the
Holy Spirit.
Christ, son of the living God,
have mercy on us.

Song of Zechariah

Ant. All nations shall come to adore you,
for you alone are holy.

Prayers

Christ our Lord is the true sun which never sets, the light
that enlightens every man who comes into the world. Let
us turn to him in prayer:

R. Lord, you are our life and our salvation.

We thank you for this day which is just beginning, Lord,
creator of the heavens, and we accept with gratitude this
mark of your love.
—We commemorate your resurrection. (*R.*)

May your spirit teach us to do your will today,
—and may your wisdom guide us. (*R.*)

Help us to share with joy in the assembly of your Church on
this Sunday,
—gathered around your table, nourished by your word and
your Body. (*R.*)

We give you thanks from our hearts,
—for your blessings towards us are beyond number. (*R.*)
Other prayers may be added
Our Father . . .

Concluding prayer of the Sunday

May the Lord bless us,
may he keep us from all evil
and lead us to life everlasting.
Amen.

Let us bless the Lord.
R. Thanks be to God.

MIDDAY PRAYER

O God, come to my assistance . . .
Glory be . . .

Hymn
Holy Spirit,
one with the Father and the Son,
deign at this hour to come down on us without delay,
and pour out your graces over our soul.

Let mouth, tongue, soul, thought and strength
make your praise resound.
Let our love be set aflame by the fire of your love,
and its heat in turn enkindle love in our neighbours.

Grant this, most loving Father,
and you, the only Son, equal to the Father,
and, with the Spirit, the Paraclete,
reigning through the ages. Amen.

Psalmody

Psalm 117   **Thanksgiving to God in the temple for his gift of salvation**

This is the stone which was rejected by you builders but which has become the head of the corner (Acts 4:11).

Ant. This day was made by the Lord, allelulia.

I
Give thanks to the Lord for he is good,
for his love has no end.

Let the sons of Israel say:
'His love has no end.'
Let the sons of Aaron say:
'His love has no end.'
Let those who fear the Lord say:
'His love has no end.'

I called to the Lord in my distress;
he answered and freed me.
The Lord is at my side; I do not fear.
What can man do against me?
The Lord is at my side as my helper:
I shall look down on my foes.

It is better to take refuge in the Lord
than to trust in men:
it is better to take refuge in the Lord
than to trust in princes. . . .
I was thrust, thrust down and falling
but the Lord was my helper.

II
The Lord is my strength and my song;
he was my saviour.
There are shouts of joy and victory
in the tents of the just.

The Lord's right hand has triumphed;
his right hand raised me up.
The Lord's right hand has triumphed;
I shall not die, I shall live and recount his deeds.
I was punished, I was punished by the Lord,
but not doomed to die.

III
Open to me the gates of holiness:
I will enter and give thanks.
This is the Lord's own gate
where the just may enter.

I will thank you for you have given answer
and you are my saviour.

The stone which the builders rejected
has become the corner stone.
This is the work of the Lord,
a marvel in our eyes.
This day was made by the Lord;
we rejoice and are glad.

O Lord, grant us salvation;
O Lord, grant success.
Blessed in the name of the Lord
is he who comes.
We bless you from the house of the Lord;
the Lord God is our light.

Go forward in procession with branches
even to the altar.
You are my God, I thank you.
My God, I praise you.
Give thanks to the Lord for he is good;
for his love has no end.

Ant. This day was made by the Lord, alleluia.

Word of God   1 Jn 4:16
We know and believe the love God has for us. God is love,
and he who abides in love abides in God, and God abides in
him.

V. The Lord our God, the Almighty, reigns.
R. Let us rejoice and exult and give him the glory.

Prayer of the Sunday
V. Let us bless the Lord.
R. Thanks be to God.

EVENING PRAYER II

O God, come to my assistance.
Lord, make haste to help me.
Glory be to the Father, and to the Son, and to the Holy Spirit.
As it was in the beginning, is now, and ever shall be, world without end. Amen. Alleluia!

Hymn

R. Alleluia! Christ is risen, alleluia!

or

R. (*in Lent*) I have power to lay down my life,
    and I have power to take it again.

I have trodden the wine press alone,
and from the peoples no one was with me.
I have laid down my life of my own free will,
and by my own power I have taken it up anew.
Fear not, I am the first and the last;
I am the living one. (*R.*)

Was it not ordained that the Christ should suffer,
and so enter into his glory?
Upon him was the chastisement that made us whole,
and with his stripes we are healed.
It was the will of the Lord to bruise him;
he has offered his life in atonement. (*R.*)

By his holy and glorious wounds
may Christ the Lord guard us and keep us.
If we have died with him, we shall also live with him;
if we endure, we shall also reign with him.
Christ yesterday and today,
the beginnings of all things and their end.
Alpha and Omega;
all time belongs to him, and all the ages. (*R.*)

Psalmody

Psalm 109   **The Messiah, king, priest and judge**

*He must reign until he has put all his enemies under his
feet* (1 Cor 15:25).

Ant. The Lord said to my Lord: 'Sit on my right.'

The Lord's revelation to my Master:†
'Sit on my right:
I will put your foes beneath your feet.'

The Lord will send from Zion your sceptre
    of power:
rule in the midst of all your foes.

A prince from the day of your birth†
on the holy mountains;
from the womb before the daybreak I begot you.

The Lord has sworn an oath he will not change.†
'You are a priest for ever,
a priest like Melchizedeck of old.'

The Master standing at your right hand
will shatter kings in the day of his great wrath . . .

He shall drink from the stream by the wayside
and therefore he shall lift up his head.

Ant. The Lord said to my Lord: 'Sit on my right.'

Psalm 113A   **The wonders of the Exodus**

*All of us who have been baptized into Christ Jesus were
baptized into his death* (Rom 6:3).

Ant. Living water will spring up before the face of the Lord,
    alleluia!

When Israel came forth from Egypt,
Jacob's sons from an alien people,
Judah became the Lord's temple,
Israel became his kingdom.

The sea fled at the sight:
the Jordan turned back on its course,
the mountains leapt like rams
and the hills like yearling sheep.

Why was it, sea, that you fled,
that you turned back, Jordan, on your course?
Mountains, that you leapt like rams,
hills, like yearling sheep?

Tremble, O earth, before the Lord,
in the presence of the God of Jacob,
who turns the rock into a pool
and flint into a spring of water.

Ant. Living water will spring up before the face of the Lord,
alleluia.

OUTSIDE LENT

Rev 19:1, 2, 5-8   **Wedding song of the Lamb**

Ant. The Lord is king, let earth rejoice, alleluia!

R. Alleluia, alleluia!
Salvation and glory and power
belong to our God, alleluia!
His judgments are true
and just.
R. Alleluia, alleluia!

Praise our God,
all you his servants, alleluia!
You who fear him,
small and great.
R. Alleluia, alleluia!

The Lord our God,
the Almighty, reigns, alleluia!
Let us rejoice and exult
and give him the glory.
R. Alleluia, alleluia!

The marriage of the Lamb
has come, alleluia!
And his bride
has made herself ready.
R. Alleluia, alleluia!

It was granted her
to be clothed, alleluia!
with fine linen
bright and pure.
R. Alleluia, alleluia!

Ant. The Lord is king, let earth rejoice, alleluia!

LENT

1 Pet 2:21–24   **New Testament Song of the suffering Servant**

Ant. For our sake God made him to be sin who knew no sin,
   so that in him we might become the righteousness of God.

Christ suffered for you,†
leaving you an example
that you should follow in his steps.
R. By his wounds you have been healed.

He committed no sin;
no guile was found on his lips.
When he was reviled,
he did not revile in return. (*R.*)

When he suffered,
he did not threaten;
but he trusted to him
who judges justly. (*R.*)

He himself bore our sins
in his body on the tree,
that we might die to sin
and live to righteousness. (*R.*)

By his wounds you have been healed.†
For you were straying like sheep,

but have now returned to the Shepherd and Guardian
of your souls. (*R.*)

Ant. For our sake God made him to be sin who knew no sin,
so that in him we might become the righteousness of God.

Word of God
2 Cor 1:3–4

Blessed be the God and Father of our Lord Jesus Christ,
the Father of mercies and God of all comfort, who comforts
us in all our affliction, so that we may be able to comfort
those who are in any affliction, with the comfort with which
we ourselves are comforted by God.

Short Response

I will give you glory,
O God my King.
V. I will bless your name for ever.
R. O God my King.
V. Glory be to the Father, and to the Son, and to the Holy
Spirit.
I will give you glory,
O God my King.

Song of the Virgin Mary

Ant. I will rejoice in God, my Saviour and my strength.

Prayers

Let us pray to Christ the Lord, for he is our head and we
the living parts of his body:

R. Lord, may your kingdom come.

Strengthen your Church throughout the world; give her
ever deeper roots in men's hearts,
—for she is the sacrament of the unity of the human race,
the mystery of the salvation which you offer to all peoples.
(*R.*)

Guide the college of bishops in union with the Pope,
—so that they may work together in unity, charity and peace
for the good of the Church. (*R.*)

Unite all Christians ever more intimately to you, for you are the divine Lord of all;
—may they proclaim your reign through the witness of their lives. (*R.*)

Grant peace to the world, we pray,
—so that men everywhere may live in reconciliation and harmony. (*R.*)

Other prayers may be added.

Give to the dead the glory of the final resurrection,
—and may we, too, share with them in eternal life. (*R.*)

Our Father . . .

Concluding prayer of the Sunday

May the Lord bless us,
may he keep us from all evil
and lead us to life everlasting.
Amen.

Let us bless the Lord.
R. Thanks be to God.

Monday I

OFFICE OF READINGS

O God, come to my assistance.
Lord, make haste to help me.
Glory be to the Father, and to the Son, and to the Holy Spirit.
As it was in the beginning, is now, and ever shall be, world without end. Amen. Alleluia!

Or, if used as first prayer of the day: O Lord, open my lips . . .

Hymn   1 Cor 13:4–10, 12–13

Love is patient and kind:†
love is not jealous or boastful;
it is not arrogant or rude.

R. Faith, hope and love abide, but the greatest of these is love.

Love does not insist on its own way,
it is not irritable or resentful;
it does not rejoice at wrong,
but rejoices in the right. (*R.*)

Love bears all things,
believes all things,
hopes all things,
endures all things. (*R.*)

Love never ends;†
as for prophecies,
they will pass away;
as for tongues,
they will cease;
as for knowledge,
it will pass away. (*R.*)

For our knowledge is imperfect
and our prophecy is imperfect;

but when the perfect comes,
the imperfect will pass away. (R.)

Now I know in part;
then I shall understand fully,
even as I have been fully understood.
So faith, hope, love abide, these three,
but the greatest of these is love. (R.)

Psalmody

Psalm 9A   Thanksgiving after victory

He shall come to judge the living and the dead.

I

Ant. God, the refuge of the poor in times of distress.

I will praise you, Lord, with all my heart;
I will recount all your wonders.
I will rejoice in you and be glad,
and sing psalms to your name, O Most High.

See how my enemies turn back,
how they stumble and perish before you.
You upheld the justice of my cause;
you sat enthroned, judging with justice.

You have checked the nations, destroyed the wicked;
you have wiped out their name for ever and ever.
The foe is destroyed, eternally ruined.
You uprooted their cities; their memory has perished.

But the Lord sits enthroned for ever.
He has set up his throne for judgment;
he will judge the world with justice,
he will judge the peoples with his truth.

For the oppressed let the Lord be a stronghold,
a stronghold in times of distress.
Those who know your name will trust you:
you will never forsake those who seek you.

Ant. God, the refuge of the poor in times of distress.

II

Ant. I will recount all your praise at the gates of the city of
Zion.

Sing psalms to the Lord who dwells in Zion.
Proclaim his mighty works among the peoples;
for the Avenger of blood has remembered them,
and has not forgotten the cry of the poor.

Have pity on me, Lord, see my sufferings,
you who save me from the gates of death;
that I may recount all your praise at the gates of the city
of Zion
and rejoice in your saving help.

The nations have fallen in the pit which they made,
their feet caught in the snare they laid.
The Lord has revealed himself, and given judgment.
The wicked are snared in the work of their own hands . . .
For the needy shall not always be forgotten
nor the hopes of the poor be in vain.

Arise, Lord, let men not prevail!
Let the nations be judged before you.
Lord, strike them with terror,
let the nations know they are but men.

Ant. I will recount all your praise at the gates of the city of
Zion.

Psalm 6   Prayer of a man chastised by God

Now is my soul troubled . . . Father, save me from this
hour (John 12:27)

Ant. Save me, O Lord, in your merciful love.

Lord, do not reprove me in your anger;
punish me not in your rage.
Have mercy on me, Lord, I have no strength;†
Lord, heal me, my body is racked;
my soul is racked with pain.

33

But you, O Lord . . . how long?
Return, Lord, rescue my soul.
Save me in your merciful love;†
for in death no one remembers you;
from the grave, who can give you praise?

I am exhausted with my groaning;†
every night I drench my pillow with tears;
I bedew my bed with weeping.
My eye wastes away with grief;
I have grown old surrounded by my foes.

Leave me, all you who do evil;
for the Lord has heard my weeping.
The Lord has heard my plea;
The Lord will accept my prayer.
All my foes will retire in confusion,
foiled and suddenly confounded.

Ant. Save me, O Lord, in your merciful love.

V. Treat your servant with love
R. And teach me your statutes.

Readings

Prayer of the day
Or alternative prayer

MORNING PRAYER

Introductory verse and Psalm
O Lord, open my lips.
And my mouth shall declare your praise.
Glory be to the Father, and to the Son, and to the Holy
Spirit.
As it was in the beginning, is now, and ever shall be, world
without end. Amen. Alleluia!

Psalm 94
Refrain: Come, ring out our joy to the Lord.

Or, if not used as first prayer of the day: O God, come to my assistance . . .

Hymn

This day God gives me
Strength of high heaven,
Sun and moon shining,
Flame in my hearth,
Flashing of lightning,
Wind in its swiftness,
Deeps of the ocean,
Firmness of earth.

This day God sends me
Strength as my steersman,
Might to uphold me,
Wisdom as guide.
Your eyes are watchful,
Your ears are listening,
Your lips are speaking,
Friend at my side.

God's way is my way,
God's shield is round me,
God's host defends me,
Saving from ill.
Angels of heaven,
Drive from me always
All that would harm me,
Stand by me still.

Rising I thank you,
Mighty and strong One,
King of creation,
Giver of rest,
Firmly confessing
Threeness of Persons,
Oneness of Godhead,
Trinity blest.

Psalmody

Psalm 5   **Morning prayer of the just man grappling with his enemies**

'In the morning you hear me' is taken to refer to Christ's
resurrection.

Ant. Attend to the sound of my cries,
   my King and my God.

To my words give ear, O Lord,
give heed to my groaning.
Attend to the sound of my cries,
my King and my God.

It is you whom I invoke, O Lord.
In the morning you hear me;
in the morning I offer you my prayer,
watching and waiting.

You are no God who loves evil;
no sinner is your guest.
The boastful shall not stand their ground
before your face.

You hate all who do evil:
you destroy all who lie.
The deceitful and bloodthirsty man
the Lord detests.

But I through the greatness of your love
have access to your house.
I bow down before your holy temple,
filled with awe.

Lead me, Lord, in your justice,†
because of those who lie in wait;
make clear your way before me.

No truth can be found in their mouths,
their heart is all mischief,
their throat a wide open grave,
all honey their speech.

Declare them guilty, O God.
Let them fail in their designs.
Drive them out for their many offences;
for they have defied you.

All those you protect shall be glad
and ring out their joy.
You shelter them; in you they rejoice,
those who love your name.

It is you who bless the just man, Lord:
you surround him with favour as with a shield.

Ant. Attend to the sound of my cries,
   my King and my God.

1 Chron 29:10–13   **Song of David**

   Blessed be the God and Father of our Lord Jesus Christ
   (Eph 1:3)

Ant. We praise your glorious name, O God.

Blessed are you, O Lord,†
the God of Israel our father,
for ever, for ages unending.

Yours, Lord, are greatness and power,†
and splendour, triumph and glory.
All is yours, in heaven and earth.

Yours, O Lord, is the kingdom,†
you are supreme over all.
Both honour and riches come from you.

You are the ruler of all,†
from your hand come strength and power,
from your hand come greatness and might.

And so, our God, we thank you
and we praise your glorious name.

Ant. We praise your glorious name, O God.

Psalm 28   God's power seen in the storm

Lo, a voice from heaven, saying, 'This is my beloved Son'
(Matthew 3:17)

Ant. Adore the Lord in his holy court.

O give the Lord you sons of God,
give the Lord glory and power;
give the Lord the glory of his name.
Adore the Lord in his holy court.

The Lord's voice resounding on the waters,
the Lord on the immensity of waters;
the voice of the Lord, full of power,
the voice of the Lord, full of spendour.

The Lord's voice shattering the cedars,
the Lord shatters the cedars of Lebanon;
he makes Lebanon leap like a calf
and Sirion like a young wild-ox.

The Lord's voice flashes flames of fire.†
The Lord's voice shaking the wilderness,
the Lord shakes the wilderness of Kadesh;
the Lord's voice rending the oak tree
and stripping the forest bare.

The God of glory thunders.
In his temple they all cry: 'Glory!'
The Lord sat enthroned over the flood;
the Lord sits as king for ever.

The Lord will give strength to his people,
the Lord will bless his people with peace.

Ant. Adore the Lord in his holy court.

Word of God   2 Thess 3:10–13
If any one will not work, let him not eat. For we hear that
some of you are living in idleness, mere busybodies, not
doing any work. Now such persons we command and exhort

in the Lord Jesus Christ to do their work in quietness and to earn their own living. Brethren, do not be weary in well-doing.

Short Response

I count on you, O Lord;
in the morning let me know your love.
V. Make me know the way I should walk:
to you I lift up my soul.
R. In the morning let me know your love.
V. Glory be to the Father, and to the Son, and to the Holy Spirit.
I count on you, O Lord;
in the morning let me know your love.

Song of Zechariah

Ant. Zechariah prophesied, saying, 'Blessed be the Lord, the God of Israel!'

Prayers

Let us turn in prayer to God, our Almighty Father, who always listens with mercy to the prayers of his children. Let us acclaim him:
R. Blessed be the Lord for ever.

May our coming day be sacred to you, Lord God,
—for you have brought light to us in baptism by your sun of righteousness. (*R.*)

Grant us your eternal wisdom,
—that it may help us and toil with us today and teach us what is pleasing to you. (*R.*)

We pray you, Lord, to keep us free from sin today,
—and to enrich us with your grace from above. (*R.*)

Be with us to aid and protect us,
—help us to live in harmony and peace. (*R.*)

Other prayers may be added

Our Father . . .

Concluding prayer

Lord, may your grace inspire all our actions and sustain them to the end, so that all our prayer and work may begin in you, and by you be completed. We make our prayer through our Lord.

May the Lord bless us,
may he keep us from all evil
and lead us to life everlasting.
Amen.

Let us bless the Lord.
R. Thanks be to God.

MIDDAY PRAYER

O God, come to my assistance . . .
Glory be . . .

Hymn

Mighty ruler, faithful God,
who arrange the successive changes in nature,
giving bright light to the morning sun
and burning heat at noon.

Put out the flames of strife
and take away the heat of passion;
grant us health of body
and true peace of soul.

Grant this, most living Father,
and you, the only Son, equal to the Father,
and, with the Spirit, the Paraclete,
reigning through the ages. Amen.

Psalmody

Psalm 18B   **Praise of God, creator and law-giver**

You must be perfect as your heavenly Father is perfect
(Matthew 5:48)

Ant. The law of the Lord gladdens the heart
and gives light to the eyes.

The law of the Lord is perfect,
it revives the soul.
The rule of the Lord is to be trusted,
it gives wisdom to the simple.

The precepts of the Lord are right,
they gladden the heart.
The command of the Lord is clear,
it gives light to the eyes.

The fear of the Lord is holy,
abiding for ever.
The decrees of the Lord are truth
and all of them just.

They are more to be desired than gold,
than the purest of gold
and sweeter are they than honey,
than honey from the comb.

So in them your servant finds instruction;
great reward is in their keeping.
But who can detect all his errors?
From hidden faults acquit me.

From presumption restrain your servant
and let it not rule me.
Then shall I be blameless,
clean from grave sin.

May the spoken words of my mouth,
the thoughts of my heart,
win favour in your sight, O Lord,
my rescuer, my rock!

Psalm 7   **Appeal to God's justice**

Depart from me, you cursed, into the eternal fire (Matthew
25:41)

I

Lord God, I take refuge in you.
From my pursuer save me and rescue me,

lest he tear me to pieces like a lion
and drag me off with no one to rescue me.

Lord God, if my hands have done wrong,†
if I have paid back evil for good,
I who saved my unjust oppressor:
then let my foe pursue me and seize me,†
let him trample my life to the ground
and lay my soul in the dust.

Lord, rise up in your anger,†
rise against the fury of my foes;
my God, awake! You will give judgment.
Let the company of nations gather round you,†
taking your seat above them on high.
The Lord is judge of the peoples.

Give judgment for me, Lord; I am just
and innocent of heart.
Put an end to the evil of the wicked!
Make the just stand firm,
you who test mind and heart,
O just God!

II

God is the shield that protects me,
who saves the upright of heart.
God is a just judge
slow to anger;
but he threatens the wicked every day,
men who will not repent.

God will sharpen his sword;
he has braced his bow and taken aim.
For them he has prepared deadly weapons;
he barbs his arrows with fire.
Here is one who is pregnant with malice,
conceives evil and brings forth lies.

He digs a pitfall, digs it deep;
and in the trap he has made he will fall.
His malice will recoil on himself;
on his own head his violence will fall.
I will thank the Lord for his justice:
I will sing to the Lord, the Most High.

Ant. The law of the Lord gladdens the heart
and gives light to the eyes.

Word of God   Rom 13:8
Owe no one anything, except to love one another; for he
who loves his neighbour has fulfilled the law.

V. The Lord is my shepherd, there is nothing I shall want.
R. Fresh and green are the pastures where he gives me
repose.

Prayer
Eternal God, Master of the vintage and of the harvest, who
give us the work we have to do and our just wages, help us
to bear the burden of each day without complaining of any
hardships you may send through Christ.

Let us bless the Lord.
R. Thanks be to God.

EVENING PRAYER

O God, come to my assistance.
Lord, make haste to help me.
Glory be to the Father, and to the Son, and to the Holy
Spirit.
As it was in the beginning, is now, and ever shall be, world
without end. Amen. Alleluia!

Hymn
Day is done, but Love unfailing
Dwells ever here;

Shadows fall, but hope, prevailing,
Calms every fear.
Loving Father, none forsaking,
Take our hearts, of Love's own making,
Watch our sleeping, guard our waking,
Be always near!

Dark descends, but Light unending
Shines through our night;
You are with us, ever lending
New strength to sight;
One in love, your truth confessing,
One in hope of heaven's blessing,
May we see, in love's possessing,
Love's endless light!

Eyes will close, but you, unsleeping,
Watch by our side;
Death may come: in Love's safe keeping
Still we abide.
God of love, all evil quelling,
Sin forgiving, fear dispelling,
Stay with us, our hearts indwelling,
This eventide!

Psalmody

Psalm 10   **The security of God's friends: a psalm of confidence**

Save, Lord; we are perishing (Matthew 8:25)

Ant. The Lord looks on the lowly.

In the Lord I have taken my refuge.†
How can you say to my soul:
'Fly like a bird to its mountain.

See the wicked bracing their bow;†
they are fixing their arrows on the string
to shoot upright men in the dark.
Foundations once destroyed,
what can the just do?'

The Lord is in his holy temple,
the Lord, whose throne is in heaven.
His eyes look down on the world;
his gaze tests mortal men.

The Lord tests the just and the wicked:
the lover of violence he hates.
He sends fire and brimstone on the wicked;
he sends a scorching wind as their lot.

The Lord is just and loves justice:
the upright shall see his face.

Ant. The Lord looks on the lowly.

Psalm 14   **A dialogue: the just man advances toward the city of God**

You have come to Mount Zion and to the city of the living God (Heb 12:22)

Ant. Let the hearts that seek the Lord rejoice.

Lord, who shall be admitted to your tent
and dwell on your holy mountain?

He who walks without fault;
he who acts with justice
and speaks the truth from his heart;
he who does not slander with his tongue;

he who does no wrong to his brother,
who casts no slur on his neighbour,
who holds the godless in disdain,
but honours those who fear the Lord;

he who keeps his pledge, come what may;
who takes no interest on a loan
and accepts no bribes against the innocent.
Such a man will stand firm for ever.

Ant. Let the hearts that seek the Lord rejoice.

Eph 1:3–10   **Song of thanks for salvation through Christ**

Ant. Blessed are those whom Christ has called together into his kingdom.

Blessed be the God and Father
of our Lord Jesus Christ,
who has blessed us in Christ
with every spiritual blessing in the heavenly places.

R. Blessed are you, God our Father,
who have blessed us in Christ.

He chose us in him
before the foundation of the world,
that we should be holy
and blameless before him. (*R.*)

He destined us in love
to be his sons through Jesus Christ,
according to the purpose of his will,†
to the praise of his glorious grace
which he freely bestowed on us in the Beloved. (*R.*)

In him we have redemption through his blood,
the forgiveness of our trespasses,
according to the riches of his grace
which he lavished upon us. (*R.*)

He has made known to us†
in all wisdom and insight
the mystery of his will,
according to his purpose
which he set forth in Christ. (*R.*)

His purpose he set forth in Christ
as a plan for the fulness of time,
to unite all things in him,
things in heaven and things on earth. (*R.*)

Ant. Blessed are those whom Christ has called together into
his kingdom.

Word of God Col 1:9–11

May you be filled with the knowledge of God's will in all spiritual wisdom and understanding, to lead a life worthy of the Lord, fully pleasing to him, bearing fruit in every good work and increasing in the knowledge of God. May you be strengthened with all power, according to his glorious might, for all endurance and patience with joy.

Short Response

I think of your name in the night-time,
I will sing of your law.

V. Remember your word to your servant, by which you gave me hope.

R. I will sing of your law.

V. Glory be to the Father, and to the Son, and to the Holy Spirit.

I think of your name in the night-time,
I will sing of your law.

Song of the Virgin Mary

Ant. My soul glorifies the Lord,
my spirit rejoices in God, my Saviour.

Prayers

God made an everlasting covenant with his people and his blessings towards them have never failed. So let our prayer to him be confident:

R. Bless your people, Lord.

Save your people, Lord
—and bless your heritage. (*R.*)

Unite all those who are proud to be called Christians,
—that the world may believe in Christ, whom you have sent. (*R.*)

Give your grace to all our friends and acquaintances,
—spread among them the knowledge and love of Christ. (*R.*)

Show your love to those about to die,
—may they see the salvation which you have promised. (R.)

Other prayers may be added

Have mercy on the dead,
—give them a share in the fellowship of all who sleep in Christ. (R.)

Our Father . . .

Concluding prayer

We offer you our service of praise, O Lord, who looked with favour on the humility of the Virgin Mary so that you might save us; grant us your help to reach the fulness of redemption. We make our prayer through our Lord.

May the Lord bless us,
may he keep us from all evil
and lead us to life everlasting.
Amen.

Let us bless the Lord.
R. Thanks be to God.

Tuesday I

OFFICE OF READINGS

O God, come to my assistance.
Lord, make haste to help me.
Glory be to the Father, and to the Son, and to the Holy Spirit.
As it was in the beginning, is now, and ever shall be, world without end. Amen. Alleluia!
Lord, open my lips . . .
Or, if used as first prayer of the day: O Lord, open my lips . . .

Hymn

Life-giving Word, come down to save your people;
Open our minds to know what you would teach us;
Grow in our hearts, O seed of heaven's harvest;
Be our true wisdom.

Word of the Father, be the word that saves us;
Lamp to our footsteps, scatter all our darkness;
Sword of the spirit, Word of God, protect us;
Be our salvation.

Psalmody

Psalm 9B   **Prayer for deliverance**

Blessed are you poor, for yours is the kingdom of God (Luke 6:20)

I

Ant. Lord God, arise, lift up your hand.

Lord, why do you stand afar off
and hide yourself in times of distress?
The poor man is devoured by the pride of the wicked:
he is caught in the schemes that others have made.

For the wicked man boasts of his heart's desires;
the covetous blasphemes and spurns the Lord.
In his pride the wicked says: 'He will not punish.
There is no God.' Such are this thoughts.

His path is ever untroubled;
your judgment is far from his mind.
His enemies he regards with contempt.†
He thinks: 'Never shall I falter:
misfortune shall never be my lot.'

His mouth is full of cursing, guile, oppression,
mischief and deceit under his tongue.
He lies in wait among the reeds;
the innocent he murders in secret.

His eyes are on the watch for the helpless man.
He lurks in hiding like a lion in his lair;
he lurks in hiding to seize the poor;
he seizes the poor man and drags him away.

He crouches, preparing to spring,
and the helpless fall beneath his strength.
He thinks in his heart: 'God forgets,
he hides his face, he does not see.'

Ant. Lord God, arise, lift up your hand.

II

Ant. O Lord, you see our sorrow.

Arise then, Lord, lift up your hand!
O God, do not forget the poor!
Why should the wicked spurn the Lord
and think in his heart: 'He will not punish'?

But you have seen the trouble and sorrow,
you note it, you take it in hand.
The helpless trusts himself to you;
for you are the helper of the orphan.

Break the power of the wicked and the sinner!
Punish his wickedness till nothing remains!
The Lord is king for ever and ever.
The heathen shall perish from the land he rules.

Lord, you hear the prayer of the poor;
you strengthen their hearts; you turn your ear

to protect the rights of the orphan and oppressed:
so that mortal man may strike terror no more.

Ant. O Lord, you see our sorrow.

Psalm 11 Appeal against lying enemies to God who is faithful

To the poor such as we are, God wished to send his Son (St Augustine)

Ant. The words of the Lord are without alloy.

Help, O Lord, for good men have vanished:
truth has gone from the sons of men.
Falsehood they speak one to another,
with lying lips, with a false heart.

May the Lord destroy all lying lips,
the tongue speaking high-sounding words,
those who say: 'Our tongue is our strength;
our lips are our own, who is our master?'

'For the poor who are oppressed and the needy who groan†
I myself will arise,' says the Lord.
'I will grant them the salvation for which they thirst.'

The words of the Lord are words without alloy,
silver from the furnace, seven times refined.

It is you, O Lord, who will take us in your care
and protect us for ever from this generation.
See how the wicked prowl on every side,
while the worthless are prized highly by the sons of men.

Ant. The words of the Lord are without alloy.

V. He guides the humble in the right path.
R. He teaches his way to the poor.

Readings

Prayer of the day
Or alternative prayer

MORNING PRAYER

Introductory verse and Psalm

O Lord, open my lips.

And my mouth shall declare your praise.

Glory be to the Father, and to the Son, and to the Holy Spirit.

As it was in the beginning, is now, and ever shall be, world without end. Amen. Alleluia!

Psalm 94

Refrain: Come, let us worship our Lord and King.

Or, if not used as first prayer of the day: O God, come to my assistance . . .

Hymn

Come, praise the Lord, the Almighty, the King of all
    nations!
Tell forth his fame, O ye peoples, with loud acclamations!
His love is sure;
Faithful his word shall endure,
Steadfast through all generations!

Praise to the Father most gracious, the Lord of creation!
Praise to his Son, the Redeemer who wrought our salvation!
O heav'nly Dove,
Praise to thee, fruit of their love.
Giver of all consolation!

Psalmody

Psalm 23   **God's solemn entry into his temple**

The gates of heaven open before Christ, as he ascends (St Irenaeus)

Ant. Such are the men who seek you,
    who seek your face, O Lord.

The Lord's is the earth and its fullness,
the world and all its peoples.
It is he who set it on the seas;
on the waters he made it firm.

Who shall climb the mountain of the Lord?
Who shall stand in his holy place?
The man with clean hands and pure heart,†
who desires not worthless things,
who has not sworn so as to deceive his neighbour.

He shall receive blessings from the Lord
and reward from the God who saves him.
Such are the men who seek him,
seek the face of the God of Jacob.

O gates, lift high your heads;†
grow higher, ancient doors.
Let him enter, the king of glory!

Who is the king of glory?
The Lord, the mighty, the valiant, the Lord, the valiant in
    war.

O gates, lift high your heads;†
grow higher, ancient doors.
Let him enter, the king of glory!

Who is he, the king of glory?
He, the Lord of armies, he is the king of glory.

Ant. Such are the men who seek you,
    who seek your face, O Lord.

Tobit 13:1–9　　　　**Song of Tobit: exile and the kingdom**

Blessed be the God and Father of our Lord Jesus Christ.
By his great mercy we have been born anew to a living
hope (1 Pet 1:3)

Ant. Exalt the king of all ages in your works.

Blessed be God! He lives for ever.
His kingdom will last from age to age.

He punishes, he also has mercy,
he leads men to the depths of the grave,
he restores them from the great destruction.
No man can escape his hand.

Proclaim him Israel's sons, amid the nations,
for it is he who scattered us among them.
Among them must we show forth his greatness
and exalt him in the presence of all living;
for he is our Lord and our God,
our Father and our God for ever.

Though he punished us because of our sins
yet he will show us his mercy again;
he will lead us out from the nations,
from those among whom we were scattered.

If you turn to him with all your heart,
with all your soul live in truth before him,
then he will turn back to you,
he will hide his face no longer.

Now think what he has done for you,
give thanks to him with all your voice.
Give praise to the Lord for his justice
and exalt the king of all ages.

In this land of exile I will thank him,
and show forth his greatness and might to the race of sinful
  men.

Sinners, come back to him,†
do what is right before him.
Who knows but he will receive you with pity?

I will sing to my God the king of heaven,
my soul shall exult in his greatness.

Ant. Exalt the king of all ages in your works.

Psalm 32   **Hymn to God's providence and power**

  The mystery hidden for ages and generations, but now made
  manifest to his saints ... Christ in you, the hope of glory
  (Col 1:26–27)

Ant. Praise is fitting for loyal hearts.

Ring out your joy to the Lord, O you just;
for praise is fitting for loyal hearts.

Give thanks to the Lord upon the harp,
with a ten-stringed lute sing him songs.
O sing him a song that is new,
play loudly, with all your skill.

For the word of the Lord is faithful
and all his works to be trusted.
The Lord loves justice and right
and fills the earth with his love.

By his word the heavens were made,
by the breath of his mouth all the stars.
He collects the waves of the ocean;
he stores up the depths of the sea.

Let all the earth fear the Lord,
all who live in the world revere him.
He spoke: and it came to be.
He commanded; it sprang into being.

He frustrates the designs of the nations,
he defeats the plans of the peoples.
His own designs shall stand for ever,
the plans of his heart from age to age.

They are happy, whose God is the Lord,
the people he has chosen as his own.
From the heavens the Lord looks forth,
he sees all the children of men.

From the place where he dwells he gazes
on all the dwellers on the earth,
he who shapes the hearts of them all
and considers all their deeds.

A king is not saved by his army,
nor a warrior preserved by his strength.
A vain hope for safety is the horse;
despite its power it cannot save.

The Lord looks on those who revere him,
on those who hope in his love,

to rescue their souls from death,
to keep them alive in famine.

Our soul is waiting for the Lord.
The Lord is our help and our shield.
In him do our hearts find joy.
We trust in his holy name.

May your love be upon us, O Lord,
as we place all our hope in you.

Ant. Praise is fitting for loyal hearts.

Word of God   Rom 13:11–13
You know what hour it is, how it is full time now for you to
wake from sleep. For salvation is nearer to us now than
when we first believed; the night is far gone, the day is at
hand. Let us then cast off the works of darkness and put on
the armour of light; let us conduct ourselves becomingly
as in the day.

Short Response
I will sing of your strength,
each morning I will acclaim your love.

V. You, O God, are my stronghold,
the God who shows me love.
R. Each morning I will acclaim your love.
V. Glory be to the Father, and to the Son, and to the Holy
Spirit.

I will sing of your strength,
each morning I will acclaim your love.

Song of Zechariah
Save us, O Lord, from the hands of all who hate us.

Prayers
Let us turn in prayer to God, who is rich in mercy towards
all who call upon him:

R. Lord, you are our God and our Father.

Almighty King, you have given us a royal priesthood in baptism;
—may we never fail to make our lives a sacrifice of praise and thanksgiving to you. (R.)

May we live this day in your presence,
—so that we may be blameless in all things. (R.)

We will bless you every hour of the day,
—we will praise your name in every circumstance. (R.)

May we bring joy today to all who are with us,
—may we never cause sorrow to anyone. (R.)

Other prayers may be added

Our Father . . .

Concluding prayer

In mercy and loving-kindness receive our morning prayer, O Lord, and cleanse our hearts, so that no evil may have power over us who have been healed by the light of your grace. We make our prayer through our Lord.

May the Lord bless us,
may he keep us from all evil
and lead us to life everlasting.
Amen.

Let us bless the Lord.
R. Thanks be to God.

MIDDAY PRAYER

O God, come to my assistance . . .
Glory be . . .

Hymn

Lord God, the strength which daily upholds all creation,
in yourself remaining unchanged
and yet determining in due order
the successive changes of the light of day.

57

Grant us light in the evening
so that life may not decay at any point of its activity,
but everlasting glory be the immediate reward
of a happy death.

Grant this, most loving Father,
and you, the only Son, equal to the Father
and, with the Spirit, the Paraclete,
reigning through the ages. Amen.

Psalmody

Psalm 118:1–8   **Hymn to the revelation of the law**

Love is the fulfilling of the law (Rom 13:10)

Ant. He is happy who walks in the ways of the Lord.

They are happy whose life is blameless,
who follow God's law!

They are happy those who do his will,
seeking him with all their hearts,
who never do anything evil
but walk in his ways.

You have laid down your precepts
to be obeyed with care.
May my footsteps be firm
to obey your statutes.

Then I shall not be put to shame
as I heed your commands.
I will thank you with an upright heart
as I learn your decrees.

I will obey your statutes:
do not forsake me.

Psalm 12   **Prayer of a man in anxiety**

*Satan demanded to have you, that he might sift you like
wheat, but I have prayed for you that your faith may not
fail* (Luke 22:31–32)

How long, O Lord, will you forget me?
How long will you hide your face?
How long must I bear grief in my soul,†
this sorrow in my heart day and night?
How long shall my enemy prevail?

Look at me, answer me, Lord my God!
Give light to my eyes lest I fall asleep in death,
lest my enemy say : 'I have overcome him';
lest my foes rejoice to see my fall.

As for me, I trust in your merciful love.
Let my heart rejoice in your saving help:
Let me sing to the Lord for his goodness to me,
singing psalms to the name of the Lord, the Most High.

Psalm 13   **Corruption and punishment of the man who rebels
against God**

Where sin increased, grace abounded all the more
(Rom 5:20)

The fool has said in his heart:
'There is no God above.'
Their deeds are corrupt, depraved;
not a good man is left.

From heaven the Lord looks down
on the sons of men
to see if any are wise,
if any seek God.

All have left the right path,
depraved, every one:
there is not a good man left,
no, not even one.

Will the evil-doers not understand?†
They eat up my people as though they ate bread:
they never pray to the Lord.

See how they tremble with fear†
without cause for fear:
for God is with the just.
You may mock the poor man's hope,
but his refuge is the Lord.

O that Israel's salvation might come from Zion!†
When the Lord delivers his people from bondage,
then Jacob will be glad and Israel rejoice.

Ant. He is happy who walks in the ways of the Lord.

Word of God   Prov 3:13–15

Happy is the man who finds wisdom,
and the man who gets understanding,
for the gain from it is better than gain from silver
and its profit better than gold.
She is more precious than jewels,
and nothing you desire can compare with her.

V. You love truth in the heart.
R. Then in the secret of my heart teach me wisdom.

Prayer

Lord, it was at this time of day that you revealed to Peter
your will for the salvation of mankind; mercifully grant
that our works may please you, and that we may love you
and do your saving will. Through Christ.

Let us bless the Lord.
R. Thanks be to God.

EVENING PRAYER

O God, come to my assistance.
Lord, make haste to help me.
Glory be to the Father, and to the Son, and to the Holy
Spirit.
As it was in the beginning, is now, and ever shall be, world
without end. Amen. Alleluia!

Hymn   John 3 : 29-31

R. He must increase,
but I must decrease.

He who has the bride is the bridegroom;
the friend of the bridegroom who stands and hears him,
rejoices greatly at the bridegroom's voice;
therefore this joy of mine is now full. (*R.*)

He who comes from above is above all;
he who is of the earth belongs to the earth,
and of the earth he speaks;
he who comes from heaven is above all. (*R.*)

Psalmody

Psalm 19   **Prayer for the king**

*I am the first and the last, and the living one; I died, and
behold I am alive for evermore* (Rev 1:17–18)

Ant. Ring out our joy to the God who saves us.

May the Lord answer in time of trial;
may the name of Jacob's God protect you.

May he send you help from his shrine
and give you support from Zion.
May he remember all your offerings
and receive your sacrifice with favour.

May he give you your heart's desire
and fulfil every one of your plans.
May we ring out our joy at your victory†
and rejoice in the name of our God.
May the Lord grant all your prayers.

I am sure now that the Lord
will give victory to his anointed,
will reply from his holy heaven
with the mighty victory of his hand.

Some trust in chariots or horses,
but we in the name of the Lord.

They will collapse and fall,
but we shall hold and stand firm.

Give victory to the king, O Lord,
give answer on the day we call.

Ant. Ring out our joy to the God who saves us.

Psalm 20   **Thanksgiving and prayer for the king**

*The risen Lord lives from age to age, throughout eternal
days* (St Irenaeus)

Ant. Arise in your strength, O Lord,
we shall sing your power.

O Lord, your strength gives joy to the king;
how your saving help makes him glad!
You have granted him his heart's desire;
you have not refused the prayer of his lips.

You came to meet him with the blessings of success,
you have set on his head a crown of pure gold.
He asked you for life and this you have given,
days that will last from age to age.

Your saving help has given him glory.
You have laid upon him majesty and splendour,
you have granted your blessings to him for ever.
You have made him rejoice with the joy of your presence.

The king has put his trust in the Lord:
through the mercy of the Most High he shall stand firm ...
O Lord, arise in your strength;
we shall sing and praise your power.

Ant. Arise in your strength, O Lord;
we shall sing your power.

Rev 4:11; 5:9, 10, 12   **Song to God the creator**
R. To the Lamb of God be glory, honour and power!

Worthy are you, our Lord and God,
to receive glory and honour and power. (*R.*)

For you created all things,
and by your will they existed and were created. (*R.*)

Worthy are you, O Lord,
to take the scroll and to open its seals. (*R.*)

For you were slain,†
and by your blood you ransomed men for God
from every tribe and tongue and people and nation. (*R.*)

You have made us a kingdom and priests to our God,
and we shall reign on earth. (*R.*)

Worthy is the Lamb who was slain,
to receive power and wealth,
and wisdom and might,
and honour and glory and blessing. (*R.*)

Word of God   1 John 3:1, 2
See what love the Father has given us, that we should be
called children of God—and so we are. Beloved, we are
God's children now; it does not yet appear what we shall
be, but we know that when he appears we shall be like him,
for we shall see him as he is.

Short Response
In you is the source of life
and in your light we see light.
V. O Lord, how precious is your love.
R. In your light we see light.
V. Glory be to the Father, and to the Son, and to the Holy
Spirit.
In you is the source of life
and in your light we see light.

Song of the Virgin Mary
Ant. My spirit rejoices in God, my Saviour.

Prayers

Let us pray to God, for he is the Lord who dwells in our midst and we are the people he has won for himself:

R. Lord, may your name be glorified in all things.

Lord, King and Ruler of all men, be with the peoples of the world and with those who exercise authority,
—may their aim be the good of all and their methods those of peace and concord, in accordance with your law. (R.)

May our youth through their dedication prove blameless before you,
—may they live without stain and in peace. (R.)

Grant that children may imitate the example of your Son,
—and go on increasing in wisdom and in grace. (R.)

Teach us to love our enemies,
—and to help them from the heart. (R.)

Other prayers may be added

Welcome the faithful departed into your eternal kingdom,
—where we also hope to reign with you one day. (R.)

Our Father . . .

Concluding prayer

Lord, God Almighty, we thank you for bringing us to the end of this day, and humbly beg you to accept our offering of prayer. We make our prayer through our Lord.

May the Lord bless us,
may he keep us from all evil
and lead us to life everlasting.
Amen.

Let us bless the Lord.
R. Thanks be to God.

Wednesday I

OFFICE OF READINGS

O God, come to my assistance.
Lord, make haste to help me.
Glory be to the Father, and to the Son, and to the Holy Spirit.
As it was in the beginning, is now, and ever shall be, world without end. Amen. Alleulia!

Or, if used as first prayer of the day : O Lord, open my lips . . .

Hymn

Word of God, come down on earth,
Living rain from heav'n descending;
Touch our hearts and bring to birth
Faith and hope and love unending.
Word almighty, we revere you;
Word made flesh, we long to hear you.

Word eternal, throned on high,
Word that brought to life creation,
Word that came from heav'n to die,
Crucified for our salvation,
Saving Word, the world restoring,
Speak to us, your love outpouring.

Psalmody

Psalm 17   David's gratitude for victory

They will see the Son of man coming in a cloud with power and great glory (Luke 21:27)

I

Ant. I love you, Lord, my strength and my salvation.

I love you, Lord, my strength,
my rock, my fortress, my saviour.
My God is the rock where I take refuge;

my shield, my mighty help, my stronghold.
The Lord is worthy of all praise:
when I call I am saved from my foes.

The waves of death rose about me;
the torrents of destruction assailed me;
the snares of the grave entangled me;
the traps of death confronted me.

In my anguish I called to the Lord;
I cried to my God for help.
From his temple he heard my voice;
my cry came to his ears.

Ant. I love you, Lord, my strength and my salvation.

II

Ant. The Lord saved me because he loved me.

Then the earth reeled and rocked;†
the mountains were shaken to their base:
they reeled at his terrible anger.
Smoke came forth from his nostrils†
and scorching fire from his mouth:
coals were set ablaze by its heat.

He lowered the heavens and came down,
a black cloud under his feet.
He came enthroned on the cherubim,
he flew on the wings of the wind.

He made the darkness his covering,
the dark waters of the clouds, his tent.
A brightness shone out before him
with hailstones and flashes of fire.

The Lord thundered in the heavens;
the Most High let his voice be heard.
He shot his arrows, scattered the foe,
flashed his lightnings, and put them to flight.

The bed of the ocean was revealed;
the foundations of the world were laid bare

at the thunder of your threat, O Lord,
at the blast of the breath of your anger.

From on high he reached down and seized me;
he drew me forth from the mighty waters.
He snatched me from my powerful foe,
from my enemies whose strength I could not match.

They assailed me in the day of my misfortune,
but the Lord was my support.
He brought me forth into freedom,
he saved me because he loved me.

Ant. The Lord saved me because he loved me.

III

Ant. You lighten my darkness, O Lord my God.

He rewarded me because I was just,
repaid me, for my hands were clean,
for I have kept the way of the Lord
and have not fallen away from my God.

For his judgments are all before me:
I have never neglected his commands.
I have always been upright before him;
I have kept myself from guilt.

He repaid me because I was just
and my hands were clean in his eyes.
You are loving with those who love you:
you show yourself perfect with the perfect.

With the sincere you show yourself sincere,
but the cunning you outdo in cunning.
For you save a humble people
but humble the eyes that are proud.

You, O Lord, are my lamp,
my God who lightens my darkness.
With you I can break through any barrier,
with my God I can scale any wall.

Ant. You lighten my darkness, O Lord my God.

V. All wondered at the gracious words
R. Which proceeded out of the mouth of God.

Readings

Prayer of the day

Or alternative prayer

MORNING PRAYER

Introductory verse and Psalm
O Lord, open my lips.
And my mouth shall declare your praise.
Glory be to the Father, and to the Son, and to the Holy Spirit.
As it was in the beginning, is now, and ever shall be, world without end. Amen. Alleluia!

Psalm 94
Refrain: Come, let us worship our Lord and Saviour.

Or, if not used as first prayer of the day: O God, come to my assistance...

Hymn
I believe in God, the Father;
I believe in God, his Son;
I believe in God, their Spirit;
Each is God, yet God is one.

I believe what God has spoken
Through his Church, whose word is true;
Boldly she proclaims his Gospel,
Ever old, yet ever new.

All my hope is in God's goodness,
Shown for us by him who died,
Jesus Christ, the world's Redeemer,
Spotless victim crucified.

All my love is Love eternal;
In that Love I love mankind.
Take my heart, O Heart once broken,
Take my soul, my strength, my mind.

Father, I have sinned against you;
Look on me with eyes of love;
Seek your wand'ring sheep, Good Shepherd;
Grant heavn's peace, O heav'nly Dove.

Bless'd be God, the loving Father;
Bless'd be God, his only Son;
Bless'd be God, all-holy Spirit;
Bless'd be God, for ever one.

Psalmody

Psalm 35   **Man's malice: God's goodness**

The hidden mystery ... Christ in you, the hope of glory
(Col 1:26, 27)

Ant. Your love, Lord, is in heaven.

Sin speaks to the sinner
in the depths of his heart.
There is no fear of God
before his eyes.

He so flatters himself in his mind
that he knows not his guilt.
In his mouth are mischief and deceit.
All wisdom is gone.

He plots the defeat of goodness
as he lies on his bed.
He has set his foot on evil ways,
he clings to what is evil.

Your love, Lord, reaches to heaven;
your truth to the skies.
Your justice is like God's mountain,
your judgments like the deep.

To both man and beast you give protection.
O Lord, how precious is your love.
My God, the sons of men find refuge
in the shelter of your wings.

They feast on the riches of your house;
they drink from the stream of your delight.
In you is the source of life
and in your light we see light.

Keep on loving those who know you,
doing justice for upright hearts.
Let the foot of the proud not crush me
nor the hand of the wicked cast me out.

See how the evil-doers have fallen!
Flung down, they shall never arise.

Ant. Your love, Lord, is in heaven.

Judith 16:15–21   **Song of Judith to God, the Creator and
protector of his people**

*By your blood you ransomed men for God from every
tribe and tongue and people and nation* (Rev 5:9)

Ant. O Lord, you are great and marvellous in might.

I will sing a new song to my God.
O Lord you are great and glorious,
unsurpassable and marvellous in might:
May the whole of your creation serve you.

For you spoke and all came into being;†
created by the breath of your mouth.
None can resist your word.

Though the heart of the mountains is shaken by the waters†
and the rocks melt before you like wax,
yet you are gracious to those who revere you.

Of little worth is the fragrance of the sacrifice we offer,†
even less is the richness that is burnt in offering;
only the man who fears the Lord is of value.

Woe to the nations that rise against my people!
In the judgment the Lord of hosts will punish them.
He will give their bodies to the fire and the worm
and they will bewail their fate for ever.

Ant. O Lord, you are great and marvellous in might.

Psalm 46   **Enthronement of God, king of Israel**

*He is seated at the right hand of the Father and his kingdom
will have no end*

Ant. Cry to God with shouts of joy.

All peoples, clap your hands,
cry to God with shouts of joy!
For the Lord, the Most High, we must fear,
great king over all the earth.

He subdues peoples under us
and nations under our feet.
Our inheritance, our glory, is from him,
given to Jacob out of love.

God goes up with shouts of joy;
the Lord goes up with trumpet blast.
Sing praise for God, sing praise,
sing praise to our king, sing praise.

God is king of all the earth.
Sing praise with all your skill.
God is king over the nations;
God reigns on his holy throne.

The princes of the peoples are assembled
with the people of Abraham's God.
The rulers of the earth belong to God,
to God who reigns over all.

Ant. Cry to God with shouts of joy.

Word of God   Tobit 4:15–16, 18–19
What you hate, do not do to any one.
Give of your bread to the hungry,

71

and of your clothing to the naked.
Seek advice from every wise man.
Bless the Lord God on every occasion;
ask him that your ways may be made straight
and that all your paths and plans may prosper.

Short Response
O Lord,
listen to my prayer.
V. And let my cry for help reach you.
R. Listen to my prayer.
V. Glory be to the Father, and to the Son, and to the Holy Spirit.
O Lord,
listen to my prayer.

Song of Zechariah
Ant. Let us serve the Lord in holiness.

Prayers
God has made himself our Father so that we might all be brothers.
Let us pray, then:
R. Sanctify your children, Lord.

May we consecrate to you with a pure heart this day which is beginning, in honour of the resurrection of your Son;
—may we make the whole day pleasing to you, with your grace to aid us in all that we do. (*R.*)

Teach us to recognize your presence in all men today,
—and to find you especially in the poor and in those who are suffering. (*R.*)

Keep our tongue from evil,
—and we shall proclaim your praise. (*R.*)

May we do all we can to live at peace with everyone today,
—never repaying evil with evil. (*R.*)

Other prayers may be added
Our Father . . .

Concluding prayer

God our Saviour, hear our prayer; help us to walk in light
and work for truth, so that we who have been born from you
as children of light may bear witness to you before all men.
We make our prayer through our Lord.

May the Lord bless us,
may he keep us from all evil
and lead us to life everlasting.
Amen.

Let us bless the Lord.
R. Thanks be to God.

MIDDAY PRAYER

O God, come to my assistance . . .
Glory be . . .

Hymn
Holy Spirit,
one with the Father and the Son,
deign at this hour to come down on us without delay
and pour out your graces over our soul.

Let mouth, tongue, soul, thought and strength
make your praise resound.
Let our love be set aflame by the fire of your love
and its heat in turn enkindle love in our neighbours.

Grant this, most loving Father,
and you the only Son, equal to the Father
and, with the Spirit, the Paraclete,
reigning through the ages. Amen.

Psalmody
Psalm 118:9–16
Ant. Blessed are you, O Lord;
teach me your statutes.

How shall the young remain sinless?
By obeying your word.
I have sought you with all my heart:
let me not stray from your commands.
I treasure your promise in my heart
lest I sin against you.
Blessed are you, O Lord;
teach me your statutes.
With my tongue I have recounted
the decrees of your lips.
I rejoiced to do your will
as though all riches were mine.
I will ponder all your precepts
and consider your paths.
I take delight in your statutes;
I will not forget your word.

Psalm 16   **God, hope of the innocent and persecuted man**

*In the days of his flesh, Jesus offered up prayers to him
who was able to save him from death, and he was heard*
(Heb 5:7)

I

Lord, hear a cause that is just,
pay heed to my cry.
Turn your ear to my prayer:
no deceit is on my lips.
From you may my judgment come forth.
Your eyes discern the truth.

You search my heart, you visit me by night.†
You test me and you find in me no wrong.
My words are not sinful as are men's words.

I kept from violence because of your word,†
I kept my feet firmly in your paths;
there was no faltering in my steps.

I am here and I call, you will hear me, O God.
Turn your ear to me; hear my words.

Display your great love,
you whose right hand saves your friends
from those who rebel against them.

Guard me as the apple of your eye.†
Hide me in the shadow of your wings
from the violent attack of the wicked.

II

My foes encircle me with deadly intent.†
Their hearts tight shut, their mouths speak proudly.
They advance against me, and now they surround me.

Their eyes are watching to strike me to the ground†
as though they were lions ready to claw
or like some young lion crouched in hiding.

Lord, arise, confront them, strike them down!
Let your sword rescue my soul from the wicked . . .
As for me, in my justice, I shall see your face
and be filled, when I awake, with the sight of your glory.

Ant. Blessed are you, O Lord,
    teach me your statutes.

Word of God   1 Pet 1:15–16
As he who called you is holy, be holy yourselves in all your conduct, since it is written, 'You shall be holy, for I am holy.'

V. The Lord is my shepherd; there is nothing I shall want.
R. Fresh and green are the pastures where he gives me repose.

Prayer
Almighty and merciful God who give us a time of rest in the middle of the day, look favourably on the work we have begun, and grant that our completed work may be pleasing to you. Through Christ.

Let us bless the Lord.
R. Thanks be to God.

EVENING PRAYER

O God, come to my assistance.
Lord, make haste to help me.
Glory be to the Father, and to the Son, and to the Holy Spirit.
As it was in the beginning, is now, and ever shall be, world without end. Amen. Alleluia!

Hymn

To God with gladness sing.
Your rock and Saviour bless;
Within his temple bring
Your songs of thankfulness!
O God of might,
To you we sing,
Enthroned as king
On heaven's height!

He cradles in his hand
The heights and depths of earth;
He made the sea and land,
He brought the world to birth!
O God most high,
We are your sheep;
On us you keep
Your shepherd's eye!

Your heav'nly Father praise,
Acclaim his only Son,
Your voice in homage raise
To him who makes all one!
O Dove of peace
On us descend
That strife may end
And joy increase.

Psalmody

Psalm 26   **Triumphant trust in God**

If God is for us, who is against us . . . who shall separate us from the love of Christ? (Rom 8:31, 35)

I

Ant. The Lord is my light and my help.

The Lord is my light and my help;
whom shall I fear?
The Lord is the stronghold of my life;
before whom shall I shrink?

When evil-doers draw near
to devour my flesh,
it is they, my enemies and foes,
who stumble and fall.

Though an army encamp against me
my heart would not fear.
Though war break out against me
even then would I trust.

There is one thing I ask of the Lord,
for this I long,
to live in the house of the Lord,
all the days of my life,
to savour the sweetness of the Lord,
to behold his temple.

For there he keeps me safe in his tent
in the day of evil.
He hides me in the shelter of his tent,
on a rock he sets me safe.

And now my head shall be raised
above my foes who surround me
and I shall offer within his tent a sacrifice of joy.
I will sing and make music for the Lord.

Ant. The Lord is my light and my help.

II

Ant. Lord, heed my call for help;
   it is your face that I seek.

O Lord, hear my voice when I call;
have mercy and answer.
Of you my heart has spoken:
'Seek his face.'

It is your face, O Lord, that I seek;
hide not your face.
Dismiss not your servant in anger;
you have been my help.

Do not abandon or forsake me,
O God my help!
Though father and mother forsake me,
the Lord will receive me.

Instruct me, Lord, in your way;
on an even path lead me.
When they lie in ambush protect me
from my enemy's greed.
False witnesses rise against me,
breathing out fury.

I am sure I shall see the Lord's goodness
in the land of the living.
Hope in him, hold firm and take heart.
Hope in the Lord!

Ant. Lord, heed my call for help;
   it is your face that I seek.

Col 1:12–20   **Song to Christ, the first-born of all creation and
                     first-born from the dead**

Ant. To you, O Lord, be glory, honour, power and majesty!

Let us give thanks to the Father,
who has qualified us
to share in the inheritance of the saints
in light.

R. Glory to you, the first-born from the dead!

He has delivered us
from the dominion of darkness
and transferred us
to the kingdom of his beloved Son,
in whom we have redemption,
the forgiveness of sins. (*R.*)

He is the image of the invisible God,
the first-born of all creation,
for in him all things were created, in heaven and on earth,
visible and invisible. (*R.*)

All things were created
through him and for him.
He is before all things,
and in him all things hold together. (*R.*)

He is the head of the body, the Church;
he is the beginning,
the first-born from the dead,
that in everything he might be pre-eminent. (*R.*)

For in him all the fulness of God was pleased to dwell,
and through him to reconcile to himself all things,
whether on earth or in heaven,
making peace by the blood of his cross. (*R.*)

Ant. To you, O Lord, be glory, honour, power and
   majesty!

Word of God   Jas 1:22–25

Be doers of the word, and not hearers only, deceiving yourselves. For if any one is a hearer of the word and not a doer,
he is like a man who observes his natural face in a mirror;
for he observes himself and goes away and at once forgets
what he was like. But he who looks into the perfect law, the
law of liberty, and perseveres, being no hearer that forgets
but a doer that acts, he shall be blessed in his doing.

Short Response

Your word, O Lord, for ever
stands firm in the heavens.

V. Your truth lasts from age to age.

R. It stands firm in the heavens.

V. Glory be to the Father, and to the Son, and to the Holy Spirit.

Your word, O Lord, for ever
stands firm in the heavens.

Song of the Virgin Mary

Ant. The Almighty works marvels for me.
Holy his name!

Prayers

Let us pray with confidence to God, since his care for the people he has chosen is without limit:

R. Lord, show us your love.

Lord, remember your Church;
—preserve her from all evil and perfect her in your love. (*R.*)

Let every people know that you alone are God,
—and Jesus Christ your Son, whom you have sent. (*R.*)

Grant that all may be well with those who are dear to us;
—send your blessing upon them and give them everlasting life. (*R.*)

Lord, we pray to you for all who labour.
—Bless the work done by their hands. (*R.*)

Other prayers may be added

Open the door of your mercy to all who have died today;
—permit them to come into your kingdom. (*R.*)

Our Father . . .

Concluding prayer

Lord, hear our prayer and protect us by day and by night, so that we who are swayed by the changes of time may become firmly established in you, our unchanging Rock. We make our prayer through our Lord.

May the Lord bless us,
may he keep us from all evil
and lead us to life everlasting.
Amen.

Let us bless the Lord.
R. Thanks be to God.

Thursday I

OFFICE OF READINGS

O God, come to my assistance.
Lord, make haste to help me.
Glory be to the Father, and to the Son, and to the Holy Spirit.
As it was in the beginning, is now, and ever shall be, world without end. Amen. Alleluia!

Or, if used as first prayer of the day: O Lord, open my lips ...

Hymn

Word that caused blind eyes to see,
Speak and heal our mortal blindness;
Deaf we are: our healer be;
Loose our tongues to tell your kindness.
Be our Word in pity spoken,
Heal the world, by our sin broken.

Word that speaks your Father's love,
One with him beyond all telling,
Word that sends us from above
God the Spirit, with us dwelling,
Word of truth, to all truth lead us,
Word of life, with one Bread feed us.

Psalmody

Psalm 17   The Lord displays his saving power

If God is for us, who is against us? (Rom 8:31)

IV

Ant. Your word shields your faithful from harm, O Lord.

As for God, his ways are perfect;
the word of the Lord, purest gold.
He indeed is the shield
of all who make him their refuge.

For who is God but the Lord?
Who is a rock but our God?
The God who girds me with strength
and makes the path safe before me.

My feet you made swift as the deer's;
you have made me stand firm on the heights.
You have trained my hands for battle
and my arms to bend the heavy bow.

Ant. Your word shields your faithful from harm, O Lord.

V

Ant. You upheld me, Lord, you trained me with care.

You gave me your saving shield;
you upheld me, trained me with care.
You gave me freedom for my steps;
my feet have never slipped.

I pursued and overtook my foes,
never turning back till they were slain.
I smote them so they could not rise;
they fell beneath my feet.

You girded me with strength for battle;
you made my enemies fall beneath me,
you made my foes take flight;
those who hated me I destroyed.

They cried, but there was no one to save them;
they cried to the Lord, but in vain.
I crushed them fine as dust before the wind;
trod them down like dirt in the streets.

You saved me from the feuds of the people
and put me at the head of the nations.
People unknown to me served me:
when they heard of me they obeyed me.

Foreign nations came to me cringing:†
foreign nations faded away.
They came trembling out of their strongholds.

Ant. You upheld me, Lord, you trained me with care.

VI

Ant. Long life to the Lord!
   Praised be the God who saves me.

Long life to the Lord, my rock!
Praised be the God who saves me,
the God who gives me redress
and subdues people under me.

You saved me from my furious foes.
You set me above my assailants
You saved me from violent men,†
so I will praise you, Lord, among the nations:
I will sing a psalm to your name.

He has given great victories to his king†
and shown his love for his anointed,
for David and his sons for ever.

Ant. Long life to the Lord!
   Praised be the God who saves me.

V. Open my eyes that I may consider
R. The wonders of your law.

Readings

Prayer of the day
Or alternative prayer

MORNING PRAYER

Introductory verse and Psalm
O Lord, open my lips.
And my mouth shall declare your praise.
Glory be to the Father, and to the Son, and to the Holy
Spirit.
As it was in the beginning, is now, and ever shall be, world
without end. Amen. Alleulia!

Psalm 94

Refrain: Come, let us worship our Lord and Master.

Or, if not used as first prayer of the day: O God, come to my assistance . . .

Hymn

We who live in Christ were born in his death:
Baptized in Christ's death, with Christ we lay in the tomb;
As God the Father's power awoke him from death,
So we were raised to walk in newness of life.

One with Christ were we in dying his death:
So one shall we be with Christ in rising again.
Our sinful selves were nailed with Christ to his cross
That, dead to sin, from sin our flesh might be free.

Dead with Christ, we yet shall rise with him too,
For this is our faith, that he who rose from the dead
Will never die; once dead, for ever he lives,
And death has power no more to conquer its King.

Once for all in death Christ died to all sin;
The life that he lives is life lived only to God.
So you like him are dead to all that is sin,
And live to God in Christ, the Saviour, our Lord.

Psalmody

Psalm 56   **Trust in God in the midst of suffering**

Father, the hour has come; glorify your Son that the Son may glorify you (John 17:1)

Ant. My soul takes shelter in you, O Lord.

Have mercy on me, God, have mercy
for in you my soul has taken refuge.
In the shadow of your wings I take refuge
till the storms of destruction pass by.

I call to God the Most High,
to God who has always been my help.
May he send from heaven and save me . . .
May God send his truth and his love.

My soul lies down among lions,
who would devour the sons of men.
Their teeth are spears and arrows,
their tongue a sharpened sword.

R. O God, arise above the heavens;
may your glory shine on earth!

They laid a snare for my steps,
my soul was bowed down.
They dug a pit in my path
but fell in it themselves.

My heart is ready, O God,†
my heart is ready.
I will sing, I will sing your praise.
Awake my soul,†
awake lyre and harp,
I will awake the dawn.

I will thank you Lord among the peoples,
praise you among the nations;
for your love reaches to the heavens
and your truth to the skies.

R. O God, arise above the heavens;
may your glory shine on earth!

Ant. My soul takes shelter in you, O Lord.

Jer 31:10–14   Song of Jeremiah: God will gather his people together in joy

He prophesied that Jesus should die to gather into one the children of God who are scattered abroad (John 11:51–52)

Ant. My people, says the Lord, shall be filled with my blessings.

O nations, hear the word of the Lord,
proclaim it to the far-off coasts.
Say: 'He who scattered Israel will gather him
and guard him as a shepherd guards his flock.'

For the Lord has ransomed Jacob,
has saved him from an overpowering hand.

They will come and shout for joy on Mount Zion,
they will stream to the blessings of the Lord,
to the corn, the new wine and the oil,
to the flocks of sheep and the herds.
Their life will be like a watered garden.
They will never be weary again.

Then the young girls will rejoice and will dance,
the men, young and old, will be glad.
I will turn their mourning into joy,
I will console them, give gladness for grief.
The priests I will again feed with plenty,
and my people shall be filled with my blessings.

Ant. My people, says the Lord, shall be filled with my blessings.

Psalm 47   **The invincible city of God**

> *He carried me away to a great high mountain, and showed me the holy city, Jerusalem* (Rev 21:10)

Ant. God brings us together in his house;
   he gives his people joy.

The Lord is great and worthy to be praised
in the city of our God.
His holy mountain rises in beauty,
the joy of all the earth.

Mount Zion, true pole of the earth,
the Great King's city!
God, in the midst of its citadels,
has shown himself its stronghold.

For the kings assembled together,
together they advanced.
They saw; at once they were astounded;
dismayed, they fled in fear.

A trembling seized them there,
like the pangs of birth,
or as the east wind destroys
the ships of Tarshish.

As we have heard, so we have seen
in the city of our God,
in the city of the Lord of hosts
which God upholds for ever.

O God, we ponder your love
within your temple.
Your praise, O God, like your name
reaches to the ends of the earth.

With justice your right hand is filled.
Mount Zion rejoices;
the people of Judah rejoice
at the sight of your judgments.

Walk through Zion, walk all round it;
count the number of its towers.
Review all its ramparts,
examine its castles,

that you may tell the next generation
that such is our God,
our God for ever and always.
It is he who leads us.

Ant. God brings us together in his house;
   he gives his people joy.

Word of God   Is 66:1–2

Thus says the Lord:
Heaven is my throne
and the earth is my footstool;
what is the house which you would build for me,
and what is the place of my rest?
All these things my hand has made,
and so all these things are mine, says the Lord.

But this is the man to whom I will look,
he that is humble and contrite in spirit,
and trembles at my word.

Short Response
Redeem me, Lord,
and show me your mercy.
V. My foot stands on level ground.
R. Show me your mercy.
V. Glory be to the Father, and to the Son, and to the Holy
Spirit.
Redeem me, Lord,
and show me your mercy.

Song of Zechariah
Ant. Blessed be the Lord who visits us like the dawn from
on high.

Prayers
Let us thank the Lord for giving us the light of this day.

R. Bless us, O Lord, and sanctify us.

All-powerful and merciful God, through your Son you
created and redeemed us.
—Sustain everything we do and plan today. (*R.*)

Give us the grace today to be tolerant with everyone,
—as you are patient and merciful toward us. (*R.*)

Let your favour be upon us this day;
—give success to the work of our hands. (*R.*)

May your peace guard our hearts and our thoughts today,
—that we may be open to truth and may seek justice. (*R.*)

Other prayers may be added
Our Father . . .

Concluding prayer

Almighty and eternal God, we pray at morning, noon and
evening that you will drive out of our hearts the darkness of

sin and fill them with the true light of Christ. Who lives
and reigns.

May the Lord bless us,
may he keep us from all evil
and lead us to life everlasting.
Amen.

Let us bless the Lord.
R. Thanks be to God.

MIDDAY PRAYER

O God, come to my assistance . . .
Glory be . . .

Hymn
Mighty ruler, faithful God,
who arrange the successive changes in nature,
giving bright light to the morning sun
and burning heat at noon.

Put out the flames of strife
and take away the heat of passion;
grant us health of body
and true peace of soul.

Grant this, most loving Father,
and you, the only Son, equal to the Father
and, with the Spirit, the Paraclete,
reigning through the ages. Amen.

Psalmody

Psalm 118:17-24

Ant. Make me walk in your truth, O Lord.

Bless your servant and I shall live
and obey your word.
Open my eyes that I may consider
the wonders of your law.

I am a pilgrim on the earth;
show me your commands.
My soul is ever consumed
in longing for your decrees.

You threaten the proud, the accursed,
who turn from your commands.
Relieve me from scorn and contempt
for I do your will.

Though princes sit plotting against me
I ponder on your statutes.
Your will is my delight;
your statutes are my counsellors.

Psalm 24   Hope in God for every need

Hope does not disappoint us (Rom 5:5)

I

To you, O Lord, I lift up my soul.†
I trust you, let me not be disappointed;
do not let my enemies triumph.
Those who hope in you shall not be disappointed,
but only those who wantonly break faith.

Lord, make me know your ways.
Lord, teach me your paths.
Make me walk in your truth, and teach me:
for you are God my saviour.

In you I hope all the day long
because of your goodness, O Lord.
Remember your mercy, Lord,
and the love you have shown from of old.
Do not remember the sins of my youth.
In your love remember me.

The Lord is good and upright.
He shows the path to those who stray,
He guides the humble in the right path;
he teaches his way to the poor.

His ways are faithfulness and love
for those who keep his covenant and will.
Lord, for the sake of your name
forgive my guilt; for it is great.

II

If anyone fears the Lord
he will show him the path he should choose.
His soul shall live in happiness
and his children shall possess the land.
The Lord's friendship is for those who revere him;
to them he reveals his covenant.

My eyes are always on the Lord;
for he rescues my feet from the snare.
Turn to me and have mercy
for I am lonely and poor.

Relieve the anguish of my heart
and set me free from my distress.
See my affliction and my toil
and take all my sins away.

See how many are my foes;
how violent their hatred for me.
Preserve my life and rescue me.
Do not disappoint me, you are my refuge.
May innocence and uprightness protect me:
for my hope is in you, O Lord.

Redeem Israel, O God,
from all its distress.

Ant. Make me walk in your truth, O Lord.

Word of God   Amos 9:6
He who builds his upper chambers in the heavens,
and founds his vault upon the earth;
who calls for the waters of the sea,
and pours them out upon the surface of the earth—
the Lord is his name.

V. His are majesty and state and power.
R. And splendour in his holy place.

Prayer

Almighty and eternal God in whom there is no darkness, no obscurity, fill our hearts with the splendour of your light, so that we who have received your commandments may walk in safety on your ways. Through Christ.

Let us bless the Lord.
R. Thanks be to God.

EVENING PRAYER

O God, come to my assistance.
Lord, make haste to help me.
Glory be to the Father, and to the Son, and to the Holy Spirit.
As it was in the beginning, is now, and ever shall be, world without end. Amen. Alleluia!

Hymn

Bless'd be the Lord our God!
With joy let heaven ring;
Before his presence let all earth
Its songs of homage bring!
His mighty deeds be told;
His majesty be praised;
To God enthroned in heav'nly light,
Let every voice be raised!

All that has life and breath,
Give thanks with heartfelt songs!
To him let all creation sing
To whom all praise belongs!
Acclaim the Father's love,
Who gave us God his Son;
Praise too the Spirit, giv'n by both,
With both for ever one!

Psalmody

Psalm 29   **Thanksgiving for recovery from sickness**

As we share abundantly in Christ's sufferings, so through Christ we share abundantly in comfort too (2 Cor 1:5)

Ant. O Lord, I cried to you for help
   and you, my God, have healed me.

I will praise you, Lord, you have rescued me
and have not let my enemies rejoice over me.

O Lord, I cried to you for help
and you, my God, have healed me.
O Lord, you have raised my soul from the dead,
restored me to life from those who sink into the grave.

Sing psalms to the Lord, you who love him,
give thanks to his holy name.
His anger lasts but a moment; his favour through life.
At night there are tears, but joy comes with dawn.

I said to myself in my good fortune:
'Nothing will ever disturb me.'
Your favour had set me on a mountain fastness,
then you hid your face and I was put to confusion.

To you, Lord, I cried,
to my God I made appeal:
'What profit would my death be, my going to the grave?
Can dust give you praise or proclaim your truth?'

The Lord listened and had pity.
The Lord came to my help.
For me you have changed my mourning into dancing,
you removed my sackcloth and girdled me with joy.
So my soul sings psalms to you unceasingly.
O Lord my God, I will thank you for ever.

Ant. O Lord, I cried to you for help
   and you, my God, have healed me.

Psalm 31   **The joy of being forgiven**

Neither do I condemn you; go, and do not sin again
(John 8:11)

Ant. Happy the man whose sin is forgiven.

Happy the man whose offence is forgiven,
whose sin is remitted.

O happy the man to whom the Lord imputes no guilt,
in whose spirit is no guile.

I kept it secret and my frame was wasted.
I groaned all the day long
for night and day your hand
was heavy upon me.
Indeed, my strength was dried up
as by the summer's heat.

But now I have acknowledged my sins;
my guilt I did not hide.
I said: 'I will confess
my offence to the Lord.'
And you, Lord, have forgiven
the guilt of my sin.

So let every good man pray to you
in the time of need.
The floods of water may reach high
but him they shall not reach.
You are my hiding place, O Lord;†
you save me from distress.
You surround me with cries of deliverance.

I will instruct you and teach you
the way you should go;
I will give you counsel
with my eye upon you.

Be not like horse and mule unintelligent,†
needing bridle and bit,

else they will not approach you.
Many sorrows has the wicked†
but he who trusts in the Lord,
loving mercy surrounds him.

Rejoice, rejoice in the Lord,
exult, you just!
O come, ring out your joy,
all you upright of heart.

Ant. Happy the man whose sin is forgiven.

Rev 11:17–18; 12:10–12   **Song of God's judgment**

Ant. The Lord our God, the Almighty, reigns.

We give thanks to you, Lord God Almighty,
who are and who were,
that you have taken your great power
and begun to reign.
R. We give thanks to you, O Lord our God.

The nations raged,
but your wrath came,
and the time for the dead to be judged,
for rewarding your servants, the prophets and saints,
and those who fear your name,
both small and great. (*R.*)

Now the salvation and the power†
and the kingdom of our God
and the authority of his Christ have come,
for the accuser of our brethren has been thrown down,
who accuses them day and night before our God. (*R.*)

And they have conquered him
by the blood of the Lamb
and by the word of their testimony,
for they loved not their lives even unto death.

Rejoice, then, O heaven
and you that dwell therein!

Ant. The Lord our God, the Almighty, reigns.

Word of God   2 Cor 10:17–18

Let him who boasts, boast of the Lord, for it is not the
man who commends himself that is accepted, but the man
whom the Lord commends.

Short Response

By your blood
you have ransomed us, Lord.

V. Men from every tribe and tongue and people and nation.

R. You have ransomed us, Lord.

V. Glory be to the Father, and to the Son, and to the Holy
Spirit.

By your blood
you have ransomed us, Lord.

Song of the Virgin Mary

Ant. His mercy is from age to age on those who fear him.

Prayers

Let us invoke God who is our strength, who is the source of
all our hope:

R. Lord, look down to us, your children.

You made an everlasting covenant with your people,
—make us always mindful of your mighty works. (*R.*)

May your Church grow in love,
—and keep the faithful always in the unity of the Spirit, in
the bond of peace. (*R.*)

Grant that the builders of our earthly city may work in
union with you,
—lest in building they labour in vain. (*R.*)

Send labourers into your harvest,
—so that your name may be honoured among all the
nations. (*R.*)

Other prayers may be added

Number all our dead relatives and benefactors among your saints,

—and admit us to their company one day.

Our Father . . .

Concluding prayer

Lord God, you bring light to the night and drive out darkness. Keep us safe from evil during the night, so that we may offer you our prayer of thanksgiving in the morning. We make our prayer through our Lord.

May the Lord bless us,
may he keep us from all evil
and lead us to life everlasting.
Amen.

Let us bless the Lord.
R. Thanks be to God.

Friday I

OFFICE OF READINGS

O God, come to my assistance.
Lord, make haste to help me.
Glory be to the Father, and to the Son, and to the Holy
Spirit.
As it was in the beginning, is now, and ever shall be, world
without end. Amen. Alleluia!

Or, if used as first prayer of the day: O Lord, open my lips . . .

Hymn
I am the holy vine,
Which God my Father tends.
Each branch that yields no fruit
My Father cuts away.
Each fruitful branch
He prunes with care
To make it yield
Abundant fruit.

If you abide in me,
I will in you abide.
Each branch to yield its fruit
Must with the vine be one.
So you shall fail
To yield your fruit
If you are not
With me one vine.

I am the fruitful vine,
and you my branches are.
He who abides in me,
I will in him abide.
So shall you yield
Much fruit, but none

If you remain
Apart from me.

Psalmody

Psalm 34   **Appeal for vindication**

> *They gathered . . . and took counsel together in order to arrest Jesus by stealth and kill him* (Matthew 26:3–4)

I

Ant. Lord, arise to help me.

O Lord, plead my cause against my foes;
fight those who fight me.
Take up your buckler and shield;
arise to help me . . .

But my soul shall be joyful in the Lord
and rejoice in his salvation.
My whole being will say:
'Lord, who is like you
who rescue the weak from the strong
and the poor from the oppressor?'

Ant. Lord, arise to help me.

II

Ant. Lord, come to my rescue.

Lying witnesses arise
and accuse me unjustly.
They repay me evil for good:
my soul is forlorn.

When they were sick I went into mourning,
afflicted with fasting.
My prayer was ever on my lips,
as though for a brother, a friend.
I went as though mourning a mother,
bowed down with grief.

Now that I am in trouble they gather,
they gather and mock me.

They take me by surprise and strike me
and tear me to pieces.
They provoke me with mockery on mockery
and gnash their teeth.

Ant. Lord, come to my rescue.

III

Ant. All the day long my tongue shall speak of your justice.

O Lord, how long will you look on?
Come to my rescue!
Save my life from these raging beasts,
my soul from these lions.
I will thank you in the great assembly
and praise you amid the throng . . .

Let there be joy for those who love my cause.
Let them say without end:
'Great is the Lord who delights
in the peace of his servant.'
Then my tongue shall speak of your justice
and all the day long of your praise.

Ant. All the day long my tongue shall speak of your justice.

V. He who is born of God.
R. He it is who hears the words of God.

Readings

Prayer of the day
Or alternative prayer

MORNING PRAYER

Introductory verse and Psalm
O Lord, open my lips.
And my mouth shall declare your praise.
Glory be to the Father, and to the Son, and to the Holy
Spirit.

As it was in the beginning, is now, and ever shall be, world without end. Amen. Alleluia!

Psalm 94

Refrain: Harden not your hearts today,
  but listen to the voice of the Lord.

Or, if not used as first prayer of the day: O God, come to my assistance . . .

Hymn   Rom 8:28–35, 37

In everything God works for good with those who love him,
who are called according to his purpose.
For those whom he foreknew he also predestined
to be conformed to the image of his Son.

R. You did not spare your own Son, but gave him up for us all.

Those whom he predestined
he also called;
and those whom he called
he also justified;
and those whom he justified
he also glorified. (*R.*)

What then shall we say?†
If God is for us,
who is against us?
He who did not spare his own Son, †
but gave him up for us all,
will he not also give us all things with him? (*R.*)

It is God who justifies,
who is to condemn?
Is it Christ Jesus, who died,
who was raised from the dead,
who is at the right hand of God,
who intercedes for us? (*R.*)

Who shall separate us
from the love of Christ?

Shall tribulation, or distress, or persecution,
or famine, or nakedness, or peril or sword?
No, in all these things we are more than conquerors
through him who loved us. (*R.*)

Psalmody

Psalm 50   **Prayer of contrition and trust**

Jesus, Son of God and Saviour, be merciful to me, a sinner.

Ant. In your kindness, Lord, blot out my sin.

Have mercy on me, God, in your kindness.
In your compassion blot out my offence.
O wash me more and more from my guilt
and cleanse me from my sin.

My offences truly I know them;
my sin is always before me.
Against you, you alone, have I sinned;
what is evil in your sight I have done.

That you may be justified when you give sentence
and be without reproach when you judge,
O see, in guilt I was born,
a sinner was I conceived.

Indeed you love truth in the heart;
then in the secret of my heart teach me wisdom
O purify me, then I shall be clean;
O wash me, I shall be whiter than snow.

Make me hear rejoicing and gladness,
that the bones you have crushed may thrill.
From my sins turn away your face
and blot out all my guilt.

A pure heart create for me, O God,
put a steadfast spirit within me.
Do not cast me away from your presence,
nor deprive me of your holy spirit.

Give me again the joy of your help;
with a spirit of fervour sustain me,
that I may teach transgressors your ways
and sinners may return to you.

O rescue me, God, my helper,
and my tongue shall ring out your goodness.
O Lord, open my lips
and my mouth shall declare your praise.

For in sacrifice you take no delight,
burnt offering from me you would refuse,
my sacrifice, a contrite spirit.
A humbled, contrite heart you will not spurn.

In your goodness, show favour to Zion:
rebuild the walls of Jerusalem.
Then you will be pleased with lawful sacrifice,†
burnt offerings wholly consumed,
then you will be offering young bulls on your altar.

Ant. In your kindness, Lord, blot out my sin.

Isaiah 45:15–26   **Song of Isaiah to the hidden God, the only Saviour**

   Lord, to whom shall we go? (John 6:68)

Ant. All Israel's sons sing your praise, O Lord.

Truly, God of Israel, the Saviour,
you are a God who lies hidden.
They will be put to shame and disgraced,
all who resist you.
They will take themselves off in dismay,
the makers of idols.

But Israel is saved by the Lord,
saved for evermore.
You will never be ashamed or disgraced
through endless ages.

For this is the word of the Lord,
the creator of heaven,

the God who made earth and shaped it,
he who made it firm.
He did not create it in vain.
he made it to be lived in.

'I am the Lord, there is no other.
I have not spoken in secret, in some dark place,
I have not said to Jacob's sons
"Search for me in vain".

I am the Lord, I speak the truth,
I proclaim what is right.
Assemble, all of you, draw near
you who have escaped from the nations.

They know nothing, who carry around
their idols made of wood
and keep on praying to a god
that cannot save them.

State your case and bring your proofs,
consult among yourselves.
Who proclaimed this beforehand,
who foretold it long ago?

Was it not I, the Lord?
There is no god but me,
a God of justice, a saviour.
There is none but me.

Turn to me and be saved,
all the ends of the earth!
For I am God, there is no other;
by myself I swear it.

It is truth that goes forth from my mouth,
a word beyond recall.
To me every knee shall bow,
every tongue shall swear.

They will say: "In the Lord alone
are victory and power.
And to him will come in dismay
all who have resisted.
Through the Lord will come victory and glory
for all Israel's sons." '

Ant. All Israel's sons sing your praise, O Lord.

Psalm 99   **Entry into the temple**

Let peace rule in your hearts . . . and be thankful (Col 3:15)

Ant. Cry out with joy to God, all the earth,
    sing to the Lord.

Cry out with joy to the Lord, all the earth.†
Serve the Lord with gladness.
Come before him, singing for joy.

Know that he, the Lord is God.†
He made us, we belong to him,
we are his people, the sheep of his flock.

Go within his gates, giving thanks.†
Enter his courts with songs of praise.
Give thanks to him and bless his name.

Indeed, how good is the Lord,†
eternal his merciful love.
He is faithful from age to age.

Ant. Cry out with joy to God, all the earth,
    sing to the Lord.

Word of God   2 Cor 13:4

Christ was crucified in weakness, but lives by the power of
God. We are weak in him, but we shall live with him by the
power of God.

Short Response

Christ, son of the living God,
have mercy on us.
V. You who are seated at the right hand of the Father,

R. Have mercy on us.

V. Glory be to the Father, and to the Son, and to the Holy Spirit.

Christ, son of the living God,
have mercy on us.

Song of Zechariah

Ant. Through the loving-kindness of the heart of our God, he visits us like the dawn from on high.

Prayers

Let us pray to God the Father, who has sent us Christ his Son, full of grace and the Holy Spirit:

R. Give us the Spirit of Christ, Lord, for we are your sons.

God, our Creator and our Father, whatever we do today may we do for your glory
—in imitation of Christ, your Son. (*R.*)

In the morning let us know your love, O Lord;
—may your joy be our strength. (*R.*)

Show us your favour, do what is for our good, grant us peace,
—so that we may have the strength of your protection today. (*R.*)

Look with favour today on those who trust in our prayers;
—give them all they need for body and soul. (*R.*)

Other prayers may be added

Our Father . . . .

Concluding prayer

O God, by the light of whose Word darkness is driven away, grant that the fire your grace has enkindled may never be extinguished by temptation. We make our prayer through our Lord.

May the Lord bless us,
may he keep us from all evil
and lead us to life everlasting.
Amen.

Let us bless the Lord.
R. Thanks be to God.

MIDDAY PRAYER

O God, come to my assistance . . .
Glory be . . .

Hymn

Lord God, the strength which daily upholds all creation,
in yourself remaining unchanged
and yet determining in due order
the successive changes of the light of day.

Grant us light in the evening
so that life may not decay at any point of its activity,
but everlasting glory be the immediate reward
of a happy death.

Grant this, most loving Father,
and you, the only Son, equal to the Father
and, with the Spirit, the Paraclete,
reigning through the ages. Amen.

Psalmody
Psalm 118:25–32

Ant. Teach me, O Lord, to do your will.

My soul lies in the dust;
by your word revive me.
I declared my ways and you answered:
teach me your statutes.

Make me grasp the way of your precepts
and I will muse on your wonders.
My soul pines away with grief;
by your word raise me up.

Keep me from the way of error
and teach me your law.
I have chosen the way of truth
with your decrees before me.

I bind myself to do your will;
Lord, do not disappoint me.
I will run the way of your commands;
you give freedom to my heart.

Psalm 25   **Prayer of a man of integrity**

*Christ gave himself up for the church that he might sanctify
her .... that she might be holy and without blemish*
(Eph 5:25, 27)

Give judgment for me, O Lord:
for I walk the path of perfection.
I trust in the Lord;
I have not wavered.

Examine me, Lord, and try me;
O test my heart and my mind,
for your love is before my eyes
and I walk according to your truth.

I never take my place with liars
and with hypocrites I shall not go.
I hate the evil-doer's company:
I will not take my place with the wicked.

To prove my innocence I wash my hands
and take my place around your altar,
singing a song of thanksgiving,
proclaiming all your wonders.

O Lord, I love the house where you dwell,
the place where your glory abides.

Do not sweep me away with sinners,
nor my life with bloodthirsty men
in whose hands are evil plots,
whose right hands are filled with gold.

As for me, I walk the path of perfection.
Redeem me and show me your mercy.
My foot stands on level ground:
I will bless the Lord in the assembly.

Psalm 27   **Prayer and thanksgiving**

All flesh shall see the salvation of God (Luke 3:6)

To you, O Lord, I call,
my rock, hear me.
If you do not heed I shall become
like those in the grave.

Hear the voice of my pleading
as I call for help,
as I lift my hands in prayer
to your holy place.

Do not drag me away with the wicked,
with the evil-doers,
who speak words of peace to their neighbours
but with evil in their hearts . . .

Blessed be the Lord for he has heard
my cry, my appeal.
The Lord is my strength and my shield;
in him my heart trusts.
I was helped, my heart rejoices
and I praise him with my song.

The Lord is the strength of his people,
the stronghold where his anointed find salvation.
Save your people; bless Israel your heritage.
Be their shepherd and carry them for ever.

Ant. Teach me, O Lord, to do your will.

Word of God   Eph 4:32

Be kind to one another, tenderhearted, forgiving one
another, as God in Christ forgave you.

V. Happy the man who fears the Lord,
R. Who takes delight in his commands.

Prayer

Lord Jesus Christ, on a day plunged into darkness, you who
were innocent were raised upon a cross for our redemption;

grant us the light we need to reach eternal life. Who live and reign.

Let us bless the Lord.
R. Thanks be to God.

EVENING PRAYER

O God, come to my assistance.
Lord, make haste to help me.
Glory be to the Father, and to the Son, and to the Holy Spirit.
As it was in the beginning, is now, and ever shall be, world without end. Amen. Alleluia!

Hymn 1 Pet 2:21-24

R. By his wounds you have been healed.

Christ suffered for you,
leaving you an example that you should follow in his steps (R.)

He committed no sin;
no guile was found on his lips.
When he was reviled,
he did not revile in return. (R.)

When he suffered,
he did not threaten,
but he trusted to him
who judges justly. (R.)

He himself bore our sins in his body on the tree,†
that we might die to sin and live to righteousness.
By his wounds you have been healed.
For you were straying like sheep,
but have now returned to the Shepherd and Guardian of
your souls. (R.)

Psalmody

Psalm 40   **Prayer of trust in sickness and betrayal**

One of you will betray me, one who is eating with me (Mark 14:18)

Ant. Blessed are the compassionate,
 for they shall obtain mercy.

Happy the man who considers the poor and the weak.
The Lord will save him in the day of evil,
will guard him, give him life, make him happy in the land
and will not give him up to the will of his foes.
The Lord will help him on his bed of pain,
he will bring him back from sickness to health.

As for me, I said: 'Lord, have mercy on me,
heal my soul for I have sinned against you.'
My foes are speaking evil against me.
'How long before he dies and his name be forgotten?'
They come to visit me and speak empty words,
their hearts full of malice, they spread it abroad.

My enemies whisper together against me.
They all weigh up the evil which is on me:
'Some deadly thing has fastened upon him,
he will not rise again from where he lies.'
Thus even my friend, in whom I trusted,
who ate my bread, has turned against me.

But you, O Lord, have mercy on me.
Let me rise once more and I will repay them.
By this I shall know that you are my friend,
if my foes do not shout in triumph over me.
If you uphold me I shall be unharmed
and set in your presence for evermore.

Blessed be the Lord, the God of Israel
from age to age. Amen. Amen.

Ant. Blessed are the compassionate,
 for they shall obtain mercy.

Psalm 45   God, the succour and strength of his people

His name shall be called Emmanuel (Matthew 1:23)

Ant. If God is for us, who is against us?
   It is God who justifies, who is to condemn?

God is for us a refuge and strength,
a helper close at hand, in time of distress:
so we shall not fear though the earth should rock,
though the mountains fall into the depths of the sea,
even though its waters rage and foam,
even though the mountains be shaken by its waves.

R. The Lord of hosts is with us:
the God of Jacob is our stronghold.

The waters of a river give joy to God's city,
the holy place where the Most High dwells.
God is within, it cannot be shaken;
God will help it at the dawning of the day.
Nations are in tumult, kingdoms are shaken:
he lifts his voice, the earth shrinks away.

R. The Lord of hosts is with us:
the God of Jacob is our stronghold.

Come, consider the works of the Lord
the redoubtable deeds he has done on the earth.
He puts an end to wars over all the earth;†
the bow he breaks, the spear he snaps.
He burns the shields with fire.
'Be still and know that I am God,
supreme among the nations, supreme on the earth!'

R. The Lord of hosts is with us:
the God of Jacob is our stronghold.

Ant. If God is for us, who is against us?
   It is God who justifies, who is to condemn?

Rev 15:3–4   Song of Moses and the Lamb

Ant. Glory to the Lamb who was slain!
   He is King for ever and ever.

Great and wonderful are your deeds,
O Lord God the Almighty!
Just and true are your ways,
O King of the ages!

R. Great are your deeds, O Lord!

Who shall not fear and glorify your name, O Lord?
For you alone are holy. (*R.*)

All nations shall come and worship you,
for your judgments have been revealed. (*R.*)

Ant. Glory to the Lamb who was slain!
   He is King for ever and ever.

Word of God   Rom 15:1–3
We who are strong ought to bear with the failings of the
weak, and not to please ourselves; let each of us please his
neighbour for his good, to edify him. For Christ did not
please himself; but, as it is written, 'The reproaches of those
who reproached you fell on me.'

Short Response
Into your hands, O Lord,
I commend my spirit.
V. It is you who will redeem me, Lord.
R. Into your hands I commend my spirit.
Glory be to the Father, and to the Son, and to the Holy
Spirit.
Into your hands, O Lord,
I commend my spirit.

Song of the Virgin Mary
Ant. Put forth your arm in strength, O Lord,
   scatter the proud, raise the lowly.

Prayers

God looks with compassion on those in want; he fills the hungry with good things. Confident of this, let us pray:

R. Let us see, O Lord, your mercy.

Most merciful Father, we pray for the suffering members of the Church:
—may they draw strength from the merits and example of Christ their Head, who offered the perfect sacrifice on the cross. (R.)

Lord, give sight to the the blind, set prisoners free,
—uphold the widow and orphan. (R.)

Arm your people for the struggle they must wage as Christians,
—that they may be able to withstand in the evil day. (R.)

Be merciful to us, Lord, in our last hour and stand with us,
—so that we may prove faithful to the end and leave the world in your peace. (R.)

Bring the dead into your eternal light
—and grant them for ever the vision of your glory. (R.)

Our Father . . .

Concluding prayer

Lord God, may the passion of your Son teach us to be ready always to carry the burden which his love makes easy to bear. Who lives and reigns.

May the Lord bless us,
may he keep us from all evil
and lead us to life everlasting.
Amen.

Let us bless the Lord.
R. Thanks be to God.

Saturday I

OFFICE OF READINGS

O God, come to my assistance.
Lord, make haste to help me.
Glory be to the Father, and to the Son, and to the Holy Spirit.
As it was in the beginning, is now, and ever shall be, world without end. Amen. Alleluia!

Or, if used as first prayer of the day: O Lord, open my lips . . .

Hymn

How deep the riches of our God,
His wisdom how sublime;
How high his judgments soar above
All judgment of mankind!

What mind has read the mind of God,
Or giv'n him counsel sure?
Who from his riches gave to God
What was not first received?

From God all things created flow;
All things through him exist;
To him for judgment all returns,
To whom all praise is due!

To God the Father, fount of grace,
Through his beloved Son
in oneness with the Holy Ghost
Be glory evermore!

Psalmody

A. THROUGHOUT THE YEAR

Psalm 130   **Song of serenity**

Learn from me, for I am gentle and lowly in heart (Matthew 11:29)

Ant. Whoever humbles himself like a child,
   he is the greatest in the kingdom of heaven.

O Lord, my heart is not proud
nor haughty my eyes.
I have not gone after things too great
nor marvels beyond me.

Truly I have set my soul
in silence and peace.
A weaned child on its mother's breast,
even so is my soul.

O Israel, hope in the Lord
both now and for ever.

Ant. Whoever humbles himself like a child,
   he is the greatest in the kingdom of heaven.

Psalm 131   **David's reign in the sanctuary of Zion**

   *The Lord God will give to him the throne of his father
   David* (Luke 1:32)

I

Ant. In the uprightness of my heart, O Lord,
   I have freely and joyously offered everything.

O Lord, remember David
and all the hardships he endured,
the oath he swore to the Lord,
his vow to the Strong One of Jacob.

'I will not enter the house where I live
nor go to the bed where I rest.
I will give no sleep to my eyes
to my eyelids will give no slumber
till I find a place for the Lord,
a dwelling for the Strong One of Jacob.'

At Ephrata we heard of the ark;
we found it in the plains of Yearim.
'Let us go to the place of his dwelling;
let us go to kneel at his footstool.'

Go up, Lord, to the place of your rest,
you and the ark of your strength.
Your priests shall be clothed with holiness:
your faithful shall ring out their joy.
For the sake of David your servant
do not reject your anointed.

Ant. In the uprightness of my heart, O Lord,
   I have freely and joyously offered everything.

II

Ant. God will give him the throne of David,
   and he will reign for ever.

The Lord swore an oath to David;
he will not go back on his word:
'A son, the fruit of your body,
will I set upon your throne.

If they keep my covenant in truth
and my laws that I have taught them,
their sons also shall rule on your throne
from age to age.'

For the Lord has chosen Zion;
he has desired it for his dwelling:
'This is my resting-place for ever,
here have I chosen to live.

I will greatly bless her produce,
I will find her poor with bread.
I will clothe her priests with salvation
and her faithful shall ring out their joy.

There the stock of David will flower:
I will prepare a lamp for my anointed.
I will cover his enemies with shame
but on him my crown shall shine.'

Ant. God will give him the throne of David,
   and he will reign for ever.

B. ADVENT, CHRISTMASTIDE, LENT AND EASTERTIDE

Psalm 104   **The story of Israel: God fulfils the promises he made to Abraham**

God works for good with those who love him, who are called according to his purpose (Rom 8:28)

I

Ant. O sing to the Lord:
  make known his deeds among the peoples.

Give thanks to the Lord, tell his name,
make known his deeds among the peoples.

O sing to him, sing his praise;
tell all his wonderful works!
Be proud of his holy name,
let the hearts that seek the Lord rejoice.

Consider the Lord and his strength;
constantly seek his face.
Remember the wonders he has done,
his miracles, the judgments he spoke.

O children of Abraham, his servant,
O sons of the Jacob he chose.
He, the Lord, is our God:
his judgments prevail in all the earth.

He remembers his covenant for ever,
his promise for a thousand generations,
the covenant he made with Abraham,
the oath he swore to Isaac.

He confirmed it for Jacob as a law,
for Israel as a covenant for ever.
He said: 'I am giving you a land,
Canaan, your appointed heritage.'

When they were few in number,
a handful of strangers in the land,
when they wandered from country to country
and from one kingdom to another,

he allowed no one to oppress them;
he admonished kings on their account:
'Do not touch my anointed;
do no harm to any of my prophets.'

Ant. O sing to the Lord:
   make known his deeds among the peoples.

II

Ant. God increased his people;
   he strengthened them against their foes.

But he called down a famine on the land;
he broke the staff that supported them.
He had sent a man before them,
Joseph, sold as a slave.

His feet were put in chains,
his neck was bound with iron,
until what he said came to pass
and the Lord's word proved him true.

Then the king sent and released him;
the ruler of the peoples set him free,
making him master of his house
and ruler of all he possessed,

to instruct his princes as he pleased
and to teach his elders wisdom.
So Israel came into Egypt,
Jacob lived in the country of Ham.

Ant. God increased his people;
   he strengthened them against their foes.

III

Ant. The Lord has set his people free:
   for his chosen ones joy and shouts of rejoicing.

He gave his people increase;
he made them stronger than their foes,
whose hearts he turned to hate his people
and to deal deceitfully with his servants.

Then he sent Moses his servant
and Aaron the man he had chosen.
Through them he showed his marvels
and his wonders in the country of Ham.

He sent darkness, and dark was made
but Egypt resisted his words.
He turned the waters into blood
and caused their fish to die.

Their land was alive with frogs,
even in the halls of their kings.
He spoke; the dog-fly came
and gnats covered the land.

He sent hail-stones in place of the rain
and flashing fire in their land.
He struck their vines and fig-trees;
he shattered the trees through their land.

He spoke; the locusts came,
young locusts, too many to be counted.
They ate up every blade in the land;
they ate up all the fruit of their fields.

He struck all the first-born in their land,
the finest flower of their sons.
He led out Israel with silver and gold.
In his tribes were none who fell behind.

Egypt rejoiced when they left
for dread had fallen upon them.
He spread a cloud as a screen
and fire to give light in the darkness.

When they asked for food he sent quails;
he filled them with bread from heaven.
He pierced the rock to give them water;
it gushed forth in the desert like a river.

For he remembered his holy word,
which he gave to Abraham his servant.

So he brought out his people with joy,
his chosen ones with shouts of rejoicing.

And he gave them the land of the nations.
They took the fruit of other men's toil,
that thus they might keep his precepts,
that thus they might observe his laws.

Ant. The Lord has set his people free:
for his chosen ones joy and shouts of rejoicing.

V. Come, consider the works of God,
R. The redoubtable deeds he has done on the earth.

Readings

Prayer of the day
Or alternative prayer

MORNING PRAYER

Introductory verse and psalm
O Lord, open my lips.
And my mouth shall declare your praise.
Glory be to the Father, and to the Son, and to the Holy
Spirit.
As it was in the beginning, is now, and ever shall be, world
without end. Amen. Alleluia!

Psalm 94
Refrain: Let us go to meet the Lord with songs of joy and
gladness.

Or, if not used as first prayer of the day: O God, come to my
assistance...

Hymn
R. Awake, O sleeper, and arise from the dead,
and Christ shall give you light.

Christ, who was manifested in the flesh,
vindicated in the Spirit,
seen by the angels,

preached among the nations,
believed on in the world,
taken up in glory. (*R.*)

Christ, who will be made manifest
at the proper time
by the blessed and only Sovereign,
the King of kings and Lord of lords,
who alone has immortality
and dwells in unapproachable light,
whom no man has ever seen or can see,
to him be honour and eternal dominion. Amen. (*R.*)

Psalmody
Psalm 118:145-152

*This is my commandment, that you love one another as I
have loved you* (John 15:12)

Ant. I rise before dawn and cry for help;
    in your Word, O Lord, I hope.

I call with all my heart; Lord, hear me,
I will keep your statutes.
I call upon you, save me
and I will do your will.

I rise before dawn and cry for help,
I hope in your word.
My eyes watch through the night
to ponder your promise.

In your love hear my voice, O Lord;
give me life by your decrees.
Those who harm me unjustly draw near:
they are far from your law.

But you, O Lord, are close:
your commands are truth.
Long have I known that your will
is established for ever.

Ant. I rise before dawn and cry for help;
in your Word, O Lord, I hope.

Ex 15:1–4, 8–13   Song of Moses to God, the Redeemer of his people

*Those who had conquered sang the song of Moses, the
servant of God* (Rev 15:2, 3)

Ant. Let us sing to the Lord, glorious his triumph!

I will sing to the Lord, glorious his triumph!
Horse and rider he has thrown into the sea!

The Lord is my strength, my song, my salvation.†
This is my God and I extol him,
my father's God and I give him praise.
The Lord is a warrior!
The Lord is his name.

The chariots of Pharaoh he hurled into the sea.
At the breath of your anger the waters piled high;
the moving waters stood up like a dam.
The deeps turned solid in the midst of the sea.

The enemy said: 'I will pursue and overtake them,†
I will divide the plunder, I shall have my will.
I will draw my sword, my hand shall destroy them.'

You blew with your breath, the sea closed over them.
They went down like lead into the mighty waters.

Who is like you among the gods, O Lord,†
who is like you, so glorious in holiness,
spreading fear through your deeds, you who do marvels.

You stretched forth your hand,
the earth engulfed them;
your love has guided the people you redeemed,
your power has led them to your holy dwelling-place . . .

You will lead them and plant them on your mountain,†
the place, O Lord, where you have made your home,
the sanctuary, Lord, which your hands have made.
The Lord will reign
for ever and ever!

Ant. Let us sing to the Lord, glorious his triumph!

Psalm 116   **World-wide call to praise God**

Christ became a servant . . . that the Gentiles might glorify God for his mercy (Rom 15:8)

Ant. O praise the Lord, all you peoples of the earth.

O praise the Lord, all you nations,
acclaim him all you peoples!

Strong is his love for us;
he is faithful for ever.

Ant. O praise the Lord, all you peoples of the earth.

Word of God   2 Cor 13:11

Brethren, mend your ways, heed my appeal, agree with one another, live in peace, and the God of love and peace will be with you.

Short Response

Ring out your joy
to God our strength.

V. Shout in triumph to the God of Jacob.

R. Ring out your joy to God our strength.

V. Glory be to the Father, and to the Son, and to the Holy Spirit.

Ring out your joy
to God our strength.

Song of Zechariah

Ant. Guide us, O Lord, into the way of peace.

Prayers

God has displayed his great love for the people he set apart for his own. Confident in this knowledge, let us ask him:

R. Give grace and peace to your people, Lord.

Almighty God, Creator, it is from you that everything has its origin,

—receive the offering which we make of ourselves and of all that belongs to us. (*R.*)

125

Enlighten us by the rays of the true Sun, Christ,
—and from the beginning of this day destroy everything
within us that tends to evil. (R.)

Control our thoughts, words and actions,
—so that our lives may prove acceptable to you today. (R.)

We pray for all those whom we shall encounter today:
—bless them, their relatives and their friends. (R.)

Other prayers may be added

Our Father . . .

Concluding prayer

Lord God, fill our hearts with the radiance of your resurrection, so that we may escape from the darkness of death into eternal life. We make our prayer through our Lord.

May the Lord bless us,
may he keep us from all evil
and lead us to life everlasting.
Amen.

Let us bless the Lord.
R. Thanks be to God.

MIDDAY PRAYER

O God, come to my assistance . . .
Glory be . . .

Hymn
Holy Spirit,
one with the Father and the Son,
deign at this hour to come down on us without delay
and pour out your graces over our soul.

Let mouth, tongue, soul, thought and strength
make your praise resound.
Let our love be set aflame by the fire of your love
and its heat in turn enkindle love in our neighbours.

126

Grant this, most loving Father,
and you, the only Son, equal to the Father,
and, with the Spirit, the Paraclete,
reigning through the ages. Amen.

Psalmody

Psalm 118:33-40

Ant. Guide me in the way of your law.

Teach me the demands of your statutes
and I will keep them to the end.
Train me to observe your law,
to keep it with my heart.

Guide me in the path of your commands;
for there is my delight.
Bend my heart to your will
and not to love of gain.

Keep my eyes from what is false:
by your word, give me life.
Keep the promise you have made
to the servant who fears you.

Keep me from the scorn I dread,
for your decrees are good.
See, I long for your precepts:
then in your justice, give me life.

Psalm 33   The fear of God and its fruit

You have tasted the kindness of the Lord (1 Peter 2:3)

I

I will bless the Lord at all times,
his praise always on my lips;
in the Lord my soul shall make its boast.
The humble shall hear and be glad.

Glorify the Lord with me.
Together let us praise his name.

I sought the Lord and he answered me;
from all my terrors he set me free.

Look towards him and be radiant;
let your faces not be abashed.
This poor man called; the Lord heard him
and rescued him from all his distress.

The angel of the Lord is encamped
around those who revere him, to rescue them.
Taste and see that the Lord is good.
He is happy who seeks refuge in him.

Revere the Lord, you his saints.
They lack nothing, those who revere him.
Strong lions suffer want and go hungry
but those who seek the Lord lack no blessing.

II

Come, children, and hear me
that I may teach you the fear of the Lord.
Who is he who longs for life
and many days, to enjoy his prosperity?

Then keep your tongue from evil
and your lips from speaking deceit.
Turn aside from evil and do good;
seek and strive after peace.

The Lord turns his face against the wicked
to destroy their remembrance from the earth.
The Lord turns his eyes to the just
and his ears to their appeal.

They call and the Lord hears
and rescues them in all their distress.
The Lord is close to the broken-hearted;
those whose spirit is crushed he will save.

Many are the trials of the just man
but from them all the Lord will rescue him.

He will keep guard over all his bones,
not one of his bones shall be broken.

Evil brings death to the wicked;
those who hate the good are doomed.

The Lord ransoms the souls of his servants.
Those who hide in him shall not be condemned.

Ant. Guide me in the way of your law.

Word of God   Jer 17:9–10
The heart is deceitful above all things, and desperately
corrupt; who can understand it? I, the Lord, search the
mind and try the heart, to give to every man according to
his ways, according to the fruit of his doings.

V. The justice of your will is eternal:
R. If you teach me I shall live.

Prayer
O Lord, fire of everlasting love, give us the fervour to love
you above all things, and our brother for your sake.
Through Christ.

Let us bless the Lord.
R. Thanks be to God.

Sunday II

EVENING PRAYER II

O God, come to my assistance.
Lord, make haste to help me.
Glory be to the Father, and to the Son, and to the Holy Spirit.
As it was in the beginning, is now, and ever shall be, world without end. Amen. Alleluia!

Hymn   2 Tim 2:11–13

R. Christ has died,
Christ is risen,
Christ will come again.

If we have died with him,
we shall also live with him;
If we endure,
we shall also reign with him. (*R.*)

If we deny him,
he will also deny us;
If we are faithless, he remains faithful—
for he cannot deny himself. Alleluia! (*R.*)

Psalmody

Psalm 118:105–112   Hymn to the revelation of the law

Love is the fulfilling of the law (Rom 13:10)

Ant. Your word is a lamp for my steps,
    a light for my path.

Your word is a lamp for my steps
and a light for my path.
I have sworn and have determined
to obey your decrees.

Lord, I am deeply afflicted:
by your word give me life.
Accept, Lord, the homage of my lips
and teach me your decrees.

Though I carry my life in my hands,
I remember your law.
Though the wicked try to ensnare me
I do not stray from your precepts

Your will is my heritage for ever,
the joy of my heart.
I set myself to carry out your statutes
in fullness, for ever.

Ant. Your word is a lamp for my steps,
    a light for my path.

Psalm 15   **Thanksgiving for God's saving action**

They will see the Son of man coming in a cloud with power
and great glory (Luke 21:27)

Ant. You will teach me the way of life,
    you will give me happiness in your presence for ever.

Preserve me, God, I take refuge in you.†
I say to the Lord: 'You are my God.
My happiness lies in you alone.'

He has put into my heart a marvellous love
for the faithful ones who dwell in his land.
Those who choose other gods increase their sorrows.†
Never will I offer their offerings of blood.
Never will I take their name upon my lips.

O Lord, it is you who are my portion and cup;
it is you yourself who are my prize.
The lot marked out for me is my delight:
welcome indeed the heritage that falls to me!

I will bless the Lord who gives me counsel,
who even at night directs my heart.

I keep the Lord ever in my sight:
since he is at my right hand, I shall stand firm.

And so my heart rejoices, my soul is glad;
even my body shall rest in safety.

For you will not leave my soul among the dead,
nor let your beloved know decay.

You will show me the path of life,†
the fullness of joy in your presence,
at your right hand happiness for ever.

Ant. You will teach me the way of life,
   you will give me happiness in your presence for ever.

Phil 2:6–11   **Song of the Easter mystery**

Ant. Christ died for our sins,
   and rose that we might live.

Though he was in the form of God,
Jesus did not count equality with God a thing to be grasped.

R. Jesus Christ is Lord
   to the glory of God the Father!

He emptied himself,†
taking the form of a servant,
being born in the likeness of men. (*R.*)

And being found in human form,†
he humbled himself and became obedient unto death,
even death on a cross. (*R.*)

Therefore God has highly exalted him
and bestowed on him the name which is above every
   name. (*R.*)

That at the name of Jesus every knee should bow,
in heaven and on earth and under the earth. (*R.*)

And every tongue confess
   that Jesus is Lord,
to the glory of God the Father.

Ant. Christ died for our sins,
   and rose that we might live.

Word of God Col 1:2–6

Grace to you and peace from God our Father.
We always thank God, the Father of our Lord Jesus Christ,
when we pray for you, because we have heard of your faith
in Christ Jesus and of the love which you have for all the
saints, because of the hope laid up for you in heaven. Of
this you have heard before in the word of the truth, the
gospel which has come to you, as indeed in the whole world
it is bearing fruit and growing—so among yourselves.

Short Response

In you, O Lord, I take refuge.
Let me never be put to shame.
V. In your justice, set me free.
R. Let me never be put to shame.
V. Glory be to the Father, and to the Son, and to the Holy
Spirit.

In you, O Lord, I take refuge.
Let me never be put to shame.

Song of the Virgin Mary

Ant. My soul glorifies the Lord who protects the lowly.

Prayers

Let us pray to God, for he is the Lord who dwells among us
and we are the people he has won for himself:

R. Be with your people, Lord, to help them.

Holy Lord, almighty Father, grant that justice may flourish
among us,
—and your people shall enjoy the blessing of peace. (*R.*)

Bring all men into your kingdom
—that your people may be saved. (*R.*)

Bless married couples with a life of harmony; may they
be faithful to you and to each other,
—may they grow in love until death. (*R.*)

133

Reward all our benefactors, Lord.
—Grant them eternal life. (R.)

Look with compassion on those who have died as a result of war, violence and hatred.
—welcome them into the peace of your kingdom and give them rest. (R.)

Our Father . . .

Concluding prayer of the Sunday

May the Lord bless us,
may he keep us from all evil
and lead us to life everlasting.
Amen.

Let us bless the Lord.
R. Thanks be to God.

OFFICE OF READINGS

O God, come to my assistance.
Lord, make haste to help me.
Glory be to the Father, and to the Son, and to the Holy Spirit.
As it was in the beginning, is now, and ever shall be, world without end. Amen. Alleluia!

Or, if used as first prayer of the day: O Lord, open my lips . . .

Hymn
R. Alleluia! Christ is risen, alleluia!

I will sing to the Lord, glorious his triumph!
Horse and rider he has thrown into the sea.
Lord, you are great, you are glorious,
wonderful in strength, none can conquer you.
God has arisen, and his foes are scattered;
those who hate him have fled before him. (R.)

He has burst the gates of bronze
and shattered the iron bars.
This God of ours is a God who saves;
the Lord our God holds the keys of death.
This is the day which the Lord has made;
let us rejoice and be glad. (*R.*)

Awake, O sleeper, and rise from the dead,
and Christ shall give you light.
For he has been raised from the dead,
never to die any more.
God has not left his soul among the dead,
nor let his beloved know decay. (*R.*)

The Lord is risen from the tomb
who hung for us upon the tree.
Beasts of the field, do not be afraid;
the pastures of the wildnerness are green again.
The tree bears its fruit once more,
vine and fig tree yield abundantly. (*R.*)

Psalmody

Psalm 103   **God's boundless care for his creation**

*If any one is in Christ, he is a new creation; the old has
passed away, behold, the new has come* (2 Cor 5:17)

I

Ant. Lord God, how great you are!

Bless the Lord, my soul!
Lord God, how great you are,
clothed in majesty and glory,
wrapped in light as in a robe!

You stretch out the heavens like a tent.
Above the rains you build your dwelling.
You make the clouds your chariot,
you walk on the wings of the wind,
you make the winds your messengers
and flashing fire your servants.

135

You founded the earth on its base,
to stand firm from age to age.
You wrapped it with the ocean like a cloak:
the waters stood higher than the mountains.

At your threat they took to flight;
at the voice of your thunder they fled.
They rose over the mountains and flowed down
to the place which you had appointed.
You set limits they might not pass
lest they return to cover the earth.

You make springs gush forth in the valleys:
they flow in between the hills.
They give drink to all the beasts of the field;
the wild-asses quench their thirst.
On their banks dwell the birds of heaven;
from the branches they sing their song.

Ant. Lord God, how great you are!

II

Ant. Earth drinks its fill of your gift, O Lord.

From your dwelling you water the hills;
earth drinks its fill of your gift.
You make the grass grow for the cattle
and the plants to serve man's needs,

that he may bring forth bread from the earth
and wine, to cheer man's heart;
oil, to make his face shine
and bread to strengthen man's heart.

The trees of the Lord drink their fill,
the cedars he planted on Lebanon;
there the birds build their nests:
on the tree-top the stork has her home.
The goats find a home on the mountains
and rabbits hide in the rocks.

You made the moon to mark the months;
the sun knows the time for its setting.
When you spread the darkness it is night
and all the beasts of the forest creep forth.
The young lions roar for their prey
and ask their food from God.

At the rising of the sun they steal away
and go to rest in their dens.
Man goes forth to his work,
to labour till evening falls.

Ant. Earth drinks its fill of your gift, O Lord.

III

Ant. God looked at his work and saw that all of it was good.

How many are your works, O Lord!†
In wisdom you have made them all.
The earth is full of your riches.

There is the sea, vast and wide,†
with its moving swarms past counting,
living things great and small.
The ships are moving there
and the monsters you made to play with.

All of these look to you
to give them their food in due season.
You give it, they gather it up:
you open your hand, they have their fill.

You hide your face, they are dismayed;†
you take back your spirit, they die,
returning to the dust from which they came.
You send forth your spirit, they are created;
and you renew the face of the earth.

May the glory of the Lord last for ever!
May the Lord rejoice in his works!
He looks on the earth and it trembles;
the mountains send forth smoke at his touch.

I will sing to the Lord all my life,
make music to my God while I live.
May my thoughts be pleasing to him.
I find my joy in the Lord.
Let sinners vanish from the earth
and the wicked exist no more.

All: Bless the Lord, my soul.

Ant. God looked at his work and saw that all of it was good.

V. Blessed are the eyes which see what you see,

R. And the ears which hear what you hear.

Readings

(Hymn of praise)

Prayer of the Sunday

MORNING PRAYER

Introductory verse and psalm

O Lord, open my lips.

And my mouth shall declare your praise.

Glory be to the Father, and to the Son, and to the Holy Spirit.

As it was in the beginning, is now, and ever shall be, world without end. Amen. Alleluia!

Psalm 94

Refrain: Come, people chosen by God,
worship your Shepherd and Guide.

Or, if not used as first prayer of the day: O God, come to my assistance . . .

Hymn

Sing, all creation, sing to God in gladness!
Joyously serve him, singing hymns of homage!
Chanting his praises, come before his presence!
Praise the Almighty!

Know that our God is Lord of all the ages!
He is our maker; we are all his creatures,
People he fashioned, sheep he leads to pasture!
Praise the Almighty!

Enter his temple, ringing out his praises!
Sing in thanksgiving as you come before him!
Blessing his bounty, glorify his greatness!
Praise the Almighty!
Great in his goodness is the Lord we worship;
Steadfast his kindness, love that knows no ending!
Faithful his word is, changeless, everlasting!
Praise the Almighty!

Psalmody

Psalm 117   **Thanksgiving in the temple for the gift of salvation**

This is the stone which was rejected by you builders, but which has become the head of the corner (Acts 4:11)

Ant. This day was made by the Lord, alleluia!

Give thanks to the Lord for he is good,
for his love has no end.
Let the sons of Israel say:
'His love has no end.'
Let the sons of Aaron say:
'His love has no end.'
Let those who fear the Lord say:
'His love has no end.'

I called to the Lord in my distress;
he answered and freed me.
The Lord is at my side; I do not fear.
What can man do against me?
The Lord is at my side as my helper:
I shall look down on my foes.

It is better to take refuge in the Lord
than to trust in men:
it is better to take refuge in the Lord
than to trust in princes . . .

I was thrust, thrust down and falling
but the Lord was my helper.
The Lord is my strength and my song;
he was my saviour.

There are shouts of joy and victory
in the tents of the just.

The Lord's right hand has triumphed;
his right hand raised me up.
The Lord's right hand has triumphed;
I shall not die, I shall live and recount his deeds.
I was punished, I was punished by the Lord,
but not doomed to die.

Open to me the gates of holiness:
I will enter and give thanks.
This is the Lord's own gate
where the just may enter.
I will thank you for you have given answer
and you are my saviour.

The stone which the builders rejected
has become the corner stone.
This is the work of the Lord,
a marvel in our eyes.
This day was made by the Lord;
we rejoice and are glad.

O Lord, grant us salvation;
O Lord, grant success.
Blessed in the name of the Lord
is he who comes.
We bless you from the house of the Lord;
the Lord God is our light.

Go forward in procession with branches
even to the altar.
You are my God, I thank you.
My God, I praise you.
Give thanks to the Lord for he is good;
for his love has no end.

Ant. This day was made by the Lord, alleluia!

Dan 3:52–57 **Song of the three children in praise of creation**

The Creator, who is blessed for ever (Rom 1:25)

Ant. Let us sing a hymn, let us bless God for ever.

You are blest, Lord God of our fathers.
To you glory and praise for evermore.

Blest your glorious holy name.
To you glory and praise for evermore.

You are blest, in the temple of your glory.
To you glory and praise for evermore.

You are blest who gaze into the depths.
To you glory and praise for evermore.

You are blest in the firmament of heaven.
To you glory and praise for evermore.

You who walk on the wings of the wind.
To you glory and praise for evermore.

May they bless you, the saints and the angels.
To you glory and praise for evermore.

From the heavens, the earth and the sea.
To you glory and praise for evermore.

You are blest, Lord God of our fathers.
To you glory and praise for evermore.

Ant. Let us sing a hymn, let us bless God for ever.

Psalm 150 **Symphony of praise to God**

*To him be glory in the Church and in Christ Jesus, for ever
and ever. Amen* (Eph 3:21)

Ant. Let everything that breathes give praise to the Lord.

Praise God in his holy place,
praise him in his mighty heavens.
Praise him for his powerful deeds,
praise his surpassing greatness.

O praise him with sound of trumpet,
praise him with lute and harp.
Praise him with timbrel and dance,
praise him with strings and pipes.

O praise him with resounding cymbals,
praise him with clashing of cymbals.
Let everything that lives and breathes
give praise to the Lord.

Ant. Let everything that breathes give praise to the Lord.

Word of God   Ez 36:25–27
I will sprinkle clean water upon you, and you shall be clean
from all your uncleannesses, and from all your idols I will
cleanse you. A new heart I will give you, and a new spirit I
will put within you; and I will take out of your flesh the
heart of stone and give you a heart of flesh. And I will put
my spirit within you, and cause you to walk in my statutes
and be careful to observe my ordinances.

Short Response
I will sing for ever
of your love, O Lord.
V. Through all ages I will sing to your name.
R. I will sing for ever of your love, O Lord.
V. Glory be to the Father, and to the Son, and to the Holy
Spirit.
I will sing for ever
of your love, O Lord.

Song of Zechariah
Ant. The Lord our God, the Almighty, reigns.
    Let us rejoice and exult and give him the glory.

Prayers
Our Saviour took flesh and came into the world to be
Emmanuel, God-with-us. Let us pray:

R. Christ, King of glory, be our light and our joy.

142

Lord Jesus Christ, you visit us like the dawn from on high;
you are the first-fruits of the resurrection to come.
—Help us to follow you so that our journey may not be in
the shadow of death, but may bring us to the light which is
eternal life. (*R.*)

Help us to recognize your goodness which you spread
abroad in all creation;
—may we contemplate your glory everywhere. (*R.*)

Keep us from falling victims to evil today, Lord.
—make us overcome evil with good. (*R.*)

We will praise you in our words and actions today, Lord,
—and our hearts shall find joy in you. (*R.*)

Other prayers may be added

Our Father . . .

Concluding prayer of the Sunday

May the Lord bless us,
may he keep us from all evil
and lead us to life everlasting.
Amen.

Let us bless the Lord.
R. Thanks be to God.

MIDDAY PRAYER

O God, come to my assistance . . .
Glory be . . .

Hymn
Mighty ruler, faithful God,
who arrange the successive changes in nature,
giving bright light to the morning sun
and burning heat at noon.

Put out the flames of strife
and take away the heat of passion;

grant us health of body
and true peace of soul.

Grant this, most loving Father,
and you, the only Son, equal to the Father
and, with the Spirit, the Paraclete,
reigning through the ages. Amen.

Psalmody

Psalm 22   **God, shepherd of his people**

The Lamb will be their shepherd, and he will guide them to springs of living water (Rev 7:17)

Ant. Guide us, Lord, to the springs of life.

The Lord is my shepherd;
there is nothing I shall want.
Fresh and green are the pastures
where he gives me repose.
Near restful waters he leads me,
to revive my drooping spirit.

He guides me along the right path;
he is true to his name.
If I should walk in the valley of darkness
no evil would I fear.
You are there with your crook and your staff;
with these you give me comfort.

You have prepared a banquet for me
in the sight of my foes.
My head you have anointed with oil;
my cup is overflowing.

Surely goodness and kindness shall follow me
all the days of my life.
In the Lord's own house shall I dwell
for ever and ever.

Psalm 75 Song after victory

They will see the Son of man coming on the clouds of heaven (Matthew 24:30)

I

God is made known in Judah;
in Israel his name is great.
He set up his tent in Jerusalem
and his dwelling place in Zion.
It was there he broke the flashing arrows,
the shield, the sword, the armour.

You, Lord, are resplendent,
more majestic than the everlasting mountains.
The warriors, despoiled, slept in death;
the hands of the soldiers were powerless.
At your threat, O God of Jacob,
horse and rider lay stunned.

II

You, you alone, strike terror.
Who shall stand when your anger is roused?
You uttered your sentence from the heavens;
the earth in terror was still
when God arose to judge,
to save the humble of the earth.

Men's anger will serve to praise you;†
its survivors surround you in joy.
Make vows to your God and fulfil them.
Let all pay tribute to him who strikes terror,†
who cuts short the breath of princes,
who strikes terror in the kings of the earth.

Ant. Guide us, Lord, to the springs of life.

Word of God Rom 8:26
The Spirit helps us in our weakness, for we do not know how to pray as we ought, but the Spirit himself intercedes for us with sighs too deep for words.

V. Lord, let my cry come before you.
R. Teach me by your word.

Prayer of the Sunday
Let us bless the Lord.
R. Thanks be to God.

EVENING PRAYER II

O God, come to my assistance.
Lord, make haste to help me.
Glory be to the Father, and to the Son, and to the Holy
Spirit.
As it was in the beginning, is now, and ever shall be, world
without end. Amen. Alleluia!

Hymn
R. Alleluia! Christ is risen, alleluia!

I have trodden the wine press alone,
and from the peoples no one was with me.
I have laid down my life of my own free will,
and by my own power I have taken it up anew.
Fear not, I am the first and the last;
I am the living one. (*R.*)

Was it not ordained that the Christ should suffer,
and so enter into his glory?
Upon him was the chastisement that made us whole,
and with his stripes we are healed.
It was the will of the Lord to bruise him;
he has offered his life in atonement. (*R.*)

By his holy and glorious wounds
may Christ the Lord guard us and keep us.
If we have died with him, we shall also live with him;
if we endure, we shall also reign with him.
Christ yesterday and today,
the beginning of all things and their end.

Alpha and Omega;
all time belongs to him, and all the ages. (*R.*)

Psalmody

Psalm 109   **The Messiah, king, priest and judge**

He must reign until he has put all his enemies under his feet (1 Cor 15:25)

Ant. The Lord said to my Lord: 'Sit on my right.'

The Lord's revelation to my Master:†
'Sit on my right:
I will put your foes beneath your feet.'

The Lord will send from Zion your sceptre of power:
rule in the midst of all your foes.

A prince from the day of your birth on the holy mountains;
from the womb before the daybreak I begot you.

The Lord has sworn an oath he will not change.†
'You are a priest for ever,
a priest like Melchizedeck of old.'

The Master standing at your right hand
will shatter kings in the day of his great wrath.

He shall drink from the stream by the wayside
and therefore he shall lift up his head.

Ant. The Lord said to my Lord: 'Sit on my right.'

Psalm 113B   **Hymn to the one true God**

You turned to God from idols to serve a living and true God (1 Thess 1:9)

Ant. Our God does whatever he wills,
in heaven or on earth.

Not to us, Lord, not to us,
but to your name give the glory
for the sake of your love and your truth,
lest the heathen say: 'Where is their God?'

But our God he is in the heavens;
he does whatever he wills.
Their idols are silver and gold,
the work of human hands.

They have mouths but they cannot speak;
they have eyes but they cannot see;
they have ears but they cannot hear;
they have nostrils but they cannot smell.

With their hands they cannot feel;†
with their feet they cannot walk.
No sound comes from their throats.
Their makers will become like them:
so will all who trust in them.

Sons of Israel, trust in the Lord;
he is their help and their shield.
Sons of Aaron, trust in the Lord;
he is their help and their shield.

You who fear him, trust in the Lord;
he is their help and their shield.
He remembers us, will give us his blessing;†
he will bless the sons of Israel.
He will bless the sons of Aaron.

The Lord will bless those who fear him,
the little no less than the great:
to you may the Lord grant increase,
to you and all your children.

May you be blessed by the Lord,
the maker of heaven and earth.
The heavens belong to the Lord
but the earth he has given to men.

The dead shall not praise the Lord,
nor those who go down into the silence.
But we who live bless the Lord
now and for ever.

Ant. Our God does whatever he wills,
  in heaven or on earth.

OUTSIDE LENT

Rev 19:1, 2, 5–8   **Wedding song of the Lamb**

Ant. Alleluia! Victory and glory and power belong to our
God.
  He reigns for ever and ever, alleluia!

R. Alleluia, alleluia!
Salvation and glory and power
belong to our God, alleluia!
His judgments are true
and just.
R. Alleluia, alleluia!

Praise our God,
all you his servants, alleluia!
You who fear him,
small and great.
R. Alleluia, alleluia!

The Lord our God,
the Almighty, reigns, alleluia!
Let us rejoice and exult
and give him the glory.
R. Alleluia, alleluia!

The marriage of the Lamb
has come, alleluia!
And his bride
has made herself ready.
R. Alleluia, alleluia!

It was granted her,
to be clothed, alleluia,

with fine linen,
bright and pure.
R. Alleluia, alleluia!

Ant. Alleluia! Victory and glory and power belong to our God.

He reigns for ever and ever, Alleluia!

LENT

1 Pet 2:21–24   **New Testament Song of the suffering Servant**

Ant. For our sake God made him to be sin who knew no sin, so that in him we might become the righteousness of God.

Christ suffered for you,†
leaving you an example
that you should follow in his steps.

R. By his wounds you have been healed.

He committed no sin;
no guile was found on his lips.
When he was reviled,
he did not revile in return (*R*.)

When he suffered,
he did not threaten;
but he trusted to him
who judges justly. (*R*.)

He himself bore our sins
in his body on the tree,
that we might die to sin
and live to righteousness.

By his wounds you have been healed.†
For you were straying like sheep,
but have now returned to the Shepherd and Guardian of your souls. (*R*.)

Ant. For our sake God made him to be sin who knew no sin, so that in him we might become the righteousness of God.

150

Word of God Eph 1:3–4

Blessed be the God and Father of our Lord Jesus Christ, who has blessed us in Christ with every spiritual blessing in the heavenly places, even as he chose us in him before the foundation of the world, that we should be holy and blameless before him in love.

Short Response

May the name of the Lord be blessed,
Alleluia, alleluia!
V. Both now and for evermore.
R. Alleluia, alleluia!
V. Glory be to the Father, and to the Son, and to the Holy Spirit.
May the name of the Lord be blessed,
Alleluia, alleluia!

Song of the Virgin Mary

Ant. Sing and rejoice, O people of God,
for lo, I come and I will dwell in the midst of you.

Prayers

Christ is able for all time to save those who draw near to God through him, since he always lives to make intercession for them. Let us turn to him, then, with full confidence:

R. Remember your people, Lord.

Lord Jesus Christ, Sun of justice, as the daylight begins to fail, we call upon you in the name of the whole human race:
—may all men one day enjoy your light, that eternal light which never fails. (*R.*)

Protect N., our Pope,
—defend him and help him. (*R.*)

Remember the people whom you have chosen, Lord,
—the place where your glory dwells. (*R.*)

Guide all travellers; may they enjoy peace and well-being;
—give them a safe journey and a happy home-coming. (*R.*)

Other prayers may be added

Welcome the souls of the faithful departed,
—pardon them and give them glory without end. (*R.*)

Our Father . . .

Concluding prayer of the Sunday

May the Lord bless us,
may he keep us from all evil
and lead us to life everlasting.
Amen.

Let us bless the Lord.
R. Thanks be to God.

Monday II

OFFICE OF READINGS

O God, come to my assistance.
Lord, make haste to help me.
Glory be to the Father, and to the Son, and to the Holy
Spirit.
As it was in the beginning, is now, and ever shall be, world
without end. Amen. Alleluia!

Or, if used as first prayer of the day: O Lord, open my lips...

Hymn 1 Cor 13:4–10, 12–13

Love is patient and kind:†
love is not jealous or boastful;
it is not arrogant or rude.

R. Faith, hope and love abide, but the greatest of these is
love.

Love does not insist on its own way,
it is not irritable or resentful;
it does not rejoice at wrong,
but rejoices in the right. (*R*.)

Love bears all things,
believes all things,
hopes all things,
endures all things. (*R*.)

Love never ends;†
as for prophecies,
they will pass away;
as for tongues,
they will cease;
as for knowledge,
it will pass away. (*R*.)

For our knowledge is imperfect
and our prophecy is imperfect;

but when the perfect comes,
the imperfect will pass away. (*R.*)

Now I know in part;
then I shall understand fully,
even as I have been fully understood.
So faith, hope, love abide, these three,
but the greatest of these is love. (*R.*)

Psalmody

Psalm 30   **Confident prayer and thanksgiving**

Father, into your hands I commit my spirit (Luke 23:46)

I

Ant. In your justice, hear me, O Lord.

In you, O Lord, I take refuge.
Let me never be put to shame.
In your justice, set me free,
hear me and speedily rescue me.

Be a rock of refuge for me,
a mighty stronghold to save me,
for you are my rock, my stronghold.
For your name's sake, lead me and guide me.

Release me from the snares they have hidden
for you are my refuge, Lord.
Into your hands I commend my spirit.
It is you who will redeem me, Lord.

O God of truth you detest
those who worship false and empty gods.
As for me, I trust in the Lord:
let me be glad and rejoice in your love.

You who have seen my affliction
and taken heed of my soul's distress,
have not handed me over to the enemy,
but set my feet at large.

Ant. In your justice, hear me, O Lord.

II

Ant. Let your face shine on your servant.

Have mercy on me, O Lord,
for I am in distress.
Tears have wasted my eyes,
my throat and my heart.

For my life is spent with sorrow
and my years with sighs.
Affliction has broken down my strength
and my bones waste away.

In the face of all my foes
I am a reproach,
an object of scorn to my neighbours
and of fear to my friends.

Those who see me in the street
run far away from me.
I am like a dead man, forgotten in men's hearts,
like a thing thrown away.

I have heard the slander of the crowd,
fear is all around me,
as they plot together against me,
as they plan to take my life.

But as for me, I trust in you, Lord,
I say: 'You are my God.
My life is in your hands,
deliver me from the hands of those who hate me.

Let your face shine on your servant.
save me in your love. . . .'

Ant. Let your face shine on your servant.

III

Ant. Blessed be the Lord who has shown me
the wonders of his love.

How great is the goodness, Lord,
that you keep for those who fear you,

that you show to those who trust you
in the sight of men.

You hide them in the shelter of your presence
from the plotting of men:
you keep them safe within your tent
from disputing tongues.

Blessed be the Lord who has shown me the wonders of his
love
in a fortified city.

'I am far removed from your sight'
I said in my alarm.
Yet you heard the voice of my plea
when I cried for help.

Love the Lord, all you saints.
He guards his faithful
but the Lord will repay to the full
those who act with pride.

Be strong, let your heart take courage,
all who hope in the Lord.

Ant. Blessed be the Lord who has shown me
the wonders of his love.

V. I obey your precepts and your will.
R. All that I do is before you.

Readings

Prayer of the day
Or alternative prayer

MORNING PRAYER

Introductory verse and Psalm

O Lord, open my lips.

And my mouth shall declare your praise.

Glory be to the Father, and to the Son, and to the Holy Spirit.

As it was in the beginning, is now, and ever shall be, world without end. Amen. Alleluia!

Psalm 94

Refrain: Let us go to meet the Lord;

let us greet him with the sound of music.

Or, if not used as first prayer of the day: O God, come to my assistance...

Hymn

This day God gives me
Strength of high heaven,
Sun and moon shining,
Flame in my hearth,
Flashing of lightning,
Wind in its swiftness,
Deeps of the ocean,
Firmness of earth.

This day God sends me
Strength as my steersman,
Might to uphold me,
Wisdom as guide.
Your eyes are watchful,
Your ears are listening,
Your lips are speaking,
Friend at my side.

God's way is my way,
God's shield is round me,
God's host defends me,
Saving from ill.

Angels of heaven,
Drive from me always
All that would harm me,
Stand by me still.

Rising I thank you,
Mighty and strong One,
King of creation,
Giver of rest,
Firmly confessing
Threeness of Persons,
Oneness of Godhead,
Trinity blest.

Psalmody

Psalm 41   **Longing for God and for his temple**

*Let him who is thirsty come, let him who desires take the
water of life* (Rev 22:17)

Ant. My soul is thirsting for God;
   when shall I see him face to face,
   the God of my life?

Like the deer that yearns
for running streams,
so my soul is yearning
for you, my God.

My soul is thirsting for God,
the God of my life;
when can I enter and see
the face of God?

My tears have become my bread,
by night, by day,
as I hear it said all the day long:
'Where is your God?'

These things will I remember
as I pour out my soul:
how I would lead the rejoicing crowd

into the house of God,
amid cries of gladness and thanksgiving,
the throng wild with joy.

Why are you cast down, my soul,
why groan within me?
Hope in God; I will praise him still,
my saviour and my God.

My soul is cast down within me
as I think of you,
from the country of Jordan and Mount Hermon,
from the Hill of Mizar.

Deep is calling on deep,
in the roar of waters:
your torrents and all your waves
swept over me.

By day the Lord will send
his loving kindness;
by night I will sing to him,
praise the God of my life.

I will say to God, my rock:
'Why have you forgotten me?
Why do I go mourning
oppressed by the foe?'

With cries that pierce me to the heart,
my enemies revile me,
saying to me all the day long:
'Where is your God?'

R. Why are you cast down, my soul,
why groan within me?
Hope in God; I will praise him still,
my saviour and my God.

Ant. My soul is thirsting for God;
when shall I see him face to face,
the God of my life?

Sir 36:1–7, 13–16   **Song of Sirach: a prayer for the deliverance of Israel**

Father, may your kingdom come (Matthew 6:10)

Ant. Show us your might, O Lord, and your compassion.

Save us, God of all things,
strike all the nations with terror;
raise your hand against foreign nations,
that they may see the greatness of your might.

Our sufferings proved your holiness to them;
let their downfall prove your glory to us.
Let them know, as we ourselves know,
that there is no other God but you.

Give us signs again, work further wonders,
clothe your hand, your right arm in glory.

Assemble all the tribes of Jacob,
as when they first received their inheritance.
Pity the poor people called by your name,
pity Israel, chosen as your first-born.

Have compassion on the holy city,
Jerusalem, the place of your rest.
Let Zion ring with your praises,
let your temple be filled with your glory.

Ant. Show us your might, O Lord, and your compassion.

Psalm 18A   **Praise of God the Creator**

You who visit us like the dawn from on high, guide us into the way of peace (Luke 1:7)

Ant. The heavens proclaim your glory, O Lord.

The heavens proclaim the glory of God
and the firmament shows forth the work of his hands.
Day unto day takes up the story
and night unto night makes known the message.

No speech, no word, no voice is heard†
yet their span goes forth through all the earth,
their words to the utmost bounds of the world.

There he has placed a tent for the sun;†
it comes forth like a bridegroom coming from his tent,
rejoices like a champion to run its course.

At the end of the sky is the rising of the sun;†
to the furthest end of the sky is its course.
There is nothing concealed from its burning heat.

Ant. The heavens proclaim your glory, O Lord.

Word of God   Jer 15:16

Your words were found, and I ate them,
and your words became to me a joy
and the delight of my heart;
for I am called by your name,
O Lord, God of hosts.

Short Response

Bend my heart to your will,
by your Word, give me life.

V. Keep the promise you have made to your servant.

R. By your Word, give me life.

V. Glory be to the Father, and to the Son, and to the Holy
Spirit.

Bend my heart to your will,
by your Word, give me life.

Song of Zechariah

Ant. Blessed be the Lord, the God of Israel!
He has visited his people and redeemed them.

Prayers

By his blood, our Saviour has made us a kingdom of priests
to offer spiritual sacrifices acceptable to God. Let our
prayer be:

R. Keep us faithful to your service, Lord.

Eternal priest, you have given your people a share in your
priesthood,
—may we always offer spiritual sacrifices acceptable to
God. (*R.*)

161

Grant us the fruits of your spirit:
—kindness, gentleness and patience. (*R.*)

Lord, may our life today be enlightened by our faith,
—may we proclaim this faith in our love and in all we do.
(*R.*)

May we try to be helpful to everyone at all times,
—may our efforts work towards their salvation. (*R.*)

Other prayers may be added

Our Father . . .

Concluding prayer

Lord, God Almighty, who have brought us to the beginning
of this day, keep us safe from sin, so that all our thoughts,
words and deeds may be pleasing to you. We make our prayer
through our Lord.

May the Lord bless us,
may he keep us from all evil
and lead us to life everlasting.
Amen.

Let us bless the Lord.
R. Thanks be to God.

MIDDAY PRAYER

O God, come to my assistance . . .
Glory be . . .

Hymn

Lord God, the strength which daily upholds all creation,
in yourself remaining unchanged
and yet determining in due order
the successive changes of the light of day.

Grant us light in the evening
so that life may not decay at any point of its activity,
but everlasting glory be the immediate reward
of a happy death.

Grant this, most loving Father,
and you, the only Son, equal to the Father
and, with the Spirit, the Paraclete,
reigning through the ages. Amen.

Psalmody

Psalm 118:41–48

Ant. Blessed are those who hear the Word of God and keep it.

Lord, let your love come upon me,
the saving help of your promise.
And I shall answer those who taunt me
for I trust in your word.

Do not take the word of truth from my mouth
for I trust in your decrees.
I shall always keep your law
for ever and ever.

I shall walk in the path of freedom
for I seek your precepts.
I will speak of your will before kings
and not be abashed.

Your commands have been my delight;
these I have loved.
I will worship your commands and love them
and ponder your statutes.

Psalm 39   Thanksgiving and further plea for help

*Sacrifices and offerings you have not desired, but a body
you have prepared for me* (Heb 10:5)

I

I waited, I waited for the Lord†
and he stooped down to me;
he heard my cry.

He drew me from the deadly pit,
from the miry clay.

He set my feet upon a rock
and made my footsteps firm.

He put a new song into my mouth,
praise of our God.
Many shall see and fear
and shall trust in the Lord.

Happy the man who has placed
his trust in the Lord
and has not gone over to the rebels
who follow false gods.

How many, O Lord, my God,†
are the wonders and designs that you have worked
    for us;
you have no equal.
Should I proclaim and speak of them,
they are more than I can tell!

You do not ask for sacrifice and offerings,
but an open ear.
You do not ask for holocaust and victim.
Instead, here am I.

In the scroll of the book it stands written
that I should do your will.
My God, I delight in your law
in the depth of my heart.

Your justice I have proclaimed
in the great assembly.
My lips I have not sealed;
you know it, O Lord.

I have not hidden your justice in my heart
but declared your faithful help.
I have not hidden your love and your truth
from the great assembly.

II

O Lord, you will not withhold
your compassion from me.
Your merciful love and your truth
will always guard me.

For I am beset with evils
too may to be counted.
My sins have fallen upon me
and my sight fails me.

They are more than the hairs of my head
and my heart sinks.
O Lord, come to my rescue,
Lord, come to my aid. . . .

O let there be rejoicing and gladness
for all who seek you.
Let them ever say: 'The Lord is great',
who love your saving help.

As for me, wretched and poor,
The Lord thinks of me.
You are my rescuer, my help,
O God, do not delay.

Ant. Blessed are those who hear the Word of God and keep it.

Word of God   Jer 31:33

This is the covenant which I will make with the house of Israel after those days, says the Lord: I will put my law within them, and I will write it upon their hearts; and I will be their God, and they shall be my people.

V. In God alone is my soul at rest.
R. He alone is my rock, my stronghold, my fortress.

Prayer

Eternal God, Master of the vintage and of the harvest, who give us the work we have to do and our just wages, help us to bear the burden of each day without complaining of any hardships you may send. Through Christ.

Let us bless the Lord.
R. Thanks be to God.

EVENING PRAYER

O God, come to my assistance.
Lord, make haste to help me.
Glory be to the Father, and to the Son, and to the Holy Spirit.
As it was in the beginning, is now, and ever shall be, world without end. Amen. Alleluia!

Hymn

Day is done, but Love unfailing
Dwells ever here;
Shadows fall, but hope, prevailing,
Calms every fear.
Loving Father, none forsaking,
Take our hearts, of Love's own making,
Watch our sleeping, guard our waking,
Be always near!

Dark descends, but Light unending
Shines through our night;
You are with us, ever lending
New strength to sight;
One in love, your truth confessing,
One in hope of heaven's blessing,
May we see, in love's possessing,
Love's endless light!

Eyes will close, but you, unsleeping,
Watch by our side;
Death may come: in Love's safe keeping
Still we abide.
God of love, all evil quelling,

Sin forgiving, fear dispelling,
Stay with us, our hearts indwelling,
This eventide!

Psalmody

Psalm 44   **Royal wedding song**

He who has the bride is the bridegroom; the friend of the bridegroom, who stands and hears him, rejoices greatly at the bridegroom's voice (John 3:29)

I

Ant. Graciousness is poured upon your lips:
  you are blessed by God for evermore.

My heart overflows with noble words.†
To the king I must speak the song I have made;
my tongue as nimble as the pen of a scribe.

You are the fairest of the children of men†
and graciousness is poured upon your lips:
because God has blessed you for evermore.

O mighty one, gird your sword upon your thigh;†
in splendour and state, ride on in triumph
for the cause of truth and goodness and right.

Take aim with your bow in your dread right hand.†
Your arrows are sharp: peoples fall beneath you.
The foes of the king fall down and lose heart.

Your throne, O God, shall endure for ever.†
A sceptre of justice is the sceptre of your kingdom.
Your love is for justice; your hatred for evil.

Therefore God, your God, has anointed you†
with the oil of gladness above other kings:
your robes are fragrant with aloes and myrrh.

From the ivory palace you are greeted with music.†
The daughters of kings are among your loved ones.
On your right stands the queen in gold of Ophir.

Ant. Graciousness is poured upon your lips:
  you are blessed by God for evermore.

167

II

Ant. Blessed are those who are invited to the marriage supper of the Lamb.

Listen, O daughter, give ear to my words:
forget your own people and your father's house.
So will the king desire your beauty:
He is your lord, pay homage to him.

And the people of Tyre shall come with gifts,
the richest of the people shall seek your favour.
The daughter of the king is clothed with splendour,
her robes embroidered with pearls set in gold.

She is led to the king with her maiden companions.†
They are escorted amid gladness and joy;
they pass within the palace of the king.

Sons shall be yours in place of your fathers:
you will make them princes over all the earth.
May this song make your name for ever remembered.
May the peoples praise you from age to age.

Ant. Blessed are those who are invited to the marriage supper of the Lamb.

Eph 1:3–10   **Song of thanks for salvation through Christ**

Ant. Blessed are those whom Christ has called together into his kingdom.

Blessed be the God and Father
of our Lord Jesus Christ,
who has blessed us in Christ
with every spiritual blessing in the heavenly places.

R. Blessed are you, God our Father,
   who have blessed us in Christ.

He chose us in him
before the foundations of the world,
that we should be holy
and blameless before him. (*R.*)

He destined us in love
to be his sons through Jesus Christ,
according to the purpose of his will,†
to the praise of his glorious grace
which he freely bestowed on us in the Beloved. (*R.*)

In him we have redemption through his blood,
the forgiveness of our trespasses,
according to the riches of his grace
which he lavished upon us. (*R.*)

He has made known to us†
in all wisdom and insight
the mystery of his will,
according to his purpose
which he set forth in Christ. (*R.*)

His purpose he set forth in Christ
as a plan for the fulness of time,
to unite all things in him,
things in heaven and things on earth. (*R.*)

Ant. Blessed are those whom Christ has called together into
his kingdom.

Word of God   1 Thess 2:13
We thank God constantly for this, that when you received
the Word of God which you heard from us, you accepted it
not as the word of men but as what it really is, the Word of
God, which is at work in you believers.

Short Response
The Lord loves justice and right;
he fills the earth with his love.
V. By his Word the heavens were made,
   by the breath of his mouth all the stars.
R. He fills the earth with his love.
V. Glory be to the Father, and to the Son, and to the Holy
Spirit.

The Lord loves justice and right;
he fills the earth with his love.

Song of the Virgin Mary

Ant. My soul glorifies the Lord.
My spirit rejoices in God, my Saviour.

Prayers

Christ loves the Church, he sustains it, he cares for it,
therefore, let us turn to him with trust:

R. Hear our prayers, Lord, grant our requests.

Grant that all men may be saved, Lord,
—and come to the knowledge of the truth. (*R.*)

Show your care for those who are out of work,
—grant that they may find steady employment soon. (*R.*)

For the oppressed let the Lord be a stronghold,
—a stronghold in times of distress. (*R.*)

Help us to fulfil your law of love,
—by teaching us to carry each other's burdens. (*R.*)

Other prayers may be added

We commend to you, Lord, all priests who have died;
—may they praise and bless you for ever in heaven. (*R.*)

Our Father . . .

Concluding prayer

Almighty God, you have strengthened us during this day;
we pray that in spite of our many shortcomings you will
accept the praise we offer you this evening in thanksgiving
for your gifts. We make our prayer through our Lord.

May the Lord bless us,
may he keep us from all evil
and lead us to life everlasting.
Amen.

Let us bless the Lord.
R. Thanks be to God.

Tuesday II

OFFICE OF READINGS

O God, come to my assistance.
Lord, make haste to help me.
Glory be to the Father, and to the Son, and to the Holy
Spirit.
As it was in the beginning, is now, and ever shall be, world
without end. Amen. Alleluia!

Or, if used as first prayer of the day: O Lord, open my lips ...

Hymn

Life-giving Word, come down to save your people;
Open our minds to know what you would teach us;
Grow in our hearts, O seed of heaven's harvest;
Be our true wisdom.

Word of the Father, be the word that saves us;
Lamp to our footsteps, scatter all our darkness;
Sword of the spirit, Word of God, protect us;
Be our salvation.

Psalmody

Psalm 36   **True and false happiness**

Blessed are the meek, for they shall inherit the earth
(Matthew 5:5)

I

Ant. Commit your life to the Lord,
and he will lead you.

Do not fret because of the wicked;
do not envy those who do evil:
for they wither quickly like grass
and fade like the green of the fields.

If you trust in the Lord and do good,
then you will live in the land and be secure.

If you find your delight in the Lord,
he will grant your heart's desire.

Commit your life to the Lord,
trust in him and he will act,
so that your justice breaks forth like the light,
your cause like the noon-day sun.

Be still before the Lord and wait in patience;
do not fret at the man who prospers;
a man who makes evil plots
to bring down the needy and the poor.

Calm your anger and forget your rage;
do not fret, it only leads to evil.
For those who do evil shall perish;
the patient shall inherit the land.

A little longer—and the wicked shall have gone.
Look at his place, he is not there.
But the humble shall own the land
and enjoy the fullness of peace.

Ant. Commit your life to the Lord
and he will lead you.

II

Ant. Turn away from evil and do good,
for the Lord will support the just.

The wicked man plots against the just
and gnashes his teeth against him;
but the Lord laughs at the wicked
for he sees that his day is at hand.

The sword of the wicked is drawn,
his bow is bent to slaughter the upright.
Their sword shall pierce their own hearts
and their bows shall be broken to pieces.

The just man's few possessions
are better than the wicked man's wealth;

for the power of the wicked shall be broken
and the Lord will support the just.

He protects the lives of the upright,
their heritage will last for ever.
They shall not be put to shame in evil days,
in time of famine their food shall not fail.

But all the wicked shall perish
and all the enemies of the Lord.
They are like the beauty of the meadows,
they shall vanish, they shall vanish like smoke.

The wicked man borrows and cannot repay,
but the just man is generous and gives.
Those blessed by the Lord shall own the land,
but those he has cursed shall be destroyed.

The Lord guides the steps of a man
and makes safe the path of one he loves.
Though he stumble he shall never fall
for the Lord holds him by the hand.

I was young and now I am old,†
but I have never seen the just man forsaken
nor his children begging for bread.
All the day he is generous and lends
and his children become a blessing.

Then turn away from evil and do good
and you shall have a home for ever;
for the Lord loves justice
and will never forsake his friends.

The unjust shall be wiped out for ever
and the children of the wicked destroyed.
The just shall inherit the land;
there they shall live for ever.

Ant. Turn away from evil and do good,
for the Lord will support the just.

III

Ant. Hope in the Lord and keep to his way.

The just man's mouth utters wisdom
and his lips speak what is right;
the law of his God is in his heart,
his steps shall be saved from stumbling.

The wicked man watches for the just
and seeks occasion to kill him.
The Lord will not leave him in his power
nor let him be condemned when he is judged.

Then wait for the Lord, keep to his way.
It is he who will free you from the wicked,
raise you up to possess the land
and see the wicked destroyed.

I have seen the wicked triumphant,
towering like a cedar of Lebanon.
I passed by again; he was gone.
I searched; he was nowhere to be found.

See the just man, mark the upright,
for the man of peace a future lies in store,
but sinners shall all be destroyed.
No future lies in store for the wicked.

The salvation of the just comes from the Lord,
their stronghold in time of distress.
The Lord helps them and delivers them
and saves them: for their refuge is in him.

Ant. Hope in the Lord and keep to his way.

V. Teach me discernment and knowledge.
R. For I trust in your commands.

Readings
Prayer of the day

Or alternative prayer

MORNING PRAYER

Introductory verse and Psalm

O Lord, open my lips.

And my mouth shall declare your praise.

Glory be to the Father, and to the Son, and to the Holy Spirit.

As it was in the beginning, is now, and ever shall be, world without end. Amen. Alleluia!

Psalm 94

Refrain: Hail the Lord, hail the rock who saves us.

Or, if not used as first prayer of the day: O God, come to my assistance...

Hymn

Come, praise the Lord, the Almighty, the King of all nations!
Tell forth his fame, O ye peoples, with loud acclamations!
His love is sure;
Faithful his word shall endure,
Steadfast through all generations!

Praise to the Father most gracious, the Lord of creation!
Praise to his Son, the Redeemer who wrought our salvation!
O heav'nly Dove,
Praise to thee, fruit of their love.
Giver of all consolation!

Psalmody

Psalm 42   Longing for God's dwelling place

I desire that they ... may be with me where I am to behold my glory which you have given me (John 17:24)

Ant. I will walk, O Lord, by the light of your truth.

Defend me, O God, and plead my cause
against a godless nation.
From deceitful and cunning men
rescue me, O God.

175

Since you, O God, are my stronghold,
why have you rejected me?
Why do I go mourning
oppressed by the foe?

O send forth your light and your truth;
let these be my guide.
Let them bring me to your holy mountain
to the place where you dwell.

And I will come to the altar of God,
the God of my joy.
My redeemer, I will thank you on the harp,
O God, my God.

Why are you cast down, my soul,
why groan within me?
Hope in God; I will praise him still,
my saviour and my God.

Ant. I will walk, O Lord, by the light of your truth.

Is 38:10–14, 17–20   **Song of Hezekiah: throes of agony, joy of recovery**

I am the Resurrection. He who believes in me, though he die, yet shall he live (John 11:25)

Ant. Lord, that you would change my sickness into health!

I said, 'So I must go away,
my life half spent,
assigned to the world below
for the rest of my years.'

I said, 'No more shall I see the Lord
in the land of the living,
no more shall I look upon men
within this world.

My home is pulled up and removed
like a shepherd's tent.

Like a weaver you have rolled up my life,
you cut it from the loom.

Between evening and morning you finish it.
I cry for help until dawn.
I suffer as though a lion
were breaking my bones.

I cry out in grief like a swallow,
I mourn like a dove.
My eyes look wearily to heaven.
Take care of me, Lord!'

You have held back my life
from the pit of doom.
You have cast far from your sight
every one of my sins.

For the world below cannot thank you,
nor death give you praise.
Those who go down to the grave
cannot hope for your mercy.

The living, the living man thanks you
as I do this day;
the father shall tell his children
of your faithful mercy.

O Lord, come to our rescue,†
and we shall sing psalms all the days of our life
in the house of the Lord.

Ant. Lord, that you would change my sickness into health!

Psalm 64   **Thanksgiving for God's gifts**

*Creation waits with eager longing ... creation itself will
be set free from its bondage to decay and obtain the
glorious liberty of the children of God* (Rom 8:19, 21)

Ant. To you, O God, praise is due in Zion!

To you our praise is due
in Zion, O God.
To you who pay our vows,
you who hear our prayer.

To you all flesh will come
with its burden of sin.
Too heavy for us, our offences,
but you wipe them away.

Blessed he whom you choose and call
to dwell in your courts.
We are filled with the blessings of your house,
of your holy temple.

You keep your pledge with wonders,
O God our saviour,
the hope of all the earth
and of far distant isles.

You uphold the mountains with your strength,
you are girded with power.
You still the roaring of the seas,†
the roaring of their waves
and the tumult of the peoples.

The ends of the earth stand in awe
at the sight of your wonders.
The lands of sunrise and sunset
you fill with your joy.

You care for the earth, give it water,
you fill it with riches.
Your river in heaven brims over
to provide its grain.

And thus you provide for the earth;
You drench its furrows,
you level it, soften it with showers,
you bless its growth.

You crown the year with your goodness.†
Abundance flows in your steps,
in the pastures of the wilderness it flows.

The hills are girded with joy,
the meadows covered with flocks,
the valleys are decked with wheat.
They shout for joy, yes, they sing.

Ant. To you, O God, praise is due in Zion!

Word of God   1 Thess 5:4–5

You are not in darkness, brethren, for that day to surprise
you like a thief. For you are all sons of light and sons of the
day; we are not of the night or of darkness.

Short Response

In you is the source of life
and in your light we see light.
V. O Lord, how precious is your love!
R. In your light we see light.
V. Glory be to the Father, and to the Son, and to the Holy
Spirit.
In you is the source of life
and in your light we see light.

Song of Zechariah

Ant. Lord, save us from the hands of all who hate us.

Prayers

By his resurrection our Saviour has brought light to the
world; let us pray to him:

R. Keep us faithful to your way, Lord Jesus.

We praise you this morning, Lord, and we celebrate your
resurrection.
—May the hope of your glory light up the day which lies
before us. (*R*.)

Receive our morning prayer,
—the first-fruits of our offering today. (*R.*)

Grant that we may advance in love of you today,
—so that everything may work for our good and the good of all men. (*R.*)

Grant, Lord, that our light may so shine before men, that they may see our good works
—and give glory to our Father who is in heaven. (*R*)

Other prayers may be added

Our Father . . .

Concluding prayer

Lord Jesus Christ, true light of all on the road of salvation, give us the strength to walk with you in the ways of peace and innocence. Who live.

May the Lord bless us,
may he keep us from evil
and lead us to life everlasting.
Amen.

Let us bless the Lord.
R. Thanks be to God.

MIDDAY PRAYER

O God, come to my assistance . . .
Glory be . . .

Hymn
Holy Spirit,
one with the Father and the Son,
deign at this hour to come down on us without delay,
and pour out your graces over our soul.

Let mouth, tongue, soul, thought and strength
make your praise resound.

Let our love be set aflame by the fire of your love,
and its heat in turn enkindle love in our neighbours.

Grant this, most loving Father,
and you, the only Son, equal to the Father
and, with the Spirit, the Paraclete,
reigning through the ages. Amen.

Psalmody

Psalm 118:49–56

Ant. In the land of exile I will keep your law.

Remember your word to your servant
by which you gave me hope.
This is my comfort in sorrow
that your promise gives me life.

Though the proud may utterly deride me
I keep to your law.
I remember your decrees of old
and these, Lord, console me.

I am seized with indignation at the wicked
who forsake your law.
Your statutes have become my song
in the land of exile.

I think of your name in the night-time
and I keep your law.
This has been my blessing,
the keeping of your precepts.

Psalm 52   Corruption and punishment of the wicked

We have all sinned and fall short of the glory of God
(Rom 3:23)

The fool has said in his heart:
'There is no God above.'
Their deeds are corrupt, depraved;
not a good man is left.

God looks down from heaven
on the sons of men,
to see if any are wise,
if any seek God.

All have left the right path;
depraved, every one.
There is not a good man left,
no, not even one.

Will the evil-doers not understand?†
They eat up my people as though they ate bread;
they never pray to God.

See how they tremble with fear
without cause for fear:
for God scatters the bones of the wicked.
They are shamed, rejected by God.

O that Israel's salvation might come from Zion!†
When God delivers his people from bondage,
then Jacob will be glad and Israel rejoice.

Psalm 53   **Prayer against enemies**

*The prophet prays to be delivered, in the name of the Lord,
from the wickedness of his persecutors* (Cassiodorus)

O God, save me by your name;
by your power, uphold my cause.
O God, hear my prayer;
listen to the words of my mouth.

For proud men have risen against me,†
ruthless men seek my life.
They have no regard for God.
But I have God for my help.
The Lord upholds my life . . .

I will sacrifice to you with willing heart
and praise your name for it is good:
for you have rescued me from all my distress
and my eyes have seen the downfall of my foes.

Ant. In the land of exile I will keep your law.

Word of God   1 Cor 12:12–13
Just as the body is one and has many members, and all the
members of the body, though many, are one body, so it is
with Christ. For by one Spirit we were all baptized into one
body—Jews or Greeks, slaves or free—and all were made
to drink of one Spirit.

V. I will thank you for evermore, for this is your doing.
R. I will proclaim that your name is good in the presence
of your friends.

Prayer
Lord, it was at this time of day that you revealed to Peter
your will for the salvation of mankind; mercifully grant
that our works may please you, and that we may love you
and do your saving will. Through Christ.

Let us bless the Lord.
R. Thanks be to God.

EVENING PRAYER

O God, come to my assistance.
Lord, make haste to help me.
Glory be to the Father, and to the Son, and to the Holy
Spirit.
As it was in the beginning, is now, and ever shall be, world
without end. Amen. Alleluia!

Hymn   John 3:29–31
R. He must increase,
but I must decrease.

He who has the bride is the bridegroom, the friend of the
bridegroom who stands and hears him
rejoices greatly at the bridegroom's voice;
therefore this joy of mine is now full. (*R.*)

He who comes from above is above all;
he who is of the earth belongs to the earth,
and of the earth he speaks;
he who comes from heaven is above all. (*R.*)

Psalmody

Psalm 48   **Wealth is deceptive**

> *It will be hard for a rich man to enter the kingdom of
> heaven* (Matthew 19:23)

I

Ant. You cannot serve God and mammon.

Hear this, all you peoples,
give heed, all who dwell in the world,
men both low and high,
rich and poor alike!

My lips will speak words of wisdom.
My heart is full of insight.
I will turn my mind to a parable,
with the harp I will solve my problem.

Why should I fear in evil days
the malice of the foes who surround me,
men who trust in their wealth,
and boast of the vastness of their riches?

For no man can buy his own ransom,
or pay a price to God for his life.
The ransom of his soul is beyond him.†
He cannot buy life without end,
nor avoid coming to the grave.

He knows that wise men and fools must both perish
and leave their wealth to others.
Their graves are their homes for ever,†
their dwelling place from age to age,
though their names spread wide through the land.

R. In his riches, man lacks wisdom:
he is like the beasts that are destroyed.

Ant. You cannot serve God and mammon.

II

Ant. Lay up for yourselves treasures in heaven, says the Lord.

This is the lot of the self-confident,
who have others at their beck and call.
Like sheep they are driven to the grave,†
where death shall be their shepherd
and the just shall become their rulers.

With the morning their outward show vanishes
and the grave becomes their home.
But God will ransom me from death
and take my soul to himself.

Then do not fear when a man grows rich,
when the glory of his house increases.
He takes nothing with him when he dies,
his glory does not follow him below.

Though he flattered himself while he lived:
'Men will praise me for doing well for myself,'
yet he will go to join his fathers,
who will never see the light any more.

R. In his riches, man lacks wisdom:
he is like the beasts that are destroyed.

Ant. Lay up for yourselves treasures in heaven, says the
Lord.

Rev 4:11; 5:9, 10, 12   **Song to God the Creator**

R. To the Lamb be glory, honour and power!

Worthy are you, our Lord and God,
to receive glory and honour and power. (*R*.)

For you created all things,
and by your will they existed and were created (*R*.)

Worthy are you, O Lord,
to take the scroll and to open its seals. (*R*.)

For you were slain,†
and by your blood you ransomed men for God
from every tribe and tongue and people and nation. (*R*.)

You have made us a kingdom and priests to our God,
and we shall reign on earth. (*R*.)

Worthy is the Lamb who was slain,
to receive power and wealth
and wisdom and might
and honour and glory and blessing. (*R*.)

Word of God   Rom 3:23–25
Since all have sinned and fall short of the glory of God,
they are justified by his grace as a gift, through the redemption which is in Christ Jesus, whom God put forward as an
expiation by his blood, to be received by faith.

Short Response
By your blood
you have ransomed us, Lord.
V. Men from every tribe and tongue and people and nation.
R. You have ransomed us, Lord.
V. Glory be to the Father, and to the Son, and to the Holy
Spirit.

By your blood
you have ransomed us, Lord.

Song of the Virgin Mary
Ant. The Lord looks on his servant in her nothingness:
the Almighty works marvels for me.

Prayers
Let us place all our hope in Christ, for he is the Shepherd
and Guardian of our souls and his care for the Church is
without limit. Let us pray:

R. Protect your people, Lord.

Lord Jesus, eternal Shepherd, protect our bishop
—and all the pastors of your Church. (*R.*)

Look with mercy on those who suffer persecution.
—and rescue them in their distress. (*R.*)

Have mercy, Lord, on those who are in want
—and give bread to the hungry. (*R.*)

Enlighten those who are appointed to the work of legislation,
—that the decrees they draw up may be wise. (*R.*)

Other prayers may be added

Come to the aid of your faithful departed, whom you have
redeemed with your precious blood;
—may they be found worthy to go in with you to the
marriage feast. (*R.*)

Our Father . . .

Concluding prayer

O Lord God, to whom both night and day belong, grant
that the light of innocence may always shine in our hearts,
so that we may attain to that light which is your dwelling-
place. We make our prayer through our Lord.

May the Lord bless us,
may he keep us from all evil

and lead us to life everlasting.
Amen.

Let us bless the Lord.
R. Thanks be to God.

Wednesday II

OFFICE OF READINGS

O God, come to my assistance.
Lord, make haste to help me.
Glory be to the Father, and to the Son, and to the Holy Spirit.
As it was in the beginning, is now, and ever shall be, world without end. Amen. Alleluia!

Or, if used as first prayer of the day: O Lord, open my lips ...

Hymn

Word of God, come down on earth,
Living rain from heav'n descending;
Touch our hearts and bring to birth
Faith and hope and love unending.
Word almighty, we revere you;
Word made flesh, we long to hear you.

Word eternal, throned on high,
Word that brought to life creation,
Word that came from heav'n to die,
Crucified for our salvation,
Saving Word, the world restoring,
Speak to us, your love outpouring.

Psalmody

Psalm 38   **Prayer of a sick man in anguish of mind**

Since all these things are to be dissolved, what sort of persons ought you to be in lives of holiness and godliness, waiting for and hastening the coming of the day of God (2 Pet 3:11–12)

I

Ant. We ourselves groan inwardly
as we wait for the redemption of our bodies.

I said: 'I will be watchful of my ways
for fear I should sin with my tongue.
I will put a curb on my lips
when the wicked man stands before me.'
I was dumb, silent and still.
His prosperity stirred my grief.

My heart was burning within me.†
At the thought of it, the fire blazed up
and my tongue burst into speech:
'O Lord, you have shown me my end,†
how short is the length of my days.
Now I know how fleeting is my life.

You have given me a short span of days;
my life is as nothing in your sight.
A mere breath, the man who stood so firm,
a mere shadow, the man passing by,
a mere breath the riches he hoards,
not knowing who will have them.'

Ant. We ourselves groan inwardly
    as we wait for the redemption of our bodies.

II

Ant. O Lord, hear my prayer;
    do not be deaf to my tears.

And now, Lord, what is there to wait for?
In you rests all my hope.
Set me free from all my sins,
do not make me the taunt of the fool.
I was silent, not opening my lips,
because this was all your doing.

Take away your scourge from me.
I am crushed by the blows of your hand.
You punish man's sins and correct him;
like the moth you devour all he treasures.
Mortal man is no more than a breath;
O Lord, hear my prayer.

O Lord, turn your ear to my cry.
Do not be deaf to my tears.
In your house I am a passing guest,
a pilgrim, like all my fathers.
Look away that I may breathe again
before I depart to be no more.

Ant. O Lord, hear my prayer;
do not be deaf to my tears.

Psalm 51   **Against the violence of calumniators**

Let him who boasts, boast of the Lord (1 Cor 1:31)

Ant. I trust in your goodness for ever and ever.

Why do you boast of your wickedness,
you champion of evil?
Why plan ruin all the day long,†
your tongue like a sharpened razor,
you master of deceit.

You love evil more than good;
lies more than truth.
You love the destructive word,
you tongue of deceit.

For this God will destroy you
and remove you for ever.
He will snatch you from your tent and uproot you
from the land of the living.

The just shall see and fear.
They shall laugh and say:
'So this is the man who refused
to take God as his stronghold,
but trusted in the greatness of his wealth
and grew powerful by his crimes.'

But I am like a growing olive tree
in the house of God.

I trust in the goodness of God
for ever and ever.

I will thank you for evermore;
for this is your doing.
I will proclaim that your name is good,
in the presence of your friends.

Ant. I trust in your goodness for ever and ever.

V. My soul is waiting for the Lord,
R. I count on his word.

Readings

Prayer of the day

Or alternative prayer

MORNING PRAYER

Introductory verse and Psalm
O Lord, open my lips.
And my mouth shall declare your praise.
Glory be to the Father, and to the Son, and to the Holy
Spirit.
As it was in the beginning, is now, and ever shall be, world,
without end. Amen. Alleluia!

Psalm 94
Refrain: The whole universe is in your hand, O Lord.

Or, if not used as first prayer of the day: O God, come to my
assistance ...

Hymn
I believe in God, the Father;
I believe in God, his Son;
I believe in God, their Spirit;
Each is God, yet God is one.

I believe what God has spoken
Through his Church, whose word is true;
Boldly she proclaims his Gospel,
Ever old, yet ever new.

All my hope is in God's goodness,
Shown for us by him who died,
Jesus Christ, the world's Redeemer,
Spotless victim crucified.

All my love is Love eternal;
In that Love I love mankind.
Take my heart, O Heart once broken,
Take my soul, my strength, my mind.

Father, I have sinned against you;
Look on me with eyes of love;
Seek your wand'ring sheep, Good Shepherd;
Grant heav'n's peace, O heav'nly Dove.

Bless'd be God, the loving Father;
Bless'd be God, his only Son;
Bless'd be God, all-holy Spirit;
Bless'd be God, for ever one.

Psalmody

Psalm 76　　　　　　　**Complaint in suffering and persecution**

Blessed be God ... who comforts us in all our affliction
(2 Cor 1:3)

Ant. You are the God who works wonders.

I cry aloud to God,
cry aloud to God that he may hear me.
In the day of my distress I sought the Lord.†
At night my hands were raised without ceasing;
my soul refused to be consoled.
I remembered my God and I groaned.
I pondered and my spirit fainted.

You withheld sleep from my eyes.
I was troubled, I could not speak.
I thought of the days of long ago
and remembered the years long past.
At night I mused within my heart.
I pondered and my spirit questioned.

'Will the Lord reject us for ever?
Will he show us his favour no more?
Has his love vanished for ever?
Has his promise come to an end?
Does God forget his mercy
or in anger withhold his compassion?'

I said: 'This is what causes my grief;
that the way of the Most High has changed.'
I remember the deeds of the Lord,
I remember your wonders of old,
I muse on all your works
and ponder your mighty deeds.

Your ways, O God, are holy.
What god is great as our God?
You are the God who works wonders.
You showed your power among the peoples.
Your strong arm redeemed your people,
the sons of Jacob and Joseph.

The waters saw you, O God,†
the waters saw you and trembled;
the depths were moved with terror.
The clouds poured down rain,†
the skies sent forth their voice;
your arrows flashed to and fro.

Your thunder rolled round the sky,
your flashes lighted up the world.
The earth was moved and trembled

when your way led through the sea,
your path through the mighty waters
and no one saw your footprints.

You guided your people like a flock
by the hand of Moses and Aaron.

Ant. You are the God who works wonders.

I Sam 2:1–10 **Song of Hannah: the Lord lifts up the lowly**

He fills the starving with good things (Luke 1:53)

Ant. It is the Lord who gives poverty and riches.
  He brings men low and raises them on high.

My heart exults in the Lord,
I find my strength in my God;
my mouth laughs at my enemies
as I rejoice in your saving help.
There is none like the Lord,†
there is no other save you.
There is no Rock like our God.

Bring your haughty words to an end,
let no boasts fall from your lips,
for the Lord is a God who knows all.
It is he who weighs men's deeds.

The bows of the mighty are broken,
but the weak are clothed with strength.
Those with plenty must labour for bread,
but the hungry need work no more.
The childless wife has children now
but the fruitful wife bears no more.

It is the Lord who gives life and death,
he brings men to the grave and back;
it is the Lord who gives poverty and riches.
He brings men low and raises them on high.

He lifts up the lowly from the dust,
from the dungheap he raises the poor
to set him in the company of princes,
to give him a glorious throne.

For the pillars of the earth are the Lord's,
on them he has set the world.
He guards the steps of his faithful,
but the wicked perish in darkness,
for no man's power gives him victory.
The enemies of the Lord shall be broken.

The Most High will thunder in the heavens,
the Lord will judge the ends of the earth.
He will give power to his king
and exalt the might of his anointed.

Ant. It is the Lord who gives poverty and riches.
He brings men low and raises them on high.

Psalm 96　　　　　**God and King, greater than all other gods**

A light to enlighten the Gentiles (Luke 2:32)

Ant. God reigns, let earth rejoice!

The Lord is king, let earth rejoice,
the many coastlands be glad.
Cloud and darkness are his raiment;
his throne, justice and right.

A fire prepares his path;
it burns up his foes on every side.
His lightnings light up the world,
the earth trembles at the sight.

The mountains melt like wax
before the Lord of all the earth.
The skies proclaim his justice;
all peoples see his glory.

Let those who serve idols be ashamed,†
those who boast of their worthless gods.
All you spirits, worship him.

196

Zion hears and is glad;†
the people of Judah rejoice
because of your judgments O Lord.

For you indeed are the Lord†
most high above all the earth
exalted far above all spirits.

The Lord loves those who hate evil:†
he guards the souls of his saints;
he sets them free from the wicked.

Light shines forth for the just
and joy for the upright of heart.
Rejoice, you just, in the Lord;
give glory to his holy name.

Ant. God reigns, let earth rejoice!

Word of God   Rom 8:35, 37
Who shall separate us from the love of Christ? Shall
tribulation, or distress, or persecution, or famine, or nakedness, or peril, or sword? No, in all these things we are more
than conquerors through him who loved us.

Short Response
I will sing of your strength;
each morning I will acclaim your love.
V. You, O God, are my stronghold,
   the God who shows me love.
R. Each morning I will acclaim your love.
V. Glory be to the Father, and to the Son, and to the Holy
Spirit.
I will sing of your strength;
each morning I will acclaim your love.

Song of Zechariah
Ant. Remember your love, O Lord,
   remember your promise to our fathers.

197

Prayers

Christ promised to stay with his Church always, to the end of time. Let us beseech him:

R. Stay with us, Lord!

Stay with us, Lord, throughout the day.
—May the light of your grace never cease to guide us. (*R*.)

Teach us to pray and to work in your Church,
—that we may work for the salvation of our brothers. (*R*.)

Lord, by our words and actions
—may we truly be the salt of the earth and light of the world. (*R*.)

May the grace of your Holy Spirit direct our hearts and our lips,
—that we may praise you always, and ever abide in your love. (*R*.)

Other prayers may be added

Concluding prayer

O Lord, fill our hearts with the light of your glory, so that we may always walk in the way of your commandments and never fall into sin. We make our prayer through our Lord.

May the Lord bless us,
may he keep us from all evil
and lead us to life everlasting.
Amen.

Let us bless the Lord.
R. Thanks be to God.

MIDDAY PRAYER

O God, come to my assistance . . .
Glory be . . .

Hymn
Mighty ruler, faithful God,
who arrange the successive changes in nature,
giving bright light to the morning sun
and burning heat at noon.

Put out the flames of strife
and take away the heat of passion;
grant us health of body
and true peace of soul.

Grant this, most loving Father,
and you, the only Son, equal to the Father,
and, with the Spirit, the Paraclete,
reigning through the ages. Amen.

Psalmody

Psalm 118:57–64

Ant. Entrust your cares to the Lord,
     and he will support you.

My part, I have resolved, O Lord,
is to obey your word.
With all my heart I implore your favour;
show the mercy of your promise.

I have pondered over my ways
and returned to your will.
I made haste and did not delay
to obey your commands.

Though the nets of the wicked ensnared me
I remembered your law.
At midnight I will rise and thank you
for your just decrees.

I am a friend of all who revere you,
who obey your precepts.
Lord, your love fills the earth.
Teach me your statutes.

Psalm 54   **Prayer of a man betrayed by his friend**

He began to be greatly distressed and troubled (Mark 14:33)

I

O God, listen to my prayer,
do not hide from my pleading,
attend to me and reply;
with my cares, I cannot rest.

I tremble at the shouts of the foe,
at the cries of the wicked;
for they bring down evil upon me.
They assail me with fury.

My heart is stricken within me,
death's terror is on me,
trembling and fear fall upon me
and horror overwhelms me.

O that I had wings like a dove
to fly away and be at rest.
So I would escape far away
and take refuge in the desert.

I would hasten to find a shelter
from the raging wind,
from the destructive storm, O Lord,
and from their plotting tongues.

For I can see nothing but violence
and strife in the city.
Night and day they patrol
high on the city walls.

It is full of wickedness and evil;
it is full of sin.

Its streets are never free
from tyranny and deceit.

II

If this had been done by an enemy
I could bear his taunts.
If a rival had risen against me,
I could hide from him.

But it is you, my own companion,
my intimate friend!
How close was the friendship between us.
We walked together in harmony in the house of God . . .

As for me, I will cry to God
and the Lord will save me.
Evening, morning and at noon
I will cry and lament.

He will deliver my soul in peace
in the attack against me:
for those who fight me are many,
but he hears my voice.

God will hear and will humble them,
the eternal judge:
for they will not amend their ways.
They have no fear of God.

The traitor has turned against his friends;
he has broken his word.
His speech is softer than butter,
but war is in his heart.
His words are smoother than oil,
but they are naked swords.

Entrust your cares to the Lord
and he will support you.
He will never allow
the just man to stumble.

But you, O God, will bring them down
to the pit of death.
Deceitful and bloodthirsty men shall not live half their days.
O Lord, I will trust in you.

Ant. Entrust your cares to the Lord,
and he will support you.

Word of God
Is 55:8–9

My thoughts are not your thoughts, neither are your ways
my ways, says the Lord. For as the heavens are higher than
the earth, so are my ways higher than your ways and my
thoughts than your thoughts.

V. O Lord, God of hosts, who is your equal?
R. You are mighty, O Lord, and truth is your garment.

Prayer

Almighty and merciful God who give us a time of rest in the
middle of the day, look favourably on the work we have
begun, and grant that our completed work may be pleasing
to you. Through Christ.

Let us bless the Lord.
R. Thanks be to God.

EVENING PRAYER

O God, come to my assistance.
Lord, make haste to help me.
Glory be to the Father, and to the Son, and to the Holy
Spirit.
As it was in the beginning, is now, and ever shall be, world
without end. Amen. Alleluia!

Hymn

To God with gladness sing.
Your rock and Saviour bless;
Within his temple bring

Your songs of thankfulness!
O God of might,
To you we sing,
Enthroned as king
On heaven's height!

He cradles in his hand
The heights and depths of earth;
He made the sea and land,
He brought the world to birth!
O God most high,
We are your sheep;
On us you keep
Your shepherd's eye!

Your heav'nly Father praise,
Acclaim his only Son,
Your voice in homage raise
To him who makes all one!
O Dove of peace
On us descend
That strife may end
And joy increase.

Psalmody

Psalm 61   **Rest in God**

May the God of hope fill you with all joy and peace in believing (Rom 15:13)

Ant. My soul is at rest in God alone.

In God alone is my soul at rest;
my help comes from him.
R. He alone is my rock, my stronghold,
my fortress: I stand firm.

How long will you all attack one man
to break him down,
as though he were a tottering wall,
or a tumbling fence?

Their plan is only to destroy:
they take pleasure in lies.
With their mouth they utter blessing
but in their heart they curse.

In God alone be at rest, my soul;
for my hope comes from him.
R. He alone is my rock, my stronghold,
my fortress: I stand firm.

In God is my safety and glory,
the rock of my strength.
Take refuge in God all you people.
Trust him at all times.
Pour out your hearts before him
for God is our refuge.

Ant. My soul is at rest in God alone.

Psalm 66   Song of blessing

> *You who once were far off have been brought near in the blood of Christ* (Eph 2:13)

Ant. Let the peoples praise you, O God;
  let all the peoples praise you.

O God, be gracious and bless us
and let your face shed its light upon us.
So will your ways be known upon earth
and all nations learn your saving help.

R. Let the peoples praise you, O God;
let all the peoples praise you.

Let the nations be glad and exult
for you rule the world with justice.
With fairness you rule the peoples,
you guide the nations on earth.

R. Let the peoples praise you, O God;
let all the peoples praise you.

The earth has yielded its fruit
for God, our God, has blessed us.
May God still give us his blessing
till the ends of the earth revere him.

Ant. Let the peoples praise you, O God;
let all the peoples praise you.

Col 1:12–20   **Song to Christ, the first-born of all creation and first-born from the dead**

Ant. To God be glory for ever and ever!
All things are from him, through him, and for him. Amen.

Let us give thanks to the Father,
who has qualified us
to share in the inheritance of the saints
in light.

R. Glory to you, the first-born from the dead!

He has delivered us
from the dominion of darkness
and transferred us
to the kingdom of his beloved Son,
in whom we have redemption,
the forgiveness of sins. (*R.*)

He is the image of the invisible God,
the first-born of all creation,
for in him all things were created, in heaven and on earth,
visible and invisible. (*R.*)

All things were created
through him and for him.
He is before all things,
and in him all things hold together. (*R.*)

He is the head of the body, the Church;
he is the beginning,
the first-born from the dead,
that in everything he might be pre-eminent. (*R.*)

For in him all the fulness of God was pleased to dwell,
and through him to reconcile to himself all things,
whether on earth or in heaven,
making peace by the blood of his cross. (*R.*)

Ant. To God be glory for ever and ever!

All things are from him, through him, and for him. Amen.

Word of God   1 Pet 5:5–7

Clothe yourselves, all of you, with humility toward one
another, for 'God opposes the proud, but gives grace to the
humble.' Humble yourselves, therefore, under the mighty
hand of God, that in due time he may exalt you. Cast all
anxieties on him, for he cares about you.

Short Response

Into your hands, Lord,
I commend my spirit.
V. It is to you who will redeem me, Lord.
R. Into your hands, Lord, I commend my spirit.
V. Glory be to the Father, and to the Son, and to the Holy
Spirit.
Into your hands, Lord,
I commend my spirit.

Song of the Virgin Mary

Ant. The Almighty works marvels for me.
Holy is his name!

Prayers

Let us pray to God the Father; he delights in overwhelming
his people with blessings, so let us say to him:

R. May grace and peace abound among us, Lord.

God of our fathers, remember your sacred covenant,
—and fill your Church with the splendour of your presence.
(*R.*)

Grant us favourable weather, Lord,
—that all may enjoy the fruits of the earth in abundance.
(*R.*)

Grant that your faithful may be responsive at all times to your Holy Spirit—so that in work and rest they may live for your glory. (*R.*)

Deliver us from all that is hurtful, O Lord,
—and bless every home. (*R.*)

Other prayers may be added

Take those who have died to the embrace of your love;
—lead us also to this crowning grace. (*R.*)

Our Father . . .

Concluding prayer

O God whose name is holy, and whose mercy is praised from generation to generation, hear the prayers of your people and grant that we may glorify you by never ceasing to praise you. We make our prayer through our Lord.

May the Lord bless us,
may he keep us from all evil
and lead us to life everlasting.
Amen.

Let us bless the Lord.
R. Thanks be to God.

Thursday II

OFFICE OF READINGS

O God, come to my assistance.
Lord, make haste to help me.
Glory be to the Father, and to the Son, and to the Holy
Spirit.
As it was in the beginning, is now, and ever shall be, world
without end. Amen. Alleluia!

Or, if used as first prayer of the day: O Lord, open my lips...

Hymn

Word that caused blind eyes to see,
Speak and heal our mortal blindness;
Deaf we are: our healer be;
Loose our tongues to tell your kindness.
Be our Word in pity spoken,
Heal the world, by our sin broken.

Word that speaks your Father's love,
One with him beyond all telling,
Word that sends us from above
God the Spirit, with us dwelling,
Word of truth, to all truth lead us,
Word of life, with one Bread feed us.

Psalmody

Psalm 43   **God's people in time of disaster**

*In all these things we are more than conquerors through
him who loved us* (Rom 8:37)

I

Ant. It was you who saved us, Lord;
    we give our thanks for ever and ever.

We heard with our own ears, O God,
our fathers have told us the story
of the things you did in their days,
you yourself, in days long ago.

To plant them you uprooted the nations:
to let them spread you laid peoples low.
No sword of their own won the land;
no arm of their own brought them victory.
It was your right hand, your arm
and the light of your face: for you loved them.

It is you, my king, my God,
who granted victories to Jacob.
Through you we beat down our foes;
in your name we trampled our aggressors.

For it was not in my bow that I trusted
nor yet was I saved by my sword:
it was you who saved us from our foes,
it was you who put our foes to shame.
All the day long our boast was in God
and we praised your name without ceasing.

Ant. It was you who saved us, Lord;
   we give you thanks for ever and ever.

II

Ant. Turn your eyes towards us; see our misery, Lord.

Yet now you have rejected us, disgraced us:
you no longer go forth with our armies.
You make us retreat from the foe
and our enemies plunder us at will.

You make us like sheep for the slaughter
and scatter us among the nations.
You sell your own people for nothing
and make no profit by the sale.

You make us the taunt of our neighbours,
the mockery and scorn of all who are near.
Among the nations, you make us a byword,
among the peoples a thing of derision.

All the day long my disgrace is before me:
my face is covered with shame

at the voice of the taunter, the scoffer,
at the sight of the foe and avenger.

Ant. Turn your eyes towards us; see our misery, Lord.

III

Ant. Stand up, Lord,
   rescue us for the sake of your name.

This befell us though we had not forgotten you;
though we had not been false to your covenant,
though we had not withdrawn our hearts;
though our feet had not strayed from your path.
Yet you have crushed us in a place of sorrows
and covered us with the shadow of death.

Had we forgotten the name of our God
or stretched out our hands to another god
would not God have found this out,
he who knows the secrets of the heart?
It is for you that we face death all the day long
and are counted as sheep for the slaughter.

Awake, O Lord, why do you sleep?
Arise, do not reject us for ever!
Why do you hide your face
and forget our oppression and misery?

For we are brought down low to the dust;
our body lies prostrate on the earth.
Stand up and come to our help!
Redeem us because of your love!

Ant. Stand up, Lord,
   rescue us for the sake of your name.

V. Lord, to whom shall we go?
R. You have the words of eternal life.

Readings

Prayer of the day

Or alternative prayer

MORNING PRAYER

Introductory verse and psalm

O Lord, open my lips.

And my mouth shall declare your praise.

Glory be to the Father, and to the Son, and to the Holy Spirit.

As it was in the beginning, is now, and ever shall be, world without end. Amen. Alleluia!

Psalm 94

Refrain: Come, let us worship the Lord.

Or, if not used as first prayer of the day: O God, come to my assistance...

Hymn

We who live in Christ were born in his death:
Baptized in Christ's death, with Christ we lay in the tomb;
As God the Father's power awoke him from death,
So we were raised to walk in newness of life.

One with Christ were we in dying his death:
So one shall we be with Christ in rising again.
Our sinful selves were nailed with Christ to his cross
That, dead to sin, from sin our flesh might be free.

Dead with Christ, we yet shall rise with him too,
For this is our faith, that he who rose from the dead
Will never die; once dead, for ever he lives,
And death has power no more to conquer its King.

Once for all in death Christ died to all sin;
The life that he lives is life lived only to God.
So you like him are dead to all that is sin,
And live to God in Christ, the Saviour, our Lord.

Psalmody

Psalm 79   **Lament for the wasted vineyard**

Come, Lord Jesus (Rev 22:20)

Ant. Stir up your might, O God,
and come to our help.

O shepherd of Israel, hear us,
you who lead Joseph's flock,
shine forth from your cherubim throne
upon Ephraim, Benjamin, Manasseh.
O Lord, rouse up your might,
O Lord, come to our help.

R. God of hosts, bring us back;
let your face shine on us and we shall be saved.

Lord God of hosts, how long
will you frown on your people's plea?
You have fed them with tears for their bread,
an abundance of tears for their drink.
You have made us the taunt of our neighbours,
our enemies laugh us to scorn.

R. God of hosts, bring us back;
let your face shine on us and we shall be saved.

You brought a vine out of Egypt;
to plant it you drove out the nations.
Before it you cleared the ground;
it took root and spread through the land.

The mountains were covered with its shadow,
the cedars of God with its boughs.
It stretched out its branches to the sea,
to the Great River it stretched out its shoots.

Then why have you broken down its walls?
It is plucked by all who pass by.
It is ravaged by the boar of the forest,
devoured by the beasts of the field.

R. God of hosts, turn again, we implore,
look down from heaven and see.

Visit this vine and protect it,
the vine your right hand has planted.

Men have burnt it with fire and destroyed it.
May they perish at the frown of your face.

May your hand be on the man you have chosen,
the man you have given your strength.
And we shall never forsake you again:
give us life that we may call upon your name.

R. God of hosts, bring us back;
let your face shine on us and we shall be saved.

Ant. Stir up your might, O God,
and come to our help.

Isaiah 12:1–6   **Song of the Redeemed**

If any one thirst, let him come to me and drink (John 7:37)

Ant. The Lord is my strength and my song.

I thank you Lord, you were angry with me
but your anger has passed and you give me comfort.

Truly, God is my salvation,
I trust, I shall not fear.

For the Lord is my strength, my song,
he became my saviour.

With joy you will draw water
from the wells of salvation.

Give thanks to the Lord, give praise to his name!
make his mighty deeds known to the peoples!

Declare the greatness of his name,
sing a psalm to the Lord!

For he has done glorious deeds,
make them known to all the earth!

People of Zion, sing and shout for joy
for great in your midst is the Holy One of Israel.

Ant. The Lord is my strength and my song.

Psalm 80   **Solemn acclamation and warning**

He who comes to me shall not hunger, and he who believes in me shall never thirst (John 6:35)

Ant. We cry out with joy to God our strength;
   the God of Jacob we acclaim.

Ring out your joy to God our strength,
shout in triumph to the God of Jacob.

Raise a song and sound the timbrel,
the sweet-sounding harp and the lute,
blow the trumpet at the new moon,
when the moon is full, on our feast.

For this is Israel's law,
a command of the God of Jacob.
He imposed it as a rule on Joseph,
when he went out against the land of Egypt.

A voice I did not know said to me:
'I freed your shoulder from the burden;
your hands were freed from the load.
You called in distress and I saved you.

I answered, concealed in the storm cloud,
at the waters of Meribah I tested you.
Listen, my people, to my warning,
O Israel, if only you would heed!

Let there be no foreign god among you,
no worship of an alien god.
I am the Lord your God,†
who brought you from the land of Egypt.
Open wide your mouth and I will fill it.

But my people did not heed my voice
and Israel would not obey,
so I left them in their stubbornness of heart
to follow their own designs.

O that my people would heed me,
that Israel would walk in my ways!

At once I would subdue their foes,
turn my hand against their enemies.

The Lord's enemies would cringe at their feet
and their subjection would last for ever.
But Israel I would feed with finest wheat
and fill them with honey from the rock.'

Ant. We cry out with joy to God our strength;
the God of Jacob we acclaim.

Word of God   Rom 14:17–19

The kingdom of God does not mean food and drink, but righteousness and peace and joy in the Holy Spirit; he who thus serves Christ is acceptable to God and approved by men. Let us then pursue what makes for peace and for mutual upbuilding.

Short Response

Rejoice, rejoice in the Lord,
exult, you just!
V. Ring out your joy, all you upright of heart.
R. Exult, you just!
V. Glory be to the Father, and to the Son, and to the Holy Spirit.
Rejoice, rejoice in the Lord,
exult, you just!

Song of Zechariah

Ant. As for you, little child,
prophet of God the Most High,
you shall go ahead of the Lord to prepare his ways before him.

Prayers

Let us pray to God our Father, who loves his children and never rejects their prayer; let us say to him:

R. Enlighten our eyes, O Lord.

We thank you, Lord, that in your Son you have given us the true light.

—May his light be with us all the days of our life. (*R.*)

Lord, may your Wisdom guide us through this day—
—that we may walk in newness of life. (*R.*)

Grant us to meet trials with constancy for your sake;
—enable us to serve you always with a great heart. (*R.*)

Direct today our thoughts, our senses, and our actions,
—and help us to co-operate with your providential guidance.
(*R.*)

Other prayers may be added

Our Father . . .

Concluding prayer

Lord, true Light and Creator of all light, we pray that our
minds may always be filled with holy thoughts and our life
filled with your praise. We make our prayer through our
Lord.

May the Lord bless us,
may he keep us from all evil
and lead us to life everlasting.
Amen.

Let us bless the Lord.
R. Thanks be to God.

MIDDAY PRAYER

O God, come to my assistance . . .
Glory be . . .

Hymn

Lord God, the strength which daily upholds all creation,
in yourself remaining unchanged
and yet determining in due order
the successive changes of the light of day.

Grant us light in the evening
so that life may not decay at any point of its activity,

216

but everlasting glory be the immediate reward
of a happy death.

Grant this, most loving Father,
and you, the only Son, equal to the Father
and, with the Spirit, the Paraclete,
reigning through the ages. Amen.

Psalmody

Psalm 118:65-72

Ant. In God I trust; I shall not fear.

Lord, you have been good to your servant
according to your word.
Teach me discernment and knowledge
for I trust in your commands.

Before I was afflicted I went astray
but now I keep your word.
You are good and your deeds are good;
teach me your statutes.

Though proud men smear me with lies
yet I keep your precepts.
Their minds are closed to good
but your law is my delight.

It was good for me to be afflicted,
to learn your statutes.
The law from your mouth means more to me
than silver and gold.

Psalm 55   Unshakable confidence in God

*While we live we are always being given up to death for
Jesus' sake, so that the life of Jesus may be manifested in
our mortal flesh* (2 Cor 4:11)

Have mercy on me, God, men crush me;
they fight me all day long and oppress me.
My foes crush me all the day long,
for many fight proudly against me.

When I fear, I will trust in you,
in God whose word I praise.
In God I trust, I shall not fear:
what can mortal man do to me?

All day long they distort my words,
all their thought is to harm me.
They band together in ambush,
track me down and seek my life . . .

You have kept an account of my wanderings;†
you have kept a record of my tears;
are they not written in your book?

Then my foes will be put to flight†
on the day that I call to you.
This I know, that God is on my side.
In God, whose word I praise,
in the Lord, whose word I praise,
in God I trust; I shall not fear:
what can mortal man do to me?

I am bound by the vows I have made you.
O God, I will offer you praise
for you rescued my soul from death,
you kept my feet from stumbling
that I may walk in the presence of God
in the light of the living.

Psalm 56   Trust in God in the midst of suffering

*Father, the hour has come; glorify your son that the Son
may glorify you* (John 17:1)

Have mercy on me, God, have mercy
for in you my soul has taken refuge.
In the shadow of your wings I take refuge
till the storms of destruction pass by.

I call to God the Most High,
to God who has always been my help.

May he send from heaven and save me . . .
May God send his truth and his love.

My soul lies down among lions,
who would devour the sons of men.
Their teeth are spears and arrows,
their tongue a sharpened sword.

R. O God, arise above the heavens;
may your glory shine on earth!

They laid a snare for my steps,
my soul was bowed down.
They dug a pit in my path
but fell in it themselves.

My heart is ready, O God,†
my heart is ready.
I will sing, I will sing your praise.
Awake my soul,†
awake lyre and harp,
I will awake the dawn.

I will thank you Lord among the peoples,
praise you among the nations;
for your love reaches to the heavens
and your truth to the skies.

R. O God, arise above the heavens;
may your glory shine on earth!

Ant. In God I trust; I shall not fear.

Word of God   Gal 5:14
The whole law is fulfilled in one word, 'You shall love your
neighbour as yourself.'

V. Though proud men smear me with lies,
R. Yet I keep your precepts.

Prayer
Almighty and eternal God in whom there is no darkness,
no obscurity, fill our hearts with the splendour of your light,

so that we who have received your commandments may walk in safety on your ways. Through Christ.

Let us bless the Lord.
R. Thanks be to God.

EVENING PRAYER

O God, come to my assistance.
Lord, make haste to help me.
Glory be to the Father, and to the Son, and to the Holy Spirit.
As it was in the beginning, is now, and ever shall be, world without end. Amen. Alleluia!

Hymn

Bless'd be the Lord our God!
With joy let heaven ring;
Before his presence let all earth
Its songs of homage bring!
His mighty deeds be told;
His majesty be praised;
To God enthroned in heav'nly light,
Let every voice be raised!

All that has life and breath,
Give thanks with heartfelt songs!
To him let all creation sing
To whom all praise belongs!
Acclaim the Father's love,
Who gave us God his Son;
Praise too the Spirit, giv'n by both,
With both for ever one!

Psalmody

Psalm 71   **The King of peace and his kingdom**

He has anointed me to preach good news to the poor (Luke 4:18)

I

Ant. In his days justice shall flourish
and abundance of peace for ever.

O God, give your judgment to the king,
to a king's son your justice,
that he may judge your people in justice
and your poor in right judgment.

May the mountains bring forth peace for the people
and the hills, justice.
May he defend the poor of the people†
and save the children of the needy
and crush the oppressor.

He shall endure like the sun and the moon
from age to age.
He shall descend like rain on the meadow,
like raindrops on the earth.

In his days justice shall flourish
and peace till the moon fails.
He shall rule from sea to sea,
from the Great River to earth's bounds.

Before him his enemies shall fall,
his foes lick the dust.
The kings of Tarshish and the sea coasts
shall pay him tribute.

The kings of Sheba and Seba
shall bring him gifts.
Before him all kings shall fall prostrate,
all nations shall serve him.

Ant. In his days justice shall flourish
and abundance of peace for ever.

II

Ant. Blessed be the Lord, God of Israel,
who alone works wonders.

For he shall save the poor when they cry
and the needy who are helpless.
He will have pity on the weak
and save the lives of the poor.

From oppression he will rescue their lives,
to him their blood is dear.
Long may he live,
may the gold of Sheba be given him.
They shall pray for him without ceasing
and bless him all the day.

May corn be abundant in the land
to the peaks of the mountains.
May its fruit rustle like Lebanon;
may men flourish in the cities like grass on the earth.

May his name be blessed for ever
and endure like the sun.
Every tribe shall be blessed in him,
all nations bless his name.

Blessed be the Lord, God of Israel,
who alone works wonders,
ever blessed his glorious name.
Let his glory fill the earth.

All: Amen! Amen!

Ant. Blessed be the Lord, God of Israel,
who alone works wonders.

Rev 11:17–18; 12:10–12　　　　　　**Song of God's judgment**

Ant. To him be glory and power for ever and ever. Amen!

We give thanks to you, Lord God Almighty,
who are and who were,
that you have taken your great power
and begun to reign.

R. We give thanks to you, O Lord our God.

The nations raged,
but your wrath came,
and the time for the dead to be judged,
for rewarding your servants, the prophets and saints,
and those who fear your name,
both small and great. (*R.*)

Now the salvation and the power†
and the kingdom of our God
and the authority of his Christ have come,
for the accuser of our brethren has been thrown down,
who accuses them night and day before our God. (*R.*)

And they have conquered him
by the blood of the Lamb
and by the word of their testimony,
for they loved not their lives even unto death.
Rejoice, then, O heaven
and you that dwell therein! (*R.*)

Ant. To him be glory and power for ever and ever. Amen!

Word of God   1 Pet 1:22–23

Having purified your souls by your obedience to the truth
for a sincere love of the brethren, love one another earnestly
from the heart. You have been born anew, not of perishable
seed but of imperishable, through the living and abiding
word of God.

Short Response
Your word, O Lord, for ever
stands firm in the heavens.
V. Your truth lasts from age to age.
R. It stands firm in the heavens.
V. Glory be to the Father, and to the Son, and to the Holy
Spirit.
Your word, O Lord, for ever
stands firm in the heavens.

Song of the Virgin Mary

Ant. His mercy is from age to age on those who fear him.

Prayers

Let us pray to God our Father who loves his children and never rejects their prayer.

R. Stay with us Lord.

Almighty and merciful God, hold Pope N. in your safe keeping.

—Grant him light and strength in his service of your Church. (*R.*)

O Lord, protect our country;

—deliver us from all harm. (*R.*)

Gather your sons and daughters around the eucharistic table

—where they will be strengthened to follow your Son more closely (*R.*)

Preserve those men and women who have consecrated themselves to you;—may they follow your Son with complete dedication. (*R.*)

Other prayers may be added

May those who have died rest in your peace for ever;—share with us their spiritual blessings. (*R.*)

Our Father . . .

Concluding prayer

Lord God, to whom we offer our evening prayer, mercifully grant that our hearts may always meditate on your law, and give us the reward of everlasting light and life. We make our prayer through our Lord.

May the Lord bless us,
may he keep us from all evil
and lead us to life everlasting.
Amen.

Let us bless the Lord.
R. Thanks be to God.

Friday II

OFFICE OF READINGS

O God, come to my assistance.
Lord, make haste to help me.
Glory be to the Father, and to the Son, and to the Holy
Spirit.
As it was in the beginning, is now, and ever shall be, world
without end. Amen. Alleluia!

Or, if used as first prayer of the day: O Lord, open my lips...

Hymn
I am the holy vine,
Which God my Father tends.
Each branch that yields no fruit
My Father cuts away.
Each fruitful branch
He prunes with care
To make it yield
Abundant fruit.

If you abide in me,
I will in you abide.
Each branch to yield its fruit
Must with the vine be one.
So you shall fail
To yield your fruit
If you are not
With me one vine.

I am the fruitful vine,
And you my branches are.
He who abides in me,
I will in him abide.
So shall you yield
Much fruit, but none

If you remain
Apart from me.

Psalmody

Psalm 37   Acknowledgement of guilt

   All his acquaintances ... stood at a distance (Luke 23:49)

I

Ant. Lord, do not rebuke me in your anger.

O Lord, do not rebuke me in your anger;
do not punish me, Lord, in your rage.
Your arrows have sunk deep in me;
your hand has come down upon me.
Through your anger all my body is sick:
through my sin, there is no health in my limbs.
My guilt towers higher than my head;
it is a weight too heavy to bear.

Ant. Lord, do not rebuke me in your anger.

II

Ant. Do not punish me, Lord, in your rage.

My wounds are foul and festering,
the result of my own folly.
I am bowed and brought to my knees.
I go mourning all the day long.

All my frame burns with fever;
all my body is sick.
Spent and utterly crushed,
I cry aloud in anguish of heart.

O Lord, you know all my longing:
my groans are not hidden from you.
My heart throbs, my strength is spent;
the very light has gone from my eyes.

My friends avoid me like a leper;
those closest to me stand afar off.

Those who plot against my life lay snares;†
those who seek my ruin speak of harm,
planning treachery all the day long.

Ant. Do not punish me, Lord, in your rage.

III

Ant. I confess that I am guilty;
     do not forsake me, O God my saviour.

But I am like a deaf man who cannot hear,
like a dumb man who cannot open his mouth.
I am like a man who hears nothing
in whose mouth is no defence.

I count on you, O Lord:
it is you, Lord God, who will answer.
I pray: 'Do not let them mock me,
those who triumph if my foot should slip.'

For I am on the point of falling
and my pain is always before me.
I confess that I am guilty
and my sin fills me with dismay.

My wanton enemies are numberless
and my lying foes are many.
They repay me evil for good
and attack me for seeking what is right.

O Lord, do not forsake me!
My God, do not stay afar off!
Make haste and come to my help,
O Lord, my God, my saviour!

Ant. I confess that I am guilty;
     do not forsake me, O God my saviour.

V. Lord, make me know your ways.

R. Lord, teach me your paths.

Readings

Prayer of the day

Or alternative prayer

MORNING PRAYER

Introductory verse and Psalm

O Lord, open my lips.
And my mouth shall declare your praise.
Glory be to the Father, and to the Son, and to the Holy Spirit.
As it was in the beginning, is now, and ever shall be, world without end. Amen. Alleluia!

Psalm 94

Refrain: At the name of Jesus, let every tongue proclaim: He is Lord!

Or, if not used as first prayer of the day: O God, come to my assistance...

Hymn   Rom 8:28–35, 37

In everything God works for good with those who love him,
who are called according to his purpose.
For those whom he foreknew he also predestined
to be conformed to the image of his Son.

R. You did not spare your own Son, but gave him up for us all.

Those whom he predestined
he also called;
and those whom he called
he also justified;
and those whom he justified
he also glorified. (*R.*)

What then shall we say?†
If God is for us,
who is against us?
He who did not spare his own Son,
but gave him up for us all,
will he not also give us all things with him? (*R.*)

It is God who justifies,
who is to condemn?

Is it Christ Jesus, who died,
who was raised from the dead,
who is at the right hand of God,
who intercedes for us? (*R.*)

Who shall separate us
from the love of Christ?
Shall tribulation, or distress, or persecution,
or famine, or nakedness, or peril or sword?
No, in all these things we are more than conquerors
through him who loved us. (*R.*)

Psalmody

Psalm 50   **Confession of guilt, promise, prayer, hope**
  Jesus, Son of God and Saviour, be merciful to me, a sinner.

Ant. A humbled heart you will not spurn, O Lord.

Have mercy on me, God, in your kindness.
In your compassion blot out my offence.
O wash me more and more from my guilt
and cleanse me from my sin.

My offences truly I know them;
my sin is always before me.
Against you, you alone, have I sinned;
what is evil in your sight I have done.

That you may be justified when you give sentence
and be without reproach when you judge,
O see, in guilt I was born,
a sinner was I conceived.

Indeed you love truth in the heart;
then in the secret of my heart teach me wisdom
O purify me, then I shall be clean;
O wash me, I shall be whiter than snow.

Make me hear rejoicing and gladness,
that the bones you have crushed may thrill.
From my sins turn away your face
and blot out all my guilt.

A pure heart create for me, O God,
put a steadfast spirit within me.
Do not cast me away from your presence,
nor deprive me of your holy spirit.

Give me again the joy of your help;
with a spirit of fervour sustain me,
that I may teach transgressors your ways
and sinners may return to you.

O rescue me, God, my helper,
and my tongue shall ring out your goodness.
O Lord, open my lips
and my mouth shall declare your praise.

For in sacrifice you take no delight,
burnt offering from me you would refuse,
my sacrifice, a contrite spirit.
A humbled, contrite heart you will not spurn.

In your goodness, show favour to Zion:
rebuild the walls of Jerusalem.
Then you will be pleased with lawful sacrifice,†
burnt offerings wholly consumed,
then you will be offered young bulls on your altar.

Ant. A humbled heart you will not spurn, O Lord.

Hab 3:2–4, 13, 16–19   **Song of Habakkuk: God executes judgment**

*Raise your heads, because your redemption is drawing
near* (Luke 21:28)

Ant. In spite of your anger, Lord, have compassion.

Lord, I have heard of your fame,
I stand in awe at your deeds.
Do them again in our days,†
in our days make them known!
In spite of your anger, have compassion.

God comes forth from Teman,
the Holy One comes from Mount Paran.

His splendour covers the sky
and his glory fills the earth.

His brilliance is like the light,†
rays flash from his hands;
there his power is hidden.
You march out to save your people,
to save the one you have anointed.

This I heard and I tremble with terror,
my lips quiver at the sound.
Weakness invades my bones,
my steps fail beneath me
yet I calmly wait for the doom
that will fall upon the people who assail us.

For even though the fig does not blossom,
nor fruit grow on the vine,
even though the olive crop fail,
and fields produce no harvest,
even though flocks vanish from the folds
and stalls stand empty of cattle.

Yet I will rejoice in the Lord
and exult in God my saviour.
The Lord my God is my strength.†
He makes me leap like the deer,
he guides me to the high places.

Ant. In spite of your anger, Lord, have compassion.

Psalm 147   **The new Jerusalem**

Come, I will show you the Bride of the Lamb (Rev 21:9)

R. O praise the Lord, Jerusalem!
Zion, praise your God!

He has strengthened the bars of your gates,
he has blessed the children within you.
He established peace on your borders,
he feeds you with finest wheat. (*R.*)

He sends out his word to the earth
and swiftly runs his command.
He showers down snow white as wool,
he scatters hoar-frost like ashes. (*R.*)

He hurls down hailstones like crumbs.
The waters are frozen at his touch;
he sends forth his word and it melts them:
at the breath of his mouth the waters flow. (*R.*)

He makes his word known to Jacob,
to Israel his laws and decrees.
He has not dealt thus with other nations;
he has not taught them his decrees. (*R.*)

Word of God Eph 1:7–10

In Christ we have redemption through his blood, the forgiveness of our trespasses, according to the riches of his grace which God lavished upon us. For he has made known to us in all wisdom and insight the mystery of his will, according to his purpose which he set forth in Christ as a plan for the fulness of time, to unite all things in him, things in heaven and things on earth.

Short Response

Christ, Son of the living God,
have mercy on us.
V. You who are seated at the right hand of the Father,
R. Have mercy on us.
V. Glory be to the Father, and to the Son, and to the Holy Spirit.
Christ, Son of the living God,
have mercy on us.

Song of Zechariah

Ant. Give light, O Lord,
    to those who dwell in the shadow of death.

Prayers

God made everything good, and for the happiness of his creatures; with this conviction let us pray:

R. Our trust is in you, Lord.

Father, in your love you have brought us to the dawn of a new day;
—make us live by the new life of baptism. (R.)

You have created all things and sustained them in being;
—enable us to be aware of your presence in all things. (R.)

Teach us to administer with care the good things you have committed to us,
—that we may prove ourselves good and faithful servants. (R.)

Grant that today we may follow you with our whole heart;
—may we always seek your face. (R.)

Other prayers may be added

Our Father . . .

Concluding prayer

Almighty God, we pray that we may sing more worthily with the saints in heaven the praises we offer you today. Through our Lord.

May the Lord bless us,
may he keep us from all evil
and lead us to life everlasting.
Amen.

Let us bless the Lord
R. Thanks be to God.

MIDDAY PRAYER

O God, come to my assistance . . .
Glory be . . .

Hymn

Holy Spirit,
one with the Father and the Son,
deign at this hour to come down on us without delay
and pour out your graces over our soul.

Let mouth, tongue, soul, thought and strength
make your praise resound.
Let our love be set aflame by the fire of your love
and its heat in turn enkindle love in our neighbours.

Grant this, most loving Father,
and you the only Son, equal to the Father
and, with the Spirit, the Paraclete,
reigning through the ages. Amen.

Psalmody

Psalm 118:73–80

Ant. Let your love console us, Lord,
according to your word.

It was your hands that made me and shaped me:
help me to learn your commands.
Your faithful will see me and rejoice
for I trust in your word.

Lord, I know that your decrees are right,
that you afflicted me justly.
Let your love be ready to console me
by your promise to your servant.

Let your love come to me and I shall live
for your law is my delight.
Shame the proud who harm me with lies
while I ponder your precepts.

Let your faithful turn to me,
those who know your will.
Let my heart be blameless in your statutes
lest I be ashamed.

Psalm 58   Appeal against proud enemies

*Your adversary, the devil, prowls around ... seeking
someone to devour* (1 Pet 5:8)

Rescue me, God, from my foes;
protect me from those who attack me.
O rescue me from those who do evil
and save me from blood-thirsty men.

See, they lie in wait for my life;
powerful men band together against me.
For no offence, no sin of mine, Lord,
for no guilt of mine they rush to take their stand. . .

But you, Lord, will laugh them to scorn.
You make light of all the nations.

O my Strength, it is you to whom I turn,†
for you, O God, are my stronghold,
the God who shows me love. . . .

As for me, I will sing of your strength
and each morning acclaim your love
for you have been my stronghold,
a refuge in the day of my distress.

O my Strength, it is you to whom I turn,†
for you, O God, are my stronghold,
the God who shows me love.

Psalm 59   After a defeat

*In the world you have tribulation, but be of good cheer, I
have overcome the world* (John 16:33)

O God, you have rejected us and broken us.
You have been angry; come back to us.

You have made the earth quake, torn it open.
Repair what is shattered for it sways.

You have inflicted hardships on your people
and made us drink a wine that dazed us.

You have given those who fear you a signal
to flee from the enemy's bow.
O come and deliver your friends,
help with your right hand and reply.

From his holy place God has made this promise:†
'I will triumph and divide the land of Shechem,
I will measure out the valley of Succoth.

Gilead is mine and Manasseh, †
Ephraim I take for my helmet,
Judah for my commander's staff.

Moab I will use for my washbowl;†
on Edom I will plant my shoe.
Over the Philistines I will shout in triumph.'

But who will lead me to conquer the fortress?
Who will bring me face to face with Edom?
Will you utterly reject us, O God,
and no longer march with our armies?

Give us help against the foe:
for the help of man is vain.
With God we shall do bravely
and he will trample down our foes.

Ant. Let your love console us, Lord,
according to your word.

Word of God   Bar 4:28–29

Just as you purposed to go astray from God, return with
tenfold zeal to seek him. For he who has brought these
calamities upon you will bring you everlasting joy with your
salvation.

V. Let the watchman count on daybreak, and Israel on the
Lord,
R. Because with the Lord there is mercy and fullness of
redemption.

Prayer

Lord Jesus Christ, on a day plunged into darkness, you who were innocent were raised upon a cross for our redemption; grant us the light we need to reach eternal life. Who live and reign.

Let us bless the Lord.
R. Thanks be to God.

EVENING PRAYER

O God, come to my assistance.
Lord, make haste to help me.
Glory be to the Father, and to the Son, and to the Holy Spirit.
As it was in the beginning, is now, and ever shall be, world without end. Amen. Alleluia!

Hymn   1 Pet 2:21–24
R. By his wounds you have been healed.

Christ suffered for you,
leaving you an example that you should follow in his steps.
  (R.)

He committed no sin;
no guile was found on his lips.
When he was reviled,
he did not revile in return. (R.)

When he suffered,
he did not threaten,
but he trusted to him
who judges justly. (R.)

He himself bore our sins in his body on the tree,†
that we might die to sin and live to righteousness.
By his wounds you have been healed.
For you were straying like sheep,
but have now returned to the Shepherd and Guardian
  of your souls. (R.)

Psalmody

Psalm 120

God the protector

They shall hunger no more, neither thirst any more; the sun shall not strike them, nor any scorching heat (Rev 7:16)

Ant. My help shall come from the Lord
who made heaven and earth.

I lift up my eyes to the mountains:
from where shall come my help?
My help shall come from the Lord
who made heaven and earth.

May he never allow you to stumble!
Let him sleep not, your guard.
No, he sleeps not nor slumbers,
Israel's guard.

The Lord is your guard and your shade;
at your right side he stands.
By day the sun shall not smite you
nor the moon in the night.

The Lord will guard you from evil,
he will guard your soul.
The Lord will guard your going and coming
both now and for ever.

Ant. My help shall come from the Lord
who made heaven and earth.

Psalm 114

Prayer of a man saved from death

Through many tribulations we must enter the kingdom of God (Acts 14:22)

Ant. You turn your ear to me, O Lord.

I love the Lord for he has heard
the cry of my appeal;
for he turned his ear to me
in the day when I called him.

They surrounded me, the snares of death,†
with the anguish of the tomb;
they caught me, sorrow and distress.
I called on the Lord's name.
O Lord my God, deliver me!

How gracious is the Lord, and just;
our God has compassion.
The Lord protects the simple hearts;
I was helpless so he saved me.

Turn back, my soul, to your rest
for the Lord has been good;
he has kept my soul from death,†
my eyes from tears
and my feet from stumbling.

I will walk in the presence of the Lord
in the land of the living.

Ant. You turn your ear to me, O Lord.

Rev 15:3–4   **Song of Moses and the Lamb**

Ant. Glory to the Lamb who was slain!
   He is King for ever and ever.

Great and wonderful are your deeds,
O Lord God the Almighty!
Just and true are your ways,
O King of the ages!

R. Great are your deeds, O Lord!

Who shall not fear and glorify your name, O Lord?
For you alone are holy. (*R.*)

All nations shall come and worship you,
for your judgments have been revealed. (*R.*)

Ant. Glory to the Lamb who was slain!
   He is King for ever and ever.

Word of God 1 Cor 2:7–10

We impart a secret and hidden wisdom of God, which God decreed before the ages for our glorification. None of the rulers of this age understood this; for if they had, they would not have crucified the Lord of glory. But, as it is written,

'What no eye has seen, nor ear heard,

nor the heart of man conceived,

what God has prepared for those who love him,'

God has revealed to us through the Spirit.

Short Response

You are blest, O Lord,

in the heavens.

V. You are worthy to receive praise and glory for all eternity.

R. You are blest, O Lord in the heavens.

V. Glory be to the Father, and to the Son, and to the Holy Spirit.

You are blest, O Lord,

in the heavens.

Song of the Virgin Mary

Ant. He casts down the mighty, the persecutors of his people.

Prayers

Let us lovingly call upon Christ, who in love and pity dried the tears of mourners; let us say to him:

R. Have mercy on your people, Lord.

Lord Jesus, who comfort the downcast, keep in mind the tears of the poor;

—sanctify their sufferings. (*R.*)

Most merciful Lord, hear the sighs of the dying;

—send an angel to visit and strengthen them. (*R.*)

May all exiles have proof of your providential care;

—bring them back to their own land, and receive them one day into the fatherland of heaven. (*R.*)

May sinners cease to refuse your love;
—may they be reconciled with your Church. (*R.*)

Other prayers may be added

In your mercy save the departed;
—may they enter into the fulness of redemption. (*R.*)

Our Father . . .

Concluding prayer

O God, whose ineffable wisdom was wonderfully made manifest in the scandal of the Cross, grant that we may so well understand the glory of your Son's Passion that we may never cease to glory in his Cross. Through our Lord.

May the Lord bless us,
may he keep us from all evil.
and lead us to life everlasting.
Amen.

Let us bless the Lord.
R. Thanks be to God.

241

Saturday II

OFFICE OF READINGS

O God, come to my assistance.
Lord, make haste to help me.
Glory be to the Father, and to the Son, and to the Holy Spirit.
As it was in the beginning, is now, and ever shall be, world without end. Amen. Alleluia!

Or, if used as first prayer of the day: O Lord, open my lips ...

Hymn

How deep the riches of our God,
His wisdom how sublime;
How high his judgments soar above
All judgment of mankind!

What mind has read the mind of God,
Or giv'n him counsel sure?
Who from his riches gave to God
What was not first received?

From God all things created flow;
All things through him exist;
To him for judgment all returns,
To whom all praise is due!

To God the Father, fount of grace,
Through his beloved Son
In oneness with the Holy Ghost
Be glory evermore!

Psalmody

A. THROUGHOUT THE YEAR

Psalm 135   **Praise of God for the marvels of creation and for the liberation of his people**

If you knew the gift of God (John 4:10)

Ant. He alone has wrought marvels,
   for his great love is without end.

I

O give thanks to the Lord for he is good,
for his great love is without end.
Give thanks to the God of gods,
for his great love is without end.
Give thanks to the Lord of lords,
for his great love is without end;

who alone has wrought marvellous works,
for his great love is without end;
whose wisdom it was made the skies,
for his great love is without end;
who fixed the earth firmly on the seas,
for his great love is without end.

It was he who made the great lights,
for his great love is without end,
the sun to rule in the day,
for his great love is without end,
the moon and stars in the night,
for his great love is without end.

II

The first-born of the Egyptians he smote,
for his great love is without end.
He brought Israel out from their midst,
for his great love is without end;
arm outstretched, with power in his hand,
for his great love is without end.

He divided the Red Sea in two,
for his great love is without end;
he made Israel pass through the midst,
for his great love is without end;
he flung Pharaoh and his force in the sea,
for his great love is without end.

III

Through the desert his people he led,
for his great love is without end.
Nations in their greatness he struck,
for his great love is without end.
Kings in their splendour he slew,
for his great love is without end. . . .

He let Israel inherit their land,
for his great love is without end.
On his servant their land he bestowed,
for his great love is without end.
He remembered us in our distress,
for his great love is without end.

And he snatched us away from our foes,
for his great love is without end.
He gives food to all living things,
for his great love is without end.
To the God of heaven give thanks,
for his great love is without end.

Ant. He alone has wrought marvels,
  for his great love is without end.

B. ADVENT, CHRISTMASTIDE, LENT AND EASTERTIDE

Psalm 105   **The story of Israel: ingratitude of man, the goodness of God**

These things were written down for our instruction, upon whom the end of the ages has come (1 Cor 10:11)

I

Ant. God saved them for the sake of his name.

O give thanks to the Lord for he is good;
for his great love is without end.
Who can tell the Lord's mighty deeds?
Who can recount all his praise?

They are happy who do what is right,
who at all times do what is just.

O Lord, remember me
out of the love you have for your people.

Come to me, Lord, with your help
that I may see the joy of your chosen ones
and may rejoice in the gladness of your nation
and share the glory of your people.

Our sin is the sin of our fathers;
we have done wrong, our deeds have been evil.
Our fathers when they were in Egypt
paid no heed to your wonderful deeds.

They forgot the greatness of your love;
at the Red Sea defied the Most High.
Yet he saved them for the sake of his name,
in order to make known his power.

He threatened the Red Sea; it dried up
and he led them through the deep as through the desert.
He saved them from the land of the foe;
he saved them from the grip of the enemy.

The waters covered their oppressors;
not one of them was left alive.
Then they believed in his words:
then they sang his praises.

Ant. God saved them for the sake of his name.

II

Ant. They forgot the God who was their saviour.

But they soon forgot his deeds
and would not wait upon his will.
They yielded to their cravings in the desert
and put God to the test in the wilderness.

He granted them the favour they asked
and sent disease among them.
Then they rebelled, envious of Moses
and of Aaron, the Lord's holy one.

The earth opened up and swallowed up Dathan
and buried the clan of Abiram.
Fire blazed up against their clan
and flames devoured the rebels.

They fashioned a calf at Horeb
and worshipped an image of metal,
exchanging the God who was their glory
for the image of a bull that eats grass.

They forgot the God who was their saviour,
who had done such great things in Egypt,
such portents in the land of Ham,
such marvels at the Red Sea.

For this he said he would destroy them,
but Moses, the man he had chosen,
stood in the breach before him,
to turn back his anger from destruction.

Then they scorned the land of promise:
they had no faith in his word.
They complained inside their tents
and would not listen to the voice of the Lord.

So he raised his hand to swear an oath
that he would lay them low in the desert;
would scatter their sons among the nations
and disperse them throughout the lands.

They bowed before the Baal of Peor;
ate offerings made to lifeless gods.
They roused him to anger with their deeds
and a plague broke out among them.

Then Phineas stood up and intervened.
Thus the plague was ended
and this was counted in his favour
from age to age for ever.

They provoked him at the waters of Meribah.
Through their fault it went ill with Moses;

for they made his heart grow bitter
and he uttered words that were rash.

Ant. They forgot the God who was their saviour.

III

Ant. Gather us, Lord, from among the nations
   that we may praise your glory.

They failed to destroy the peoples
as the Lord had given command,
but instead they mingled with the nations
and learned to act like them.

They worshipped the idols of the nations
and these became a snare to entrap them.
They even offered their own sons
and their daughters in sacrifice to demons.

They shed the blood of the innocent,
the blood of their sons and daughters
whom they offered to the idols of Canaan.
The land was polluted with blood.

So they defiled themselves by their deeds
and broke their marriage bond with the Lord
till his anger blazed against his people:
he was filled with horror at his chosen ones.

So he gave them into the hand of the nations
and their foes became their rulers.
Their enemies became their oppressors;
they were subdued beneath their hand.

Time after time he rescued them,†
but in their malice they dared to defy him
and sank low through their guilt.
In spite of this he paid heed to their distress,
so often as he heard their cry.

For their sake he remembered his covenant.
In the greatness of his love he relented

and he let them be treated with mercy
by all who held them captive.

O Lord, our God, save us!
Gather us from among the nations
that we may thank your holy name
and make it our glory to praise you.

Blessed be the Lord, God of Israel,
for ever, from age to age.
Let all the people cry out:
'Amen! Amen! Alleluia!'

Ant. Gather us, Lord, from among the nations
that we may praise your glory.

V. Lord, make me know your ways.
R. Lord, teach me your paths.

Readings

Prayer of the day
Or alternative prayer

MORNING PRAYER

Introductory verse and psalm
O Lord, open my lips.
And my mouth shall declare your praise.
Glory be to the Father, and to the Son, and to the Holy
Spirit.
As it was in the beginning, is now, and ever shall be, world
without end. Amen. Alleluia!

Psalm 94
Refrain: Let us go to meet the Lord with songs of joy and
gladness.

Or, if not used as first prayer of the day: O God, come to my
assistance...

Hymn
R. Awake, O sleeper, and arise from the dead,
and Christ shall give you light.

Christ, who was manifested in the flesh,
vindicated in the Spirit,
seen by the angels,
preached among the nations,
believed on in the world,
taken up in glory. (*R.*)

Christ, who will be made manifest
at the proper time
by the blessed and only Sovereign,
the King of kings and Lord of lords,
who alone has immortality
and dwells in unapproachable light,
whom no man has ever seen or can see,
to him be honour and eternal dominion. Amen. (*R.*)

Psalmody

Psalm 91 **God guides the life of men with wisdom and justice**

By this my Father is glorified, that you bear much fruit
(John 15:8)

Ant. It is good to give thanks to the Lord.

It is good to give thanks to the Lord
to make music to your name, O Most High,
to proclaim your love in the morning
and your truth in the watches of the night,
on the ten-stringed lyre and the lute,
with the murmuring sound of the harp.

Your deeds, O Lord, have made me glad;
for the work of your hands I shout with joy.
O Lord, how great are your works!
How deep are your designs!
The foolish man cannot know this
and the fool cannot understand.

Though the wicked spring up like grass
and all who do evil thrive,
they are doomed to be eternally destroyed;

but you, Lord, are eternally on high.
See how your enemies perish;
all doers of evil are scattered.

To me you give the wild-ox's strength;
you anoint me with the purest oil.
My eyes looked in triumph on my foes;
my ears heard gladly of their fall.
The just will flourish like the palm-tree
and grow like a Lebanon cedar.

Planted in the house of the Lord
they will flourish in the courts of our God,
still bearing fruit when they are old,
still full of sap, still green,
to proclaim that the Lord is just.
in him, my rock, there is no wrong.

Ant. It is good to give thanks to the Lord.

Deut 32:1–12   Song of Moses: God's love for his people

How often would I have gathered your children together!
(Matthew 23:27)

Ant. I shall praise the name of the Lord.
    O give glory to this God of ours!

Listen, O heavens and I will speak,
let the earth hear the words on my lips,
May my teaching fall like the rain,
my speech descend like the dew,
like rain drops on the young green,
like showers falling on the grass.

For I shall praise the name of the Lord,
O give glory to this God of ours!
The Rock—his deeds are perfect,
and all his ways are just,
a faithful God, without deceit,
a God who is right and just.

Those whom he begot unblemished
have become crooked, false, perverse.
Is it thus you repay the Lord,
O senseless and foolish people?
Is he not your father who created you,
he who made you, on whom you depend?

Remember the days of old,
consider the years that are past;
ask your father and he will show you,
ask your elders and they will tell you.

When the Most High gave the nations their heritage
and disposed men according to his plan,
in fixing the boundaries of the nations
he thought first of Israel's sons.
For Israel was the Lord's possession,
Jacob the one he had chosen.

God found him in a wilderness,
in fearful, desolate wastes;
he surrounded him, he lifted him up,
he kept him as the apple of his eye.

Like an eagle that watches its nest,
that hovers over its young,
so he spread his wings; he took him,
placed him on his outstretched wings.
The Lord alone was his guide
and no other god was with him.

Ant. I shall praise the name of the Lord.
    O give glory to this God of ours!

Psalm 8   **God's majesty, man's dignity**

*He has put all things under his feet and has made him the
head over all things for the Church* (Eph 1:22)

R. How great is your name, O Lord our God,
through all the earth!

Your majesty is praised
above the heavens;
on the lips of children and of babes†
you have found praise to foil your enemy,
to silence the foe and the rebel.

When I see the heavens, the work of your hands,
the moon and the stars which you arranged,
what is man that you should keep him in mind,
mortal man that you care for him?

Yet you have made him little less than a god;
with glory and honour you crowned him,
gave him power over the works of your hand,
put all things under his feet.

All of them, sheep and cattle,
yes, even the savage beasts,
birds of the air, and fish
that make their way through the waters.

R. How great is your name, O Lord our God,
through all the earth!

Word of God   Rom 12:18, 20, 21
Live peaceably with all. If your enemy is hungry, feed him;
if he is thirsty, give him drink. Do not be overcome by evil,
but overcome evil with good.

Short Response
I call with all my heart.
Lord, hear me.
V. Give me life by your decrees.
R. Lord, hear me.
V. Glory be to the Father, and to the Son, and to the Holy
Spirit.
I call with all my heart.
Lord, hear me.

252

Song of Zechariah

Ant. Enlighten those in darkness, Lord;
  guide us into the way of peace.

Prayers

Christ wants us to see himself in all our brothers, but especially in those who are suffering; let us pray to him:

R. Make us perfect in charity, Lord.

In celebrating this morning your Son's resurrection
—may we receive the fruits of his redemption. (*R.*)

Lord, may we bear witness to you;
—may we offer ourselves as an oblation to the Father, holy, pleasing to him for your sake. (*R.*)

Make us see yourself reflected in all we meet;
—may we minister to you in them. (*R.*)

In the morning, Lord, fill us with your love,
—that we may be glad and rejoice in you. (*R.*)

Other prayers may be added

Our Father . . .

Prayer

May our lips, our soul and our life praise you, O Lord, and since our very being is your gift, so may our whole life be entirely yours. We make our prayer through our Lord.

May the Lord bless us,
may he keep us from all evil
and lead us to life everlasting.
Amen.

Let us bless the Lord.
R. Thanks be to God.

MIDDAY PRAYER

O God, come to my assistance . . .
Glory be . . .

Hymn

Mighty ruler, faithful God,
who arrange the successive changes in nature,
giving bright light to the morning sun
and burning heat at noon.

Put out the flames of strife
and take away the heat of passion;
grant us health of body
and true peace of soul.

Grant this, most loving Father,
and you, the only Son, equal to the Father,
and, with the Spirit, the Paraclete,
reigning through the ages. Amen.

Psalmody

Psalm 118:81–88

Ant. You are my refuge, Lord.

I yearn for your saving help;
I hope in your word.
My eyes yearn to see your promise.
When will you console me?

Though parched and exhausted with waiting
I remember your statutes.
How long must your servant suffer?
When will you sentence my oppressors?

For me the proud have dug pitfalls,
against your law.
Your commands are all true; then help me
when lies oppress me.

They almost made an end of me on earth
but I kept your precepts.
Because of your love give me life
and I will do your will.

Psalm 60   **Prayer for the king**

*He has delivered us from the dominion of darkness and
transferred us to the kingdom of his beloved Son* (Col 1:13)

O God, hear my cry!
Listen to my prayer!
From the end of the earth I call:
my heart is faint.

On the rock too high for me to reach
set me on high,
O you who have been my refuge,
my tower against the foe.

Let me dwell in your tent for ever
and hide in the shelter of your wings.
For you, O God, hear my prayer
and grant me the heritage of those who fear you.

May you lengthen the life of the king:
may his years cover many generations.
May he ever sit enthroned before God:
bid love and truth be his protection.

So I will always praise your name
and day after day fulfil my vows.

Psalm 63   **The defeat of God's enemies**

*I have a baptism to be baptized with, and how I am con-
strained until it is accomplished!* (Luke 12:50)

Hear my voice, O God, as I complain,
guard my life from dread of the foe.
Hide me from the band of the wicked,
from the throng of those who do evil.

They sharpen their tongues like swords;
they aim bitter words like arrows
to shoot at the innocent from ambush,
shooting suddenly and recklessly.

They scheme their evil course;
they conspire to lay secret snares.
They say: 'Who will see us?
Who can search out our crimes?'

He will search who searches the mind
and knows the depths of the heart.
God has shot an arrow at them
and dealt them sudden wounds.
Their own tongue has brought them to ruin
and all who see them mock.

Then all men will fear;†
they will tell what God has done.
They will understand God's deeds.
The just will rejoice in the Lord†
and fly to him for refuge.
All the upright hearts will glory.

Ant. You are my refuge, Lord.

Word of God   Deut 8:5–6

As a man disciplines his son, the Lord your God disciplines
you. So you shall keep the commandments of the Lord your
God, by walking in his ways and by fearing him.

V. Guide me in the paths of your commands,
R. For there is my delight.

Prayer

O Lord, fire of everlasting love, give us the fervour to love
you above all things, and our brother for your sake.
Through Christ.

Let us bless the Lord.
R. Thanks be to God.

Sunday III

EVENING PRAYER I

O God, come to my assistance.
Lord, make haste to help me.
Glory be to the Father, and to the Son, and to the Holy Spirit.
As it was in the beginning, is now, and ever shall be, world without end. Amen. Alleluia!

Hymn 2 Tim 2:11–13

R. Christ has died,
   Christ is risen,
   Christ will come again.

If we have died with him,
we shall also live with him:
If we endure,
we shall also reign with him. (R.)

If we deny him,
he will also deny us;
If we are faithless, he remains faithful—
for he cannot deny himself. Alleluia!

Psalmody

Psalm 115   Thanksgiving in the temple after recovery from sickness

Through him, let us continually offer up a sacrifice of praise to God (Heb 13:15)

Ant. My vows to the Lord I will fulfil
   in the presence of all his people.

I trusted, even when I said:
'I am sorely afflicted,'
and when I said in my alarm:
'No man can be trusted.'

How can I repay the Lord
for his goodness to me?
The cup of salvation I will raise;
I will call on the Lord's name.

My vows to the Lord I will fulfil
before all his people.
O precious in the eyes of the Lord
is the death of his faithful.

Your servant, Lord, your servant am I;
you have loosened my bonds.
A thanksgiving sacrifice I make:
I will call on the Lord's name.

My vows to the Lord I will fulfil
before all his people,
in the courts of the house of the Lord,
in your midst, O Jerusalem.

Ant. My vows to the Lord I will fulfil
in the presence of all his people.

Psalm 112   **To the God of glory and compassion: a hymn of worship**

*He has cast the mighty from their thrones and has raised
the lowly* (Luke 1:52)

Ant. May the name of the Lord be blessed,
now and for evermore.

Praise, O servants of the Lord,
praise the name of the Lord!
May the name of the Lord be blessed
both now and for evermore!
From the rising of the sun to its setting
praised be the name of the Lord!

High above all nations is the Lord,
above the heavens his glory.

Who is like the Lord, our God,
who has risen on high to his throne
yet stoops from the heights to look down,
to look down upon heaven and earth?

From the dust he lifts up the lowly,
from the dungheap he raises the poor
to set him in the company of princes,
yes, with the princes of his people.
To the childless wife he gives a home
and gladdens her heart with children.

Ant. May the name of the Lord be blessed,
    now and for evermore.

Phil 2:6–11   **Song of the Easter mystery**

Ant. Christ died for our sins,
    and rose that we might live.

Though he was in the form of God,
Jesus did not count equality with God a thing to be grasped.

R. Jesus Christ is Lord
    to the glory of God the Father!

He emptied himself,†
taking the form of a servant,
being born in the likeness of men. (*R.*)

And being found in human form,†
he humbled himself and became obedient unto death,
even death on a cross. (*R.*)

Therefore God has highly exalted him
and bestowed on him the name which is above every name.
    (*R.*)

That at the name of Jesus every knee should bow,
in heaven and on earth and under the earth. (*R.*)

And every tongue confess that Jesus is Lord,
to the glory of God the Father.

Ant. Christ died for our sins,
    and rose that we might live.

Word of God   Heb 13:20–21

May the God of peace who brought again from the dead
our Lord Jesus, the great shepherd of the sheep, by the
blood of the eternal covenant, equip you with everything
good that you may do his will, working in you that which
is pleasing in his sight, through Jesus Christ, to whom be
glory for ever and ever. Amen.

Short Response

By your blood
you have ransomed us, Lord.
V. Men from every tribe and tongue and people and nation.
R. You have ransomed us, Lord.
V. Glory be to the Father, and to the Son, and to the Holy
Spirit.
By your blood
you have ransomed us, Lord.

Song of the Virgin Mary

Ant. Blessed are you among women,
    and blessed is the fruit of your womb.

Prayers

God protects and helps the people whom he has chosen as
his own, that they may have joy. Let us pray to him:

R. All our trust is in you, Lord.

Father of mercy, we implore you for our Holy Father,
Pope N.
—shelter him under your protecting care, and give him
grace to grow in holiness. (*R.*)

Look with pity on the homeless;
—may they find a dwelling-place worthy of human dignity.
(*R.*)

Give and increase the fruits of the earth,
—that all men may have the food they need each day. (*R.*)

May the sick look with faith on the passion of Christ;
—may they find strength as they share his sufferings. (*R.*)

Other prayers may be added

Let your loving-kindness go with those on their last journey;
—admit them to heavenly mansions.

Our Father . . .

Concluding prayer of the Sunday

May the Lord bless us,
may he keep us from all evil
and lead us to life everlasting.
Amen.

Let us bless the Lord.
R. Thanks be to God.

OFFICE OF READINGS

O God, come to my assistance.
Lord, make haste to help me.
Glory be to the Father, and to the Son, and to the Holy
Spirit.
As it was in the beginning, is now, and ever shall be, world
without end. Amen. Alleluia!

Or, if used as first prayer of the day: O Lord, open my lips . . .

Hymn
R. Alleluia! Christ is risen, alleluia!
R. (*in Lent*) If we have died with him, we shall also live
with him.

I will sing to the Lord, glorious his triumph!
Horse and rider he has thrown into the sea.
Lord, you are great, you are glorious,
wonderful in strength, none can conquer you.
God has arisen, and his foes are scattered;
those who hate him have fled before him. (*R.*)

He has burst the gates of bronze
and shattered the iron bars.
This God of ours is a God who saves;
the Lord our God holds the keys of death.
This is the day which the Lord has made;
let us rejoice and be glad. (*R.*)

Awake, O sleeper, and rise from the dead,
and Christ shall give you light.
For he has been raised from the dead,
never to die any more.
God has not left his soul among the dead,
nor let his beloved know decay.
The Lord is risen from the tomb
who hung for us upon the tree. (*R.*)

Beasts of the field, do not be afraid;
the pastures of the wilderness are green again;
the tree bears its fruit once more,
vine and fig tree yield abundantly. (*R.*)

Psalmody

Psalm 144   **Praise of God's grandeur**

*God raised us up . . . that in the coming ages he might show
the immeasurable riches of his grace in kindness towards
us in Christ Jesus* (Eph 2:7)

I

Ant. Day after day I will bless you, alleluia!

I will give you glory, O God my King,
I will bless your name for ever.

I will bless you day after day
and praise your name for ever.
The Lord is great, highly to be praised,
his greatness cannot be measured.

Age to age shall proclaim your works,
shall declare your mighty deeds,
shall speak of your splendour and glory,
tell the tale of your wonderful works.

They will speak of your terrible deeds,
recount your greatness and might.
They will recall your abundant goodness;
age to age shall ring out your justice.

Ant. Day after day I will bless you, alleluia!

II

Ant. Your kingdom, Lord, is an everlasting kingdom,
alleluia!

The Lord is kind and full of compassion,
slow to anger, abounding in love.
How good is the Lord to all,
compassionate to all his creatures.

All your creatures shall thank you, O Lord,
and your friends shall repeat their blessing.
They shall speak of the glory of your reign
and declare your might, O God.

to make known to men your mighty deeds
and the glorious splendour of your reign.
Yours is an everlasting kingdom;
your rule lasts from age to age.

The Lord is faithful in all his words
and loving in all his deeds.
The Lord supports all who fall
and raises all who are bowed down.

The eyes of all creatures look to you
and you give them their food in due time.
You open wide your hand,
grant the desires of all who live.

Ant. Your kingdom, Lord, is an everlasting kingdom,
alleluia!

III

Ant. The Lord is true in all his words
and loving in all his deeds.

The Lord is just in all his ways
and loving in all his deeds.
He is close to all who call him,
who call on him from their hearts.

He grants the desires of those who fear him,
he hears their cry and he saves them.
The Lord protects all who love him;
but the wicked he will utterly destroy.

Let me speak the praise of the Lord,†
let all mankind bless his holy name
for ever, for ages unending.

Ant. The Lord is true in all his words
and loving in all his deeds.

V. You shall know that you are my disciples,
R. If you keep my words.

Readings

(Hymn of Praise)

Prayer of the Sunday

MORNING PRAYER

Introductory verse and Psalm
O Lord, open my lips.
And my mouth shall declare your praise.

Glory be to the Father, and to the Son, and to the Holy Spirit.

As it was in the beginning, is now, and ever shall be, world without end. Amen. Alleluia.

Psalm 94

Refrain: Come, let us worship the Lord our God.

Or, if not used as first prayer of the day: O God, come to my assistance . . .

Hymn

Sing, all creation, sing to God in gladness!
Joyously serve him, singing hymns of homage!
Chanting his praises, come before his presence!
Praise the Almighty!

Know that our God is Lord of all the ages!
He is our maker; we are all his creatures,
People he fashioned, sheep he leads to pasture!
Praise the Almighty!

Enter his temple, ringing out his praises!
Sing in thanksgiving as you come before him!
Blessing his bounty, glorify his greatness!
Praise the Almighty!

Great in his goodness is the Lord we worship;
Steadfast his kindness, love that knows no ending!
Faithful his word is, changeless, everlasting!
Praise the Almighty!

Psalmody

Psalm 92   **Praise of God, king of the world**

The Lord our God, the Almighty, reigns. Let us rejoice and exult and give him glory (Rev 19:6–7)

Ant. Alleluia! The Lord reigns, clothed with majesty, alleluia, alleluia!

The Lord is king, with majesty enrobed;†
the Lord has robed himself with might,
he has girded himself with power.

The world you made firm, not to be moved;†
your throne has stood firm from of old.
From all eternity, O Lord, you are.

The waters have lifted up, O Lord,†
the waters have lifted up their voice,
the waters have lifted up their thunder.

Greater than the roar of mighty waters,†
more glorious than the surgings of the sea,
the Lord is glorious on high.

Truly your decrees are to be trusted.†
Holiness is fitting to your house, O Lord,
until the end of time.

Ant. Alleluia! The Lord reigns, clothed with majesty, alleluia, alleluia!

Dan 3:57–88, 56   **Song of the universe**

Creation waits with eager longing . . . for the Creator, who is blessed for ever (Rom 1:25)

Ant. In the midst of the flames the children sang,
    Blessed be God, alleluia!

O all you works of the Lord, O bless the Lord.
R. To him be highest glory and praise for ever.

And you, angels of the Lord, O bless the Lord.
R. To him be highest glory and praise for ever.

And you, the heavens of the Lord, O bless the Lord.
And you, clouds of the sky, O bless the Lord.
And you, all armies of the Lord, O bless the Lord.
R. To him be highest glory and praise for ever.

And you, sun and moon, O bless the Lord.
And you, the stars of the heav'ns, O bless the Lord.
And you, showers and rain, O bless the Lord.
R. To him be highest glory and praise for ever.

And you, all you breezes and winds, O bless the Lord.
And you, fire and heat, O bless the Lord.

And you, cold and heat, O bless the Lord.
R. To him be highest glory and praise for ever.

And you, showers and dew, O bless the Lord.
And you, frosts and cold, O bless the Lord.
And you, frost and snow, O bless the Lord.
R. To him be highest glory and praise for ever.

And you, night-time and day, O bless the Lord.
And you, darkness and light, O bless the Lord.
And you, lightning and clouds, O bless the Lord.
R. To him be highest glory and praise for ever.

O let the earth bless the Lord.
R. To him be highest glory and praise for ever.

And you, mountains and hills, O bless the Lord.
And you, all plants of the earth, O bless the Lord.
And you, fountains and springs, O bless the Lord.
R. To him be highest glory and praise for ever.

And you, rivers and seas, O bless the Lord.
And you, creatures of the sea, O bless the Lord.
And you, every bird in the sky, O bless the Lord.
And you, wild beasts and tame, O bless the Lord.
R. To him be highest glory and praise for ever.

And you, children of men, O bless the Lord.
R. To him be highest glory and praise for ever.

O Israel, bless the Lord, O bless the Lord.
And you, priests of the Lord, O bless the Lord.
And you, servants of the Lord, O bless the Lord.
R. To him be highest glory and praise for ever.

And you spirits and souls of the just, O bless the Lord,
And you holy and humble of heart, O bless the Lord.
Ananias, Azarias, Mizael, O bless the Lord.
R. To him be highest glory and praise for ever.

May you be blessed, O Lord, in the heavens.
R. To you be highest glory and praise for ever.

Ant. In the midst of the flames the children sang,
  Blessed be God, alleluia!

Psalm 148   Cosmic praise

> *To him who sits upon the throne and to the Lamb be blessing
> and honour and glory and might for ever and ever* (Rev
> 5:13)

Ant. Alleluia! Praise the Lord from the heavens, alleluia,
alleluia!

Praise the Lord from the heavens,
praise him in the heights.
Praise him, all his angels,
praise him, all his host.

Praise him, sun and moon,
praise him, shining stars.
Praise him, highest heavens
and the waters above the heavens.

Let them praise the name of the Lord.
He commanded: they were made.
He fixed them for ever,
gave a law which shall not pass away.

Praise the Lord from the earth,
sea creatures and all oceans,
fire and hail, snow and mist,
stormy winds that obey his word;

all mountains and hills,
all fruit trees and cedars,
beasts, wild and tame,
reptiles and birds on the wing;

all earth's kings and peoples,
earth's princes and rulers;
young men and maidens,
old men together with children.

Let them praise the name of the Lord
for he alone is exalted.

The splendour of his name
reaches beyond heaven and earth.

He exalts the strength of his people.
He is the praise of all his saints,
of the sons of Israel,
of the people to whom he comes close.

Ant. Alleluia! Praise the Lord from the heavens, alleluia, alleluia!

Word of God   Ez 37:12–14

Thus says the Lord God: Behold, I will open your graves, and raise you from your graves, O my people; and I will bring you home into the land of Israel. And you shall know that I am the Lord, when I open your graves, and raise you from your graves, O my people. And I will put my Spirit within you, and you shall live, and I will place you in your own land; then you shall know that I, the Lord, have spoken, and I have done it, says the Lord.

Short Response

Give the Lord glory and power.
Alleluia, alleluia!
V. Give the Lord the glory of his name.
R. Alleluia, alleluia!
V. Glory be to the Father, and to the Son, and to the Holy Spirit.
Give the Lord glory and power.
Alleluia, alleluia!

Song of Zechariah

Ant. Behold, I make all things new. I am the Alpha and the Omega, the beginning and the end.

Prayers

Let us pray to God our Father who listens to those who seek him. Let us say:

269

R. Glory be to you for ever.

Blessed are you, O God, giver of light.

—It is for your glory that you have awakened us to a new day. (*R.*)

By the Resurrection of your Son you have filled the world with light;

—diffuse this light among all peoples through the work of your Church. (*R.*)

You enlightened the minds of your Son's disciples by the gift of the Holy Spirit;

—send the same Spirit upon the Church, that she may be ever faithful to you. (*R.*)

Light of all the nations, remember those still groping in darkness.

—Give them spiritual sight, that they may recognize you as the only true God. (*R.*)

Other prayers may be added

Our Father . . .

Concluding prayer of the Sunday

May the Lord bless us,
may he keep us from all evil
and lead us to life everlasting.
Amen.

Let us bless the Lord.
R. Thanks be to God.

MIDDAY PRAYER

O God, come to my assistance . . .
Glory be . . .

Hymn

Lord God, the strength which daily upholds all creation,
in yourself remaining unchanged
and yet determining in due order
the successive changes of the light of day.

Grant us light in the evening
so that life may not decay at any point of its activity,
but everlasting glory be the immediate reward
of a happy death.

Grant this, most loving Father,
and you, the only Son, equal to the Father
and, with the Spirit, the Paraclete,
reigning through the ages. Amen.

Psalmody

Psalm 117   **Thanksgiving in the temple for the gift of salvation**

This is the stone which was rejected by you builders, but which has become the head of the corner (Acts 4:11)

Ant. The Lord God is our light.

I

Give thanks to the Lord for he is good,
for his love has no end.

Let the sons of Israel say:
'His love has no end.'
Let the sons of Aaron say:
'His love has no end.'
Let those who fear the Lord say:
'His love has no end.'

I called to the Lord in my distress;
he answered and freed me.

The Lord is at my side; I do not fear.
What can man do against me?
The Lord is at my side as my helper:
I shall look down on my foes.

It is better to take refuge in the Lord
than to trust in men:
it is better to take refuge in the Lord
than to trust in princes. . .
I was thrust, thrust down and falling
but the Lord was my helper.

II

The Lord is my strength and my song;
he was my saviour.
There are shouts of joy and victory
in the tents of the just.

The Lord's right hand has triumphed;
his right hand raised me up.
The Lord's right hand has triumphed.
I shall not die, I shall live and recount his deeds.
I was punished, I was punished by the Lord,
but not doomed to die.

III

Open to me the gates of holiness:
I will enter and give thanks.
This is the Lord's own gate
where the just may enter.
I will thank you for you have given answer
and you are my saviour.

The stone which the builders rejected
has become the corner stone.
This is the work of the Lord,
a marvel in our eyes.
This day was made by the Lord;
we rejoice and are glad.

O Lord, grant us salvation;
O Lord, grant success.
Blessed in the name of the Lord
is he who comes.
We bless you from the house of the Lord;
the Lord God is our light.

Go forward in procession with branches
even to the altar.
You are my God, I thank you.
My God, I praise you.
Give thanks to the Lord for he is good;
for his love has no end.

Ant. The Lord God is our light.

Word of God   Eph 1:5–6
God destined us in love to be his sons through Jesus Christ,
according to the purpose of his will, to the praise of his
glorious grace which he freely bestowed on us in the
Beloved.

V. As a father has compassion on his sons,
R. The Lord has pity on those who fear him.

Prayer of the Sunday
Let us bless the Lord.
R. Thanks be to God.

EVENING PRAYER II

O God, come to my assistance.
Lord, make haste to help me.
Glory be to the Father, and to the Son, and to the Holy
Spirit.
As it was in the beginning, is now, and ever shall be, world
without end. Amen. Alleluia!

Hymn
R. Alleluia! Christ is risen, alleluia!

I have trodden the wine press alone,
and from the peoples no one was with me.
I have laid down my life of my own free will,
and by my power I have taken it up anew.
Fear not, I am the first and the last;
I am the living one. (R.)

Was it not ordained that the Christ should suffer,
and so enter into his glory?
Upon him was the chastisement that made us whole,
and with his stripes we are healed.
It was the will of the Lord to bruise him;
he has offered his life in atonement. (R.)

By his holy and glorious wounds
may Christ the Lord guard us and keep us.
If we have died with him, we shall also live with him;
if we endure, we shall also reign with him.
Christ yesterday and today,
the beginning of all things and their end.
Alpha and Omega;
all time belongs to him, and all the ages. (R.)

Psalmody

Psalm 109   **The Messiah, king, priest and judge**

*He must reign until he has put all his enemies under his
feet* (1 Cor 15:25)

Ant. The Lord said to my Lord: 'Sit on my right.'

The Lord's revelation to my Master:†
'Sit on my right:
I will put your foes beneath your feet.'

The Lord will send from Zion your sceptre of power:
rule in the midst of all your foes.

A prince from the day of your birth on the holy mountains;
from the womb before the daybreak I begot you.

The Lord has sworn an oath he will not change.†
'You are a priest for ever,
a priest like Melchizedeck of old.'

The Master standing at your right hand
will shatter kings in the day of his great wrath. . . .

He shall drink from the stream by the wayside
and therefore he shall lift up his head.

Ant. The Lord said to my Lord: 'Sit on my right.'

Psalm 110   **To God the Almighty, faithful and true**

*Great and wonderful are your deeds, O Lord God, the
Almighty* (Rev 15:5)

Ant. Great are the works of the Lord,
to be pondered and loved.

I will thank the Lord with all my heart
in the meeting of the just and their assembly.
Great are the works of the Lord;
to be pondered by all who love them.

Majestic and glorious his work,
his justice stands firm for ever.
He makes us remember his wonders.
The Lord is compassion and love.

He gives food to those who fear him;
keeps his covenant ever in mind.
He has shown his might to his people
by giving them the lands of the nations.

His works are justice and truth:
his precepts are all of them sure,
standing firm for ever and ever:
they are made in uprightness and truth.

He has sent deliverance to his people†
and established his covenant for ever.
Holy his name, to be feared.

To fear the Lord is the beginning of wisdom;†
all who do so prove themselves wise.
His praise shall last for ever!

Ant. Great are the works of the Lord,
   to be pondered and loved.

OUTSIDE LENT

Rev 19:1, 2, 5, 8   **Wedding song of the Lamb**

Ant. The Lord is king, let earth rejoice, alleluia!

R. Alleluia, alleluia!

Salvation and glory and power
belong to our God, alleluia!
His judgments are true
and just.

R. Alleluia, alleluia!

Praise our God,
all you his servants, alleluia!
You who fear him,
small and great.

R. Alleluia, alleluia!

The Lord our God,
the Almighty, reigns, alleluia!
Let us rejoice and exult
and give him the glory.

R. Alleluia, alleluia!

The marriage of the Lamb
has come, alleluia!
And his bride
has made herself ready.

R. Alleluia, alleluia!

It was granted her
to be clothed, alleluia!
with fine linen,
bright and pure.

R. Alleluia, alleluia!

Ant. The Lord is king, let earth rejoice, alleluia!

LENT

1 Pet 2:21–24   **New Testament Song of the suffering Servant**

Ant. For our sake God made him to be sin who knew no sin,
   so that in him we might become the righteousness of God.

Christ suffered for you,†
leaving you an example
that you should follow in his steps.

R. By his wounds you have been healed.

He committed no sin;
no guile was found on his lips.
When he was reviled,
he did not revile in return.
When he suffered,
he did not threaten;
but he trusted to him
who judges justly. (*R.*)

He himself bore our sins
in his body on the tree,
that we might die to sin
and live to righteousness.

By his wounds you have been healed.†
For you were straying like sheep,
but have now returned to the Shepherd and Guardian
   of your souls. (*R.*)

Ant. For our sake God made him to be sin who knew no sin,
   so that in him we might become the righteousness of God.

Word of God   1 Pet 1:3–5

Blessed be the God and Father of our Lord Jesus Christ!

By his great mercy we have been born anew to a living hope through the resurrection of Jesus Christ from the dead, and to an inheritance which is imperishable, undefiled, and unfading, kept in heaven for you, who by God's power are guarded through faith for a salvation ready to be revealed in the last time.

Short Response

May the name of the Lord be blessed,
alleluia, alleluia!
V. Now and for evermore.
R. Alleluia, alleluia!
V. Glory be to the Father, and to the Son, and to the Holy Spirit.
May the name of the Lord be blessed,
alleluia, alleluia!

Song of the Virgin Mary

Ant. Let my soul praise the Lord; he loves the just, he raises those who fall.

Prayers

The world once created by God was recreated by the redemption and is always being restored by divine love; let us beseech God and say:

R. Renew the wonderful works of your love, O Lord.

We give thanks to you, O God, because all creation reveals your power;
—your providence is made manifest in your guidance of the world. (*R.*)

For the sake of your Son, who proclaimed peace and victory through his cross,
—set free those who are bound by fear and despair. (*R.*)

To all those who love and seek justice
—grant that they may co-operate in peace to build a better world. (*R.*)

Be with the oppressed, console the unhappy, deliver captives,
provide bread for the hungry, strengthen the infirm.
—Let the victory of the cross shine out in all of them. (*R.*)

Other prayers may be added

As you so wonderfully recalled your Son from death after
three days,
—lead those who have died to eternal life. (*R.*)

Our Father . . .

Concluding prayer of the Sunday

May the Lord bless us,
may he keep us from all evil
and lead us to life everlasting.
Amen.

Let us bless the Lord.
R. Thanks be to God.

Monday III

OFFICE OF READINGS

O God, come to my assistance.
Lord, make haste to help me.
Glory be to the Father, and to the Son, and to the Holy
Spirit.
As it was in the beginning, is now, and ever shall be, world
without end. Amen. Alleluia.

Or, if used as first prayer of the day: O Lord, open my lips...

Hymn   1 Cor 13:4–10, 12–13

Love is patient and kind:†
love is not jealous or boastful;
it is not arrogant or rude.

R. Faith, hope and love abide, but the greatest of these is
love.

Love does not insist on its own way,
it is not irritable or resentful;
it does not rejoice at wrong,
but rejoices in the right. (*R.*)

Love bears all things,
believes all things,
hopes all things,
endures all things. (*R.*)

Love never ends;†
as for prophecies,
they will pass away;
as for tongues,
they will cease;
as for knowledge,
it will pass away. (*R.*)

For our knowledge is imperfect
and our prophecy is imperfect;

but when the perfect comes,
the imperfect will pass away. (*R.*)

Now I know in part;†
then I shall understand fully,
even as I have been fully understood.
So faith, hope, love abide, these three,
but the greatest of these is love. (*R.*)

Psalmody

Psalm 49   **True and false worship of God**

> *By grace you have been saved through faith; and this is*
> *not your own doing, it is the gift of God* (Eph 2:8)

I

Ant. Our God comes, he keeps silence no longer.

The God of gods, the Lord,†
has spoken and summoned the earth,
from the rising of the sun to its setting.
Out of Zion's perfect beauty he shines.
Our God comes, he keeps silence no longer.

Before him fire devours,
around him tempest rages.
He calls on the heavens and the earth
to witness his judgment of his people.

'Summon before me my people
who made covenant with me by sacrifice.'
The heavens proclaim his justice,
for he, God, is the judge.

Ant. Our God comes, he keeps silence no longer.

II

Ant. Pay your sacrifice of thanksgiving to God.

'Listen my people, I will speak;
Israel, I will testify against you,
for I am God your God.
I accuse you, lay the charge before you.

I find no fault with your sacrifices,
your offerings are always before me.
I do not ask more bullocks from your farms,
nor goats from among your herds.

For I own all the beasts of the forest,
beasts in their thousands on my hills.
I know all the birds in the sky,
all that moves in the field belong to me.

Were I hungry, I would not tell you,
for I own the world and all it holds.
Do you think I eat the flesh of bulls,
or drink the blood of goats?

Pay your sacrifice of thanksgiving to God
and render him your votive offerings.
Call on me in the day of distress.
I will free you and you shall honour me.'

Ant. Pay your sacrifices of thanksgiving to God.

III

Ant. I desire steadfast love and not sacrifice.

God says to the wicked:†
'But how can you recite my commandments
and take my covenant on your lips,
you who despise my law
and throw my words to the winds,

you who see a thief and go with him;
who throw in your lot with adulterers,
who unbridle your mouth for evil
and whose tongue is plotting crime,

you who sit and malign your brother
and slander your own mother's son.
You do this, and should I keep silence?
Do you think that I am like you?

Mark this, you who never think of God,
lest I seize you and you cannot escape;
a sacrifice of thanksgiving honours me
and I will show God's salvation to the upright.'

Ant. I desire steadfast love and not sacrifice.

V. I am the Lord your God.
R. Listen, my people, to my law.

Readings

Prayer of the day

Or alternative prayer

MORNING PRAYER

Introductory verse and psalm
O Lord, open my lips.
And my mouth shall declare your praise.
Glory be to the Father, and to the Son, and to the Holy
Spirit.
As it was in the beginning, is now, and ever shall be, world
without end. Amen. Alleluia!

Psalm 94
Refrain: Come, ring out our joy to the Lord.

Or, if not used as first prayer of the day: O God, come to my
assistance...

Hymn
This day God gives me
Strength of high heaven,
Sun and moon shining,
Flame in my hearth,
Flashing of lightning,
Wind in its swiftness,
Deeps of the ocean,
Firmness of earth.

This day God sends me
Strength as my steersman,
Might to uphold me,
Wisdom as guide.
Your eyes are watchful,
Your ears are listening,
Your lips are speaking,
Friend at my side.

God's way is my way,
God's shield is round me,
God's host defends me,
Saving from ill.
Angels of heaven,
Drive from me always
All that would harm me,
Stand by me still.

Rising I thank you,
Mighty and strong One,
King of creation,
Giver of rest,
Firmly confessing
Threeness of Persons,
Oneness of Godhead,
Trinity blest.

Psalmody

Psalm 83   **Love and longing for God's temple in Zion**

*Here we have no lasting city, but we seek the city which
is to come* (Heb 13:14)

Ant. They are happy, who dwell in your house, O Lord.

How lovely is your dwelling place,
Lord, God of hosts.

My soul is longing and yearning,
is yearning for the courts of the Lord.

My heart and my soul ring out their joy
to God, the living God.

The sparrow herself finds a home
and the swallow a nest for her brood;
she lays her young by your altars,
Lord of hosts, my king and my God.

They are happy, who dwell in your house,
for ever singing your praise.
They are happy, whose strength is in you,
in whose hearts are the roads to Zion.

As they go through the Bitter Valley†
they make it a place of springs,
the autumn rain covers it with blessings.
They walk with ever growing strength,
they will see the God of gods in Zion.

O Lord God of hosts, hear my prayer,
give ear, O God of Jacob.
Turn your eyes, O God, our shield,
look on the face of your anointed.

One day within your courts
is better than a thousand elsewhere.
The threshold of the house of God
I prefer to the dwellings of the wicked.

For the Lord God is a rampart, a shield;
he will give us his favour and glory.
The Lord will not refuse any good
to those who walk without blame.

Lord, God of hosts,
happy the man who trusts in you!

Ant. They are happy, who dwell in your house, O Lord.

Is 2:2–5   **Song of Isaiah: Jerusalem, city of peace**

All nations shall come and worship you (Rev 15:4)

Ant. Come, let us go to the house of the Lord.

It shall come to pass in the latter days†
that the mountain of the house of the Lord
shall be established as the highest of the mountains;
it shall be raised above the hills;
and all the nations shall flow to it.

And many peoples shall come, and say:†
'Come, let us go up to the mountain of the Lord,
to the house of the God of Jacob,
that he may teach us his ways
and that we may walk in his paths.'
For out of Zion shall go forth the law,
and the word of the Lord from Jerusalem.

He shall judge between the nations,
and shall decide for many peoples;
and they shall beat their swords into ploughshares,
and their spears into pruning hooks;
nation shall not lift up sword against nation,
neither shall they learn war any more.

O house of Jacob, come,
let us walk in the light of the Lord.

Ant. Come, let us go to the house of the Lord.

Psalm 95   **The universal reign of the true God**

They sing a new song before the throne and before the Lamb (Rev 14:3)

Ant. Sing a new song to the Lord,
day after day proclaim his help.

O sing a new song to the Lord,†
sing to the Lord all the earth.
O sing to the Lord, bless his name.

Proclaim his help day by day,†
tell among the nations his glory
and his wonders among all the peoples.

The Lord is great and worthy of praise,†
to be feared above all gods;
the gods of the heathens are naught.

It was the Lord who made the heavens,†
his are majesty and state and power
and splendour in his holy place.

Give the Lord, you families of peoples,†
give the Lord glory and power,
give the Lord the glory of his name.

Bring an offering and enter his courts,†
worship the Lord in his temple.
O earth, tremble before him.

Proclaim to the nations: 'God is king.'†
The world he made firm in its place;
he will judge the peoples in fairness.

Let the heavens rejoice and earth be glad,
let the sea and all within it thunder praise,
let the land and all it bears rejoice,
all the trees of the wood shout for joy

at the presence of the Lord for he comes,
he comes to rule the earth.
With justice he will rule the world,
he will judge the peoples with his truth.

Ant. Sing a new song to the Lord,
day after day proclaim his help.

Word of God Jas 2:12–13
So speak and so act as those who are to be judged under
the law of liberty. For judgment is without mercy to one
who has shown no mercy; yet mercy triumphs over judgment.

287

Short Response

Lord, heal my soul,

for I have sinned against you.

V. I said: Have mercy on me, Lord,

R. For I have sinned against you.

V. Glory be to the Father, and to the Son, and to the Holy Spirit.

Lord, heal my soul,

for I have sinned against you.

Song of Zechariah

Ant. Blessed be the Lord, the God of Israel!

He has visited his people and redeemed them.

Prayers

Let us pray to God, who put men into the world to work together in harmony for his glory; let us say to him:

R. Lord, show us how to glorify you.

O God, Maker of us all, we praise you:

—you made this world, and have preserved our life in it even to this day. (*R.*)

Look upon us as we begin our daily tasks.

—Since we are engaged in your work, help us to do it in accordance with your will. (*R.*)

Render our work so fruitful for our fellow-men today,

—that with them and for them we may rebuild a world pleasing to you. (*R.*)

To us and to all those we encounter today

—grant joy and peace. (*R.*)

Other prayers may be added

Our Father . . .

Concluding prayer

O Lord God, King of heaven and earth, we pray you to govern and sanctify our hearts and bodies, our words and works, according to your law and commandments, so that

288

today and for ever we may rejoice in your freedom and
salvation. We make our prayer through our Lord.

May the Lord bless us,
may he keep us from all evil
and lead us to life everlasting.
Amen.

Let us bless the Lord.
R. Thanks be to God.

MIDDAY PRAYER

O God, come to my assistance . . .
Glory be . . .

Hymn

Holy Spirit,
one with the Father and the Son,
deign at this hour to come down on us without delay,
and pour out your graces over our soul.

Let mouth, tongue, soul, thought and strength
make your praise resound.
Let our love be set aflame by the fire of your love,
and its heat in turn enkindle love in our neighbours.

Grant this, most loving Father,
and you, the only Son, equal to the Father,
and, with the Spirit, the Paraclete,
reigning through the ages. Amen.

Psalmody

Psalm 118:89-96

Ant. It is you, O Lord,
   who are my hope since my youth.

Your word, O Lord, for ever
stands firm in the heavens:
your truth lasts from age to age,
like the earth you created.

By your decree it endures to this day;
for all things serve you.
Had your law not been my delight
I would have died in my affliction.

I will never forget your precepts
for with them you give me life.
Save me, for I am yours
since I seek your precepts.

Though the wicked lie in wait to destroy me
yet I ponder on your will.
I have seen that all perfection has an end
but your command is boundless.

Psalm 70   **Prayer in old age**

He who endures to the end will be saved (Matthew 24:13)

I

In you, O Lord, I take refuge;
let me never be put to shame.
In your justice rescue me, free me:
pay heed to me and save me.

Be a rock where I can take refuge,†
a mighty stronghold to save me;
for you are my rock, my stronghold.
Free me from the hand of the wicked,
from the grip of the unjust, of the oppressor.

It is you, O Lord, who are my hope,
my trust, O Lord, since my youth.
On you I have leaned from my birth,†
from my mother's womb you have been my help.
My hope has always been in you.

My fate has filled many with awe
but you are my strong refuge.
My lips are filled with your praise,
with your glory all the day long.

Do not reject me now that I am old;
when my strength fails do not forsake me.

For my enemies are speaking about me;
those who watch me take counsel together saying:
'God has forsaken him; follow him,
seize him; there is no one to save him.'
O God, do not stay far off:
my God, make haste to help me . . .

II

But as for me, I will always hope
and praise you more and more.
My lips will tell of your justice†
and day by day of your help
though I can never tell it all.

I will declare the Lord's mighty deeds
proclaiming your justice, yours alone.
O God, you have taught me from my youth
and I proclaim your wonders still.

Now that I am old and grey-headed,
do not forsake me, God.
Let me tell of your power to all ages,
praise your strength and justice to the skies,
tell of you who have worked such wonders.
O God, who is like you?

You have burdened me with bitter troubles
but you will give me back my life.
You will raise me from the depths of the earth;
you will exalt me and console me again.

So I will give you thanks on the lyre
for your faithful love, my God.
To you will I sing with the harp
to you, the Holy One of Israel.
When I sing to you my lips shall rejoice
and my soul, which you have redeemed.

And all day long my tongue
shall tell the tale of your justice:
for they are put to shame and disgraced,
all those who seek to harm me.

Ant. It is you, O Lord,
   who are my hope since my youth.

Word of God   Rom 7:5–6

While we were living in the flesh, our sinful passions,
aroused by the law, were at work in our members to bear
fruit for death. But now we are discharged from the law,
dead to that which held us captive, so that we serve not
under the old written code but in the new life of the Spirit.

V. O Lord, I cried to you for help,
R. And you, my God, have healed me.

Prayer

Eternal God, Master of the vintage and of the harvest,
who give us the work we have to do and our just wages,
help us to bear the burden of each day without complaining
of any hardships you may send. Through Christ.

Let us bless the Lord.
R. Thanks be to God.

EVENING PRAYER

O God, come to my assistance.
Lord, make haste to help me.
Glory be to the Father, and to the Son, and to the Holy
Spirit.
As it was in the beginning, is now, and ever shall be, world
without end. Amen. Alleluia!

Hymn

Day is done, but Love unfailing
Dwells ever here;
Shadows fall, but hope, prevailing,

Calms every fear.
Loving Father, none forsaking,
Take our hearts, of Love's own making,
Watch our sleeping, guard our waking,
Be always near!

Dark descends, but Light unending
Shines through our night;
You are with us, ever lending
New strength to sight;
One in love, your truth confessing,
One in hope of heaven's blessing,
May we see, in love's possessing,
Love's endless light!

Eyes will close, but you, unsleeping,
Watch by our side;
Death may come: in Love's safe keeping
Still we abide.
God of love, all evil quelling,
Sin forgiving, fear dispelling,
Stay with us, our hearts indwelling,
This eventide!

Psalmody

Psalm 122   Trust in God

*Blessed are those servants whom the master finds awake
when he comes ... he will have them sit at table, and he
will come and serve them* (Luke 12:37)

Ant. To you we lift up our eyes,
you who dwell in the heavens.

To you have I lifted up my eyes,
you who dwell in the heavens:
my eyes, like the eyes of slaves
on the hand of their lords.

Like the eyes of a servant
on the hand of her mistress,

293

so our eyes are on the Lord our God
till he show us his mercy.

Have mercy on us, Lord, have mercy.
We are filled with contempt.
Indeed all too full is our soul with the scorn of the rich,
with the proud man's disdain.

Ant. To you we lift up our eyes,
  you who dwell in the heavens.

Psalm 123   **Thanksgiving for help in crisis**

  *The Lord said to Paul, Do not be afraid, for I am with
  you* (Acts 18:9)

Ant. Our help is in the name of the Lord,
  who made heaven and earth.

'If the Lord had not been on our side,'
this is Israel's song.
'If the Lord had not been on our side
when men rose against us,
then would they have swallowed us alive
when their anger was kindled.

Then would the waters have engulfed us,
the torrent gone over us;
over our head would have swept
the raging waters.'

Blessed be the Lord who did not give us
a prey to their teeth!
Our life, like a bird, has escaped
from the snare of the fowler.

Indeed the snare has been broken
and we have escaped.
Our help is in the name of the Lord,
who made heaven and earth.

Ant. Our help is in the name of the Lord,
  who made heaven and earth.

Eph 1:3–10   Song of thanks for salvation through Christ

Ant. Blessed are those whom Christ has called together into
his kingdom.

Blessed be the God and Father
of our Lord Jesus Christ,
who has blessed us in Christ
with every spiritual blessing in the heavenly places.

R. Blessed are you, God our Father,
    who have blessed us in Christ.

He chose us in him
before the foundation of the world,
that we should be holy
and blameless before him. (*R.*)

He destined us in love
to be his sons through Jesus Christ,
according to the purpose of his will,
to the praise of his glorious grace
which he freely bestowed on us in the Beloved. (*R.*)

In him we have redemption through his blood,
the forgiveness of our trespasses,
according to the riches of his grace which he lavished upon
    us. (*R.*)

He has made known to us†
in all wisdom and insight
the mystery of his will,
according to his purpose
which he set forth in Christ. (*R.*)

His purpose he set forth in Christ
as a plan for the fulness of time,
to unite all things in him,
things in heaven and things on earth. (*R.*)

Ant. Blessed are those whom Christ has called together into his kingdom.

Word of God Jas 4:11–12

Do not speak evil against one another, brethren. He that speaks evil against a brother or judges his brother, speaks evil against the law and judges the law. But if you judge the law, you are not a doer of the law but a judge. There is one lawgiver and judge, he who is able to save and to destroy. But who are you that you judge your neighbour?

Short Response

Into your hands, O Lord,
I commend my spirit.
V. It is you who will redeem me, Lord.
R. Into your hands, O Lord, I commend my spirit.
V. Glory be to the Father, and to the Son, and to the Holy Spirit.
Into your hands, O Lord,
I commend my spirit.

Song of the Virgin Mary

Ant. My soul glorifies the Lord,
my spirit rejoices in God, my Saviour.

Prayers

God wants all men to be saved; let us pray to him:

R. Draw all men to yourself, Lord.

Blessed are you, Lord, who redeemed us from the slavery of sin by the precious blood of your Son;
—grant us the glorious liberty of the children of God. (*R.*)

Endow with plentiful grace our Bishop N. and all bishops of the Church,
—that they may fulfil their ministry with joyful zeal. (*R.*)

Grant to all who explore the truth to find what they seek;
—may they be led to seek ever more. (*R.*)

Lord, keep orphans, widows and all the destitute in the shelter of your love.
—Help them in their need, and make them feel that you are near. (*R.*)

Other prayers may be added

Mercifully receive those who have died into your holy city
—where you will be all in all. (*R.*)

Our Father . . .

Concluding prayer

O God, whom we rightly celebrate as Eternal Light, you have brought us to this evening in which we pray you to enlighten our hearts and forgive us our sins. We make our prayer through our Lord.

May the Lord bless us,
may he keep us from all evil
and lead us to life everlasting.
Amen.

Let us bless the Lord.
R. Thanks be to God.

Tuesday III

OFFICE OF READINGS

O God, come to my assistance.
Lord, make haste to help me.
Glory be to the Father, and to the Son, and to the Holy
Spirit.
As it was in the beginning, is now, and ever shall be, world
without end. Amen. Alleluia!

Or, if used as first prayer of the day: O Lord open my lips...

Hymn

Life-giving Word, come down to save your people;
Open our minds to know what you would teach us;
Grow in our hearts, O seed of heaven's harvest;
Be our true wisdom.

Word of the Father, be the word that saves us;
Lamp to our footsteps, scatter all our darkness;
Sword of the spirit, Word of God, protect us;
Be our salvation.

Psalmody

Psalm 67   **Triumphant hymn of thanks**

*He who descended is he who also ascended far above all
   the heavens* (Eph 4:10)

I

Ant. Let God arise, let his foes be scattered.

Let God arise, let his foes be scattered.†
Let those who hate him flee before him.
As smoke is blown away so will they be blown away.
Like wax that melts before the fire,
so the wicked shall perish at the presence of God.

But the just shall rejoice at the presence of God,
they shall exult and dance for joy.

O sing to the Lord, make music to his name;†
make a highway for him who rides on the clouds.
Rejoice in the Lord, exult at his presence.

Father of the orphan, defender of the widow,
such is God in his holy place.
God gives the lonely a home to live in;†
he leads the prisoners forth into freedom:
but rebels must dwell in a parched land.

When you went forth, O God, at the head of your people,
when you marched across the desert, the earth trembled:
the heavens melted at the presence of God,
at the presence of God, Israel's God.

You poured down, O God, a generous rain:
when your people were starved you gave them new life.
It was there that your people found a home,
prepared in your goodness, O God, for the poor.

Ant. Let God arise, let his foes be scattered.

II

Ant. This God of ours is a God who saves;
to the Lord belong the keys of death.

The Lord gives the word to the bearers of good tidings:
'The Almighty has defeated a numberless army
and kings and armies are in flight, in flight
while you were at rest among the sheepfolds.'

At home the women already share the spoil.
They are covered with silver as the wings of a dove,
its feathers brilliant with shining gold
and jewels flashing like snow on Mount Zalmon.

The mountains of Bashan are mighty mountains;
high-ridged mountains are the mountains of Bashan.
Why look with envy, you high-ridged mountains,†
at the mountain where God has chosen to dwell?
It is there that the Lord shall dwell for ever.

The chariots of God are thousands upon thousands.
The Lord has come from Sinai to the holy place.
You have gone up on high; you have taken captives,†
receiving men in tribute, O God,
even those who rebel, into your dwelling, O Lord.

May the Lord be blessed day after day.
He bears our burdens, God our saviour.
This God of ours is a God who saves.
The Lord our God holds the keys of death.
And God will smite the head of his foes,
the crown of those who persist in their sins.

The Lord said: 'I will bring them back from Bashan;
I will bring them back from the depth of the sea.
Then your feet will tread in their blood
and the tongues of your dogs take their share of the foe.'

Ant. This God of ours is a God who saves;
　to the Lord belong the keys of death.

III

Ant. Kingdoms of the earth, sing to God!

They see your solemn procession, O God,
the procession of my God, of my king, to the sanctuary:
the singers in the forefront, the musicians coming last,
between them, maidens sounding their timbrels.

'In festive gatherings, bless the Lord;
bless God, O you who are Israel's sons.'
There is Benjamin, least of the tribes, at the head,†
Judah's princes, a mighty throng,
Zebulun's princes, Naphtali's princes.

Show forth, O God, show forth your might,
your might, O God, which you have shown for us.
For the sake of your temple high in Jerusalem
may kings come to you bringing their tribute.

Threaten the wild beast that dwells in the reeds,†
the bands of the mighty and lords of the peoples.

Let them bow down offering silver.
Scatter the peoples who delight in war.†
Princes will make their way from Egypt:
Ethiopia will stretch out her hands to God.

Kingdoms of the earth, sing to God, praise the Lord
who rides on the heavens, the ancient heavens.
He thunders his voice, his mighty voice.
Come, acknowledge the power of God.

His glory is over Israel;†
his might is in the skies.
God is to be feared in his holy place.
He is the Lord, Israel's God.†
He gives strength and power to his people.
Blessed be God!

Ant. Kingdoms of the earth, sing to God!

V. The Word of the Lord is faithful.
R. And all his works to be trusted.

Readings

Prayer of the day
Or alternative prayer

MORNING PRAYER

Introductory verse and psalm
O Lord, open my lips.
And my mouth shall declare your praise.
Glory be to the Father, and to the Son, and to the Holy
Spirit.
As it was in the beginning, is now, and ever shall be, world
without end. Amen. Alleluia!

Psalm 94

Refrain: Come, let us worship our Lord and King.

Or, if not used as first prayer of the day: O God come to my
assistance

Hymn

Come, praise the Lord, the Almighty, the King of all
nations!
Tell forth his fame, O ye peoples, with loud acclamations!
His love is sure;
Faithful his word shall endure,
Steadfast through all generations!

Praise to the Father most gracious, the Lord of creation!
Praise to his Son, the Redeemer who wrought our salvation!
O heav'nly Dove,
Praise to thee, fruit of their love.
Giver of all consolation!

Psalmody

Psalm 84   **The coming age of peace and justice**

*Through our Saviour who came down on earth, God has
blessed the earth* (Origen)

Ant. Exalt the Lord our God;
  bow down before him.

O Lord, you once favoured your land
and revived the fortunes of Jacob,
you forgave the guilt of your people
and covered all their sins.
You averted all your rage,
you calmed the heat of your anger.

Revive us now, God, our helper!
Put an end to your grievance against us.
Will you be angry with us for ever,
will your anger never cease?

Will you not restore again our life
that your people may rejoice in you?
Let us see, O Lord, your mercy
and give us your saving help.

I will hear what the Lord God has to say,
a voice that speaks of peace,
peace for his people and his friends
and those who turn to him in their hearts.
His help is near for those who fear him
and his glory will dwell in our land.

Mercy and faithfulness have met;
justice and peace have embraced.
Faithfulness shall spring from the earth
and justice look down from heaven.

The Lord will make us prosper
and our earth shall yield its fruit.
Justice shall march before him
and peace shall follow his steps.

Ant. Exalt the Lord our God;
   bow down before him.

Is 26:1–4, 7–9, 12   **Song of victory**

   Once you were no people, but now you are God's people
   (1 Pet 2:10)

Ant. Earnestly do I seek you, Lord;
   my soul yearns for you.

We have a strong city;
he sets up salvation as walls and bulwarks.
Open the gates,
that the righteous nation which keeps faith may enter in.

You keep him in perfect peace,†
whose mind is stayed on you,
because he trusts in you.
Trust in the Lord for ever,
for the Lord God is an everlasting rock.

The way of the righteous is level;
you make smooth the path of the righteous.
In the path of your judgments, O Lord,
we wait for you.

My soul yearns for you in the night,
my spirit within me earnestly seeks you.
For when your judgments are in the earth,
the inhabitants of the world learn righteousness.

O Lord, you will ordain peace for us;
you have wrought for us all our works.

Ant. Earnestly do I seek you, Lord;
  my soul yearns for you.

Psalm 66   Song of blessing

*You who once were far off have been brought near in the
blood of Christ* (Eph 2:13)

Ant. Let all the peoples praise you, O God,
  let all the peoples praise you.

O God, be gracious and bless us
and let your face shed its light upon us.
So will your ways be known upon earth
and all nations learn your saving help.

R. Let the peoples praise you, O God;
let all the peoples praise you.

Let the nations be glad and exult
for you rule the world with justice.
With fairness you rule the peoples,
you guide the nations on earth.

R. Let the peoples praise you, O God;
let all the peoples praise you.

The earth has yielded its fruit
for God, our God, has blessed us.
May God still give us his blessing
till the ends of the earth revere him.

Ant. Let the peoples praise you, O God;
let all the peoples praise you.

Word of God   1 John 4:14–15

We have seen and testify that the Father has sent his Son
as the Saviour of the world. Whoever confesses that Jesus
is the Son of God, God abides in him, and he in God.

Short Response

Christ, Son of the living God,
have mercy on us.
V. You who are seated at the right hand of the Father,
R. Have mercy on us.
V. Glory be to the Father, and to the Son, and to the Holy
Spirit.
Christ, Son of the living God,
have mercy on us.

Song of Zechariah

Ant. Lord, save us from the hands of all who hate us.

Prayers

Let us pray to God, who in every age remembers his holy
covenant; let us say to him:

R. Lord, remember your people.

O God, our refuge and our strength, listen to the praises of
your Church at the dawning of this day;
—teach her to glorify your majesty unceasingly. (*R.*)

Lord, our hope and strength, we put our trust in you;
—let us never be put to shame. (*R.*)

Look upon our frailty and come to help us:
—without you we can do nothing. (*R.*)

Keep in mind the poor and suffering, that this new day may
not be a burden to them,
—but rather a solace and a joy. (*R.*)

Other prayers may be added

Our Father . . .

Concluding prayer

O God, who created all things good and beautiful, grant that we may begin this day joyfully in your name, and perform all our works in the love of you and of our fellow-men. We make our prayer through our Lord.

May the Lord bless us,
may he keep us from all evil
and lead us to life everlasting.
Amen.

Let us bless the Lord.
R. Thanks be to God.

MIDDAY PRAYER

O God, come to my assistance . . .
Glory be . . .

Hymn

Mighty ruler, faithful God,
who arrange the successive changes in nature,
giving bright light to the morning sun
and burning heat at noon.

Put out the flames of strife
and take away the heat of passion;
grant us health of body
and true peace of soul.

Grant this, most loving Father,
and you, the only Son, equal to the Father
and, with the Spirit, the Paraclete,
reigning through the ages. Amen.

Psalmody

Psalm 118:97–104

Ant. Lord, guard my life from dread of the foe.

Lord, how I love your law!
It is ever in my mind.

Your command makes me wiser than my foes;
for it is mine for ever.

I have more insight than all who teach me
for I ponder your will.
I have more understanding than the old
for I keep your precepts.

I turn my feet from evil paths
to obey your word.
I have not turned away from your decrees;
you yourself have taught me.

Your promise is sweeter to my taste
than honey in the mouth.
I gain understanding from your precepts
and so I hate false ways.

Psalm 73   **God's people mourn over the ruined temple**

Destroy this temple, and in three days I will raise it up
(John 2:19)

I

Why, O God, have you cast us off for ever?
Why blaze with anger against the sheep of your pasture?
Remember your people whom you chose long ago,†
the tribe you redeemed to be your own possession,
the mountain of Zion where you made your dwelling.

Turn your steps to these places that are utterly ruined!
The enemy has laid waste the whole of the sanctuary.
Your foes have made uproar in your house of prayer:†
they have set up their emblems, their foreign emblems,
high above the entrance to the sanctuary.

Their axes have battered the wood of its doors.
They have struck together with hatchet and pickaxe.
O God, they have set your sanctuary on fire:
they have razed and profaned the place where you dwell.

They said in their hearts: 'Let us utterly crush them:
let us burn every shrine of God in the land.'
There is no sign from God, nor have we a prophet,
we have no one to tell us how long it will last.

How long, O God, is the enemy to scoff?
Is the foe to insult your name for ever?
Why, O Lord, do you hold back your hand?
Why do you keep your right hand hidden?

II

Yet God is our king from time past,
the giver of help through all the land.
It was you who divided the sea by your might,
who shattered the heads of the monsters in the sea.

It was you who crushed Leviathan's heads
and gave him as food to the untamed beasts.
It was you who opened springs and torrents;
it was you who dried up ever-flowing rivers.

Yours is the day and yours is the night.
It was you who appointed the light and the sun:
it was you who fixed the bounds of the earth:
you who made both summer and winter.

Remember this, Lord, and see the enemy scoffing;
a senseless people insults your name.
Do not give Israel, your dove, to the hawk
nor forget the life of your poor servants for ever.

Remember your covenant;
every cave in the land is a place where violence makes its
    home.
Do not let the oppressed return disappointed;
let the poor and the needy bless your name.

Arise, O God, and defend your cause!
Remember how the senseless revile you all the day.
Do not forget the clamour of your foes,
the daily increasing uproar of your foes.

Ant. Lord, guard my life from dread of the foe.

Word of God   Deut 15:7–8

If there is among you a poor man, one of your brethren, in any of your towns within your land which the Lord your God gives you, you shall not harden your heart or shut your hand against your poor brother, but you shall open your hand to him, and lend him sufficient for his need, whatever it may be.

V. Lord, you hear the prayer of the poor.
R. You strengthen their hearts.

Prayer

Lord, it was at this time of day that you revealed to Peter your will for the salvation of mankind; mercifully grant that our works may please you, and that we may love you and do your saving will. Through Christ.

Let us bless the Lord.
R. Thanks be to God.

EVENING PRAYER

O God, come to my assistance.
Lord, make haste to help me.
Glory be to the Father, and to the Son, and to the Holy Spirit.
As it was in the beginning, is now, and ever shall be, world without end. Amen. Alleluia!

Hymn   John 3:29–31

R. He must increase,
but I must decrease.

He who has the bride is the bridegroom;
the friend of the bridegroom who stands and hears him
rejoices greatly at the bridegroom's voice;
therefore this joy of mine is now full. (*R.*)

He who comes from above is above all;
he who is of the earth belongs to the earth,
and of the earth he speaks;
he who comes from heaven is above all. (*R.*)

Psalmody

Psalm 125   **Song of the returned exiles**

As you share in our sufferings, you will also share in our comfort (2 Cor 1:7)

Ant. Those who sow in tears
 will sing when they reap.

When the Lord delivered Zion from bondage,
it seemed like a dream.
Then was our mouth filled with laughter,
on our lips there were songs.

The heathens themselves said:
'What marvels the Lord worked for them!'
What marvels the Lord worked for us!
Indeed we were glad.

Deliver us, O Lord, from our bondage
as streams in dry land.
Those who are sowing in tears
will sing when they reap.

They go out, they go out, full of tears,
carrying seed for the sowing:
they come back, they come back, full of song,
carrying their sheaves.

Ant. Those who sow in tears
 will sing when they reap.

Psalm 124   **God rescues his people from the hands of their foes**

Peace upon the Israel of God! (Gal 6:16)

Ant. The Lord surrounds his people
 both now and for ever.

Those who put their trust in the Lord
are like Mount Zion, that cannot be shaken, that stands for
  ever.

Jerusalem! The mountains surround her,
so the Lord surrounds his people both now and for ever.

For the sceptre of the wicked shall not rest
over the land of the just
for fear that the hands of the just
should turn to evil.

Do good, Lord, to those who are good,
to the upright of heart;
but the crooked and those who do evil, drive them away!
On Israel, peace!

Ant. The Lord surrounds his people
  both now and for ever.

Rev 4:11; 5:9, 10, 12　　　　　　**Song to God the Creator**

R. To the Lamb of God be glory, honour and power!

Worthy are you, our Lord and God,
to receive glory and honour and power. (*R.*)

For you created all things,
and by your will they existed and were created. (*R.*)

Worthy are you, O Lord,
to take the scroll and to open its seals. (*R.*)

For you were slain,†
and by your blood you ransomed men for God
from every tribe and tongue and people and nation. (*R.*)

You have made us a kingdom and priests to our God,
and we shall reign on earth. (*R.*)

Worthy is the Lamb who was slain,
to receive power and wealth
and wisdom and might
and honour and glory and blessing. (*R.*)

311

Word of God Jas 2:5

Listen, my beloved brethren. Has not God chosen those who are poor in the world to be rich in faith and heirs of the kingdom which he has promised to those who love him?

Short Response

In the day of my distress I sought the Lord.
At night my hands were raised without ceasing.
V. I remember the deeds of the Lord,
  I remember your wonders of old.
R. At night my hands were raised without ceasing.
V. Glory be to the Father, and to the Son, and to the Holy Spirit.
In the days of my distress I sought the Lord.
At night my hands were raised without ceasing.

Song of the Virgin Mary
Ant. My spirit rejoices in God, my Saviour.

Prayers

God has established his people in hope. Let us pray to him:

R. You are the hope of your people, Lord.

We give you thanks, Lord, who have enriched us in Christ in every way,
—with the word of truth and with understanding. (*R.*)

O God, the hearts of all rulers are in your hand; give of your own wisdom to those who govern our country,
—that their plans may originate in you, and they themselves be pleasing to you in heart and deed. (*R.*)

It is by your gift that artists are able to express your beauty;
—use their work to brighten our world with hope and joy. (*R.*)

You never allow us to be tried beyond our strength;
—fortify the weak, and raise up those who have fallen. (*R.*)

Other prayers may be added

By your Son you have promised that the departed will be raised to life at the last day;
—be ever mindful of those who have left this life. *(R.)*

Our Father . . .

Concluding prayer

May our evening prayer rise up to you, merciful Lord, and may your blessing come down upon us and make us safe both now and for evermore. We make our prayer through our Lord.

May the Lord bless us,
may he keep us from all evil
and lead us to life everlasting.
Amen.

Let us bless the Lord.
R. Thanks be to God.

Wednesday III

OFFICE OF READINGS

O God, come to my assistance.
Lord, make haste to help me.
Glory be to the Father, and to the Son, and to the Holy Spirit.
As it was in the beginning, is now, and ever shall be, world without end. Amen. Alleluia!

Or, if used as first prayer of the day: O Lord, open my lips...

Hymn

Word of God, come down on earth,
Living rain from heav'n descending;
Touch our hearts and bring to birth
Faith and hope and love unending.
Word almighty, we revere you;
Word made flesh, we long to hear you.

Word eternal, throned on high,
Word that brought to life creation,
Word that came from heav'n to die,
Crucified for our salvation,
Saving Word, the world restoring,
Speak to us, your love outpouring.

Psalmody

Psalm 88   God is faithful to the promise made to David

God has brought to Israel a Saviour of David's posterity, as he promised (Acts 13:23)

Ant. Love and truth walk in your presence, Lord.

I

I will sing for ever of your love, O Lord;
through all ages my mouth will proclaim your truth.
Of this I am sure, that your love lasts for ever,
that your truth is firmly established as the heavens.

' I have made a covenant with my chosen one;
I have sworn to David my servant:
I will establish your dynasty for ever
and set up your throne through all ages.'

The heavens proclaim your wonders, O Lord;
the assembly of your holy ones proclaims your truth.
For who in the skies can compare with the Lord
or who is like the Lord among the sons of God?

A God to be feared in the council of the holy ones,
great and dreadful to all around him.
O Lord God of hosts, who is your equal?
You are mighty, O Lord, and truth is your garment.

It is you who rule the sea in its pride;
it is you who still the surging of its waves.
It is you who trod Rahab underfoot like a corpse,
scattering your foes with your mighty arm.

The heavens are yours, the world is yours.
It is you who founded the earth and all it holds;
it is you who created the North and the South.
Tabor and Hermon shout with joy at your name.

Yours is a mighty arm, O Lord;
your hand is strong, your right hand ready.
Justice and right are the pillars of your throne,
love and truth walk in your presence.

Happy the people who acclaim such a king,
who walk, O Lord, in the light of your face,
who find their joy every day in your name,
who make your justice the source of their bliss.

For it is you, O Lord, who are the glory of their strength;
it is by your favour that our might is exalted:
for our ruler is in the keeping of the Lord;
our king in the keeping of the Holy One of Israel.

Ant. Love and truth walk in your presence, Lord.

II

Ant. You are the Son of God,
    descended from David according to the flesh.

Of old you spoke in a vision.
To your friends the prophets you said:
'I have set the crown on a warrior,
I have exalted one chosen from the people.

I have found David my servant
and with my holy oil anointed him.
My hand shall always be with him
and my arm shall make him strong.

The enemy shall never outwit him
nor the evil man oppress him.
I will beat down his foes before him
and smite those who hate him.

My truth and my love shall be with him;
by my name his might shall be exalted.
I will stretch out his hand to the Sea
and his right hand as far as the River.

He will say to me: 'You are my father,
my God, the rock who saves me.'
And I will make him my first-born,
the highest of the kings of the earth.

I will keep my love for him always;
for him my covenant shall endure.
I will establish his dynasty for ever,
make his throne as lasting as the heavens.'

Ant. You are the Son of God,
    descended from David according to the flesh.

III

Ant. I have preserved the dynasty of David, my servant, for
ever.

'If his sons forsake my law
and refuse to walk as I decree

and if ever they violate my statutes,
refusing to keep my commands;

then I will punish their offences with the rod,
then I will scourge them on account of their guilt.
But I will never take back my love:
my truth will never fail.

I will never violate my covenant
nor go back on the word I have spoken.
Once for all, I have sworn by my holiness.
" I will never lie to David.

His dynasty shall last for ever.
In my sight his throne is like the sun;
like the moon, it shall endure for ever,
a faithful witness in the skies." '

Ant. I have preserved the dynasty of David, my servant, for ever.

V. Lord, in you is the source of life.
R. In your light we see light.

Readings

Prayer of the day

Or alternative prayer

MORNING PRAYER

Introductory verse and psalm
O Lord, open my lips.
And my mouth shall declare your praise.
Glory be to the Father, and to the Son, and to the Holy Spirit.
As it was in the beginning, is now, and ever shall be, world without end. Amen. Alleluia!

Psalm 94
Refrain: Come, let us worship our Lord and Saviour.

Or, if not used as first prayer of the day: O God, come to my assistance...

Hymn

I believe in God, the Father;
I believe in God, his Son;
I believe in God, their Spirit;
Each is God, yet God is one.

I believe what God had spoken
Through his Church, whose word is true;
Boldly she proclaims his Gospel,
Ever old, yet ever new.

All my hope is in God's goodness,
Shown for us by him who died,
Jesus Christ, the world's Redeemer,
Spotless victim crucified.

All my love is Love eternal;
In that Love I love mankind.
Take my heart, O Heart once broken,
Take my soul, my strength, my mind.

Father, I have sinned against you;
Look on me with eyes of love;
Seek your wand'ring sheep, Good Shepherd;
Grant heav'n's peace, O heav'nly Dove.

Bless'd be God, the loving Father;
Bless'd be God, his only Son;
Bless'd be God, all-holy Spirit;
Bless'd be God, for ever one.

Psalmody

Psalm 85   Lament in suffering and persecution

> *Blessed be God ... who comforts us in all our affliction*
> (2 Cor 1:3)

Ant. Give heed, O Lord, to my prayer,
and deliver me.

Turn you ear, O Lord, and give answer
for I am poor and needy.

Preserve my life, for I am faithful:
save the servant who trusts in you.

You are my God, have mercy on me, Lord,
for I cry to you all the day long.
Give joy to your servant, O Lord,
for you I lift up my soul.

O Lord, you are good and forgiving,
full of love to all who call.
Give heed, O Lord, to my prayer
and attend to the sound of my voice.

In the day of distress I will call
and surely you will reply.
Among the gods there is none like you, O Lord;
nor work to compare with yours.

All the nations shall come to adore you
and glorify your name, O Lord:
for you are great and do marvellous deeds,
you who alone are God.

Show me, Lord, your way†
so that I may walk in your truth.
Guide my heart to fear your name.

I will praise you, Lord my God, with all my heart
and glorify your name for ever;
for your love to me has been great:
you have saved me from the depths of the grave.

The proud have risen against me;†
ruthless men seek my life:
to you they pay no need.

But you, God of mercy and compassion,
slow to anger, O Lord,
abounding in love and truth,
turn and take pity on me.

O give your strength to your servant
and save your handmaid's son.

Show me a sign of your favour†
that my foes may see to their shame
that you console me and give me your help.

Ant. Give heed, O Lord, to my prayer,
and deliver me.

Is 33:13–16　　　　　Song of Isaiah: The Lord, the just judge

*The promise is to you and to your children and to all that
are far off* (Acts 2:39)

Ant. Blessed is he who walks righteously.

Hear, you who are far off,
what I have done;
and you who are near,
acknowledge my might.

R. Thanks be to you for the marvellous deeds you have
done!

The sinners in Zion are afraid;
trembling has seized the godless:
'Who among us can dwell with the devouring fire?
Who among us can dwell with everlasting burnings?' (*R.*)

He who walks righteously and speaks uprightly,
who despises the gain of oppressions,
who shakes his hands,
lest they hold a bribe,
who stops his ears from hearing of bloodshed
and shuts his eyes from looking upon evil. (*R.*)

He will dwell on the heights;
his place of defence will be the fortresses of rocks;
his bread will be given him,
his water will be sure. (*R.*)

Ant. Blessed is he who walks righteously.

Psalm 97　　　　　God, victor and judge

You shall be my witnesses ... to the end of the earth
(Acts 1:8)

320

Ant. Lord Jesus, you are indeed
    the Saviour of the world!

Sing a new song to the Lord
for he has worked wonders.
His right hand and his holy arm
have brought salvation.

The Lord has made known his salvation;
has shown his justice to the nations.
He has remembered his truth and love
for the house of Israel.

All the ends of the earth have seen
the salvation of our God.
Shout to the Lord all the earth,
ring out your joy.

Sing psalms to the Lord with the harp
with the sound of music.
With trumpets and the sound of the horn
acclaim the King, the Lord.

Let the sea and all within it, thunder;
the world, and all its peoples.
Let the rivers clap their hands
and the hills ring out their joy

at the presence of the Lord: for he comes,
he comes to rule the earth.
He will rule the world with justice
and the peoples with fairness.

Ant. Lord Jesus, you are indeed
    the Saviour of the world!

Word of God   Job 1:21; 2:10
Naked I came from my mother's womb, and naked shall
I return; the Lord gave, and the Lord has taken away;
blessed be the name of the Lord. Shall we receive good at
the hand of God, and shall we not receive evil?

Short Response

In you I take refuge, Lord;
let me never be put to shame.

V. In your justice rescue me, free me.

R. Let me never be put to shame.

V. Glory be to the Father, and to the Son, and to the Holy Spirit.

In you I take refuge, Lord;
let me never be put to shame.

Song of Zechariah

Ant. Let us serve the Lord in holiness:
it is he who saves us from the hands of our foes.

Prayers

Let us pray Christ, who feeds and cherishes the Church, for which he gave his life; let us say to him:

R. Look upon your Church, O Lord.

Christ, shepherd of your Church, we thank you for your gift of life and light.

—May this grace be a source of joy for us. (*R.*)

Look with compassion upon the flock gathered together in your name;

—of those entrusted to you by the Father, let no one be lost. (*R.*)

Lead your Church in the way of your commandments;
—may the Holy Spirit keep her ever faithful. (*R.*)

Give new life to your Church at the table of the Word and the Eucharist;

—in the strength of that food may she follow you rejoicing. (*R.*)

Other prayers may be added

Our Father . . .

Concluding prayer

O God who created us in your wisdom and govern us in your providence, we pray you to fill our minds with your light, so that our lives may be pleasing to you always. We make our prayer through our Lord.

May the Lord bless us,
may he keep us from all evil
and lead us to life everlasting.
Amen.

Let us bless the Lord.
R. Thanks be to God.

MIDDAY PRAYER

O God, come to my assistance . . .
Glory be . . .

Hymn

Lord God, the strength which daily upholds all creation,
in yourself remaining unchanged
and yet determining in due order
the successive changes of the light of day.

Grant us light in the evening
so that life may not decay at any point of its activity,
but everlasting glory be the immediate reward
of a happy death.

Grant this, most loving Father,
and you, the only Son, equal to the Father
and, with the Spirit, the Paraclete,
reigning through the ages. Amen.

Psalmody

Psalm 118:105–112

Ant. Arise, Lord, and defend your cause.

Your word is a lamp for my steps
and a light for my path.
I have sworn and have determined
to obey your decrees.

Lord, I am deeply afflicted:
by your word give me life.
Accept, Lord, the homage of my lips
and teach me your decrees.

Though I carry my life in my hands,
I remember your law.
Though the wicked try to ensnare me
I do not stray from your precepts.

Your will is my heritage for ever,
the joy of my heart.
I set myself to carry out your statutes
in fulness, for ever.

Psalm 69   Cry to God for help

My eyes have seen your salvation (Luke 2:30)

O God, make haste to my rescue,
Lord, come to my aid . . .

Let there be rejoicing and gladness
for all who seek you.
Let them say for ever: 'God is great,'
who love your saving help.

As for me, wretched and poor,
come to me, O God.
You are my rescuer, my help,
O Lord, do not delay.

Psalm 74   Judge of the world

*He has cast the mighty from their thrones and has raised
the lowly* (Luke 1:52)

We give thanks to you, O God,†
we give thanks and call upon your name.
We recount your wonderful deeds.

'When I reach the appointed time,
then I will judge with justice.
Though the earth and all who dwell in it may rock,
it is I who uphold its pillars.

I say to the boastful: "Do not boast,"
to the wicked: "Do not flaunt your strength,
do not flaunt your strength on high.
Do not speak with insolent pride." '

For neither from the east nor from the west,
nor from desert or mountains comes judgment,
but God himself is the judge.
One he humbles, another he exalts.

The Lord holds a cup in his hand,
full of wine, foaming and spiced.
He pours it; they drink it to the dregs:
all the wicked on the earth must drain it.

As for me, I will rejoice for ever
and sing psalms to Jacob's God.
He shall break the power of the wicked,
while the strength of the just shall be exalted.

Ant. Arise, Lord, and defend your cause.

Word of God   1 Cor 13:8–10, 13
Love never ends; as for prophecies, they will pass away;
as for tongues, they will cease; as for knowledge, it will pass
away. For our knowledge is imperfect and our prophecy is
imperfect; but when the perfect comes, the imperfect will
pass away. So faith, hope, love abide, these three; but the
greatest of these is love.

V. May your love be upon us, O Lord,
R. As we place all our hope in you.

Prayer
Almighty and merciful God who give us a time of rest in
the middle of the day, look favourably on the work we have
begun, and grant that our completed work may be pleasing
to you. Through Christ.

Let us bless the Lord.
R. Thanks be to God.

EVENING PRAYER

O God, come to my assistance.
Lord, make haste to help me.
Glory be to the Father, and to the Son, and to the Holy Spirit.
As it was in the beginning, is now, and ever shall be, world without end. Amen. Alleluia!

Hymn
To God with gladness sing.
Your rock and Saviour bless;
Within his temple bring
Your songs of thankfulness!
O God of might,
To you we sing,
Enthroned as king
On heaven's height!

He cradles in his hand
The heights and depths of earth;
He made the sea and land,
He brought the world to birth!
O God most high,
We are your sheep;
On us you keep
Your shepherd's eye!

Your heav'nly Father praise,
Acclaim his only Son,
Your voice in homage raise
To him who makes all one!
O Dove of peace
On us descend
That strife may end
And joy increase.

Psalmody

Psalm 126 God, our only hope

You are God's building (1 **Cor** 3:9)

Ant. May the Lord build us a house,
   may the Lord watch over the city.

If the Lord does not build the house,
in vain do its builders labour;
if the Lord does not watch over the city,
in vain does the watchman keep vigil.

In vain is your earlier rising,
your going later to rest,
you who toil for the bread you eat:
when he pours gifts on his beloved while they slumber.

Truly sons are a gift from the Lord,
a blessing, the fruit of the womb.
Indeed the sons of youth
are like arrows in the hand of a warrior.

O the happiness of the man,
who has filled his quiver with these arrows!
He will have no cause for shame
when he disputes with his foes in the gateways.

Ant. May the Lord build us a house,
   may the Lord watch over the city.

Psalm 130 Song of serenity

Learn from me, for I am gentle and lowly in heart (Matthew
   11:29)

Ant. Hope in the Lord
   both now and for ever.

O Lord, my heart is not proud
nor haughty my eyes.
I have not gone after things too great
nor marvels beyond me.
Truly I have set my soul
in silence and peace.

A weaned child on its mother's breast,
even so is my soul.

O Israel, hope in the Lord
both now and for ever.

Ant. Hope in the Lord
both now and for ever.

Col 1:12–20   **Song to Christ, the first-born of all creation and
first-born from the dead**

Ant. To you, O Lord, be glory, honour, power and majesty!

Let us give thanks to the Father,
who has qualified us
to share in the inheritance of the saints
in light.

R. Glory to you, the first-born from the dead!

He has delivered us
from the dominion of darkness
and transferred us
to the kingdom of his beloved Son,
in whom we have redemption,
the forgiveness of sins. (*R.*)

He is the image of the invisible God,
the first-born of all creation,
for in him all things were created, in heaven and on earth,
visible and invisible. (*R.*)

All things were created
through him and for him.
He is before all things,
and in him all things hold together. (*R.*)

He is the head of the body, the Church;
he is the beginning,
the first-born from the dead,
that in everything he might be pre-eminent. (*R.*)

For in him all the fulness of God was pleased to dwell,
and through him to reconcile to himself all things,
whether on earth or in heaven,
making peace by the blood of his cross. (*R.*)

Ant. To you, O Lord, be glory, honour, power and majesty!

Word of God
Eph 3:20–21

To him who by the power at work within us is able to do far more abundantly than all that we ask or think, to him be glory in the church and in Christ Jesus to all generations, for ever and ever. Amen.

Short Response
Cry out with joy to God all the earth,
O render him glorious praise.
V. Before you all the earth shall bow.
R. O render him glorious praise.
V. Glory be to the Father, and to the Son, and to the Holy Spirit.
Cry out with joy to God all the earth,
O render him glorious praise.

Song of the Virgin Mary
Ant. The Almighty works marvels for me.
    Holy his name!

Prayers
Let us pray to God through our mediator Jesus Christ. Let us say to him:

R. Pour out your love upon us, Lord.

We thank you, for from eternity you have chosen us as your people;
—and you have called us to receive the glory of Jesus our Lord. (*R.*)

Unite all who bear the name of Christian;
—may they all be of one mind in the word of truth, and one in heart by fervent charity. (*R.*)

Creator of the universe, whose incarnate Son undertook to work by the side of his fellow-men;
—have mercy on all who earn their bread in the sweat of their brow. (R.)

Keep in mind also those who spend themselves in the service of their fellow-men.
—Do not let them be discouraged by failure or misunderstanding. (R.)

Other prayers may be added

Have mercy on those who have died;
—let not the evil spirit have any hold over them. (R.)

Our Father . . .

Concluding prayer

O Lord, in your loving-kindness, hear the cry of your Church and grant her the forgiveness of sins. May your grace increase her dedication to your service, and your protection free her from fear and anxiety. We make our prayer through our Lord.

May the Lord bless us,
may he keep us from all evil
and lead us to life everlasting.
Amen.

Let us bless the Lord.
R. Thanks be to God.

Thursday III

OFFICE OF READINGS

O God, come to my assistance.
Lord, make haste to help me.
Glory be to the Father, and to the Son, and to the Holy
Spirit.
As it was in the beginning, is now, and ever shall be, world
without end. Amen. Alleluia!

Or, if used as first prayer of the day: O Lord, open my lips...

Hymn

Word that caused blind eyes to see,
Speak and heal our mortal blindness;
Deaf we are: our healer be;
Loose our tongues to tell your kindness.
Be our Word in pity spoken,
Heal the world, by our sin broken.

Word that speaks your Father's love,
One with him beyond all telling,
Word that sends us from above
God the Spirit, with us dwelling,
Word of truth, to all truth lead us,
Word of life, with one Bread feed us.

Psalmody

Psalm 88   **Lament for the fall of the house of David**

He has raised up for us a mighty Saviour in the house of
David (Luke 1:69)

IV

Ant. Turn your eyes towards us;
see our plight, O Lord.

You have spurned, rejected,
you are angry with the one you have anointed.

You have broken your covenant with your servant
and dishonoured his crown in the dust.

You have broken down all his walls
and reduced his fortress to ruins.
He is despoiled by all who pass by:
he has become the taunt of his neighbours.

You have exalted the right hand of his foes;
you have made all his enemies rejoice.
You have made his sword give way,
you have not upheld him in battle.

You have brought his glory to an end;
you have hurled his throne to the ground.
You have cut short the years of his youth;
you have heaped disgrace upon him.

Ant. Turn your eyes towards us;
   see our plight, O Lord.

V

Ant. I am the root and the offspring of David,
   the bright morning star.

How long, O Lord? Will you hide yourself for ever?
How long will your anger burn like a fire?
Remember, Lord, the shortness of my life
and how frail you have made the sons of men.
What man can live and never see death?
Who can save himself from the grasp of the grave?

Where are your mercies of the past, O Lord,
which you have sworn in your faithfulness to David?
Remember, Lord, how your servant is taunted,
how I have to bear all the insults of the peoples.
Thus your enemies taunt me, O Lord,
mocking your anointed at every step.

Blessed be the Lord for ever.
Amen, amen!

Ant. I am the root and the offspring of David,
  the bright morning star.

Psalm 89   **The Eternal, man's resting place in this short life**

*With the Lord one day is as a thousand years, and a
thousand years as one day* (2 Pet 3:8)

Ant. Our years pass away like grass,
  but you, you are God from one generation to the next.

O Lord, you have been our refuge
from one generation to the next.
Before the mountains were born†
or the earth or the world brought forth,
you are God, without beginning or end.

You turn men back into dust and say:
'Go back, sons of men.'
To your eyes a thousand years are like yesterday, come and
    gone,
no more than a watch in the night.

You sweep men away like a dream,
like grass which springs up in the morning.
In the morning it springs up and flowers:
by evening it withers and fades.

So we are destroyed in your anger
struck with terror in your fury.
Our guilt lies open before you;
our secrets in the light of your face.

All our days pass away in your anger.
Our life is over like a sigh.
Our span is seventy years
or eighty for those who are strong.

And most of these are emptiness and pain.
They pass swiftly and we are gone.
Who understands the power of your anger
and fears the strength of your fury?

Make us know the shortness of our life
that we may gain wisdom of heart.
Lord, relent! Is your anger for ever?
Show pity to your servants.

In the morning, fill us with your love;
we shall exult and rejoice all our days.
Give us joy to balance our affliction
for the years when we knew misfortune.

Show forth your work to your servants;
let your glory shine on their children.
Let the favour of the Lord be upon us:†
give success to the work of our hands;
give success to the work of our hands.

Ant. Our years pass away like grass,
but you, you are God from one generation to the next.

V. Lord, make me know your ways.
R. Lord, teach me your paths.

Readings

Prayer of the day
Or alternative prayer

MORNING PRAYER

Introductory verse and psalm
O Lord, open my lips.
And my mouth shall declare your praise.
Glory be to the Father, and to the Son, and to the Holy
Spirit.
As it was in the beginning, is now, and ever shall be, world
without end. Amen. Alleluia!

Psalm 94
Refrain: Come, let us worship our Lord and Master.

Or, if not used as first prayer of the day: O God, come to my
assistance...

Hymn

We who live in Christ were born in his death:
Baptized in Christ's death, with Christ we lay in the tomb;
As God the Father's power awoke him from death,
So we were raised to walk in newness of life.

One with Christ were we in dying his death:
So one shall we be with Christ in rising again.
Our sinful selves were nailed with Christ to his cross
That, dead to sin, from sin our flesh might be free.

Dead with Christ, we yet shall rise with him too,
For this is our faith, that he who rose from the dead
Will never die; once dead, for ever he lives,
And death has power no more to conquer its King.

Once for all in death Christ died to all sin;
The life that he lives is life lived only to God.
So you like him are dead to all that is sin,
And live to God in Christ, the Saviour, our Lord.

Psalmody

Psalm 86   **God's city, mother of all nations**

The Jerusalem above is free, and she is our mother (Gal
4:26)

Ant. All the earth sings your glory,
   holy city of God.

On the holy mountain is his city
cherished by the Lord.
The Lord prefers the gates of Zion
to all Jacob's dwellings.
Of you are told glorious things,
O city of God!

'Babylon and Egypt I will count
among those who know me;
Philistia, Tyre, Ethiopia,
these will be her children

and Zion shall be called "Mother"
for all shall be her children.'

It is he, the Lord Most High,
who gives each his place.
In his register of peoples he writes:
'These are her children'
and while they dance they will sing:
'In you all find their home.'

Ant. All the earth sings your glory,
holy city of God.

Is 40:10–17   **Song of Isaiah: the good news of salvation**

Behold, I am coming soon! (Rev 22:7)

Ant. Behold, the Lord God! He comes with might,
a light to the eyes of his children.

Behold the Lord God comes with might,
and his arm rules for him;
behold his reward is with him,
and his recompense before him.

R. Blessed is he who comes!

He will feed his flock like a shepherd,
he will gather the lambs in his arms,
he will carry them in his bosom,
and gently lead those that are with young. (*R.*)

Who has measured the waters in the hollow of his hand
and marked off the heavens with a span,
enclosed the dust of the earth in a measure†
and weighed the mountains in scales
and the hills in a balance? (*R.*)

Who has directed the Spirit of the Lord,
or as his counsellor has instructed him?
Whom did he consult for his enlightenment,
and who taught him the path of justice,
taught him knowledge,
and showed him the way of understanding? (*R.*)

Behold, the nations are like a drop from a bucket,
and are accounted as the dust on the scales;
behold, he takes up the isles
like fine dust. (*R.*)

Lebanon would not suffice for fuel,
nor are its beasts enough for a burnt offering.
All the nations are as nothing before him,
they are accounted by him as less than nothing and emptiness. (*R.*)

Ant. Behold, the Lord God! He comes with might,
   a light to the eyes of his children.

Psalm 98   **The power and holiness of God**

   Holy, holy, holy is the Lord.

Ant. Exalt the Lord our God,
   bow down before him.

The Lord is king; the peoples tremble.
He is throned on the cherubim; earth quakes.

The Lord is great in Zion.
He is supreme over all the peoples.
Let them praise his name, so terrible and great.
He is holy, full of power.

You are a king who loves what is right;†
you have established equity, justice and right;
you have established them in Jacob.

Exalt the Lord our God;†
bow down before Zion, his footstool.
He the Lord is holy.

Among his priests were Aaron and Moses,†
among those who invoked his name was Samuel.
They invoked the Lord and he answered.

To them he spoke in the pillar of cloud.†
They did his will; they kept the law,
which he, the Lord, had given.

O Lord our God, you answered them†.
For them you were a God who forgives;
yet you punished all their offences.

Exalt the Lord our God;†
bow down before his holy mountain
for the Lord our God is holy.

Ant. Exalt the Lord our God,
   bow down before him.

Word of God 1 Pet 4:9–10

Practise hospitality ungrudgingly to one another. As each
has received a gift, employ it for one another, as good
stewards of God's varied grace.

Short Response

I will bless the Lord
everywhere and at all times.
V. His praise is always on my lips
R. Everywhere and at all times.
V. Glory be to the Father, and to the Son, and to the Holy
Spirit.
I will bless the Lord
everywhere and at all times.

Song of Zechariah

Ant. Blessed be the Lord,
   who visits us like the dawn from on high.

Prayers

Let us give thanks to God, who in his love leads and
nourishes his people; let us say:

R. Glory to you, Lord, for ever!

Lord and King of the universe, we bless that great love of
yours
—which has wonderfully created but more wonderfully
redeemed us. (*R*.)

As we begin this day, fill our hearts with zeal in your service,

—that all our thoughts and actions may be for your glory.
(R).

Cleanse our hearts of unwholesome desire;
—may we always be intent upon your will. (R.)

Give us heart-felt sympathy for the needs of our brothers;
—may our fraternal affection never fail them. (R.)

Other prayers may be added

Our Father . . .

Concluding prayer

Almighty, eternal God, with the coming of the dawn from
on high, our Lord Jesus Christ, let the light of your glory
shine upon all who dwell in the shadow of death. We make
our prayer through our Lord.

May the Lord bless us,
may he keep us from all evil
and lead us to life everlasting.
Amen.

Let us bless the Lord.
R. Thanks be to God.

MIDDAY PRAYER

O God, come to my assistance . . .
Glory be . . .

Hymn

Holy Spirit,
one with the Father and the Son,
deign at this hour to come down on us without delay
and pour out your graces over our soul.

Let mouth, tongue, soul, thought and strength
make your praise resound.
Let our love be set aflame by the fire of your love
and its heat in turn enkindle love in our neighbours.

339

Grant this, most loving Father,
and you the only Son, equal to the Father
and, with the Spirit, the Paraclete,
reigning through the ages. Amen.

Psalmody

Psalm 118:113–120

Ant. If you uphold me by your promise,
  your servant shall live.

I have no love for half-hearted men:
my love is for your law.
You are my shelter, my shield;
I hope in your word.

Leave me, you who do evil;
I will keep God's command.
If you uphold me by your promise I shall live;
let my hopes not be in vain.

Sustain me and I shall be saved
and ever observe your statutes.
You spurn all who swerve from your statutes;
their cunning is in vain.

You throw away the wicked like dross:
so I love your will.
I tremble before you in terror;
I fear your decrees.

Psalm 78   **National lament over the destruction of Jerusalem**

  *Would that even today you knew the things that make for
  peace* (Luke 19:41)

O God, the nations have invaded your land,†
they have profaned your holy temple.
They have made Jerusalem a heap of ruins.
They have handed over the bodies of your servants†
as food to feed the birds of heaven
and the flesh of your faithful to the beasts of the earth.

They have poured out blood like water in Jerusalem,
leaving no one to bury the dead.
We have become the taunt of our neighbours,
the mockery and scorn of those who surround us.
How long, O Lord? Will you be angry for ever,
how long will your anger burn like fire? . . .

Do not hold the guilt of our fathers against us.†
Let your compassion hasten to meet us
for we are in the depths of distress.
O God our saviour, come to our help,
come for the sake of the glory of your name.
O Lord our God, forgive us our sins;
rescue us for the sake of your name.

Why should the nations say:
'Where is their God?'
Let us see the nations around us repaid with vengeance
for the blood of your servants that was shed!
Let the groans of the prisoners come before you;
let your strong arm reprieve those condemned to die . . .

But we, your people, the flock of your pasture,†
will give you thanks for ever and ever.
We will tell your praise from age to age.

Psalm 79   **Lament for the wasted vineyard**

Come, Lord Jesus! (Rev 22:20)

O shepherd of Israel, hear us,
you who lead Joseph's flock,
shine forth from your cherubim throne
upon Ephraim, Benjamin, Manasseh.
O Lord, rouse up your might,
O Lord, come to our help.

R. God of hosts, bring us back;
let your face shine on us and we shall be saved.

Lord God of hosts, how long
will you frown on your people's plea?

341

You have fed them with tears for their bread,
an abundance of tears for their drink.
You have made us the taunt of our neighbours,
our enemies laugh us to scorn.

R. God of hosts, bring us back;
let your face shine on us and we shall be saved.

You brought a vine out of Egypt;
to plant it you drove out the nations.
Before it you cleared the ground;
it took root and spread through the land.

The mountains were covered with its shadow,
the cedars of God with its boughs.
It stretched out its branches to the sea,
to the Great River it stretched out its shoots.

Then why have you broken down its walls?
It is plucked by all who pass by.
It is ravaged by the boar of the forest,
devoured by the beasts of the field.

God of hosts, turn again, we implore,
look down from heaven and see.
Visit this vine and protect it,
the vine your right hand has planted.
Men have burnt it with fire and destroyed it.
May they perish at the frown of your face.

May your hand be on the man you have chosen,
the man you have given your strength.
And we shall never forsake you again:
give us life that we may call upon your name.

R. God of hosts, bring us back;
let your face shine on us and we shall be saved.

Ant. If you uphold me by your promise,
your servant shall live.

Word of God 2 Sam 7:23–24

What other nation on earth is like your people Israel, whom God went to redeem to be his people, making himself a name, and doing for them great and terrible things, by driving out before his people a nation and its gods? And you established for yourself your people Israel to be your people for ever; and you, O Lord, became their God.

V. You, Lord, are close:
R. Your commands are truth.

Prayer

Almighty and eternal God, in whom there is no darkness, no obscurity, fill our hearts with the splendour of your light, so that we who have received your commandments may walk in safety on your ways. Through Christ.

Let us bless the Lord.
R. Thanks be to God.

EVENING PRAYER

O God, come to my assistance.
Lord make haste to help me.
Glory be to the Father, and to the Son, and to the Holy Spirit.
As it was in the beginning, is now, and ever shall be, world without end. Amen. Alleluia!

Hymn

Bless'd be the Lord our God!
With joy let heaven ring;
Before his presence let all earth
Its songs of homage bring!
His mighty deeds be told;
His majesty be praised;
To God enthroned in heav'nly light,
Let every voice be raised!

All that has life and breath,
Give thanks with heartfelt songs!
To him let all creation sing
To whom all praise belongs!
Acclaim the Father's love,
Who gave us God his Son;
Praise too the Spirit, giv'n by both,
With both for ever one!

Psalmody

Psalm 131   **David's reign at the sanctuary at Zion**

The Lord God will give to him the throne of his father David (Luke 1:32)

I

Ant. The Lord has chosen Jerusalem
for his dwelling.

O Lord, remember David
and all the hardships he endured,
the oath he swore to the Lord,
his vow to the Strong One of Jacob.

'I will not enter the house where I live
nor go to the bed where I rest.
I will give no sleep to my eyes
to my eyelids will give no slumber
till I find a place for the Lord,
a dwelling for the Strong One of Jacob.'

At Ephrata we heard of the ark;
we found it in the plains of Yearim.
'Let us go to the place of his dwelling;
let us go to kneel at his footstool.'

Go up, Lord, to the place of your rest,
you and the ark of your strength.
Your priests shall be clothed with holiness:

your faithful shall ring out their joy.
For the sake of David your servant
do not reject your anointed.

Ant. The Lord has chosen Jerusalem
   for his dwelling.

II

Ant. Your faithful shall ring out their joy, O Lord,
   as they enter the place where you dwell.

The Lord swore an oath to David;
he will not go back on his word:
'A son, the fruit of your body,
will I set upon your throne.

If they keep my covenant in truth
and my laws that I have taught them,
their sons also shall rule
on your throne from age to age.'

For the Lord has chosen Zion;
he has desired it for his dwelling:
'This is my resting-place for ever,
here have I chosen to live.

I will greatly bless her produce,
I will fill her poor with bread.
I will clothe her priests with salvation
and her faithful shall ring out their joy.

There the stock of David will flower:
I will prepare a lamp for my anointed.
I will cover his enemies with shame
but on him my crown shall shine.'

Ant. Your faithful shall ring out their joy, O Lord,
   as they enter the place where you dwell.

Rev 11:17–18, 12:10–12   **Song of God's judgment**

Ant. The Lord our God, the Almighty, reigns.

We give thanks to you, Lord God Almighty,

who are and who were,
that you have taken your great power
and begun to reign.

R. We give thanks to you, O Lord our God.

The nations raged,
but your wrath came,
and the time for the dead to be judged,
for rewarding your servants, the prophets and saints,
and those who fear your name,
both small and great. (*R.*)

Now the salvation and the power†
and the kingdom of our God
and the authority of his Christ have come,
for the accuser of our brethren has been thrown down,
who accuses them day and night before our God. (*R.*)

And they have conquered him
by the blood of the Lamb
and by the word of their testimony,
for they loved not their lives even unto death.
Rejoice, then, O heaven
and you that dwell therein! (*R.*)

Ant. The Lord our God, the Almighty, reigns.

Word of God   1 Pet 3:8–9
All of you, have unity of spirit, sympathy, love of the
brethren, a tender heart and a humble mind. Do not return
evil for evil or reviling for reviling; but on the contrary
bless, for to this you have been called, that you may obtain
a blessing.

Short Response
You are blest, O Lord,
in the heavens.

V. Worthy are you to receive praise and glory for all eternity.

R. You are blest, O Lord, in the heavens.

V. Glory be to the Father, and to the Son, and to the Holy Spirit.

You are blest, O Lord,
in the heavens.

Song of the Virgin Mary

Ant. His mercy is from age to age
  on those who fear him.

Prayers

Let us pray to God, the Creator, shepherd and helper of his people; let us say to him:

R. Hear us, O God our refuge.

We bless you, Lord, who have graciously called us to your holy Catholic Church.

—Keep us always united to her. (*R*.)

You have called Pope N. to watch over all the churches;
—endow him with confident faith, living hope and increasing charity. (*R*.)

Convert the sinner, and strengthen those who have lapsed.
—Grant to all the grace of repentance and salvation. (*R*.)

You allowed your Son to live in an alien land;
—look, therefore, with compassion on those who live far from their family and homeland. (*R*.)

Other prayers may be added

Give to all the departed who have put their trust in you
—the peace of eternal rest. (*R*.)

Our Father . . .

Concluding prayer

Almighty God, at the ending of this day we bring you an offering of thanks, and we beg you in your mercy to forgive whatever sins we have committed because of our human frailty. We make our prayer through our Lord.

May the Lord bless us,
may he keep us from all evil
and lead us to life everlasting.
Amen.

Let us bless the Lord.
R. Thanks be to God.

Friday III

OFFICE OF READINGS

O God, come to my assistance.
Lord, make haste to help me.
Glory be to the Father, and to the Son, and to the Holy
Spirit.
As it was in the beginning, is now, and ever shall be, world
without end. Amen. Alleluia!

Or, if used as first prayer of the day: O Lord, open my lips...

Hymn

I am the holy vine,
Which God my Father tends.
Each branch that yields no fruit
My Father cuts away.
Each fruitful branch
He prunes with care
To make it yield
Abundant fruit.

If you abide in me,
I will in you abide.
Each branch to yield its fruit
Must with the vine be one.
So you shall fail
To yield your fruit
If you are not
With me one vine.

I am the fruitful vine,
And you my branches are.
He who abides in me,
I will in him abide.
So shall you yield
Much fruit, but none
If you remain
Apart from me.

Psalmody

Psalm 68   Cry from the depths of sorrow

Father, save me from this hour (John 12:27)

I

Ant. I am wearied with my crying
   while I wait for my God.

Save me, O God,
for the waters have risen to my neck.

I have sunk into the mud of the deep
and there is no foothold.
I have entered the waters of the deep
and the waves overwhelm me.

I am wearied with all my crying,
my throat is parched.
My eyes are wasted away
from looking for my God.

More numerous than the hairs on my head
are those who hate me without cause.
Those who attack me with lies
are too much for my strength.

How can I restore
what I have never stolen?
O God, you know my sinful folly;
my skins you can see.

Let not those who hope in you be put to shame
through me, Lord of hosts:
let not those who seek you be dismayed
through me, God of Israel.

It is for you that I suffer taunts,
that shame covers my face,
that I have become a stranger to my brothers,
an alien to my own mother's sons.

I burn with zeal for your house
and taunts against you fall on me.

When I afflict my soul with fasting
they make it a taunt against me.
When I put on sackcloth in mourning
then they make me a byword,
the gossip of men at the gates,
the subject of drunkard's songs.

Ant. I am wearied with my crying
    while I wait for my God.

II

Ant. They offered me poison for my food,
    they gave me vinegar in my thirst.

This is my prayer to you,
my prayer for your favour.
In your great love, answer me, O God,
with your help that never fails:
rescue me from sinking in the mud;
save me from my foes.

Save me from the waters of the deep
lest the waves overwhelm me.
Do not let the deep engulf me
nor death close its mouth on me.

Lord, answer, for your love is kind;
in your compassion, turn towards me.
Do not hide your face from your servant;
answer quickly for I am in distress.
Come close to my soul and redeem me;
ransom me pressed by my foes.

You know how they taunt and deride me;
my oppressors are all before you.
Taunts have broken my heart;
I have reached the end of my strength.

I looked in vain for compassion, for consolers;
not one could I find.

For food they gave me poison;
in my thirst they gave me vinegar to drink . . .

Ant. They offered me poison for my food,
   they gave me vinegar in my thirst.

III

Ant. The hearts of those who seek God will revive.

As for me in my poverty and pain
let your help, O God, lift me up.
I will praise God's name with a song;
I will glorify him with thanksgiving.
A gift pleasing God more than oxen,
more than beasts prepared for sacrifice.

The poor when they see it will be glad
and God-seeking hearts will revive;
for the Lord listens to the needy
and does not spurn his servants in their chains.
Let the heavens and the earth give him praise,
the sea and all its living creatures.

For God will bring help to Zion†
and rebuild the cities of Judah
and men shall dwell there in possession.
The sons of his servants shall inherit it;
those who love his name shall dwell there.

Ant. The hearts of those who seek God will revive.

V. Lord, make me know your ways.
R. Lord, teach me your paths.

Readings

Prayer of the day

Or alternative prayer

352

MORNING PRAYER

Introductory verse and psalm

O Lord, open my lips.

And my mouth shall declare your praise.

Glory be to the Father, and to the Son, and to the Holy Spirit.

As it was in the beginning, is now, and ever shall be, world without end. Amen. Alleluia!

Psalm 94

Refrain: Harden not your hearts today,
   but listen to the voice of the Lord.

Or, if not used as first prayer of the day: O God, come to my assistance...

Hymn   Rom 8:28–35, 37

In everything God works for good with those who love him,
who are called according to his purpose.

For those whom he foreknew he also predestined
to be conformed to the image of his Son.

R. You did not spare your own Son, but gave him up for us all.

Those whom he predestined
he also called;
and those whom he called
he also justified;
and those whom he justified
he also glorified. (*R.*)

What then shall we say?†
If God is for us,
who is against us?
He who did not spare his own Son,
but gave him up for us all,
will he not also give us all things with him? (*R.*)

It is God who justifies,
who is to condemn?

Is it Christ Jesus, who died,
who was raised from the dead,
who is at the right hand of God,
who intercedes for us? (*R.*)

Who shall separate us
from the love of Christ?
Shall tribulation, or distress, or persecution,
or famine, or nakedness, or peril, or sword?
No, in all these things we are more than conquerors
through him who loved us. (*R.*)

Psalmody

Psalm 50   **Confession of a sinner; promise, prayer and hope**

Jesus, Son of God and Saviour, have mercy on me, a sinner

Ant. Lord, cleanse me from my guilt.

Have mercy on me, God, in your kindness.
In your compassion blot out my offence.
O wash me more and more from my guilt
and cleanse me from my sin.

My offences truly I know them;
my sin is always before me.
Against you, you alone, have I sinned;
what is evil in your sight I have done.

That you may be justified when you give sentence
and be without reproach when you judge,
O see, in guilt I was born,
a sinner was I conceived.

Indeed you love truth in the heart;
then in the secret of my heart teach me wisdom.
O purify me, then I shall be clean;
O wash me, I shall be whiter than snow.

Make me hear rejoicing and gladness,
that the bones you have crushed may thrill.
From my sins turn away your face
and blot out all my guilt.

A pure heart create for me, O God,
put a steadfast spirit within me.
Do not cast me away from your presence,
nor deprive me of your holy spirit.

Give me again the joy of your help;
with a spirit of fervour sustain me,
that I may teach transgressors your ways
and sinners may return to you.

O rescue me, God, my helper,
and my tongue shall ring out your goodness.
O Lord, open my lips
and my mouth shall declare your praise.

For in sacrifice you take no delight,
burnt offering from me you would refuse,
my sacrifice, a contrite spirit.
A humbled, contrite heart you will not spurn.

In your goodness, show favour to Zion:
rebuild the walls of Jerusalem.
Then you will be pleased with lawful sacrifice,†
burnt offerings wholly consumed,
then you will be offered young bulls on your altar.

Ant. Lord, cleanse me from my guilt.

Jer 14:17–21   Song of Jeremiah: lament of the people during a famine

The kingdom of God is at hand; repent, and believe in the gospel (Mark 1:15)

Ant. Have mercy on us, Lord, have mercy on us.

Let my eyes run down with tears night and day,
and let them not cease,
for the virgin daughter of my people is smitten with a great
    wound,
with a very grievous blow.
If I go out into the field,
behold, those slain by the sword!

355

And if I enter the city,
behold, the diseases of famine!

For both prophet and priest ply their trade through the land,
and have no knowledge.

Have you utterly rejected Judah?
Does your soul loathe Zion?
Why have you smitten us
so that there is no healing for us?

We looked for peace,
but no good came;
for a time of healing,
but behold, terror.

We acknowledge our wickedness, O Lord,†
and the iniquity of our fathers,
for we have sinned against you.

Do not spurn us, for your name's sake;†
do not dishonour your glorious throne;
remember and do not break your covenant with us.

Ant. Have mercy on us, Lord, have mercy on us.

Psalm 99   Entry into the temple

*Let the peace of Christ rule in your hearts ... and be
thankful* (Col 3:15)

Ant. We come before you, Lord,
singing for joy.

Cry out with joy to the Lord, all the earth.†
Serve the Lord with gladness.
Come before him, singing for joy.

Know that he, the Lord, is God.†
He made us, we belong to him,
we are his people, the sheep of his flock.

Go within his gates, giving thanks.†
Enter his courts with songs of praise.
Give thanks to him and bless his name.

Indeed, how good is the Lord,†
eternal his merciful love.
He is faithful from age to age.

Ant. We come before you, Lord,
singing for joy.

Word of God
2 Cor 12:9–10

I will all the more gladly boast of my weaknesses, that the power of Christ may rest upon me. For the sake of Christ, then, I am content with weaknesses, insults, hardships, persecutions, and calamities; for when I am weak, then I am strong.

Short Response
Our Lord is great
and almighty.
V. His wisdom can never be measured.
R. Our Lord is great and almighty.
V. Glory be to the Father, and to the Son, and to the Holy Spirit.
Our Lord is great
and almighty.

Song of Zechariah
Ant. A Saviour is given us
through the loving-kindness of the heart of our God.

Prayers
Christ was born, died, and rose again for his people; let us pray to him, saying:

R. Lord, save us whom you have ransomed by your blood.

Blessed are you, O Christ, the Saviour of men:
—you did not refuse to undergo the passion and cross, but ransomed us by your blood. (*R.*)

You promised that from your side would flow streams of living water.
—Through the mystery of the cross, pour out your Spirit on all mankind. (*R.*)

357

You sent the disciples to preach the Gospel to all nations;
—help those who proclaim the victory of the cross. (*R.*)

You have given the sick and the needy a share in your cross;
—give them also fortitude and patience. (*R.*)

Other prayers may be added

Concluding prayer

Almighty Father, pour out your grace into our hearts, that we may always walk in the way of your commandments by following you, our King and Leader. We make our prayer through our Lord.

May the Lord bless us,
may he keep us from all evil
and lead us to life everlasting.
Amen.

Let us bless the Lord.
R. Thanks be to God.

MIDDAY PRAYER

O God, come to my assistance . . .
Glory be . . .

Hymn

Mighty ruler, faithful God,
who arrange the successive changes in nature,
giving bright light to the morning sun
and burning heat at noon.

Put out the flames of strife
and take away the heat of passion;
grant us health of body
and true peace of soul.

Grant this, most loving Father,
and you, the only Son, equal to the Father

and, with the Spirit, the Paraclete,
reigning through the ages. Amen.

Psalmody

Psalm 21   **Prayer of the suffering servant**

*Was it not necessary that the Christ should suffer these
things and enter into his glory?* (Luke 24:26)

Ant. All people shall worship before him.

I

My God, my God, why have you forsaken me?
You are far from my plea and the cry of my distress.
O my God, I call by day and you give no reply;
I call by night and I find no peace.

Yet you, O God, are holy,
enthroned on the praises of Israel.
In you our fathers put their trust;
they trusted and you set them free.
When they cried to you, they escaped.
In you they trusted and never in vain.

But I am a worm and no man,
the butt of men, laughing-stock of the people.
All who see me deride me.
They curl their lips, they toss their heads.
'He trusted in the Lord, let him save him;
let him release him if this is his friend.'

Yes, it was you who took me from the womb,
entrusted me to my mother's breast.
To you I was committed from my birth,
from my mother's womb you have been my God.

II

Do not leave me alone in my distress;
come close, there is none else to help.

Many bulls have surrounded me,
fierce bulls of Bashan close me in.
Against me they open wide their jaws,
like lions, rending and roaring.

Like water I am poured out,
disjointed are all my bones.
My heart has become like wax,
it is melted within my breast.
Parched as burnt clay is my throat,
my tongue cleaves to my jaws.

Many dogs have surrounded me,
a band of the wicked beset me.
They tear holes in my hands and my feet
and lay me in the dust of death.

I can count every one of my bones.
These people stare at me and gloat;
they divide my clothing among them.
They cast lots for my robe.

O Lord, do not leave me alone,
my strength, make haste to help me!
Rescue my soul from the sword,
my life from the grip of these dogs.
Save my life from the jaws of these lions,
my poor soul from the horns of these oxen.

I will tell of your name to my brethren
and praise you where they are assembled.

III

'You who fear the Lord give him praise;†
all sons of Jacob, give him glory.
Revere him, Israel's sons.

For he has never despised
nor scorned the poverty of the poor.
From him he has not hidden his face,
but he heard the poor man when he cried.'

You are my praise in the great assembly.
My vows I will pay before those who fear him.
The poor shall eat and shall have their fill.†
They shall praise the Lord, those who seek him.
May their hearts live for ever and ever!

All the earth shall remember and return to the Lord,†
all families of the nations worship before him
for the kingdom is the Lord's; he is ruler of the nations.
They shall worship him, all the mighty of the earth;
before him shall bow all who go down to the dust.

And my soul shall live for him,
my children serve him.
They shall tell of the Lord to generations yet to come,†
declare his faithfulness to peoples yet unborn:
'These things the Lord has done.'

Ant. All people shall worship before him.

Word of God   Rom 3:21–22

Now the righteousness of God has been manifested apart
from law, although the law and the prophets bear witness
to it, the righteousness of God through faith in Jesus Christ
for all who believe.

V. In him do our hearts find joy.
R. We trust in his holy name.

Prayer

Lord Jesus Christ, on a day plunged into darkness, you who
were innocent were raised upon a cross for our redemption;
grant us the light we need to reach eternal life. Who live.

Let us bless the Lord.
R. Thanks be to God.

EVENING PRAYER

O God, come to my assistance.
Lord, make haste to help me.

Glory be to the Father, and to the Son, and to the Holy Spirit.

As it was in the beginning, is now, and ever shall be, world without end. Amen. Alleluia!

Hymn   1 Pet 2:21–24

R. By his wounds you have been healed.

Christ suffered for you,
leaving you an example that you should follow in his steps. (R.)

He committed no sin;
no guile was found on his lips.
When he was reviled,
he did not revile in return. (R.)

When he suffered,
he did not threaten,
but he trusted to him
who judges justly. (R.)

He himself bore our sins in his body on the tree,†
that we might die to sin and live to righteousness.
By his wounds you have been healed.
For you were straying like sheep,
but have now returned to the Shepherd and Guardian
   of your souls. (R.)

Psalmody

Psalm 134   Anthology of praise

You are God's own people, that you may declare the wonderful deeds of him who called you out of darkness into his marvellous light (1 Pet 2:9)

Ant. I know the Lord is great,
   that our Lord is high above all gods.

Praise the name of the Lord,
praise him, servants of the Lord,
who stand in the house of the Lord
in the courts of the house of our God.

Praise the Lord for the Lord is good.
Sing a psalm to his name for he is loving.
For the Lord has chosen Jacob for himself
and Israel for his own possession.

For I know the Lord is great,
that our Lord is high above all gods.
The Lord does whatever he wills,
in heaven, on earth, in the seas.

He summons clouds from the ends of the earth;†
makes lightning produce the rain;
from his treasures he sends forth the wind.

The first-born of the Egyptians he smote,
of man and beast alike.
Signs and wonders he worked†
in the midst of your land, O Egypt,
against Pharaoh and all his servants.

Nations in their greatness he struck
and kings in their splendour he slew. . .
He let Israel inherit their land;
on his people their land he bestowed.

Ant. I know the Lord is great,
    that our Lord is high above all gods.

II

Ant. Sons of Israel, bless the Lord;
    sing a song to his name for he is loving.

Lord, your name stands for ever,
unforgotten from age to age:
for the Lord does justice for his people;
the Lord takes pity on his servants.

Pagan idols are silver and gold,
the work of human hands.
They have mouths but they cannot speak;
they have eyes but they cannot see.

They have ears but they cannot hear;
there is never a breath on their lips.
Their makers will become like them
and so will all who trust in them!

Sons of Israel, bless the Lord!
Sons of Aaron, bless the Lord!
Sons of Levi, bless the Lord!
You who fear him, bless the Lord!

From Zion may the Lord be blessed,
he who dwells in Jerusalem!

Ant. Sons of Israel, bless the Lord;
    sing a song to his name for he is loving.

Rev 15:3–4   **Song of Moses and the Lamb**

R. Great are your deeds, O Lord!

Great and wonderful are your deeds,
O Lord God the Almighty!
Just and true are your ways,
O King of the ages!

R. Great are your deeds, O Lord!

Who shall not fear and glorify your name, O Lord?
For you alone are holy. (*R.*)

All nations shall come and worship you,
for your judgments have been revealed. (*R.*)

Word of God   Jas 1:2–4

Count it all joy, my brethren, when you meet various trials,
for you know that the testing of your faith produces steadfastness. And let steadfastness have its full effect, that you
may be perfect and complete, lacking in nothing.

Short Response
O God, save me
by your name.

V. In your goodness, set me free.
R. Save me by your name.
V. Glory be to the Father, and to the Son, and to the Holy Spirit.
O God, save me
by your name.

Song of the Virgin Mary
Ant. Lord, put forth your arm in strength,
scatter the proud-hearted, raise the lowly.

Prayers
God gave up his own Son to atone for our sins and raised him up for our justification. Let us pray:

R. Have mercy on your people, Lord.

Lord, hear our supplications and spare us as we confess our sins.
—in your mercy, grant us pardon and peace. (*R.*)

O God, you said through your Apostle: Where sin increased, grace abounded all the more.
—In your abundant mercy, pardon our sins. (*R*).

O Lord, we have sinned greatly, but we know that your mercy is infinite;
—bring us back, that we may be healed. (*R.*)

Lord, save your people from their sins;
—may they once again be pleasing to you. (*R.*)

Other prayers may be added

O God, you opened paradise to the thief who acknowledged your Son.
—Do not shut out from heaven those who have died. (*R.*)

Our Father . . .

Concluding prayer

Holy Father, by whose will Christ your Son paid the price of our salvation, grant us so to live that, by sharing in his sufferings, we may come to know the power of his resurrection. We make our prayer through our Lord.

May the Lord bless us,
may he keep us from all evil
and lead us to life everlasting.
Amen.

Let us bless the Lord.
R. Thanks be to God.

Saturday III

OFFICE OF READINGS

O God, come to my assistance.
Lord, make haste to help me.
Glory be to the Father, and to the Son, and to the Holy
Spirit.
As it was in the beginning, is now, and ever shall be, world
without end. Amen. Alleluia!

Or, if used as first prayer of the day: O Lord open my lips...

Hymn

How deep the riches of our God,
His wisdom how sublime;
How high his judgments soar above
All judgment of mankind!

What mind has read the mind of God,
Or giv'n him counsel sure?
Who from his riches gave to God
What was not first received?

From God all things created flow;
All things through him exist;
To him for judgment all returns,
To whom all praise is due!

To God the Father, fount of grace,
Through his beloved Son
In oneness with the Holy Ghost
Be glory evermore!

Psalmody

Psalm 106   Thanksgiving: God rescues his people from their difficulties
during the course of their history

*You know the word which he sent to Israel, preaching good
news of peace by Jesus Christ* (Acts 10:36)

I

Ant. Let them thank the Lord for his love,
  for the wonders he does for men.

'O give thanks to the Lord for he is good;
for his great love is without end.'

Let them say this, the Lord's redeemed,
whom he redeemed from the hand of the foe
and gathered from far-off lands,
from east and west, north and south.

Some wandered in the desert, in the wilderness,
finding no way to a city they could dwell in.
Hungry they were and thirsty;
their soul was fainting within them.

Then they cried to the Lord in their need
and he rescued them from their distress
and he led them along the right way,
to reach a city they could dwell in.

Let them thank the Lord for his love,
for the wonders he does for men.
For he satisfies the thirsty soul;
he fills the hungry with good things.

Some lay in darkness and in gloom,
prisoners in misery and chains,
having defied the words of God
and spurned the counsels of the Most High.
He crushed their spirit with toil;
they stumbled; there was no one to help.

Then they cried to the Lord in their need
and he rescued them from their distress.
He led them forth from darkness and gloom
and broke their chains to pieces.

Let them thank the Lord for his goodness,
for the wonders he does for men:

for he bursts the gates of bronze
and shatters the iron bars.

Some were sick on account of their sins
and afflicted on account of their guilt.
They had a loathing for every food;
they came close to the gates of death.

Then they cried to the Lord in their need
and he rescued them from their distress.
He sent forth his word to heal them
and saved their life from the grave.

Let them thank the Lord for his love,
for the wonders he does for men.
Let them offer a sacrifice of thanks
and tell of his deeds with rejoicing.

II

Some sailed to the sea in ships
to trade on the mighty waters.
These men have seen the Lord's deeds,
the wonders he does in the deep.

For he spoke; he summoned the gale,†
tossing the waves of the sea up to heaven and back
    into the deep;
their soul melted away in their distress.

They staggered, reeled like drunken men,
for all their skill was gone.
Then they cried to the Lord in their need
and he rescued them from their distress.

He stilled the storm to a whisper:
all the waves of the sea were hushed.
They rejoiced because of the calm
and he led them to the haven they desired.

Let them thank the Lord for his love,
the wonders he does for men.

Let them exalt him in the gathering of the people
and praise him in the meeting of the elders.

III

He changes streams into a desert,
springs of water into thirsty ground,
a fruitful land into a salt waste,
for the wickedness of those who live there.

But he changes desert into streams,
thirsty ground into springs of water.
There he settles the hungry
and they build a city to dwell in.

They sow fields and plant their vines;
these yield crops for the harvest.
He blesses them; they grow in numbers.
He does not let their herds decrease.

He pours contempt upon princes,
makes them wander in trackless wastes.
They diminish, are reduced to nothing
by oppression, evil and sorrow.

But he raises the needy from distress;
makes families numerous as a flock.
The upright see it and rejoice
but all who do wrong are silenced.

Whoever is wise, let him heed these things
and consider the love of the Lord.

Ant. Let them thank the Lord for his love,
 for the wonders he does for men.

V. Come, consider the works of the Lord,
R. The redoubtable deeds he has done on the earth.

Readings

Prayer of the day

Or alternative prayer

MORNING PRAYER

Introductory verse and Psalm

O Lord, open my lips.

And my mouth shall declare your praise.

Glory be to the Father, and to the Son, and to the Holy Spirit.

As it was in the beginning, is now, and ever shall be, world without end. Amen. Alleluia!

Psalm 94

Refrain: Let us go to meet the Lord with songs of joy and gladness.

Or, if not used as first prayer of the day: O God come to my assistance...

Hymn

R. Awake, O sleeper, and arise from the dead,
  and Christ shall give you light.

Christ, who was manifested in the flesh,
vindicated in the Spirit,
seen by the angels,
preached among the nations,
believed on in the world,
taken up in glory. (*R.*)

Christ, who will be made manifest
at the proper time
by the blessed and only Sovereign,
the King of kings and Lord of lords,
who alone has immortality
and dwells in unapproachable light,
whom no man has ever seen or can see,
to him be honour and eternal dominion. Amen. (*R.*)

Psalmody

Psalm 118:145–152

  Love is the fulfilling of the law (Rom 13:10)

Ant. Lord, remember your word,
  my comfort in sorrow.

I call with all my heart; Lord, hear me,
I will keep your statutes.
I call upon you, save me
and I will do your will.

I rise before dawn and cry for help,
I hope in your word.
My eyes watch through the night
to ponder your promise.

In your love hear my voice, O Lord;
give me life by your decrees.
Those who harm me unjustly draw near:
they are far from your law.

But you, O Lord, are close:
your commands are truth.
Long have I known that your will
is established for ever.

Ant. Lord, remember your word,
  my comfort in sorrow.

Wis 9:1–12   **Song: prayer for wisdom**

  I will give you a mouth and wisdom which none of your
  adversaries will be able to withstand or contradict (Luke
  21:15)

R. Give me the wisdom that comes from you.

O God of my fathers and Lord of mercy,
who have made all things by your word,
and by your wisdom have formed man
to have dominion over the creatures you have made,
and rule the world in holiness and righteousness,
and pronounce judgment in uprightness of soul
give me the wisdom that sits by your throne,
and do not reject me from among your servants.

R. Give me the wisdom that comes from you.

For I am your slave
and the son of your maidservant,
a man who is weak and short-lived,
with little understanding of judgment and laws;
for even if one is perfect among the sons of men,†
yet without the wisdom that comes from you
he will be regarded as nothing. (R)

You have chosen me to be king of your people
and to be judge over your sons and daughters.
You have given command to build a temple on your holy
    mountain
and an altar in the city of your habitation,
a copy of the holy tent
which you had prepared from the beginning. (R).

With you is wisdom, who knows your works
and was present when you made the world,
and who understands what is pleasing in your sight
and what is right according to your commandments. (R.)

Send her forth from the holy heavens,
and from the throne of your glory send her,
that she may be with me and toil,
and that I may learn what is pleasing to you. (R.)

For she knows and understands all things,†
and she will guide me wisely in my actions
and guard me with her glory.
Then my works will be acceptable,†
and I shall judge your people justly,
and shall be worthy of the throne of my father. (R.)

Psalm 116   **World-wide call to praise God**

Christ became a servant . . . that the Gentiles might glorify
God for his mercy (Rom 15:8)

Ant. O praise the Lord;
    strong is his love for us.

O praise the Lord, all you nations,
acclaim him all you peoples!

Strong is his love for us;
he is faithful for ever.

Ant. O praise the Lord;
strong is his love for us.

Word of God   Phil 2:14–15

Do all things without grumbling or questioning, that you
may be blameless and innocent, children of God without
blemish in the midst of a crooked and perverse generation,
among whom you shine as lights in the world.

Short Response

Your deeds, O Lord, have made me glad;
for the work of your hands I shout with joy.

V. O Lord, how deep are your designs!

R. For the work of your hands I shout with joy.

V. Glory be to the Father, and to the Son, and to the Holy
Spirit.

You deeds, O Lord, have made me glad;
for the work of your hands I shout with joy.

Song of Zechariah

Ant. Guide us, Lord, into the way of peace.

Prayers

It was God who set Mary the Mother of Christ above all
creatures in heaven and earth. Let us pray:

R. Look upon the Mother of your Son, and hear our prayer.

Father of mercies, we thank you for giving us Mary to be
our mother and example;

—make us holy through her intercession. (*R.*)

By your grace Mary kept all your words in her heart, and
became your faithful servant.

—Make us, through her intercession, your true servants and
true disciples of her Son. (*R.*)

374

By your power the Holy Spirit overshadowed Mary and she conceived a Son;
—grant us the fruits of the Holy Spirit through her intercession. (*R*).

God, who gave Mary the strength to stand beneath the cross and filled her with joy at the resurrection of your Son,
—through her intercession help us in tribulation, and strengthen our hope. (*R*.)

Other prayers may be added

Our Father . . .

Concluding prayer

O God, the well-spring of salvation, grant that we may so praise you day by day on earth, that our praises may become the never-ending song of heaven. We make our prayer through our Lord.

May the Lord bless us,
may he keep us from all evil
and lead us to life everlasting.
Amen.

Let us bless the Lord.
R. Thanks be to God.

MIDDAY PRAYER

O God, come to my assistance . . .
Glory be . . .

Hymn

Lord God, the strength which daily upholds all creation,
in yourself remaining unchanged
and yet determining in due order
the successive changes of the light of day.

Grant us light in the evening
so that life may not decay at any point of its activity,

but everlasting glory be the immediate reward
of a happy death.

Grant this, most loving Father,
and you, the only Son, equal to the Father
and, with the Spirit, the Paraclete,
reigning through the ages. Amen.

Psalmody

Psalm 118:121–128

Ant. I am your servant, make me understand;
    then I shall know your will.

I have done what is right and just:
let me not be oppressed.
Vouch for the welfare of your servant
lest the proud oppress me.

My eyes yearn for your saving help
and the promise of your justice.
Treat your servant with love
and teach me your statutes.

I am your servant, make me understand;
then I shall know your will.
It is time for the Lord to act
for your law has been broken.

That is why I love your commands
more than finest gold.
That is why I rule my life by your precepts:
I hate false ways.

Psalm 33   Fear of God and its fruit

    You have tasted the kindness of the Lord (1 Pet 2:3)

I

I will bless the Lord at all times,
his praise always on my lips;
in the Lord my soul shall make its boast.
The humble shall hear and be glad.

Glorify the Lord with me.
Together let us praise his name.
I sought the Lord and he answered me;
from all my terrors he set me free.

Look towards him and be radiant;
let your faces not be abashed.
This poor man called; the Lord heard him
and rescued him from all his distress.

The angel of the Lord is encamped
around those who revere him, to rescue them.
Taste and see that the Lord is good.
He is happy who seeks refuge in him.

Revere the Lord, you his saints.
They lack nothing, those who revere him.
Strong lions suffer want and go hungry
but those who seek the Lord lack no blessing.

II

Come, children, and hear me
that I may teach you the fear of the Lord.
Who is he who longs for life
and many days, to enjoy his prosperity?

Then keep your tongue from evil
and your lips from speaking deceit.
Turn aside from evil and do good;
seek and strive after peace.

The Lord turns his face against the wicked
to destroy their remembrance from the earth.
The Lord turns his eyes to the just
and his ears to their appeal.

They call and the Lord hears
and rescues them in all their distress.
The Lord is close to the broken-hearted;
those whose spirit is crushed he will save.

Many are the trials of the just man
but from them all the Lord will rescue him.
He will keep guard over all his bones,
not one of his bones shall be broken.

Evil brings death to the wicked;
those who hate the good are doomed.
The Lord ransoms the souls of his servants.
Those who hide in him shall not be condemned.

Ant. I am your servant, make me understand;
    then I shall know your will.

Word of God   Hos 6:6

I desire steadfast love and not sacrifice,
the knowledge of God, rather than burnt offerings.

V. O purify me, then I shall be clean;
R. O wash me, I shall be whiter than snow.

Prayer

O Lord, fire of everlasting love, give us the fervour to love
you above all things, and our brother for your sake.
Through Christ.

Let us bless the Lord.
R. Thanks be to God.

Sunday IV

EVENING PRAYER I

O God, come to my assistance.
Lord, make haste to help me.
Glory be to the Father, and to the Son, and to the Holy Spirit.
As it was in the beginning, is now, and ever shall be, world without end. Amen. Alleluia!

Hymn   2 Tim 2:11–13

R. Christ has died,
   Christ is risen,
   Christ will come again.

If we have died with him,
we shall also live with him:
If we endure,
we shall also reign with him. (R.)

If we deny him,
he will also deny us;
If we are faithless, he remains faithful—
for he cannot deny himself. Alleluia! (R.)

Psalmody

Psalm 121   Greeting to Jerusalem

You have come to Mount Zion and to the city of the living God, the heavenly Jerusalem (Heb 12:22)

Ant. Give peace, O Lord, to those who count on you.

I rejoiced when I heard them say:
'Let us go to God's house.'
And now our feet are standing
within your gates, O Jerusalem.

Jerusalem is built as a city
strongly compact.

It is there that the tribes go up,
the tribes of the Lord.

For Israel's law it is,
there to praise the Lord's name.
There were set the thrones of judgment
of the house of David.

For the peace of Jerusalem pray:
'Peace be to your homes!
May peace reign in your walls,
in your palaces, peace!'

For love of my brethren and friends
I say: 'Peace upon you!'
For love of the house of the Lord
I will ask for your good.

Ant. Give peace, O Lord, to those who count on you.

Psalm 129   **Prayer of repentance and trust**

He will save his people from their sins (Matthew 1:21)

Ant. With the Lord there is mercy
and fulness of redemption.

Out of the depths I cry to you, O Lord,
Lord, hear my voice!
O let your ears be attentive
to the voice of my pleading.

If you, O Lord, should mark our guilt,
Lord, who would survive?
But with you is found forgiveness:
for this we revere you.

My soul is waiting for the Lord,
I count on his word.
My soul is longing for the Lord
more than watchman for daybreak.
Let the watchman count on daybreak
and Israel on the Lord.

Because with the Lord there is mercy
and fulness of redemption,
Israel indeed he will redeem
from all its iniquity.

Ant. With the Lord there is mercy
and fulness of redemption.

Phil 2:6–11   **Song of the Easter mystery**

Ant. Christ died for our sins,
and rose that we might live.

Though he was in the form of God,
Jesus did not count equality with God a thing to be grasped.

R. Jesus Christ is Lord
to the glory of God the Father!

He emptied himself,†
taking the form of a servant,
being born in the likeness of men. (*R.*)

And being found in human form,†
he humbled himself and became obedient unto death,
even death on a cross. (*R.*)

Therefore God has highly exalted him
and bestowed on him the name which is above every
name. (*R.*)

That at the name of Jesus every knee should bow,
in heaven and on earth and under the earth. (*R.*)

And every tongue confess that Jesus is Lord,
to the glory of God the Father.

Ant. Christ died for our sins,
and rose that we might live.

Word of God   2 Pet 1:19–21
We were eyewitnesses of his majesty, for we were with him
on the holy mountain. And we have the prophetic word
made more sure. You will do well to pay attention to this

as to a lamp shining in a dark place, until the day dawns and the morning star rises in your hearts. First of all you must understand this, that no prophecy of scripture is a matter of one's own interpretation, because no prophecy ever came by the impulse of man, but men moved by the Holy Spirit spoke from God.

Short Response
Your Word, O Lord,
stands firm in the heavens.
V. Your truth lasts from age to age.
R. It stands firm in the heavens.
V. Glory be to the Father, and to the Son, and to the Holy Spirit.
Your Word, O Lord,
stands firm in the heavens.

Song of the Virgin Mary
Ant. Blessed are you among women,
   and blessed is the fruit of your womb.

Prayers
Christ had pity on the hungry, and gave them food in their need. Let us remember this and pray:

R. Lord, save us by your love.

Lord, we acknowledge that all the good things we have received today come from your goodness:
—let them not return to you empty, but remain with us to bear fruit in good and honest hearts. (*R.*)

O God who are the light and salvation of all peoples, protect those whom you have sent to be your witnesses throughout the world;
—kindle in them the fire of the Holy Spirit. (*R.*)

Teach us, Lord, to build a more human world;
—teach us to respect the dignity of our brothers. (*R.*)

Heavenly Physician, comfort those who suffer in mind or body, and give peace to the dying;
—visit us with your mercy, and heal us. (*R.*)

Other prayers may be added

We pray that you will include those who have died among your blessed ones
—whose names are written in the book of life. (*R.*)

Our Father . . .

Concluding prayer of the Sunday
May the Lord bless us,
may he keep us from all evil
and lead us to life everlasting.
Amen.

Let us bless the Lord.
R. Thanks be to God.

OFFICE OF READINGS

O God, come to my assistance.
Lord, make haste to help me.
Glory be to the Father, and to the Son, and to the Holy Spirit.
As it was in the beginning, is now, and ever shall be, world without end. Amen. Alleluia!

Or, if used as first prayer of the day: O Lord, open my lips . . .

Hymn
R. Alleluia! Christ is risen, alleluia!
R. (*in Lent*) If we have died with him, we shall also live with him.

I will sing to the Lord, glorious his triumph!
Horse and rider he has thrown into the sea.
Lord, you are great, you are glorious,
wonderful in strength, none can conquer you.
God has arisen, and his foes are scattered;
those who hate him have fled before him. (*R.*)

He has burst the gates of bronze
and shattered the iron bars.
This God of ours is a God who saves;
the Lord our God holds the keys of death.
This is the day which the Lord has made;
let us rejoice and be glad. (*R.*)

Awake, O sleeper, and rise from the dead,
and Christ shall give you light.
For he has been raised from the dead,
never to die any more.
God has not left his soul among the dead,
nor let his beloved know decay. (*R.*)

The Lord is risen from the tomb
who hung for us upon the tree.
Beasts of the field, do not be afraid;
the pastures of the wilderness are green again;
the tree bears its fruit once more,
vine and fig tree yield abundantly. (*R.*)

Psalmody

Psalm 23   **God's solemn entry into his temple**

*The gates of heaven open before Christ as he ascends to
heaven* (St Irenaeus)

Ant. He, the Lord of armies,
  he is the king of glory.

The Lord's is the earth and its fulness,
the world and all its peoples.
It is he who set it on the seas;
on the waters he made it firm.

Who shall climb the mountain of the Lord?
Who shall stand in his holy place?
The man with clean hands and pure heart,†
who desires not worthless things,
who has not sworn so as to deceive his neighbour.

He shall receive blessings from the Lord
and reward from the God who saves him.
Such are the men who seek him,
seek the face of the God of Jacob.

O gates, lift high your heads;†
grow higher, ancient doors.
Let him enter, the king of glory!

Who is the king of glory?
The Lord, the mighty, the valiant, the Lord, the valiant in
war.

O gates, lift high your heads;†
grow higher, ancient doors.
Let him enter the king of glory!

Who is he, the king of glory?
He, the Lord of armies, he is the king of glory.

Ant. He, the Lord of armies,
  he is the king of glory.

Psalm 65   A people's thanksgiving

*You were slain, and by your blood you ransomed men for
God from every tribe . . . and have made them a kingdom
and priests to our God* (Rev 5:9)

I

Ant. All you nations, bless our God,
  the God who gave life to our souls. Alleluia!

Cry out with joy to God all the earth,
O sing to the glory of his name.
O render him glorious praise.
Say to God: 'How tremendous your deeds!

Because of the greatness of your strength
your enemies cringe before you.
Before you all the earth shall bow;
shall sing to you, sing to your name!'

385

Come and see the works of God,
tremendous his deeds among men.
He turned the sea into dry land,
they passed through the river dry-shod.

Let our joy then be in him;
he rules for ever by his might.
His eyes keep watch over the nations:
let rebels not rise against him.

O peoples, bless our God,
let the voice of his praise resound,
of the God who gave life to our souls
and kept our feet from stumbling.

For you, O God, have tested us,
you have tried us as silver is tried:
you led us, God, into the snare;
you laid a heavy burden on our backs.

You let men ride over our heads;†
we went through fire and through water
but then you brought us relief.

Ant. All you nations, bless our God,
    the God who gave life to our souls. Alleluia!

II

Ant. Listen, and I will tell you
    what the Lord has done for my soul.

Burnt offering I bring to your house;
to you I will pay my vows,
the vows which my lips have uttered,
which my mouth spoke in my distress.

I will offer burnt offerings of fatlings†
with the smoke of burning rams.
I will offer bullocks and goats.

Come and hear, all who fear God.
I will tell what he did for my soul:

to him I cried aloud,
with high praise ready on my tongue.

If there had been evil in my heart,
the Lord would not have listened.
But truly God has listened;
he has heeded the voice of my prayer.

Blessed be God who did not reject my prayer
nor withhold his love from me.

Ant. Listen, and I will tell you
what the Lord has done for my soul.

V. The Word of God is living and active,
R. Sharper than any two-edged sword.

Readings

(Hymn of praise)

Prayer of the Sunday

MORNING PRAYER

Introductory verse and psalm
O Lord, open my lips.
And my mouth shall declare your praise.
Glory be to the Father, and to the Son, and to the Holy
Spirit.
As it was in the beginning, is now, and ever shall be, world
without end. Amen. Alleluia!

Psalm 94
Refrain: Come, people chosen by God,
worship your Shepherd and Guide.

Or, if not used as first prayer of the day: O God come to my
assistance . . .

Hymn
Sing, all creation, sing to God in gladness!
Joyously serve him, singing hymns of homage!

Chanting his praises, come before his presence!
Praise the Almighty!

Know that our God is Lord of all the ages!
He is our maker; we are all his creatures,
People he fashioned, sheep he leads to pasture!
Praise the Almighty!

Enter his temple, ringing out his praises!
Sing in thanksgiving as you come before him!
Blessing his bounty, glorify his greatness!
Praise the Almighty!

Great in his goodness is the Lord we worship;
Steadfast his kindness, love that knows no ending!
Faithful his word is, changeless, everlasting!
Praise the Almighty!

Psalmody

Psalm 117   **Thanksgiving in the temple for the gift of salvation**

*This is the stone which was rejected by you builders, but
which has become the head of the corner* (Acts 4:11)

Ant. Proclaim that the Lord is good,
   that his love is without end.

Give thanks to the Lord for he is good,
for his love has no end.

Let the sons of Israel say:
'His love has no end.'
Let the sons of Aaron say:
'His love has no end.'
Let those who fear the Lord say:
'His love has no end.'

I called to the Lord in my distress;
he answered and freed me.
The Lord is at my side; I do not fear.
What can man do against me?
The Lord is at my side as my helper:
I shall look down on my foes.

It is better to take refuge in the Lord
than to trust in men:
it is better to take refuge in the Lord
than to trust in princes . . .

I was thrust, thrust down and falling
but the Lord was my helper.
The Lord is my strength and my song;
he was my saviour.
There are shouts of joy and victory
in the tents of the just.

The Lord's right hand has triumphed;
his right hand raised me up.
The Lord's right hand has triumphed;
I shall not die, I shall live and recount his deeds.
I was punished, I was punished by the Lord,
but not doomed to die.

Open to me the gates of holiness:
I will enter and give thanks.
This is the Lord's own gate
where the just may enter.
I will thank you for you have given answer
and you are my saviour.

The stone which the builders rejected
has become the corner stone.
This is the work of the Lord,
a marvel in our eyes.
This day was made by the Lord;
we rejoice and are glad.

O Lord, grant us salvation;
O Lord, grant success.
Blessed in the name of the Lord
is he who comes.
We bless you from the house of the Lord;
the Lord God is our light.

Go forward in procession with branches
even to the altar.
You are my God, I thank you.
My God, I praise you
Give thanks to the Lord for he is good;
for his love has no end.

Ant. Proclaim that the Lord is good,
that his love is without end.

Dan 3:52–57   Song of the three children in praise of creation

The Creator ... who is blessed for ever (Rom 1:25)

Ant. Let us sing a hymn,
let us bless God for ever.

You are blest, Lord God of our fathers.
R. To you glory and praise for evermore.

Blest your glorious holy name.
R. To you glory and praise for evermore.

You are blest, in the temple of your glory.
R. To you glory and praise for evermore.

You are blest who gaze into the depths.
R. To you glory and praise for evermore.

You are blest in the firmanent of heaven.
R. To you glory and praise for evermore.

You who walk on the wings of the wind.
R. To you glory and praise for evermore.

May they bless you, the saints and the angels.
R. To you glory and praise for evermore.

From the heavens, the earth and the sea.
R. To you glory and praise for evermore.

You are blest, Lord God of our fathers.
R. To you glory and praise for evermore.

Ant. Let us sing a hymn,
let us bless God for ever.

Psalm 150 Symphony of praise to God

To him be glory in the Church and in Christ Jesus, for ever and ever. Amen (Eph 3:21)

Ant. Let everything that breathes give praise to the Lord.

Praise God in his holy place,
praise him in his mighty heavens.
Praise him for his powerful deeds,
praise his surpassing greatness.

O praise him with sound of trumpet,
praise him with lute and harp.
Praise him with timbrel and dance,
praise him with strings and pipes.

O praise him with resounding cymbals,
praise him with clashing of cymbals.
Let everything that lives and that breathes
give praise to the Lord.

Ant. Let everything that breathes give praise to the Lord.

Word of God Rom 8:18–21

I consider that the sufferings of this present time are not worth comparing with the glory that is to be revealed to us. For the creation waits with eager longing for the revealing of the sons of God; for the creation was subjected to futility, not of its own will but by the will of him who subjected it in hope; because the creation itself will be set free from its bondage to decay and obtain the glorious liberty of the children of God.

Short Response

The Lord loves justice and right;
he fills the earth with his love.
V. By his Word the heavens were made,
by the breath of his mouth all the stars.
R. He fills the earth with his love.
V. Glory be to the Father, and to the Son, and to the Holy Spirit.

The Lord loves justice and right;
he fills the earth with his love.

Song of Zechariah

Ant. To him who conquers I will give the morning star,
and I will confess his name before my Father.

Prayers

Let us offer our praise and prayer to the God who knows
what we need:

R. We praise you, Lord, and put our trust in you.

We bless you, almighty God, King of the universe.
—Although we are sinners, you have called us to the
knowledge of your truth. (*R.*)

O God, who have opened to us the gates of your mercy,
look graciously upon us;
—grant that we may never depart from your way. (*R.*)

Lord, since we celebrate the resurrection of your beloved
Son;
—grant us his peace and joy. (*R.*)

Lord, grant the spirit of prayer and praise to your people,
—that in all things we may offer you thanksgiving. (*R.*)

Other prayers may be added

Our Father . . .

Concluding prayer of the Sunday

May the Lord bless us,
may he keep us from all evil
and lead us to life everlasting.
Amen.

Let us bless the Lord.
R. Thanks be to God.

MIDDAY PRAYER

O God, come to my assistance . . .
Glory be . . .

Hymn
Holy Spirit,
one with the Father and the Son,
deign at this hour to come down on us without delay,
and pour out your graces over our soul.

Let mouth, tongue, soul, thought and strength
make your praise resound.
Let our love be set aflame by the fire of your love,
and its heat in turn enkindle love in our neighbours.

Grant this, most loving Father,
and you, the only Son, equal to the Father,
and, with the Spirit, the Paraclete,
reigning through the ages. Amen.

Psalmody

Psalm 22   **God, shepherd and host**

*The Lamb . . . will be their shepherd, and he will guide them
to springs of living water* (Rev 7:17)

Ant. If anyone eats of this bread,
   he will live for ever.

The Lord is my shepherd;
there is nothing I shall want.
Fresh and green are the pastures
where he gives me repose.
Near restful waters he leads me,
to revive my drooping spirit.

He guides me along the right path;
he is true to his name.
If I should walk in the valley of darkness
no evil would I fear.

393

You are there with your crook and your staff;
with these you give me comfort.

You have prepared a banquet for me
in the sight of my foes.
My head you have anointed with oil;
my cup is overflowing.

Surely goodness and kindness shall follow me
all the days of my life.
In the Lord's own house shall I dwell
for ever and ever.

Psalm 75   **Song after victory**

*They will see the Son of man coming on the clouds of
heaven* (Matthew 24:30)

I

God is made known in Judah;
in Israel his name is great.
He set up his tent in Jerusalem
and his dwelling place in Zion.
It was there he broke the flashing arrows,
the shield, the sword, the armour.

You, Lord, are resplendent,
more majestic than the everlasting mountains.
The warriors, despoiled, slept in death;
the hands of the soldiers were powerless.
At your threat, O God of Jacob,
horse and rider lay stunned.

II

You, you alone, strike terror.
Who shall stand when your anger is roused?
You uttered your sentence from the heavens;
the earth in terror was still
when God arose to judge,
to save the humble of the earth.

Men's anger will serve to praise you;†
its survivors surround you in joy.
Make vows to your God and fulfil them.
Let all pay tribute to him who strikes terror,†
who cuts short the breath of princes,
who strikes terror in the kings of the earth.

Ant. If anyone eats of this bread,
    he will live for ever.

Word of God   Deut 10:12

What does the Lord your God require of you, but to fear the Lord your God, to walk in all his ways, to love him, to serve the Lord your God with all your heart and with all your soul.

V. They are happy who do his will,
R. Seeking him with all their hearts.

Prayer of the Sunday
Let us bless the Lord.
R. Thanks be to God.

EVENING PRAYER II

O God, come to my assistance.
Lord, make haste to help me.
Glory be to the Father, and to the Son, and to the Holy Spirit.
As it was in the beginning, is now, and ever shall be, world without end. Amen. Alleluia!

Hymn
R. Alleluia! Christ is risen, alleluia!
R. (*in Lent*) I have power to lay down my life,
    and I have power to take it again.

I have trodden the wine press alone,
and from the peoples no one was with me.
I have laid down my life of my own free will,

and by my own power I have taken it up anew.
Fear not, I am the first and the last;
I am the living one. (*R*.)

Was it not ordained that the Christ should suffer,
and so enter into his glory?
Upon him was the chastisement that made us whole,
and with his stripes we are healed.
It was the will of the Lord to bruise him;
he has offered his life in atonement. (*R*.)

By his holy and glorious wounds
may Christ the Lord guard us and keep us.
If we have died with him, we shall also live with him;
if we endure, we shall also reign with him.
Christ yesterday and today,
the beginning of all things and their end.
Alpha and Omega;
all time belongs to him, and all the ages. (*R*.)

Psalmody

Psalm 109   **The Messiah, king, priest and judge**

*He must reign until he has put all his enemies under his
feet* (1 Cor 15:25)

Ant. The Lord said to my Lord: 'Sit on my right.'

The Lord's revelation to my Master:†
'Sit on my right:
I will put your foes beneath your feet.'

The Lord will send from Zion your sceptre of power:
rule in the midst of all your foes.

A prince from the day of your birth on the holy mountains;
from the womb before the daybreak I begot you.

The Lord has sworn an oath he will not change.†
'You are a priest for ever,
a priest like Melchizedeck of old.'

The Master standing at your right hand
will shatter kings in the day of his great wrath . . .

He shall drink from the stream by the wayside
and therefore he shall lift up his head.

Ant. The Lord said to my Lord: 'Sit on my right.'

Psalm 111   **Praise of the fear of the Lord. Its fruit**

*Walk as children of light, for the fruit of light is found in
all that is good and right and true* (Eph 5:8–9)

Ant. Happy the man who delights in your law.

Happy the man who fears the Lord,
who takes delight in his commands.
His sons will be powerful on earth;
the children of the upright are blessed.

Riches and wealth are in his house;
his justice stands firm for ever.
He is a light in the darkness for the upright:
he is generous, merciful and just.

The good man takes pity and lends,
he conducts his affairs with honour.
The just man will never waver:
he will be remembered for ever.

He has no fear of evil news;
with a firm heart he trusts in the Lord.
With a steadfast heart he will not fear;
he will see the downfall of his foes.

Open-handed, he gives to the poor;†
his justice stands firm for ever.
His head will be raised in glory.

The wicked man sees and is angry,†
gnashes his teeth and pines away;
the desire of the wicked leads to doom.

Ant. Happy the man who delights in your law.

OUTSIDE LENT

Rev 19:1, 2, 5–8   **Wedding song of the Lamb**

Ant. Alleluia! Victory and glory and power belong to our
God.
 He reigns for ever and ever, alleluia!

R. Alleluia, alleluia!
Salvation and glory and power
belong to our God, alleluia!
His judgments are true
and just.
R. Alleluia, alleluia!

Praise our God,
all you his servants, alleluia!
You who fear him,
small and great.
R. Alleluia, alleluia!

The Lord our God,
the Almighty, reigns, alleluia!
Let us rejoice and exult
and give him the glory.
R. Alleluia, alleluia!

The marriage of the Lamb
has come, alleluia!
And his bride
has made herself ready.
R. Alleluia, alleluia!

It was granted her
to be clothed, alleluia!
with fine linen,
bright and pure.
R. Alleluia, alleluia!

Ant. Alleluia! Victory and glory and power belong to our
God.
 He reigns for ever and ever, alleluia!

LENT

1 Pet 2:21–24   New Testament Song of the suffering Servant

Ant. For our sake God made him to be sin who knew no sin,
   so that in him we might become the righteousness of God.

Christ suffered for you,†
leaving you an example
that you should follow in his steps.

R. By his wounds you have been healed.

He committed no sin;
no guile was found on his lips.
When he was reviled,
he did not revile in return. (*R.*)

When he suffered,
he did not threaten;
but he trusted to him
who judges justly. (*R.*)

He himself bore our sins
in his body on the tree,
that we might die to sin
and live to righteousness.

By his wounds you have been healed.†
For you were straying like sheep,
but have now returned to the Shepherd and Guardian
of your souls. (*R.*)

Ant. For our sake God made him to be sin who knew no sin,
   so that in him we might become the righteousness of God.

Word of God   Heb 12:22–24
You have come to Mount Zion and to the city of the living
God, the heavenly Jerusalem, and to innumerable angels in
festal gathering, and to the assembly of the first-born who
are enrolled in heaven, and to a judge who is God of all,
and to the spirits of just men made perfect, and to Jesus, the
mediator of a new covenant, and to the sprinkled blood
that speaks more graciously than the blood of Abel.

Short Response

By your blood
you have ransomed us, Lord.

V. Men of every tribe and tongue and people and nation.

R. You have ransomed us, Lord.

V. Glory be to the Father, and to the Son, and to the Holy Spirit.

By your blood
you have ransomed us, Lord.

Song of the Virgin Mary

Ant. The Lord your God is in your midst;
    he renews you in his love.

Prayers

Let us pray to God from whom comes every perfect gift, and say:

R. Lord, hear my prayer.

Father and Lord of all, who sent your Son into this world, so that your Name might be glorified in every place,
—strengthen your Church to bear witness to you among all nations. (*R.*)

O God, may we humbly receive the teaching of your apostles;
—may we conform our lives to the truths of our faith. (*R.*)

O God, who love the righteous,
—do justice for those who suffer unjustly. (*R.*)

O God, set prisoners free, open the eyes of the blind;
—lift up all who are bowed down, and watch over those who travel. (*R.*)

O God, through your Son, bring to a joyful resurrection
—those who have fallen asleep in your peace. (*R.*)
Our Father . . .

Concluding prayer of the Sunday

May the Lord bless us,

may he keep us from all evil
and lead us to life everlasting.
Amen.

Let us bless the Lord.
R. Thanks be to God.

Monday IV

OFFICE OF READINGS

O God, come to my assistance.
Lord, make haste to help me.
Glory be to the Father, and to the Son, and to the Holy
Spirit.
As it was in the beginning, is now, and ever shall be, world
without end. Amen. Alleluia!

Or, if used as first prayer of the day: O Lord, open my lips . . .

Hymn   1 Cor 13:4–10, 12–13

Love is patient and kind:†
love is not jealous or boastful;
it is not arrogant or rude.

R. Faith, hope and love abide, but the greatest of these is
love.

Love does not insist on its own way,
it is not irritable or resentful;
it does not rejoice at wrong,
but rejoices in the right. (*R.*)

Love bears all things,
believes all things,
hopes all things,
endures all things. (*R.*)

Love never ends;†
as for prophecies,
they will pass away;
as for tongues,
they will cease;
as for knowledge,
it will pass away. (*R.*)

For our knowledge is imperfect
and our prophecy is imperfect;

but when the perfect comes,
the imperfect will pass away. (*R.*)

Now I know in part;
then I shall understand fully,
even as I have been fully understood.
So faith, hope, love abide, these three,
but the greatest of these is love. (*R.*)

Psalmody

Psalm 72   **Why do the wicked prosper?**

Blessed is he who takes no offence at me (Matthew 11:6)

I

Ant. God is good to Israel,
  to those who are pure of heart.

How good God is to Israel,
to those who are pure of heart.
Yet my feet came close to stumbling,
my steps had almost slipped
for I was filled with envy of the proud
when I saw how the wicked prosper.

For them there are no pains;
their bodies are sound and sleek.
They have no share in men's sorrows;
they are not stricken like others.

So they wear their pride like a necklace,
they clothe themselves with violence.
Their hearts overflow with malice,
their minds seethe with plots.

They scoff; they speak with malice;
from on high they plan oppression.
They have set their mouths in the heavens
and their tongues dictate to the earth.

So the people turn to follow them
and drink in all their words.

They say: 'How can God know?
Does the Most High take any notice?'
Look at them, such are the wicked,
but untroubled, they grow in wealth.

Ant. God is good to Israel,
   to those who are pure of heart.

II

Ant. Your laughter will give way to tears,
   your joy to mourning.

How useless to keep my heart pure
and wash my hands in innocence,
when I was stricken all day long,
suffered punishment day after day.
Then I said, 'If I should speak like that,
I should betray the race of your sons.'

I strove to fathom this problem,
too hard for my mind to understand,
until I pierced the mysteries of God
and understood what becomes of the wicked.

How slippery the paths on which you set them;
you make them slide to destruction.
How suddenly they come to their ruin,
wiped out, destroyed by terrors.
Like a dream one wakes from, O Lord,
when you wake you dismiss them as phantoms.

Ant. Your laughter will give way to tears,
   your joy to mourning.

III

Ant. To be near God is my happiness.

And so when my heart grew embittered
and when I was cut to the quick,
I was stupid and did not understand,
no better than a beast in your sight.

404

Yet I was always in your presence;
you were holding me by my right hand.
You will guide me by your counsel
and so you will lead me to glory.

What else have I in heaven but you?
Apart from you I want nothing on earth.
My body and my heart faint for joy;
God is my possession for ever.

All those who abandon you shall perish;
you will destroy all those who are faithless.
To be near God is my happiness.
I have made the Lord God my refuge.
I will tell of all your works
at the gates of the city of Zion.

Ant. To be near God is my happiness.

V. It is your face, O Lord, that I seek.
R. I will do your will.

Readings

Prayer of the day

Or alternative prayer

MORNING PRAYER

O Lord, open my lips.
And my mouth shall declare your praise.
Glory be to the Father, and to the Son, and to the Holy
Spirit.
As it was in the beginning, is now, and ever shall be, world
without end. Amen. Alleluia!

Psalm 94

Refrain: Let us go to meet the Lord;
   let us greet him with the sound of music.

Or, if not used as first prayer of the day: O God, come to my assistance . . .

Hymn

This day God gives me
Strength of high heaven,
Sun and moon shining,
Flame in my hearth,
Flashing of lightning,
Wind in its swiftness,
Deeps of the ocean,
Firmness of earth.

This day God sends me
Strength as my steersman,
Might to uphold me,
Wisdom as guide.
Your eyes are watchful,
Your ears are listening,
Your lips are speaking,
Friend at my side.

God's way is my way,
God's shield is round me,
God's host defends me,
Saving from ill.
Angels of heaven,
Drive from me always
All that would harm me,
Stand by me still.

Rising I thank you,
Mighty and strong One,
King of creation,
Giver of rest,
Firmly confessing
Threeness of Persons,
Oneness of Godhead,
Trinity blest.

Psalmody

Psalm 89 **The Eternal, man's resting-place in this short life**

*With the Lord one day is as a thousand years and a thousand
years as one day* (2 Pet 3:8)

Ant. In the morning, fill us with your love;
we shall exult and rejoice all our days.

O Lord, you have been our refuge
from one generation to the next.
Before the mountains were born†
or the earth or the world brought forth,
you are God, without beginning or end.

You turn men back into dust and say:
'Go back, sons of men.'
To your eyes a thousand years are like yesterday, come and
gone,
no more than a watch in the night.

You sweep men away like a dream,
like grass which springs up in the morning.
In the morning it springs up and flowers:
by evening it withers and fades.

So we are destroyed in your anger
struck with terror in your fury.
Our guilt lies open before you;
our secrets in the light of your face.

All our days pass away in your anger.
Our life is over like a sigh.
Our span is seventy years
or eighty for those who are strong.

And most of these are emptiness and pain.
They pass swiftly and we are gone.
Who understands the power of your anger
and fears the strength of your fury?

Make us know the shortness of our life
that we may gain wisdom of heart.
Lord, relent! Is your anger for ever?
Show pity to your servants.

In the morning, fill us with your love;
we shall exult and rejoice all our days.
Give us joy to balance our affliction
for the years when we knew misfortune.

Show forth your work to your servants;
let your glory shine on their children.
Let the favour of the Lord be upon us:†
give success to the work of our hands;
give success to the work of our hands.

Ant. In the morning, fill us with your love;
we shall exult and rejoice all our days.

Is 42:10–16   **A new song to the Lord in his triumph**

Be of good cheer, I have overcome the world (John 16:33)

Ant. Praise the Lord, you peoples of the earth.

R. Sing to the Lord a new song,
his praise to the end of the earth!

Let the sea roar and all that fills it,
the coastlands and their inhabitants;
let the desert and its cities lift up their voice,
the villages that Kedar inhabits. (*R.*)

Let the inhabitants of Sela sing for joy,
let them shout from the top of the mountains.
Let them give glory to the Lord,
and declare his praise in the coastlands. (*R*).

The Lord goes forth like a mighty man,
like a man of war he stirs up his fury;
he cries out, he shouts aloud,
he shows himself mighty against his foes. (*R.*)

For a long time I have held my peace,
I have kept still and restrained myself;
now I will cry out like a woman in travail,
I will gasp and pant. (*R.*)

I will lay waste mountains and hills,
and dry up all their herbage;
I will turn the rivers into islands,
and dry up the pools. (*R.*)

And I will lead the blind
in a way that they know not;
in paths that they have not known
I will guide them. (*R.*)

I will turn the darkness before them into light,
the rough places into level ground.
These are the things I will do,
and I will not forsake them. (*R.*)

Ant. Praise the Lord, you peoples of the earth.

Psalm 145   **Praise of God's fidelity**

> *Go out quickly to the streets and lanes . . . and bring in the
> poor and maimed and blind and lame* (Luke 14:21)

Ant. The Lord will reign for ever, alleluia!

My soul, give praise to the Lord;†
I will praise the Lord all my days,
make music to my God while I live.

Put no trust in princes,
in mortal men in whom there is no help.
Take their breath, they return to clay
and their plans that day come to nothing.

He is happy who is helped by Jacob's God,
whose hope is in the Lord his God,
who alone made heaven and earth,
the seas and all they contain.

It is he who keeps faith for ever,
who is just to those who are oppressed.
It is he who gives bread to the hungry,
the Lord, who sets prisoners free,

the Lord who gives sight to the blind,
who raises up those who are bowed down,
the Lord, who protects the stranger
and upholds the widow and orphan.

It is the Lord who loves the just
but thwarts the path of the wicked.
The Lord will reign for ever,
Zion's God, from age to age.

Ant. The Lord will reign for ever, alleluia!

Word of God
Jud 8:25–27

Let us give thanks to the Lord our God, who is putting us
to the test as he did our forefathers. Remember what he
did with Abraham, and how he tested Isaac, and what
happened to Jacob in Mesopotamia in Syria, while he was
keeping the sheep of Laban, his mother's brother. For he
has not tried us with fire, as he did them, to search their
hearts, nor has he taken revenge upon us; but the Lord
scourges those who draw near to him, in order to admonish
them.

Short Response
Your deeds, O Lord, have made me glad;
for the work of your hands I shout with joy.
V. O Lord, how deep are your designs!
R. For the work of your hands I shout with joy.
V. Glory be to the Father, and to the Son, and to the Holy
Spirit.
Your deeds, O Lord, have made me glad;
for the work of your hands I shout with joy.

Song of Zechariah

Ant. Zechariah prophesied, saying:
Blessed be the Lord, the God of Israel!

Prayers

Let us pray to God who hears and saves those who hope in him:

R. We praise you, we hope in you, O Lord.

We thank you, O God, who are rich in mercy
—for the great love with which you have loved us. (*R.*)

O God, who are ceaselessly at work throughout the world,
—make all things new by the power of your Holy Spirit. (*R.*)

O God, open our eyes and the eyes of our fellow-men,
—that we may see your wonderful works today. (*R.*)

O God, who have called us to your service,
—make us, we pray, worthy stewards of your wondrous grace in our service of our fellow-men. (*R.*)

Other prayers may be added

Our Father . . .

Concluding prayer

O God who gave the earth to men that they might keep and cultivate it, and who made the sun to shine for their benefit, grant us the light of your grace, so that during this day we may faithfully work for your glory and the good of our fellow-men. We make our prayer through our Lord.

May the Lord bless us,
may he keep us from all evil
and lead us to life everlasting.
Amen.

Let us bless the Lord.
R. Thanks be to God.

MIDDAY PRAYER

O God, come to my assistance . . .
Glory be . . .

Hymn

Mighty ruler, faithful God,
who arrange the successive changes in nature,
giving bright light to the morning sun
and burning heat at noon.

Put out the flames of strife
and take away the heat of passion;
grant us health of body
and true peace of soul.

Grant this, most loving Father,
and you, the only Son, equal to the Father,
and with the Spirit, the Paraclete,
reigning through the ages. Amen.

Psalmody

Psalm 118:129–136

Ant. I called, and the Lord answered me.

Your will is wonderful indeed;
therefore I obey it.
The unfolding of your word gives light
and teaches the simple.

I open my mouth and I sigh
as I yearn for your commands.
Turn and show me your mercy;
show justice to your friends.

Let my steps be guided by your promise;
let no evil rule me.
Redeem me from man's oppression
and I will keep your precepts.

Let your face shine on your servant
and teach me your decrees.
Tears stream from my eyes
because your law is disobeyed.

Psalm 81   **Judgment on corrupt authority**

Do not pronounce judgment before the time, before the Lord comes (1 Cor 4:5)

God stands in the divine assembly.
In the midst of the gods he gives judgment.

'How long will you judge unjustly
and favour the cause of the wicked?
Do justice for the weak and the orphan,
defend the afflicted and the needy.
Rescue the weak and the poor;
set them free from the hand of the wicked.

Unperceiving, they grope in the darkness
and the order of the world is shaken.
I have said to you: 'You are gods
and all of you, sons of the Most High.'
And yet, you shall die like men,
you shall fall like any of the princes.'

Arise, O God, judge the earth,
for you rule all the nations.

Psalm 119   **Among treacherous strangers: a pilgrimage song**

Behold, we are going up to Jerusalem, and everything that is written of the Son of man by the prophets will be accomplished (Luke 18:31)

To the Lord in the hour of my distress
I call and he answers me.
'O Lord, save my soul from lying lips,
from the tongue of the deceitful.'

What shall he pay you in return,
O treacherous tongue?

The warrior's arrows sharpened
and coals, red-hot, blazing.

Alas, that I abide a stranger in Meshech,
dwell among the tents of Kedar!

Long enough have I been dwelling
with those who hate peace.
I am for peace, but when I speak,
they are for fighting.

Ant. I called, and the Lord answered me.

Word of God   Ez 20:5
Thus says the Lord God: On the day when I chose Israel,
I swore to the seed of the house of Jacob, making myself
known to them in the land of Egypt, I swore to them, saying,
I am the Lord your God.

V. Sons of Israel, trust in the Lord;
R. He is their help and their shield.

Prayer
Eternal God, Master of the vintage and of the harvest, who
give us the work we have to do and our just wages, help us
to bear the burden of each day without complaining of any
hardships you may send. Through Christ.

Let us bless the Lord.
R. Thanks be to God.

EVENING PRAYER

O God, come to my assistance.
Lord, make haste to help me.
Glory be to the Father, and to the Son, and to the Holy
Spirit.
As it was in the beginning, is now, and ever shall be, world
without end. Amen. Alleluia!

Hymn

Day is done, but Love unfailing
Dwells ever here;
Shadows fall, but hope, prevailing,
Calms every fear.
Loving Father, none forsaking,
Take our hearts, of Love's own making,
Watch our sleeping, guard our waking,
Be always near!

Dark descends, but Light unending
Shines through our night;
You are with us, ever lending
New strength to sight;
One in love, your truth confessing,
One in hope of heaven's blessing,
May we see, in love's possessing,
Love's endless light!

Eyes will close, but you, unsleeping,
Watch by our side;
Death may come: in Love's safe keeping
Still we abide.
God of love, all evil quelling,
Sin forgiving, fear dispelling,
Stay with us, our hearts indwelling,
This eventide!

Psalmody

Psalm 135 **Praise of God for the marvels of creation and redemption**

If you knew the gift of God (John 4:10)

I

Ant. O give thanks to the Lord,
   for his great love is without end.

O give thanks to the Lord for he is good,
for his great love is without end.
Give thanks to the God of gods,

415

for his great love is without end.
Give thanks to the Lord of lords,
for his great love is without end;

who alone has wrought marvellous works,
for his great love is without end;
whose wisdom it was made the skies,
for his great love is without end;
who fixed the earth firmly on the seas,
for his great love is without end.

It was he who made the great lights,
for his great love is without end,
the sun to rule in the day,
for his great love is without end,
the moon and stars in the night,
for his great love is without end.

II

The first-born of the Egyptians he smote,
for his great love is without end.
He brought Israel out from their midst,
for his great love is without end;
arm outstretched, with power in his hand,
for his great love is without end.

He divided the Red Sea in two,
for his great love is without end;
he made Israel pass through the midst,
for his great love is without end;
he flung Pharaoh and his force in the sea,
for his great love is without end.

Through the desert his people he led,
for his great love is without end.
Nations in their greatness he struck,
for his great love is without end.
Kings in their splendour he slew,
for his great love is without end . . .

He let Israel inherit their land,
for his great love is without end.
On his servant their land he bestowed,
for his great love is without end.
He remembered us in our distress,
for his great love is without end.

And he snatched us away from our foes,
for his great love is without end.
He gives food to all living things,
for his great love is without end.
To the God of heaven give thanks,
for his great love is without end.

Ant. O give thanks to the Lord,
for his great love is without end.

Eph 1:3–10   Song of thanks for salvation through Christ

Ant. Blessed are those whom Christ has called together into
his kingdom.

Blessed be the God and Father
of our Lord Jesus Christ,
who has blessed us in Christ
with every spiritual blessing in the heavenly places.

R. Blessed are you, God our Father,
who have blessed us in Christ.

He chose us in him
before the foundation of the world,
that we should be holy
and blameless before him. (*R.*)

He destined us in love
to be his sons through Jesus Christ,
according to the purpose of his will,†
to the praise of his glorious grace
which he freely bestowed on us in the Beloved. (*R.*)

In him we have redemption through his blood,
the forgiveness of our trespasses,

417

according to the riches of his grace
which he lavished upon us. (R.)

He has made known to us†
in all wisdom and insight
the mystery of his will,
according to his purpose
which he set forth in Christ. (R.)

His purpose he set forth in Christ
as a plan for the fulness of time,
to unite all things in him,
things in heaven and things on earth. (R.)

Ant. Blessed are those whom Christ has called together into
his kingdom.

Word of God   1 Thess 3:12–13
May the Lord make you increase and abound in love to
one another and to all men, as we do to you, so that he may
establish your hearts unblamable in holiness before our
God and Father, at the coming of our Lord Jesus with all
his saints.

Short Response
Bend my heart to your will;
by your Word, give me life.
V. Keep the promise you have made to your servant.
R. By your Word, give me life.
V. Glory be to the Father, and to the Son, and to the Holy
Spirit.
Bend my heart to your will;
by your Word, give me life.

Song of the Virgin Mary
Ant. My soul glorifies the Lord,
    my spirit rejoices in God, my Saviour.

Prayers
Let us pray to God who never deserts those who hope in
him, saying:

R. Hear and answer us, O Lord our God.

O God the Giver of light, enlighten your Church,
—that she may preach to all men the great mystery of the lovingkindness which was made visible in the flesh of your Son. (R.)

Lord God, protect the priests and ministers of your Church,
—so that while they preach to others, they themselves may remain faithful in your service. (R.)

O God, you made peace for the world through the blood of your Son on the cross.
—We pray you, avert the sin of discord and the scourge of war. (R.)

O God, pour your abundant grace upon married people,
—that they may more perfectly show forth the mystery of your Church. (R.)

Other prayers may be added

Through your great mercy, Lord, grant to all the departed the pardon of their sins;
—may they enjoy a new life in the company of your saints. (R.)

Our Father . . .

Concluding prayer

Stay with us, Lord Jesus, for it is nearly evening. Be our companion on the road, enkindle our hearts and stir up our hope, so that we and all our fellow-men may learn to know you in the scriptures and in the breaking of bread. You live and reign.

May the Lord bless us,
may he keep us from all evil
and lead us to life everlasting.
Amen.

Let us bless the Lord.
R. Thanks be to God.

Tuesday IV

OFFICE OF READINGS

O God, come to my assistance.
Lord, make haste to help me.
Glory be to the Father, and to the Son, and to the Holy
Spirit.
As it was in the beginning, is now, and ever shall be, world
without end. Amen. Alleluia!

Or, if used as first prayer of the day: O Lord, open my lips...

Hymn
Life-giving Word, come down to save your people;
Open our minds to know what you would teach us;
Grow in our hearts, O seed of heaven's harvest;
Be our true wisdom.

Word of the Father, be the word that saves us;
Lamp to our footsteps, scatter all our darkness;
Sword of the spirit, Word of God, protect us;
Be our salvation.

Psalmody

Psalm 101   **Prayer in distress**

God comforts us in all our afflictions (2 Cor 1:4)

I

Ant. O Lord, listen to my prayer:
   do not hide your face from me.

O Lord, listen to my prayer
and let my cry for help reach you.
Do not hide your face from me
in the day of my distress.
Turn your ear towards me
and answer me quickly when I call.

For my days are vanishing like smoke,
my bones burn away like a fire.
My heart is withered like the grass.
I forget to eat my bread.
I cry with all my strength
and my skin clings to my bones.

I have become like a pelican in the wilderness,
like an owl in desolate places.
I lie awake and I moan
like some lonely bird on a roof.
All day long my foes revile me;
those who hate me use my name as a curse.

The bread I eat is ashes;
my drink is mingled with tears.
In your anger, Lord, and your fury
you have lifted me up and thrown me down.
My days are like a passing shadow
and I wither away like the grass.

Ant. O Lord, listen to my prayer:
　do not hide your face from me.

II

Ant. Lord, hear the cry of the poor.

But you, O Lord, will endure for ever
and your name from age to age.
You will arise and have mercy on Zion:†
for this is the time to have mercy;
yes, the time appointed has come,
for your servants love her very stones,
are moved with pity even for her dust.

The nations shall fear the name of the Lord
and all the earth's kings your glory,
when the Lord shall build up Zion again
and appear in all his glory.
Then he will turn to the prayers of the helpless;
he will not despise their prayers.

Let this be written for ages to come
that a people yet unborn may praise the Lord;
for the Lord leaned down from his sanctuary on high.
He looked down from heaven to the earth
that he might hear the groans of the prisoners
and free those condemned to die.

The sons of your servants shall dwell untroubled
and their race shall endure before you
that the name of the Lord may be proclaimed in Zion
and his praise in the heart of Jerusalem,
when peoples and kingdoms are gathered together
to pay their homage to the Lord.

Ant. Lord, hear the cry of the poor.

III

Ant. Lord you founded the earth,
and the heavens are the work of your hands.

He has broken my strength in mid-course;
he has shortened the days of my life.
I say to God: 'Do not take me away before my days are
complete,
you, whose days last from age to age.

Long ago you founded the earth
and the heavens are the work of your hands.
They will perish but you will remain.
They will all wear out like a garment.
You will change them like clothes that are changed.
But you neither change, nor have an end.'

Ant. Lord, you founded the earth,
and the heavens are the work of your hands.

V. Lord, make me know your ways,
R. For to you I lift up my soul.

Readings

Prayer of the day

Or alternative prayer

422

MORNING PRAYER

Introductory verse and psalm

O Lord, open my lips.

And my mouth shall declare your praise.

Glory be to the Father, and to the Son, and to the Holy Spirit.

As it was in the beginning, is now, and ever shall be, world without end. Amen. Alleluia!

Psalm 94

Refrain: Hail the Lord, hail the rock who saves us.

Or, if not used as first prayer of the day: O God, come to my assistance...

Hymn

Come, praise the Lord, the Almighty, the King of all nations!

Tell forth his fame, O ye peoples, with loud acclamations!

His love is sure;

Faithful his word shall endure,

Steadfast through all generations!

Praise to the Father most gracious, the Lord of creation!

Praise to his Son, the Redeemer who wrought our salvation!

O heav'nly Dove,

Praise to thee, fruit of their love.

Giver of all consolation!

Psalmody

Psalm 100   A pattern for rulers

If you love me, you will keep your commandments (John 14:15)

Ant. I will sing to the Lord,

I will walk with blameless heart.

My song is of mercy and justice;

I sing to you, O Lord.

I will walk in the way of perfection.

O when, Lord, will you come?

I will walk with blameless heart
within my house;
I will not set before my eyes
whatever is base.

I will hate the ways of the crooked;
they shall not be my friends.
The false-hearted must keep far away;
the wicked I disown.

The man who slanders his neighbour in secret
I will bring to silence.
The man of proud looks and haughty heart
I will never endure.

I look to the faithful in the land
that they may dwell with me.
He who walks in the way of perfection
shall be my friend.

No man who practises deceit
shall live within my house.
No man who utters lies
shall stand before my eyes.

Morning by morning I will silence
all the wicked in the land,
uprooting from the Lord's city
all who do evil.

Ant. I will sing to the Lord,
   I will walk with blameless heart.

Dan 3:3, 4, 6, 11–18   **Song of Azariah**

   *Repent, therefore, and turn again, that your sins may be
   blotted out (Acts 3:19)*

R. Blessed are you, Lord God of our fathers;
   your name is glorified for ever.

For you are just
in all that you have done to us,

424

and all your works are true and your ways right,
and all your judgments are truth. (*R.*)

For we have sinned
and lawlessly departed from you,
and have sinned in all things
and have not obeyed your commandments. (*R.*)

For your name's sake†
do not give us up utterly,
and do not break your covenant. (*R.*)

Do not withdraw your mercy from us
for the sake of Abraham your beloved
and for the sake of Isaac your servant
and Israel your holy one, to whom you promised
to make their descendants as many as the stars of heaven
and as the sand on the shore of the sea. (*R.*)

For we, O Lord, have become fewer than any nation,†
and are brought low this day in all the world
because of our sins. (*R.*)

And at this time there is no prince, or prophet, or leader,
no burnt offering, or sacrifice, or oblation, or incense,
no place to make an offering before you
or to find mercy. (*R.*)

Yet with a contrite heart and a humble spirit
may we be accepted,
as though it were with burnt offerings of rams and bulls,
and with tens of thousands of fat lambs. (*R.*)

Such may our sacrifice be in your sight this day,
and may we wholly follow you,
for there will be no shame
for those who trust in you. (*R.*)

And now with all our heart
we follow you,
we fear you
and seek your face.

Ant. Blessed are you, Lord God of our fathers;
   your name is glorified for ever.

Psalm 134   Anthology of praise

   You are God's own people, that you may declare the
   wonderful deeds of him who called you out of darkness
   into his marvellous light (1 Pet 2:9)

Ant. Whatever the Lord wills, he does.

Praise the name of the Lord,
praise him, servants of the Lord,
who stand in the house of the Lord
in the courts of the house of our God.

Praise the Lord for the Lord is good.
Sing a psalm to his name for he is loving.
For the Lord has chosen Jacob for himself
and Israel for his own possession.

For I know the Lord is great,
that our Lord is high above all gods.
The Lord does whatever he wills,
in heaven, on earth, in the seas.

He summons clouds from the ends of the earth;†
makes lightning produce the rain;
from his treasuries he sends forth the wind.

The first-born of the Egyptians he smote,
of man and beast alike.
Signs and wonders he worked†
in the midst of your land, O Egypt,
against Pharaoh and all his servants.

Nations in their greatness he struck
and kings in their splendour he slew . . .
He let Israel inherit their land;
on his people their land he bestowed.

426

Lord, your name stands for ever,
unforgotten from age to age:
for the Lord does justice for his people;
the Lord takes pity on his servants . . .

Ant. Whatever the Lord wills, he does.

Word of God   Is 55:1

Ho, every one who thirsts,
come to the waters;
and he who has no money,
come, buy and eat!
Come, buy wine and milk
without money and without price.

Short Response

In you is the source of life
and in your light we see light.
V. O Lord, how precious is your love!
R. In your light we see light.
V. Glory be to the Father, and to the Son, and to the Holy
Spirit.
In you is the source of life
and in your light we see light.

Song of Zechariah

Ant. Lord, save us from the hands of all who hate us.

Prayers

God strengthens our hope in him by granting us the joy
of praising him in these morning hours. So let us pray:

R. For the glory of your name, Lord, hear us.

O God and Father of our Saviour Jesus Christ,
—we thank you for the knowledge and undying life which
you have given us through your Son. (*R.*)

O God, grant us a humble heart,
—that men and women may work for one another in the
love of Christ. (*R.*)

427

Lord, send forth your Spirit into the hearts of your servants,
—that our brotherly love may be sincere and unfeigned. (*R.*)

O God, who commanded man to labour and subdue the earth,
—grant that our work may glorify you and sanctify our brethren. (*R.*)

Other prayers may be added

Our Father . . .

Concluding prayer

Lord, increase our faith, so that our lips may utter that perfect praise which is the gift of heaven. We make our prayer through our Lord.

May the Lord bless us,
may he keep us from all evil
and lead us to life everlasting.
Amen.

Let us bless the Lord.
R. Thanks be to God.

MIDDAY PRAYER

O God, come to my assistance . . .
Glory be . . .

Hymn

Lord God, the strength which daily upholds all creation,
in yourself remaining unchanged
and yet determining in due order
the successive changes of the light of day.

Grant us light in the evening
so that life may not decay at any point of its activity,
but everlasting glory be the immediate reward
of a happy death.

Grant this, most loving Father,
and you, the only Son, equal to the Father

and, with the Spirit, the Paraclete,
reigning through the ages. Amen.

Psalmody

Psalm 118:137–144

Ant. Lord, let my prayer come into your presence.

Lord, you are just indeed;
your decrees are right.
You have imposed your will with justice
and with absolute truth.

I am carried away by anger
for my foes forget your word.
Your promise is tried in the fire,
the delight of your servant.

Although I am weak and despised
I remember your precepts.
Your justice is eternal justice
and your law is truth.

Though anguish and distress have seized me,
I delight in your commands.
The justice of your will is eternal:
if you teach me, I shall live.

Psalm 87   Prayer in desolation

This is your hour, and the power of darkness (Luke 22:53)

I

Lord my God, I call for help by day;
I cry at night before you.
Let my prayer come into your presence.
O turn your ear to my cry.

For my soul is filled with evils;
my life is on the brink of the grave.
I am reckoned as one in the tomb:
I have reached the end of my strength,

429

like one alone among the dead;
like the slain lying in their graves;
like those you remember no more,
cut off, as they are, from your hand.

You have laid me in the depths of the tomb,
in places that are dark, in the depths.
Your anger weighs down upon me:
I am drowned beneath your waves.

You have taken away my friends
and made me hateful in their sight.
Imprisoned, I cannot escape;
my eyes are sunken with grief.

II

I call to you, Lord, all the day long;
to you I stretch out my hands.
Will you work your wonders for the dead?
Will the shades stand and praise you?

Will your love be told in the grave
or your faithfulness among the dead?
Will your wonders be known in the dark
or your justice in the land of oblivion?

As for me, Lord, I call to you for help:
in the morning my prayer comes before you.
Lord, why do you reject me?
Why do you hide your face?

Wretched, close to death from my youth,
I have borne your trials; I am numb.
Your fury has swept down upon me;
your terrors have utterly destroyed me.

They surround me all the day like a flood,
they assail me all together.
Friend and neighbour you have taken away:
my one companion is darkness.

Ant. Lord, let my prayer come into your presence.

Word of God Is 55:10–11

As the rain and the snow come down from heaven, and return not thither but water the earth, making it bring forth and sprout, giving seed to the sower and bread to the eater, so shall my word be that goes forth from my mouth; it shall not return to me empty, but it shall accomplish that which I purpose, and prosper in the thing for which I sent it.

V. Your word is a lamp for my steps
R. And a light for my path.

Prayer

Lord, it was at this time of day that you revealed to Peter your will for the salvation of mankind; mercifully grant that our works may please you, and that we may love you and do your saving will. Through Christ.

Let us bless the Lord.
R. Thanks be to God.

EVENING PRAYER

O God, come to my assistance.
Lord, make haste to help me.
Glory be to the Father, and to the Son, and to the Holy Spirit.
As it was in the beginning, is now, and ever shall be, world without end. Amen. Alleluia!

Hymn John 3:29–31

R. He must increase,
but I must decrease.

He who has the bride is the bridegroom;
the friend of the bridegroom who stands and hears him
rejoices greatly at the bridegroom's voice;
therefore this joy of mine is now full. (*R.*)

He who comes from above is above all;
he who is of the earth belongs to the earth,
and of the earth he speaks;
he who comes from heaven is above all. (*R.*)

Psalmody

Psalm 136   Homesickness in exile

> *While we are at home in the body, we are away from the
> Lord* (2 Cor 5:6)

Ant. Sing to us, they said, one of Zion's songs.

By the rivers of Babylon
there we sat and wept, remembering Zion;
on the poplars that grew there
we hung up our harps.

For it was there that they asked us,
our captors, for songs, our oppressors, for joy.
'Sing to us,' they said,
'one of Zion's songs.'

O how could we sing the song of the Lord
on alien soil?
If I forget you, Jerusalem,
let my right hand wither!

O let my tongue cleave to my mouth
if I remember you not,
if I prize not Jerusalem
above all my joys . . .

Ant. Sing to us, they said, one of Zion's songs.

Psalm 137   Thanksgiving to a faithful God

> *The kings of the earth shall bring their glory into the holy
> city* (Rev 21:24)

Ant. I will bless you, Lord, before the angels.

I thank you, Lord, with all my heart,
you have heard the words of my mouth.

Before the angels I will bless you.
I will adore before your holy temple.

I thank you for your faithfulness and love
which excel all we ever knew of you.
On the day I called, you answered;
you increased the strength of my soul.

All earth's kings shall thank you
when they hear the words of your mouth.
They shall sing of the Lord's ways:
'How great is the glory of the Lord!'

The Lord is high yet he looks on the lowly
and the haughty he knows from afar.
Though I walk in the midst of affliction
you give me life and frustrate my foes.

You stretch out your hand and save me,
your hand will do all things for me.
Your love, O Lord, is eternal,
discard not the works of your hands.

Ant. I will bless you, Lord, before the angels.

Rev 4:11; 5:9, 10, 12   **Song to God the Creator**

R. To the Lamb of God be glory, honour and power!

Worthy are you, our Lord and God
to receive glory and honour and power. (*R*)

For you created all things,
and by your will they existed and were created. (*R.*)

Worthy are you, O Lord,
to take up the scroll and to open its seals. (*R*)

For you were slain,†
and by your blood you ransomed men for God
from every tribe and tongue and people and nation. (*R.*)

You have made us a kingdom and priests to our God,
and we shall reign on earth. (*R*)

433

Worthy is the Lamb who was slain,
to receive power and wealth
and wisdom and might
and honour and glory and blessing. (*R.*)

Word of God   Col 3:16
Let the word of Christ dwell in you richly, as you teach and admonish one another in all wisdom, and as you sing psalms and hymns and spiritual songs with thankfulness in your hearts to God.

Short Response
I will sing for ever
of the love of the Lord.
V. I will bless his name for ever,
   from age to age.
R. I will sing for ever of the love of the Lord.
V. Glory be to the Father, and to the Son, and to the Holy Spirit.
I will sing for ever
of the love of the Lord.

Song of the Virgin Mary
Ant. The Lord looks on his servant in her nothingness;
   the Almighty works marvels for me.

Prayers
Let us pray to Christ who gives strength and power to his people:

R. Hear and grant our prayer, O Lord,
   and we shall ever praise you.

O Christ, you are our strength;
—grant faith and constancy to your faithful, whom you have called to your truth. (*R.*)

According to your mind, O Lord, guide those who rule over us;
—inspire their minds to govern us in peace. (*R.*)

O God, who fed the Hebrews in the desert with manna and satisfied the crowds by the miracle of the five loaves,
—teach us to help, from our own store, those who suffer hunger. (*R.*)

O God, strengthen the weak and the faint-hearted;
—comfort the sick and suffering. (*R.*)

Other prayers may be added

Lord, when you come to be glorified in all who have believed in you,
—grant a blessed life and resurrection to all who have fallen asleep in you. (*R.*)

Our Father . . .

Concluding prayer

As we pray in your presence, Lord, we beg of your mercy the grace to keep ever in our hearts the words we speak with our lips. We make our prayer through our Lord.

May the Lord bless us,
may he keep us from all evil
and lead us to life everlasting.
Amen.

Let us bless the Lord.
R. Thanks be to God.

Wednesday IV

OFFICE OF READINGS

O God, come to my assistance.
Lord, make haste to help me.
Glory be to the Father, and to the Son, and to the Holy
Spirit.
As it was in the beginning, is now, and ever shall be, world
without end. Amen. Alleluia!

Or, if used as the first prayer of the day: O Lord, open my lips...

Hymn

Word of God, come down on earth,
Living rain from heav'n descending;
Touch our hearts and bring to birth
Faith and hope and love unending.
Word almighty, we revere you;
Word made flesh, we long to hear you.

Word eternal, throned on high,
Word that brought to life creation,
Word that came from heav'n to die,
Crucified for our salvation,
Saving Word, the world restoring,
Speak to us, your love outpouring.

Psalmody

Psalm 102   **Praise of God's love**

He visits us like the dawn from on high (Luke 1:78)

I

Ant. Give thanks to the Lord, O my soul,
  and never forget all his blessings.

My soul, give thanks to the Lord,
all my being, bless his holy name.
My soul, give thanks to the Lord
and never forget all his blessings.

It is he who forgives all your guilt,
who heals every one of your ills,
who redeems your life from the grave,
who crowns you with love and compassion,
who fills your life with good things,
renewing your youth like an eagle's.

The Lord does deeds of justice,
gives judgment for all who are oppressed.
He made known his ways to Moses
and his deeds to Israel's sons.

Ant. Give thanks to the Lord, O my soul,
and never forget all his blessings.

II

Ant. As a father has compassion on his sons,
the Lord has pity on those who fear him.

The Lord is compassion and love,
slow to anger and rich in mercy.
His wrath will come to an end;
he will not be angry for ever.
He does not treat us according to our sins
nor repay us according to our faults.

For as the heavens are high above the earth
so strong is his love for those who fear him.
As far as the east is from the west
so far does he remove our sins.

As a father has compassion on his sons,
the Lord has pity on those who fear him;
for he knows of what we are made,
he remembers that we are dust.

As for man, his days are like grass;
he flowers like the flower of the field;
the wind blows and he is gone
and his place never sees him again.

Ant. As a father has compassion on his sons,
the Lord has pity on those who fear him.

III

Ant. My soul, give thanks to the Lord.

But the love of the Lord is everlasting
upon those who hold him in fear;
his justice reaches out to children's children†
when they keep his covenant in truth,
when they keep his will in their mind.

The Lord has set his sway in heaven
and his kingdom is ruling over all.
Give thanks to the Lord, all his angels,†
mighty in power, fulfilling his word,
who heed the voice of his word.

Give thanks to the Lord, all his hosts,
his servants who do his will.
Give thanks to the Lord, all his works,†
in every place where he rules.
My soul, give thanks to the Lord!

Ant. My soul, give thanks to the Lord.

V. Open my eyes,
R. That I may see the wonders of your law.

Readings

Prayer of the day

Or alternative prayer

MORNING PRAYER

Introductory verse and psalm

O Lord, open my lips.
And my mouth shall declare your praise.
Glory be to the Father, and to the Son, and to the Holy Spirit.
As it was in the beginning, is now, and ever shall be, world without end. Amen. Alleluia!

Psalm 94

Refrain: The whole universe is in your hand, O Lord.

Or, if not used as first prayer of the day: O God, come to my assistance...

Hymn

I believe in God, the Father;
I believe in God, his Son;
I believe in God, their Spirit;
Each is God, yet God is one.

I believe what God has spoken
Through his Church, whose word is true;
Boldly she proclaims his Gospel,
Ever old, yet ever new.

All my hope is in God's goodness,
Shown for us by him who died,
Jesus Christ, the world's Redeemer,
Spotless victim crucified.

All my love is Love eternal;
In that Love I love mankind.
Take my heart, O Heart once broken,
Take my soul, my strength, my mind.

Father, I have sinned against you;
Look on me with eyes of love;
Seek your wand'ring sheep, Good Shepherd;
Grant heav'n's peace, O heav'nly Dove.

Bless'd be God, the loving Father;
Bless'd be God, his only Son;
Bless'd be God, all-holy Spirit;
Bless'd be God, for ever one.

Psalmody

Psalm 107   God, the hope of his people

The Son of God was raised above the heavens, and his glory has been preached through all the earth (Arnobius)

Ant. Send forth your light and your truth, O Lord.

439

My heart is ready, O God;
I will sing, sing your praise.
Awake, my soul;†
awake, lyre and harp.
I will awake the dawn.

I will thank you, Lord, among the peoples,
praise you among the nations;
for your love reaches to the heavens
and your truth to the skies.
O God, arise above the heavens;
may your glory shine on earth!

O come and deliver your friends;
help with your right hand and reply.
From his holy place God has made this promise:†
'I will triumph and divide the land of Shechem;
I will measure out the valley of Succoth.

Gilead is mine and Manasseh.†
Ephraim I take for my helmet,
Judah for my commander's staff . . .

But who will lead me to conquer the fortress?
Who will bring me face to face with Edom?
Will you utterly reject us, O God,
and no longer march with our armies?

Give us help against the foe:
for the help of man is vain.
With God we shall do bravely
and he will trample down our foes.'

Ant. Send forth your light and your truth, O Lord.

Is 61:10–62:5　　　　　**Song of joy: the new Jerusalem**

*Christ gave himself up . . . so that he might present the
Church to himself in splendour* (Eph 5:27)

Ant. The Lord has filled me with joy;
he has clothed me with the garment of holiness.

I will greatly rejoice in the Lord,
my soul shall exult in my God;
for he has clothed me with the garments of salvation,
he has covered me with the robe of righteousness,
as a bridegroom decks himself with a garland,
and as a bride adorns herself with her jewels.

For as the earth brings forth its shoots,
and as a garden causes what is sown in it to spring up,
so the Lord God will cause righteousness and praise to
   spring forth
before all the nations.

For Zion's sake I will not keep silent,
and for Jerusalem's sake I will not rest
until her vindication goes forth as brightness,
and her salvation as a burning torch.

The nations shall see your vindication,
and all the kings your glory;
and you shall be called by a new name
which the mouth of the Lord will give.

You shall be a crown of beauty
in the hand of the Lord,
and a royal diadem
in the hand of your God.

You shall no more be termed Forsaken,
and your land shall no more be termed Desolate;
but you shall be called My delight in her,
and your land Married;
for the Lord delights in you,
and your land shall be married.

For as a young man marries a virgin,
so shall your sons marry you,
and as the bridegroom rejoices over the bride,
so shall your God rejoice over you.

Ant. The Lord has filled me with joy;
he has clothed me with the garment of holiness.

Psalm 143   **Appeal of the king for victory and peace**

> *God raised us up with Christ ... that in the coming ages*
> *he might show the immeasurable riches of his grace in*
> *kindness towards us in Christ Jesus* (Eph 2:7)

Ant. A new song I will sing to you, O God.

Blessed be the Lord, my rock†
who trains my arms for battle,
who prepares my hands for war.

He is my love, my fortress;
he is my stronghold, my saviour,
my shield, my place of refuge.
He brings peoples under my rule.

Lord, what is man that you care for him,
mortal man, that you keep him in mind;
man, who is merely a breath
whose life fades like a passing shadow?

Lower your heavens and come down;
touch the mountains; wreathe them in smoke.
Flash your lightnings; rout the foe,
shoot your arrows and put them to flight.

Reach down from heaven and save me;
draw me out from the mighty waters,
from the hands of alien foes†
whose mouths are filled with lies,
whose hands are raised in perjury.

To you, O God, will I sing a new song;
I will play on the ten-stringed lute
to you who give kings their victory,
who set David your servant free ...

Ant. A new song I will sing to you, O God.

442

Word of God Deut 4:39-40

Know this day, and lay it to your heart, that the Lord is God in heaven above and on the earth beneath; there is no other. Therefore you shall keep his statutes and his commandments which I command you this day.

Short Response

I call with all my heart,
Lord, hear me.
V. Give me life by your decrees.
R. Lord, hear me.
V. Glory be to the Father, and to the Son, and to the Holy Spirit.
I call with all my heart,
Lord, hear me.

Song of Zechariah

Ant. Remember your love, O Lord,
remember your promise to our fathers.

Prayers

God has loved us from all eternity. With faith and love, let us say to him:

R. Lord, you are our everlasting help.

Blessed are you, holy Father;
—you have called us out of darkness into your marvellous light. (*R.*)

Lord, you have revealed yourself to men,
—increase our faith in your Word. (*R.*)

Lord, may we live out our lives in your love;
—may all men learn to live in your harmony and peace. (*R.*)

Lord, give us the grace to resist temptation, to bear tribulation with patience,
—to give thanks in prosperity. (*R.*)

Other prayers may be added

Our Father . . .

Concluding prayer

Lord, remember your holy covenant, renewed by the sacrament of the blood of the Lamb, and grant that your people may obtain forgiveness of their sins, while they penetrate ever more deeply the mystery of their redemption. We make our prayer through our Lord.

May the Lord bless us,
may he keep us from all evil
and lead us to life everlasting.
Amen.

Let us bless the Lord.
R. Thanks be to God.

MIDDAY PRAYER

O God, come to my assistance . . .
Glory be . . .

Hymn
Holy Spirit,
one with the Father and the Son,
deign at this hour to come down on us without delay
and pour out your graces over our soul.

Let mouth, tongue, soul, thought and strength
make your praise resound.
Let our love be set aflame by the fire of your love
and its heat in turn enkindle love in our neighbours.

Grant this, most loving Father,
and you the only Son, equal to the Father
and, with the Spirit, the Paraclete,
reigning through the ages. Amen.

Psalmody

Psalm 118:145–152
Ant. You, O Lord, are close.

I call with all my heart; Lord, hear me,
I will keep your statutes.
I call upon you, save me
and I will do your will.

I rise before dawn and cry for help,
I hope in your word.
My eyes watch through the night
to ponder your promise.

In your love hear my voice, O Lord;
give me life by your decrees.
Those who harm me unjustly draw near:
they are far from your law.

But you, O Lord, are close:
your commands are truth.
Long have I known that your will
is established for ever.

Psalm 93   **God, the judge and vindicator**

*The Lord is an avenger in all these sins: he has not called
us for uncleanness, but in holiness* (1 Thess 4:6)

I

O Lord, avenging God,
avenging God, appear!
Judge of the earth, arise,
give the proud what they deserve!

How long, O Lord, shall the wicked,
how long shall the wicked triumph?
They bluster with arrogant speech;
the evil-doers boast to each other.

They crush your people, Lord,
they afflict the ones you have chosen.
They kill the widow and the stranger
and murder the fatherless child.

445

And they say: 'The Lord does not see;
the God of Jacob pays no need.'
Mark this, most senseless of people;
fools, when will you understand?

Can he who made the ear, not hear?
Can he who formed the eye, not see?
Will he who trains nations, not punish?
Will he who teaches men, not have knowledge?
The Lord knows the thoughts of men.
He knows they are no more than a breath.

II

Happy the man whom you teach, O Lord,
whom you train by means of your law:
to him you give peace in evil days
while the pit is being dug for the wicked.

The Lord will not abandon his people
nor forsake those who are his own:
for judgment shall again be just
and all true hearts shall uphold it.

Who will stand up for me against the wicked?
Who will defend me against those who do evil?
If the Lord were not to help me,
I would soon go down into the silence.

When I think: 'I have lost my foothold';
your mercy, Lord, holds me up.
When cares increase in my heart
your consolation calms my soul.

Can judges who do evil be your friends?
They do injustice under cover of law;
they attack the life of the just
and condemn innocent blood.

As for me, the Lord will be a stronghold;
my God will be the rock where I take refuge.
He will repay them for their wickedness,†

destroy them for their evil deeds.
The Lord, our God, will destroy them.

Ant. You, O Lord, are close.

Word of God Col 3:17

Whatever you do, in word or deed, do everything in the
name of the Lord Jesus, giving thanks to God the Father
through him.

V. A thanksgiving sacrifice I make;
R. I will call on the Lord's name.

Prayer

Almighty and merciful God who give us a time of rest in the
middle of the day, look favourably on the work we have
begun, and grant that our completed work may be pleasing
to you. Through Christ.

Let us bless the Lord.
R. Thanks be to God.

EVENING PRAYER

O God, come to my assistance.
Lord, make haste to help me.
Glory be to the Father, and to the Son, and to the Holy
Spirit.
As it was in the beginning, is now, and ever shall be, world
without end. Amen. Alleluia!

Hymn

To God with gladness sing.
Your rock and Saviour bless;
Within his temple bring
Your songs of thankfulness!
O God of might,
To you we sing,
Enthroned as king
On heaven's height!

447

He cradles in his hand
The heights and depths of earth;
He made the sea and land,
He brought the world to birth!
O God most high,
We are your sheep;
On us you keep
Your shepherd's eye!

Your heav'nly Father praise,
Acclaim his only Son,
Your voice in homage raise
To him who makes all one!
O Dove of peace
On us descend
That strife may end
And joy increase.

Psalmody

Psalm 138 The hound of heaven

Who has known the mind of the Lord, or who has been his counsellor? (Rom 11:34)

I

Ant. You search me, Lord, and you know me.

O Lord, you search me and you know me,†
you know my resting and my rising,
you discern my purpose from afar.
You mark when I walk or lie down,
all my ways lie open to you.

Before ever a word is on my tongue
you know it, O Lord, through and through.
Behind and before you besiege me,
your hand ever laid upon me.
Too wonderful for me, this knowledge,
too high, beyond my reach.

O where can I go from your spirit,
or where can I flee from your face?
If I climb the heavens, you are there.
If I lie in the grave, you are there.

If I take the wings of the dawn
and dwell at the sea's furthest end,
even there your hand would lead me,
your right hand would hold me fast.

If I say: 'Let the darkness hide me
and the light around me be night,'
even darkness is not dark for you
and the night is as clear as the day.

Ant. You search me, Lord, and you know me.

II

Ant. Lord, I know the wonders of your creation.

For it was you who created my being,
knit me together in my mother's womb.
I thank you for the wonder of my being,
for the wonders of all your creation.

Already you knew my soul,
my body held no secret from you
when I was being fashioned in secret
and moulded in the depths of the earth.

Your eyes saw all my actions,
they were all of them written in your book;
every one of my days was decreed
before one of them came into being.

To me, how mysterious your thoughts,
the sum of them not to be numbered!
If I count them, they are more than the sand;
to finish, I must be eternal, like you . . .

O search me, God, and know my heart.
O test me and know my thoughts.

See that I follow not the wrong path
and lead me in the path of life eternal.

Ant. Lord, I know the wonders of your creation.

Col 1:12–20   **Song to Christ, the first-born of all creation and first-born from the dead**

Ant. To God be glory for ever and ever!
   All things are from him, through him, and for him. Amen.

Let us give thanks to the Father,
who has qualified us
to share in the inheritance of the saints
in light.

R. Glory to you, the first-born from the dead!

He has delivered us
from the dominion of darkness
and transferred us
to the kingdom of his beloved Son,
in whom we have redemption,
the forgiveness of sins. (*R.*)

He is the image of the invisible God,
the first-born of all creation,
for in him all things were created, in heaven and on earth,
visible and invisible. (*R*).

All things were created
through him and for him.
He is before all things,
and in him all things hold together. (*R.*)

He is the head of the body, the Church;
he is the beginning,
the first-born from the dead,
that in everything he might be pre-eminent. (*R.*)

For in him all the fulness of God was pleased to dwell,
and through him to reconcile to himself all things,
whether on earth or in heaven,
making peace by the blood of his cross. (*R.*)

Ant. To God be glory for ever and ever!
All things are from him, through him, and for him. Amen.

Word of God 1 Pet 4:10–11

As each has received a gift, employ it for one another:
whoever speaks, as one who utters oracles of God; whoever
renders service, as one who renders it by the strength which
God supplies; in order that in everything God may be
glorified through Jesus Christ. To him belong glory and
dominion for ever and ever. Amen.

Short Response
I think of your name in the night time;
I will sing of your law.
V. Remember your word to your servant
   by which you gave me hope.
R. I will sing of your law.
V. Glory be to the Father, and to the Son, and to the Holy
Spirit.
I think of your name in the night time;
I will sing of your law.

Song of the Virgin Mary
Ant. The Almighty works marvels for me.
   Holy his name!

Prayers
Let us pray to God whose love reaches to the heavens,
saying:

R. May all who hope in you, O Lord, rejoice.

Lord, you sent your Son not to judge the world, but to save
it;
—grant that his glorious death may be our salvation. (*R.*)

451

O God, from the beginning you created man and woman:
—may all families live in sincere love. (R.)

O God grant perseverance to those whom you have called
to a life of chastity for the sake of the kingdom of heaven
—may they be faithful in following your Son. (R.)

Other prayers may be added

O God, you sent your Son into the world to save sinners;
—grant to all the dead the forgiveness of their sins. (R.)

Our Father . . .

Concluding prayer

Lord, you fill the hungry with good things. In your mercy,
remember us now and transform our poverty in the
abundance of your riches. We make our prayer through our
Lord.

May the Lord bless us,
may he keep us from all evil
and lead us to life everlasting.
Amen.

Let us bless the Lord.
R. Thanks be to God.

Thursday IV

OFFICE OF READINGS

O God, come to my assistance.
Lord, make haste to help me.
Glory be to the Father, and to the Son, and to the Holy
Spirit.
As it was in the beginning, is now, and ever shall be, world
without end. Amen. Alleluia!

Or, if used as first prayer of the day: O Lord, open my lips...

Hymn

Word that caused blind eyes to see,
Speak and heal our mortal blindness;
Deaf we are: our healer be;
Loose our tongues to tell your kindness.
Be our Word in pity spoken,
Heal the world, by our sin broken.

Word that speaks your Father's love,
One with him beyond all telling,
Word that sends us from above
God the Spirit, with us dwelling,
Word of truth, to all truth lead us,
Word of life, with one Bread feed us.

Psalmody

Psalm 43   **God's people in time of disaster: a national lament**

*In all these things we are more than conquerors through
him who loved us* (Rom 8:37)

I

Ant. It is your right hand, O Lord,
  that brings victory.

We heard with our own ears, O God,
our fathers have told us the story
of the things you did in their days,
you yourself, in days long ago.

To plant them you uprooted the nations:
to let them spread you laid peoples low.
No sword of their own won the land;
no arm of their own brought them victory.
It was your right hand, your arm
and the light of your face: for you loved them.

It is you, my king, my God,
who granted victories to Jacob.
Through you we beat down our foes;
in your name we trampled our aggressors.

For it was not in my bow that I trusted
nor yet was I saved by my sword:
it was you who saved us from our foes,
it was you who put our foes to shame.
All the day long our boast was in God
and we praised your name without ceasing.

Ant. It is your right hand, O Lord,
  that brings victory.

II

Ant. Do not hide your face far from me.

Yet now you have rejected us, disgraced us:
you no longer go forth with our armies.
You make us retreat from the foe
and our enemies plunder us at will.

You make us like sheep for the slaughter
and scatter us among the nations.
You sell your own people for nothing
and make no profit by the sale.

You make us the taunt of our neighbours,
the mockery and scorn of all who are near.
Among the nations, you make us a byword,
among the peoples a thing of derision.
All the day long my disgrace is before me:
my face is covered with shame

at the voice of the taunter, the scoffer,
at the sight of the foe and avenger.

Ant. Do not hide your face far from me.

III

Ant. Awake, Lord, come to our help.
Do not reject us for ever.

This befell us though we had not forgotten you;
though we had not been false to your covenant,
though we had not withdrawn our hearts;
though our feet had not strayed from your path.
Yet you have crushed us in a place of sorrows
and covered us with the shadow of death.

Had we forgotten the name of our God
or stretched out our hands to another god
would not God have found this out,
he who knows the secrets of the heart?
It is for you that we face death all the day long
and are counted as sheep for the slaughter.

Awake, O Lord, why do you sleep?
Arise, do not reject us for ever!
Why do you hide your face
and forget our oppression and misery?

For we are brought down low to the dust;
our body lies prostrate on the earth.
Stand up and come to our help!
Redeem us because of your love!

Ant. Awake, Lord, come to our help.
Do not reject us for ever.

V. Let your face shine on your servant.
R. Teach me your decrees.

Readings

Prayer of the day

Or alternative prayer.

MORNING PRAYER

Introductory verse and psalm

O Lord, open my lips.

And my mouth shall declare your praise.

Glory be to the Father, and to the Son, and to the Holy Spirit.

As it was in the beginning, is now, and ever shall be, world without end. Amen. Alleluia!

Psalm 94

Refrain: Come, let us worship our Lord and Master.

Or, if not used as first prayer of the day: O God, come to my assistance...

Hymn

We who live in Christ were born in his death:
Baptized in Christ's death, with Christ we lay in the tomb;
As God the Father's power awoke him from death,
So we were raised to walk in newness of life.

One with Christ were we in dying his death:
So one shall we be with Christ in rising again.
Our sinful selves were nailed with Christ to his cross
That, dead to sin, from sin our flesh might be free.

Dead with Christ, we yet shall rise with him too,
For this is our faith, that he who rose from the dead
Will never die; once dead, for ever he lives,
And death has power no more to conquer its King.

Once for all in death Christ died to all sin;
The life that he lives is life lived only to God.
So you like him are dead to all that is sin,
And live to God in Christ, the Saviour, our Lord.

Psalmody

Psalm 142   **Prayer in desolation**

A man is not justified by works of the law, but through faith in Jesus (Gal 2:16)

456

Ant. Lord, turn your ear to my prayer;
   listen to my appeal.

Lord, listen to my prayer:†
turn your ear to my appeal.
You are faithful, you are just; give answer.
Do not call your servant to judgment
for no one is just in your sight.

The enemy pursues my soul;
he has crushed my life to the ground;
he has made me dwell in darkness
like the dead, long forgotten.
Therefore my spirit fails;
my heart is numb within me.

I remember the days that are past:
I ponder all your works.
I muse on what your hand has wrought†
and to you I stretch out my hands.
Like a parched land my soul thirsts for you.

Lord, make haste and give me answer;
for my spirit fails within me.
Do not hide your face
lest I become like those in the grave.

In the morning let me know your love
for I put my trust in you.
Make me know the way I should walk:
to you I lift up my soul.

Rescue me, Lord, from my enemies;
I have fled to you for refuge.
Teach me to do your will
for you, O Lord, are my God.
Let your good spirit guide me
in ways that are level and smooth.

For your name's sake, Lord, save my life;
in your justice save my soul from distress . . .

Ant. Lord, turn your ear to my prayers;
listen to my appeal.

Is 66:10–14   **Song of Isaiah: joy and consolation in the holy city**

The Jerusalem above is free, and she is our mother (Gal 4:26)

Ant. Prosperity shall be extended to you like a river,
O Jerusalem!

Rejoice with Jerusalem, and be glad for her,
all you who love her;
rejoice with her in joy,
all you who mourn over her;

That you may suck and be satisfied
with her consoling breasts;
that you may drink deeply with delight
from the abundance of her glory.

For thus says the Lord:†
Behold, I will extend prosperity to her like a river,
and the wealth of the nations like an overflowing stream;
and you shall suck, you shall be carried upon her hip,
and dandled upon her knees.

As one whom his mother comforts,†
so I will comfort you;
you shall be comforted in Jerusalem.

You shall see, and your heart shall rejoice;
your bones shall flourish like the grass;
and it shall be known†
that the hand of the Lord is with his servants,
and his indignation is against his enemies.

Ant. Prosperity shall be extended to you like a river,
O Jerusalem!

Psalm 146   **Praise to God the giver of life**

The Lamb of God will guide them to springs of living water
(Rev 7:17)

Ant. Praise the Lord, for he is good;
  sing to the Lord.

Praise the Lord for he is good;†
sing to our God for he is loving:
to him our praise is due.

The Lord builds up Jerusalem
and brings back Israel's exiles,
he heals the broken-hearted,
he binds up all their wounds.
He fixes the number of the stars;
he calls each one by its name.

Our Lord is great and almighty;
his wisdom can never be measured.
The Lord raises the lowly;
he humbles the wicked to the dust.
Sing to the Lord, giving thanks;
sing psalms to our God with the harp.

He covers the heavens with clouds;
he prepares the rain for the earth,
making mountains sprout with grass
and with plants to serve man's needs.
He provides the beasts with their food
and young ravens that call upon him.

His delight is not in horses
nor his pleasure in warriors' strength.
The Lord delights in those who revere him,
in those who wait for his love.

Ant. Praise the Lord, for he is good;
  sing to the Lord.

Word of God   Eph 2:10
We are God's workmanship, created in Christ Jesus for
good works, which he prepared beforehand, that we should
walk in them.

Short Response

How many are your works, O Lord!
In wisdom you have made them all.
V. The earth is full of your riches.
R. In wisdom you have made them all.
V. Glory be to the Father, and to the Son, and to the Holy Spirit.
How many are your works, O Lord!
in wisdom you have made them all.

Song of Zechariah

Ant. As for you, little child, prophet of God the Most High, you shall go ahead of the Lord to prepare his ways before him.

Prayers

Let us pray to God who gives salvation to his people; let us say to him:

R. You are our life, O Lord.

Blessed are you, Father of our Lord Jesus Christ, for by your mercy we have been born anew to a living hope,
—through the resurrection of Jesus Christ from the dead. (*R.*)

O God, who created man after your own image and renewed him in Christ,
—we pray you to conform us to the image of your Son. (*R.*)

Our hearts are wounded by envy and hatred;
—fill them, Lord, with the love of the Holy Spirit. (*R.*)

Give work today to all who labour, give food to the hungry and comfort to the sorrowing;
—give grace and salvation to all men. (*R.*)

Other prayers may be added

Our Father . . .

Concluding prayer

Lord, may the knowledge of our salvation be to us an ever living reality, so that delivered from the hands of our

enemies, we may serve you faithfully all the days of our life.
We make our prayer through our Lord.

May the Lord bless us,
may he keep us from all evil
and lead us to life everlasting.
Amen.

Let us bless the Lord.
R. Thanks be to God.

MIDDAY PRAYER

O God, come to my assistance . . .
Glory be . . .

Hymn

Mighty ruler, faithful God,
who arrange the successive changes in nature,
giving bright light to the morning sun
and burning heat at noon.

Put out the flames of strife
and take away the heat of passion;
grant us health of body
and true peace of soul.

Grant this, most loving Father,
and you, the only Son, equal to the Father
and, with the Spirit, the Paraclete,
reigning through the ages. Amen.

Psalmody

Psalm 118:153–160

Ant. May the Lord bless you:
  On Israel, peace!

See my affliction and save me
for I remember your law.
Uphold my cause and defend me;
by your promise, give me life.

461

Salvation is far from the wicked
who are heedless of your statutes.
Numberless, Lord, are your mercies;
with your decrees give me life.

Though my foes and oppressors are countless
I have not swerved from your will.
I look at the faithless with disgust;
they ignore your promise.

See how I love your precepts;
in your mercy give me life.
Your word is founded on truth:
your decrees are eternal.

Psalm 127   **The just man's blessings of home**

Christ loved the Church and gave himself up for her ...
that she might be holy and without blemish (Eph 5:25, 27)

O blessed are those who fear the Lord
and walk in his ways!

By the labour of your hands you shall eat.
You will be happy and prosper;
your wife like a fruitful vine
in the heart of your house;
your children like shoots of the olive,
around your table.

Indeed thus shall be blessed
the man who fears the Lord.
May the Lord bless you from Zion
all the days of your life!
May you see your children's children in a happy Jerusalem!
On Israel, peace!

Psalm 128   **Prayer of a persecuted man**

Five times I have received at the hands of the Jews the
forty lashes less one (2 Cor 11:24)

'They have pressed me hard from my youth,'
this is Israel's song.
'They have pressed me hard from my youth
but could never destroy me.

They ploughed my back like ploughmen,
drawing long furrows.
But the Lord who is just, has destroyed
the yoke of the wicked.'

Let them be shamed and routed,
those who hate Zion!
Let them be like grass on the roof
that withers before it flowers.

With that no reaper fills his arms,
no binder makes his sheaves
and those passing by will not say:†
'On you the Lord's blessing!'
'We bless you in the name of the Lord.'

Ant. May the Lord bless you:
On Israel, peace!

Word of God   Wis 1:1–2

Love righteousness, rulers of the earth,
think of the Lord with uprightness,
and seek him with sincerity of heart;
because he is found by those who do not put him to the test,
and manifests himself to those who do not distrust him.

V. He is close to all who call him,
R. Who call on him from their hearts.

Prayer

Almighty and eternal God in whom there is no darkness, no
obscurity, fill our hearts with the splendour of your light,
so that we who have received your commandments may walk
in safety on your ways. Through Christ.

Let us bless the Lord.
R. Thanks be to God.

463

EVENING PRAYER

O God, come to my assistance.
Lord, make haste to help me.
Glory be to the Father, and to the Son, and to the Holy Spirit.
As it was in the beginning, is now, and ever shall be, world without end. Amen. Alleluia!

Hymn

Bless'd be the Lord our God!
With joy let heaven ring;
Before his presence let all earth
Its songs of homage bring!
His mighty deeds be told;
His majesty be praised;
To God enthroned in heav'nly light,
Let every voice be raised!

All that has life and breath,
Give thanks with heartfelt songs!
To him let all creation sing
To whom all praise belongs!
Acclaim the Father's love,
Who gave us God his Son;
Praise too the Spirit, giv'n by both,
With both for ever one!

Psalmody

Psalm 143   **Appeal of the king for victory and peace**

God raised us up with Christ ... that in the coming ages he might show the immeasurable riches of his grace in kindness towards us in Christ Jesus (Eph 2:7)

Ant. Blessed be the Lord,
   my stronghold, my saviour!

Blessed be the Lord, my rock†
who trains my arms for battle,
who prepares my hands for war.

He is my love, my fortress;
he is my stronghold, my saviour,
my shield, my place of refuge.
He brings peoples under my rule.

Lord, what is man that you care for him,
mortal man, that you keep him in mind;
man, who is merely a breath
whose life fades like a passing shadow?

Lower your heavens and come down;
touch the mountains; wreathe them in smoke.
Flash your lightnings; rout the foe,
shoot your arrows and put them to flight.

Reach down from heaven and save me;
draw me out from the mighty waters,
from the hands of alien foes†
whose mouths are filled with lies,
whose hands are raised in perjury.

Ant. Blessed be the Lord,
   my stronghold, my saviour!

II

Ant. Happy the people whose God is the Lord.

To you, O God, will I sing a new song;
I will play on the ten-stringed lute
to you who give kings their victory,
who set David your servant free.

You set him free from the evil sword;
you rescued him from alien foes
whose mouths were filled with lies,
whose hands were raised in perjury.

Let our sons then flourish like saplings
grown tall and strong from their youth:
our daughters graceful as columns,
adorned as though for a palace.

Let our barns be filled to overflowing
with crops of every kind;
our sheep increasing by thousands,†
myriads of sheep in our fields,
our cattle heavy with young,

no ruined wall, no exile,
no sound of weeping in our streets.
Happy the people with such blessings;
happy the people whose God is the Lord.

Ant. Happy the people whose God is the Lord.

Rev 11:17-18; 12:10-12   Song of God's judgment

Ant. To him be glory and power,
   for ever and ever. Amen.

We give thanks to you, Lord God almighty,
who are and who were,
that you have taken your great power
and begun to reign.

R. We give thanks to you, O Lord our God.

The nations raged,
but your wrath came,
and the time for the dead to be judged,
for rewarding your servants, the prophets and saints,
and those who fear your name,
both small and great. (*R*.)

Now the salvation and the power†
and the kingdom of our God
and the authority of his Christ have come,
for the accuser of our brethren has been thrown down,
who accuses them day and night before our God. (*R*.)

And they have conquered him
by the blood of the Lamb
and by the word of their testimony,
for they loved not their lives even unto death.
Rejoice, then, O heaven
and you that dwell therein! (R.)

Ant. To him be glory and power,
for ever and ever. Amen.

Word of God   Col 1:23
Continue in the faith, stable and steadfast, not shifting from
the hope of the gospel which you heard, which has been
preached to every creature under heaven.

Short Response
I think of your name in the night time;
I will sing of your law.
V. Remember your word to your servant
by which you gave me hope.
R. I will sing of your law.
V. Glory be to the Father, and to the Son, and to the Holy
Spirit.
I think of your name in the night time;
I will sing of your law.

Song of the Virgin Mary
Ant. His mercy is from age to age
on those who fear him.

Prayers
The Lord is the light and joy of all the living. Let us pray:
R. Give us, Lord, light, peace and salvation.

O God, the Father of light, you desire that all men should be
saved and come to know your truth;
—guide the catechumens of your Church, that they may see
your light. (R.)

Mark not our guilt, O Lord,
—for with you is found forgiveness. (R.)

O God, whose will it is that man's mind should seek out the secrets of nature and so rule the earth,
—grant that all branches of science and art may serve your glory and promote the well-being of man. (*R.*)

O God, we beseech you, grant to all religious families the grace they need, so that they may remain faithful in their search for perfection,
—and bear witness to your Name. (*R.*)

Other prayers may be added

Lord, since no one can shut what you open:
—lead out into your light those who sit in darkness and the shadow of death. (*R.*)

Our Father . . .

Concluding prayer

Graciously receive our evening prayer, O Lord, and grant that we may follow in the footsteps of your Son, and bring forth fruit in patience. We make our prayer through our Lord.

May the Lord bless us,
may he keep us from all evil
and lead us to life everlasting.
Amen.

Let us bless the Lord.
R. Thanks be to God.

Friday IV

OFFICE OF READINGS

O God, come to my assistance.
Lord, make haste to help me.
Glory be to the Father, and to the Son, and to the Holy Spirit.
As it was in the beginning, is now, and ever shall be, world without end. Amen. Alleluia!

Or, if used as first prayer of the day: O Lord, open my lips...

Hymn
I am the holy vine,
Which God my Father tends.
Each branch that yields no fruit
My Father cuts away.
Each fruitful branch
He prunes with care
To make it yield
Abundant fruit.

If you abide in me,
I will in you abide.
Each branch to yield its fruit
Must with the vine be one.
So you shall fail
To yield your fruit
If you are not
With me one vine.

I am the fruitful vine,
And you my branches are.
He who abides in me,
I will in him abide.
So shall you yield

Much fruit, but none
If you remain
Apart from me.

Psalmody

A. THROUGHOUT THE YEAR

Psalm 49   **True and false worship of God**

*By grace you have been saved through faith, and this is not
your doing, it is the gift of God* (Eph 2:8)

I

Ant. The Lord summons the heavens and the earth
  to the trial of his people.

The God of gods, the Lord,†
has spoken and summoned the earth,
from the rising of the sun to its setting.

Out of Zion's perfect beauty he shines.
Our God comes, he keeps silence no longer.

Before him fire devours,
around him tempest rages.
He calls on the heavens and the earth
to witness his judgment of his people.

'Summon before me my people
who made covenant with me by sacrifice.'
The heavens proclaim his justice,
for he, God, is the judge.

Ant. The Lord summons the heavens and the earth
  to the trial of his people.

II

Ant. Pay your sacrifice of thanksgiving to God.

'Listen, my people, I will speak;
Israel, I will testify against you,
for I am God your God.
I accuse you, lay the charge before you.

I find no fault with your sacrifices,
your offerings are always before me.
I do not ask more bullocks from your farms,
nor goats from among your herds.

For I own all the beasts of the forest,
beasts in their thousands on my hills.
I know all the birds in the sky,
all that moves in the field belongs to me.

Were I hungry, I would not tell you,
for I own the world and all it holds.
Do you think I eat the flesh of bulls,
or drink the blood of goats?

Pay your sacrifice of thanksgiving to God
and render him your votive offerings.
Call on me in the day of distress.
I will free you and you shall honour me.'

Ant. Pay your sacrifice of thanksgiving to God.

III

Ant. I desire steadfast love and not sacrifice.

But God says to the wicked:†
'But how can you recite my commandments
and take my covenant on your lips,
you who despise my law
and throw my words to the winds,

you who see a thief and go with him;
who throw in your lot with adulterers,
who unbridle your mouth for evil
and whose tongue is plotting crime,

you who sit and malign your brother
and slander your own mother's son.
You do this, and should I keep silence?
Do you think that I am like you?

Mark this, you who never think of God,
lest I seize you and you cannot escape;
a sacrifice of thanksgiving honours me
and I will show God's salvation to the upright.'

Ant. I desire steadfast love and not sacrifice.

B. ADVENT, CHRISTMAS, LENT AND EASTER

Psalm 77　　　　God's patience and man's ingratitude: the lesson of
　　　　　　　　past history

*These things happened to them as a warning, but they were
written down for our instruction* (1 Cor 10:11)

I

Ant. Give ear to the words of the Lord.

Give heed, my people, to my teaching;
turn your ear to the words of my mouth.
I will open my mouth in a parable
and reveal hidden lessons of the past.

The things we have heard and understood,
the things our fathers have told us
we will not hide from their children
but will tell them to the next generation:

the glories of the Lord and his might
and the marvellous deeds he has done,
the witness he gave to Jacob,
the law he established in Israel.

He gave a command to our fathers
to make it known to their children
that the next generation might know it,
the children yet to be born.

They too should arise and tell their sons
that they too should set their hope in God
and never forget God's deeds
but keep every one of his commands:

472

so that they might not be like their fathers,
a defiant and rebellious race,
a race whose heart was fickle,
whose spirit was unfaithful to God.

The sons of Ephraim, armed with the bow,
turned back in the day of battle.
They failed to keep God's covenant
and would not walk according to his law.

They forgot the things he had done,
the marvellous deeds he had shown them.
He did wonders in the sight of their fathers,
in Egypt, in the plains of Zoan.

He divided the sea and led them through
and made the waters stand up like a wall.
By day he led them with a cloud:
by night, with a light of fire.

He split the rocks in the desert.
He gave them plentiful drink as from the deep.
He made streams flow out from the rock
and made waters run down like rivers.

Ant. Give ear to the words of the Lord.

II

Ant. The Lord worked wonders for our fathers.

Yet still they sinned against him;
they defied the Most High in the desert.
In their heart they put God to the test
by demanding the food they craved.

They even spoke against God.†
They said: 'Is it possible for God
to prepare a table in the desert?

It was he who struck the rock,
water flowed and swept down in torrents.
But can he also give us bread?
Can he provide meat for his people?'

When he heard this the Lord was angry.
A fire was kindled against Jacob,
his anger rose against Israel for having no faith in God;
for refusing to trust in his help.

Yet he commanded the clouds above
and opened the gates of heaven.
He rained down manna for their food,
and gave them bread from heaven.

Mere men ate the bread of angels.
He sent them abundance of food:
he made the east wind blow from heaven
and roused the south wind by his might.

He rained food on them like dust,
winged fowl like the sands of the sea.
He let it fall in the midst of their camp
and all around their tents.

So they ate and had their fill;
for he gave them all they craved.

But before they had sated their craving,†
while the food was still in their mouths,
God's anger rose against them.
He slew the strongest among them,
struck down the flower of Israel.

Ant. The Lord worked wonders for our fathers.

III

Ant. He rained down manna for their food
and gave them bread from heaven.

Despite this they went on sinning;
they had no faith in his wonders:
so he ended their days like a breath
and their years in sudden ruin.

When he slew them then they would seek him,
return and seek him in earnest.

They would remember that God was their rock,
God the Most High their redeemer.

But the words they spoke were mere flattery;
they lied to him with their lips.
For their hearts were not truly with him;
they were not faithful to his covenant.

Yet he who is full of compassion
forgave their sin and spared them.
So often he held back his anger
when he might have stirred up his rage.

He remembered they were only men,
a breath that passes never to return.

Ant. He rained down manna for their food
and gave them bread from heaven.

V. I am the Lord your God:
R. Listen, my people, to my law.

Readings

Prayer of the day
Or alternative prayer

MORNING PRAYER

Introductory verse and psalm
O Lord, open my lips.
And my mouth shall declare your praise.
Glory be to the Father, and to the Son, and to the Holy
Spirit.
As it was in the beginning, is now, and ever shall be, world
without end. Amen. Alleluia!

Psalm 94

Refrain: Harden not your hearts today,
but listen to the voice of the Lord.

Or, if not used as first prayer of the day: O God, come to my
assistance...

Hymn Rom 8:28–35, 37

In everything God works for good with those who love him,
who are called according to his purpose.
For those whom he foreknew he also predestined
to be conformed to the image of his Son.

R. You did not spare your own Son, but gave him up for us
all.

Those whom he predestined
he also called;
and those whom he called
he also justified;
and those whom he justified
he also glorified. (*R.*)

What then shall we say?†
If God is for us,
who is against us?
He who did not spare his own Son,†
but gave him up for us all,
will he not also give us all things with him? (*R.*)

It is God who justifies,
who is to condemn?
Is it Christ Jesus, who died,
who was raised from the dead,
who is at the right hand of God,
who intercedes for us? (*R.*)

Who shall separate us
from the love of Christ?
Shall tribulation, or distress, or persecution,
or famine, or nakedness, or peril or sword?
No, in all these things we are more than conquerors
through him who loved us. (*R.*)

Psalmody

Psalm 50 **Prayer of contrition and trust**

Jesus, Son of God and Saviour, have mercy on me, a sinner

Ant. O my God, purify me, and I shall be clean;
   wash my soul, and I shall be whiter than snow.

Have mercy on me, God, in your kindness.
In your compassion blot out my offence.
O wash me more and more from my guilt
and cleanse me from my sin.

My offences truly I know them;
my sin is always before me.
Against you, you alone, have I sinned;
what is evil in your sight I have done.

That you may be justified when you give sentence
and be without reproach when you judge,
O see, in guilt I was born,
a sinner was I conceived.

Indeed you love truth in the heart;
then in the secret of my heart teach me wisdom.
O purify me, then I shall be clean;
O wash me, I shall be whiter than snow.

Make me hear rejoicing and gladness,
that the bones you have crushed may thrill.
From my sins turn away your face
and blot out all my guilt.

A pure heart create for me, O God,
put a steadfast spirit within me.
Do not cast me away from your presence,
nor deprive me of your holy spirit.

Give me again the joy of your help;
with a spirit of fervour sustain me,
that I may teach transgressors your ways
and sinners may return to you.

O rescue me, God, my helper,
and my tongue shall ring out your goodness.
O Lord, open my lips
and my mouth shall declare your praise.

For in sacrifice you take no delight,
burnt offering from me you would refuse,
my sacrifice, a contrite spirit.
A humbled, contrite heart you will not spurn.

In your goodness, show favour to Zion:
rebuild the walls of Jerusalem.
Then you will be pleased with lawful sacrifice,†
burnt offerings wholly consumed,
then you will be offered young bulls on your altar.

Ant. O my God, purify me, and I shall be clean;
   wash my soul, and I shall be whiter than snow.

Tob 13:8–11, 13–15   Song of thanks for the deliverance of the people
   We are the temple of the living God (2 Cor 6:16)

Ant. Our sons are a gift from the Lord.

Let all men speak,
and give him thanks in Jerusalem.
O Jerusalem, the holy city,†
he will afflict you for the deeds of your sons,
but again he will show mercy to the sons of the righteous.

Give thanks worthily to the Lord,†
and praise the King of the ages,
that his tent may be raised for you again with joy.

May he cheer those within you who are captives,†
and love those within you who are distressed,
to all generations for ever.

Many nations will come from afar
to the name of the Lord God,
bearing gifts in their hands,
gifts for the king of heaven.
Generations of generations
will give you joyful praise.

Rejoice and be glad
for the sons of the righteous,

for they will be gathered together,
and will praise the Lord of the righteous.

How blessed are those who love you!
They will rejoice in your peace.
Blessed are those who grieved
over all your afflictions,
for they will rejoice for you upon seeing all your glory,
and they will be made glad for ever.

Ant. Our sons are a gift from the Lord.

Psalm 147   **Hymn to a renewed Jerusalem**

Come, and I will show you the bride of the Lamb (Rev 21:9)

Ant. O praise the Lord, Jerusalem!

O praise the Lord, Jerusalem!
Zion, praise your God!

He has strengthened the bars of your gates,
he has blessed the children within you.
He established peace on your borders,
he feeds you with finest wheat.

He sends out his word to the earth
and swiftly runs his command.
He showers down snow white as wool,
he scatters hoar-frost like ashes.

He hurls down hailstones like crumbs.
The waters are frozen at his touch;
he sends forth his word and it melts them:
at the breath of his mouth the waters flow.

He makes his word known to Jacob,
to Israel his laws and decrees.
He has not dealt thus with other nations;
he has not taught them his decrees.

Ant. O praise the Lord, Jerusalem!

Word of God Gal 2:20

I have been crucified with Christ; it is no longer I who live, but Christ who lives in me; and the life I now live in the flesh I live by faith in the Son of God, who loved me and gave himself for me.

Short Response

I will sing of your strength;
each morning I will acclaim your love.

V. You, O God, are my stronghold,
   the God who shows me love.

R. Each morning I will acclaim your love.

V. Glory be to the Father, and to the Son, and to the Holy Spirit.

I will sing of your strength;
each morning I will acclaim your love.

Song of Zechariah

Ant. Light of Christ, rescue us from our night.

Prayers

God takes care of all those whom he has created and redeemed through his Son. Let us pray:

R. Show forth your might, Lord, on our behalf.

God of mercy, guide our steps on the way of holiness;
—may our thoughts always dwell on what is pure, just and honourable. (*R.*)

For your name's sake, do not abandon us;
do not reject your covenant, O God. (*R.*)

Lord, accept our contrite and humble hearts:
—those who trust in you shall not be disappointed. (*R.*)

O God who have called us in Christ to a royal priesthood,
—grant that we may offer you spiritual sacrifices, and proclaim your power. (*R.*)

Other prayers may be added

Our Father . . .

Concluding prayer

Grant us abundant grace, O Lord, and help us to fulfil your commandments, so that we may be comforted in this life and attain the joys of the life to come. We make our prayer through our Lord.

or

Enlighten the hearts of your faithful, Lord. Be our ever-present shield and help. We make our prayer through our Lord.

May the Lord bless us,
may he keep us from all evil
and lead us to life everlasting.
Amen.

Let us bless the Lord.
R. Thanks be to God.

MIDDAY PRAYER

O God, come to my assistance . . .
Glory be . . .

Hymn
Lord God, the strength which daily upholds all creation,
in yourself remaining unchanged
and yet determining in due order
the successive changes of the light of day.

Grant us light in the evening
so that life may not decay at any point of its activity,
but everlasting glory be the immediate reward
of a happy death.

Grant this, most loving Father,
and you, the only Son, equal to the Father
and, with the Spirit, the Paraclete,
reigning through the ages. Amen.

481

Psalmody

Psalm 118:161–168

Ant. Do not abandon me, O God my help.

Though princes oppress me without cause
I stand in awe of your word.
I take delight in your promise
like one who finds a treasure.

Lies I hate and detest
but your law is my love.
Seven times a day I praise you
for your just decrees.

The lovers of your law have great peace;
they never stumble.
I await your saving help, O Lord,
I fulfil your commands.

My soul obeys your will
and loves it dearly.
I obey your precepts and your will;
all that I do is before you.

Psalm 132   **The blessings of unity**

*The company of those who believed were of one heart and
soul* (Acts 4:32)

How good and how pleasant it is,
brothers dwelling in unity!

It is like precious oil upon the head
running down upon the beard,
running down upon Aaron's beard
upon the collar of his robes.

It is like the dew of Hermon which falls
on the heights of Zion.
For there the Lord gives his blessing,
life for ever.

Psalm 139   Complaint against the cunning and violence of the enemy

The Son of man is betrayed into the hands of sinners
(Matthew 26:45)

Rescue me, Lord, from evil men;
from the violent keep me safe,
from those who plan evil in their hearts
and stir up strife every day;
who sharpen their tongue like an adder's,
with the poison of viper on their lips.

Lord, guard me from the hands of the wicked;
from the violent keep me safe;
they plan to make me stumble.
The proud have hidden a trap,
have spread out lines in a net,
set snares across my path.

I have said to the Lord: 'You are my God.'
Lord, hear the cry of my appeal!
Lord my God, my mighty help,
you shield my head in the battle.
Do not grant the wicked their desire
nor let their plots succeed . . .

I know that the Lord will avenge the poor,
that he will do justice for the needy.
Truly the just will praise your name:
the upright shall live in your presence.

Ant. Do not abandon me, O God my help.

Word of God   1 John 3:14

We know that we have passed out of death into life,
because we love the brethren.

V. The Lord is at my side as my helper.
R. I shall look down on my foes.

Prayer

Lord Jesus Christ, on a day plunged into darkness, you
who were innocent were raised upon a cross for our re-

demption; grant us the light we need to reach eternal life.
Who live and reign.

Let us bless the Lord.
R. Thanks be to God.

EVENING PRAYER

O God, come to my assistance.
Lord, make haste to help me.
Glory be to the Father, and to the Son, and to the Holy
Spirit.
As it was in the beginning, is now, and ever shall be, world
without end. Amen. Alleluia!

Hymn   1 Pet 2:21–24

R. By his wounds you have been healed.

Christ suffered for you,
leaving you an example that you should follow in his steps.
  (R.)

He committed no sin;
no guile was found on his lips.
When he was reviled,
he did not revile in return. (R.)

When he suffered,
he did not threaten,
but he trusted to him
who judges justly. (R.)

He himself bore our sins in his body on the tree,†
that we might die to sin and live to righteousness.
By his wounds you have been healed.
For you were straying like sheep,
but have now returned to the Shepherd and Guardian
  of your souls. (R.)

Psalmody

Psalm 144

Praise of God's grandeur

God raised us up .... that in the coming ages he might show the immeasurable riches of his grace in kindness towards us in Christ Jesus (Eph 2:7)

I

Ant. I give you glory, O God my King,
  I bless your name for ever.

I will give you glory, O God my King.
I will bless your name for ever.

I will bless you day after day
and praise your name for ever.
The Lord is great, highly to be praised,
his greatness cannot be measured.

Age to age shall proclaim your works,
shall declare your mighty deeds,
shall speak of your splendour and glory,
tell the tale of your wonderful works.

They will speak of your terrible deeds,
recount your greatness and might.
They will recall your abundant goodness;
age to age shall ring out your justice.

The Lord is kind and full of compassion,
slow to anger, abounding in love.
How good is the Lord to all,
compassionate to all his creatures.

All your creatures shall thank you, O Lord,
and your friends shall repeat their blessing.
They shall speak of the glory of your reign
and declare your might, O God,

to make known to men your mighty deeds
and the glorious splendour of your reign.
Yours is an everlasting kingdom;
your rule lasts from age to age.

Ant. I give you glory, O God my King,
  I bless your name for ever.

II

Ant. The eyes of all creatures look to you, O Lord.

The Lord is faithful in all his words
and loving in all his deeds.
The Lord supports all who fall
and raises all who are bowed down.

The eyes of all creatures look to you
and you give them their food in due time.
You open wide your hand,
grant the desires of all who live.

The Lord is just in all his ways
and loving in all his deeds.
He is close to all who call him,
who call on him from their hearts.

He grants the desires of those who fear him,
he hears their cry and he saves them.
The Lord protects all who love him;
but the wicked he will utterly destroy.

Let me speak the praise of the Lord,†
let all mankind bless his holy name
for ever, for ages unending.

Ant. The eyes of all creatures look to you, O Lord.

Rev. 15: 3–4   **Song of Moses and the Lamb**

Ant. Glory be to the Lamb who was slain!
  he is King for all eternity.

Great and wonderful are your deeds,
O Lord God, the Almighty!
Just and true are your ways,
O King of the ages!

R. Great and wonderful are your deeds, O Lord!

Who shall not fear and glorify your name, O Lord?
For you alone are holy. (*R.*)

All nations shall come and worship you,
for your judgments have been revealed. (*R.*)

Ant. Glory to the Lamb who was slain!
   He is King for all eternity.

Word of God
Rom 8:1-2

There is now no condemnation for those who are in Christ
Jesus. For the law of the Spirit of life in Christ Jesus has set
me free from the law of sin and death.

Short Response
Heal my soul, O Lord,
for I have sinned against you.
V. I said: Lord, have mercy on me,
R. For I have sinned against you.
V. Glory be to the Father, and to the Son, and to the Holy
Spirit.
Heal my soul, O Lord,
for I have sinned against you.

Song of the Virgin Mary
Ant. He casts down the mighty,
   the persecutors of his people.

Prayers
Let us call upon Christ our Saviour:

R. Lord, have mercy!

Christ, comforter of the poor in spirit, you know our
weakness; you know we are prone to fall;
—May our strength be in your forgiveness. (*R.*)

May our human nature, so apt to displease you,
—always be restored by your forgiveness. (*R.*)

Lord, who are offended by sin and appeased by repentance,
—turn away the scourge of your anger which our sins
deserve. (*R.*)

487

You forgave the sins of the contrite woman and placed the lost sheep upon your shoulders;
—do not deprive us of your mercy. (*R.*)

Other prayers may be added

Open the gates of heaven to all those who, while they lived, hoped in you;
—for their sake you did not hesitate to endure the cross. (*R.*)

Our Father . . .

Concluding prayer

Almighty and merciful God who willed that Christ should suffer to save the world, grant that your people may take fire from your love, and offer themselves to you as a living sacrifice.
We make our prayer through our Lord.

May the Lord bless us,
may he keep us from all evil
and lead us to life everlasting.
Amen.

Let us bless the Lord.
R. Thanks be to God.

Saturday IV

OFFICE OF READINGS

O God, come to my assistance.
Lord, make haste to help me.
Glory be to the Father, and to the Son, and to the Holy Spirit.
As it was in the beginning, is now, and ever shall be, world without end. Amen. Alleluia!

Or, if used as the first prayer of the day: O Lord, open my lips...

Hymn

How deep the riches of our God,
His wisdom how sublime;
How high his judgments soar above
All judgment of mankind!

What mind has read the mind of God,
Or giv'n him counsel sure?
Who from his riches gave to God
What was not first received?

From God all things created flow;
All things through him exist;
To him for judgment all returns,
To whom all praise is due!

To God the Father, fount of grace,
Through his beloved Son
In oneness with the Holy Ghost
Be glory evermore!

Psalmody

A. THROUGHOUT THE YEAR

Psalm 54   Prayer of a man betrayed by his friend

He began to be greatly distressed and troubled (Mark 14:33)

I

Ant. I tremble at the shouts of the foe:
    Lord, hear my prayer.

O God, listen to my prayer,
do not hide from my pleading,
attend to me and reply;
with my cares, I cannot rest.

I tremble at the shouts of the foe,
at the cries of the wicked;
for they bring down evil upon me.
They assail me with fury.

My heart is stricken within me,
death's terror is on me,
trembling and fear fall upon me
and horror overwhelms me.

O that I had wings like a dove
to fly away and be at rest.
So I would escape far away
and take refuge in the desert.

I would hasten to find a shelter
from the raging wind,
from the destructive storm, O Lord,
and from their plotting tongues.

For I can see nothing but violence
and strife in the city.
Night and day they patrol
high on the city walls.

It is full of wickedness and evil;
it is full of sin.
Its streets are never free
from tyranny and deceit.

Ant. I tremble at the shouts of the foe:
    Lord, hear my prayer.

II

Ant. As for me, I will call on God;
   the Lord will save me.

If this had been done by an enemy
I could bear his taunts.
If a rival had risen against me,
I could hide from him.

But it is you, my own companion,
my intimate friend!
How close was the friendship between us.
We walked together in harmony in the house of God ...

As for me, I will cry to God
and the Lord will save me.
Evening, morning and at noon
I will cry and lament.

Ant. As for me, I will call on God;
   the Lord will save me.

III

Ant. O Lord, I will trust in you:
   you will deliver my soul in peace.

He will deliver my soul in peace
in the attack against me:
for those who fight me are many,
but he hears my voice.

God will hear and will humble them,
the eternal judge:
for they will not amend their ways.
They have no fear of God.

The traitor has turned against his friends;
he has broken his word.
His speech is softer than butter,
but war is in his heart.
His words are smoother than oil,
but they are naked swords.

Entrust your cares to the Lord
and he will support you.
He will never allow
the just man to stumble.

But you, O God, will bring them down
to the pit of death.
Deceitful and bloodthirsty men shall not live half their days.
O Lord, I will trust in you.

Ant. O Lord, I will trust in you:
   you will deliver my soul in peace.

B. ADVENT, CHRISTMASTIDE, LENT AND EASTER

Psalm 77   **God's patience and man's ingratitude: the lesson of past history**

These things happened to them as a warning, but they were written down for our instruction (1 Cor 10:11)

Ant. Give ear to the words of the Lord.

IV

How often they defied him in the wilderness
and caused him pain in the desert!

Yet again they put God to the test
and grieved the Holy One of Israel.
They did not remember his deeds
nor the day he saved them from the foe;

when he worked his miracles in Egypt,
his wonders in the plains of Zoan:
when he turned their rivers into blood
and made their streams impossible to drink.

He sent dog-flies against them to devour them
and swarms of frogs to molest them.
He gave their crops to the grub,
the fruit of their labour to the locust.

He destroyed their vines with hail,
their sycamore trees with frost.

He gave up their cattle to plague,
their flocks and herds to pestilence.

He turned on them the heat of his anger, fury, rage and
    havoc,
a troop of destroying angels.

He gave free course to his anger.†
He did not spare them from death
but gave their lives to the plague.
He struck all the first-born in Egypt,
the finest flower in the dwellings of Ham.

V

Then he brought forth his people like sheep;
like a flock he guided them in the desert.
He led them safely with nothing to fear,
while the sea engulfed their foes.

So he brought them to his holy land,
to the mountain which his right hand had won.
He drove out the nations before them,
and divided the land for their heritage.

Their tents he gave as a dwelling
to each one of Israel's tribes.
Still they put God to the proof and defied him;
they refused to obey the Most High.

They strayed, as faithless as their fathers,
like a bow on which the archer cannot count.
They angered him with their mountain shrines;
made him jealous with the idols they served.

God saw this and was filled with fury:
he utterly rejected Israel.
He forsook his dwelling place in Shiloh,
the tent where he lived among men.

He gave his ark into captivity,
his glorious ark into the hands of the foe.

He gave up his people to the sword,
in his anger against his chosen ones.

So war devoured their young men,
their maidens had no wedding songs;
their priests fell by the sword
and their widows made no lament.

VI

Then the Lord awoke as if from sleep,
like a warrior overcome with wine.
He struck his enemies from behind
and put them to everlasting shame.

He rejected the tent of Joseph;
He did not choose the tribe of Ephraim
but he chose the tribe of Judah,
the hill of Zion which he loves.

He built his shrine like the heavens,
or like the earth which he made firm for ever.
And he chose David his servant
and took him away from the sheepfolds.

From the care of the ewes he called him†
to be shepherd of Jacob his people,
of Israel his own possession.
He tended them with blameless heart,
with discerning mind he led them.

Ant. Give ear to the words of the Lord.

V. Come, consider the works of the Lord,
R. The redoubtable deeds he has done on the earth.

Readings

Prayer of the day

Or alternative prayer

MORNING PRAYER

Introductory verse and psalm

O Lord, open my lips.

And my mouth shall declare your praise.

Glory be to the Father, and to the Son, and to the Holy Spirit.

As it was in the beginning, is now, and ever shall be, world without end. Amen. Alleluia!

Psalm 94

Refrain: Let us go to meet the Lord
   with songs of joy and gladness.

Or, if not used as first prayer of the day: O God, come to my assistance..,

Hymn

R. Awake, O sleeper, and arise from the dead,
   and Christ shall give you light.

Christ, who was manifested in the flesh,
vindicated in the Spirit,
seen by the angels,
preached among the nations,
believed on in the world,
taken up in glory. (*R.*)

Christ, who will be made manifest
at the proper time
by the blessed and only Sovereign,
the King of kings and Lord of lords,
who alone has immortality
and dwells in unapproachable light,
whom no man has ever seen or can see,
to him be honour and eternal dominion. Amen. (*R.*)

Psalmody

Psalm 91   **God guides the life of man with wisdom and justice**

By this my Father is glorified, that you bear much fruit (John 15:8)

Ant. It is good to give thanks to the Lord,
to make music to your name, O Most High.

It is good to give thanks to the Lord
to make music to your name, O Most High,
to proclaim your love in the morning
and your truth in the watches of the night,
on the ten-stringed lyre and the lute,
with the murmuring sound of the harp.

Your deeds, O Lord, have made me glad;
for the work of your hands I shout with joy.
O Lord, how great are your works!
How deep are your designs!
The foolish man cannot know this
and the fool cannot understand.

Though the wicked spring up like grass
and all who do evil thrive,
they are doomed to be eternally destroyed;
but you, Lord, are eternally on high.
See how your enemies perish;
all doers of evil are scattered.

To me you give the wild-ox's strength;
you anoint me with the purest oil.
My eyes looked in triumph on my foes;
my ears heard gladly of their fall.
The just will flourish like the palm-tree
and grow like a Lebanon cedar.

Planted in the house of the Lord
they will flourish in the courts of our God,
still bearing fruit when they are old,
still full of sap, still green,
to proclaim that the Lord is just.
In him, my rock, there is no wrong.

Ant. It is good to give thanks to the Lord,
to make music to your name, O Most High.

Ez 36:24–28   Song of Ezechiel: God renews his people

*They shall be his people, and God himself will be with them
and be their God* (Rev 21:3)

Ant. Lord, give us a new heart,
    and put a new spirit within us.

I will take you from the nations,†
and gather you from all the countries,
and bring you into your own land.

I will sprinkle clean water upon you,†
and you shall be clean from all your uncleannesses,
and from all your idols I will cleanse you.

A new heart I will give you,
and a new spirit I will put within you;
and I will take out of your flesh the heart of stone
and give you a heart of flesh.

And I will put my spirit within you,†
and cause you to walk in my statutes
and be careful to observe my ordinances.

You shall dwell in the land
which I gave to your fathers;
and you shall be my people,
and I will be your God.

Ant. Lord, give us a new heart,
    and put a new spirit within us.

Psalm 8   God's majesty, man's dignity

*We see Jesus, who for a little while was made lower than
the angels, crowned with glory and honour* (Heb 2:9)

R. How great is your name, O Lord our God,
through all the earth!

Your majesty is praised
above the heavens;
on the lips of children and of babes†
you have found praise to foil your enemy,
to silence the foe and the rebel. (*R.*)

When I see the heavens, the work of your hands,
the moon and the stars which you arranged,
what is man that you should keep him in mind,
mortal man that you care for him? (*R.*)

Yet you have made him little less than a god;
with glory and honour you crowned him,
gave him power over the works of your hand,
put all things under his feet. (*R.*)

All of them, sheep and cattle,
yes, even the savage beasts,
birds of the air, and fish
that make their way through the waters. (*R.*)

R. How great is your name, O Lord our God,
through all the earth!

Word of God   Phil 4:8–9
Brethren, whatever is true, whatever is honourable, whatever
is just, whatever is pure, whatever is lovely, whatever is
gracious, if there is any excellence, if there is anything
worthy of praise, think about these things; and the God of
peace will be with you.

Short Response
In the morning let me know your love,
for I put my trust in you.
V. Make me know the way I should walk:
R. For I put my trust in you.
V. Glory be to the Father, and to the Son, and to the Holy
Spirit.
In the morning let me know your love,
for I put my trust in you.

Song of Zechariah
Ant. Enlighten those in darkness, Lord;
    guide us into the way of peace.

Prayers

Let us call upon God who, through his Son, gave hope and life to the world, and say to him:

R. Lord, hear us.

Lord and Father of us all, who have brought us to the beginning of this day,
—grant that we may live our lives in union with Christ, and to the praise of your glory. (*R*.)

You have poured into our hearts faith, hope and love;
—grant that they may always abide with us. (*R*.)

May our eyes always be on you, Lord,
—that we may answer quickly when you call. (*R*.)

Defend us from all wicked snares and deceptions;
—always keep our feet from stumbling. (*R*.)

Other prayers may be added

Our Father . . .

Concluding prayer

Almighty and eternal God, splendour of true light and everlasting day, we pray at the beginning of this new day that the darkness of sin may be driven from our minds, and the radiance of your coming may shine upon us. We make our prayer through our Lord.

May the Lord bless us,
may he keep us from all evil
and lead us to life everlasting.
Amen.

Let us bless the Lord.
R. Thanks be to God.

MIDDAY PRAYER

O God, come to my assistance . . .
Glory be . . .

Hymn
Holy Spirit,
one with the Father and the Son,
deign at this hour to come down on us without delay
and pour out your graces over our soul.

Let mouth, tongue, soul, thought and strength
make your praise resound.
Let our love be set aflame by the fire of your love
and its heat in turn enkindle love in our neighbours.

Grant this, most loving Father,
and you, the only Son, equal to the Father
and, with the Spirit, the Paraclete,
reigning through the ages. Amen.

Psalmody

Psalm 118:169–176

Ant. Stretch out your hand to help me,
  for I have chosen your commandments.

Lord, let my cry come before you:
teach me by your word.
Let my pleading come before you;
save me by your promise.

Let my lips proclaim your praise
because you teach me your statutes.
Let my tongue sing your promise
for your commands are just.

Let your hand be ready to help me,
since I have chosen your precepts.
Lord, I long for your saving help
and your law is my delight.

Give life to my soul that I may praise you.
Let your decrees give me help.
I am lost like a sheep; seek your servant
for I remember your commands.

Psalm 44   **Royal wedding song**

*He who has the bride is the bridegroom; the friend of the
bridegroom, who stands and hears him, rejoices greatly at
the bridegroom's voice* (John 3:29)

I

My heart overflows with noble words.†
To the king I must speak the song I have made;
my tongue as nimble as the pen of a scribe.

You are the fairest of the children of men†
and graciousness is poured upon your lips:
because God has blessed you for evermore.

O mighty one, gird your sword upon your thigh;†
in splendour and state, ride on in triumph
for the cause of truth and goodness and right.

Take aim with your bow in your dread right hand.†
Your arrows are sharp; peoples fall beneath you.
The foes of the king fall down and lose heart.

Your throne, O God, shall endure for ever.†
A sceptre of justice is the sceptre of your kingdom.
Your love is for justice; your hatred for evil.

Therefore God, your God, has anointed you†
with the oil of gladness above other kings:
your robes are fragrant with aloes and myrrh.

From the ivory palace you are greeted with music.†
The daughters of kings are among your loved ones.
On your right stands the queen in gold of Ophir.

II

Listen, O daughter, give ear to my words:
forget your own people and your father's house.

So will the king desire your beauty:
He is your lord, pay homage to him.

And the people of Tyre shall come with gifts,
the richest of the people shall seek your favour.
The daughter of the king is clothed with splendour,
her robes embroidered with pearls set in gold.

She is led to the king with her maiden companions.†
They are escorted amid gladness and joy;
they pass within the palace of the king.

Sons shall be yours in place of your fathers:
you will make them princes over all the earth.
May this song make your name for ever remembered.
May the peoples praise you from age to age.

Ant. Stretch out your hand to help me,
for I have chosen your commandments.

Word of God   Dan 6:26–27

Tremble and fear before God,
for he is the living God,
enduring for ever;
his kingdom shall never be destroyed,
and his dominion shall be to the end.
He delivers and rescues,
he works signs and wonders
in heaven and on earth.

V. The Lord is great, highly to be praised.
R. His greatness cannot be measured.

Prayer

O Lord, fire of everlasting love, give us the fervour to love
you above all things, and our brother for your sake.
Through Christ our Lord.

Let us bless the Lord.
R. Thanks be to God.

Night Prayer

When night prayer is celebrated in common, it may begin with a brief reflection on our Christian living, or with an act of penance.

O God, come to my assistance.
R. Lord, make haste to help me.

Glory be to the Father, and to the Son, and to the Holy Spirit.
As it was in the beginning, is now, and ever shall be, world without end. Amen. Alleluia!

Hymn

Before the day is finished, Creator of the world,
we earnestly ask of you
that, in keeping with your mercy,
you be our protector and defence.

Keep far away all evil dreams
and phantoms of the night,
and overcome our enemy
lest we should be defiled.

Grant this, most loving Father,
and you, the only Son, equal to the Father
and, with the Spirit, the Paraclete,
reigning through the ages. Amen.

SUNDAYS I and III

Psalmody

Psalm 90   **Under the wing of God's protection**

Let not your hearts be troubled, neither let them be afraid
(John 14:7)

Ant. Under the shadow of his wings,
we shall not fear the night.

He who dwells in the shelter of the Most High
and abides in the shade of the Almighty

says to the Lord: 'My refuge,
my stronghold, my God in whom I trust!'
It is he who will free you from the snare of the fowler
who seeks to destroy you;
he will conceal you with his pinions
and under his wings you will find refuge.

You will not fear the terror of the night
nor the arrow that flies by day,
nor the plague that prowls in the darkness
nor the scourge that lays waste at noon.

A thousand may fall at your side,
ten thousand fall at your right,
you, it will never approach;
his faithfulness is buckler and shield.

Your eyes have only to look
to see how the wicked are repaid,
you who have said: 'Lord, my refuge!'
and have made the Most High your dwelling.

Upon you no evil shall fall,
no plague approach where you dwell.
For you has he commanded his angels,
to keep you in all your ways.

They shall bear you upon their hands
lest you strike your foot against a stone.
On the lion and the viper you will tread
and trample the young lion and the dragon.

His love he set on me, so I will rescue him;
protect him for he knows my name.
When he calls I shall answer: 'I am with you.'
I will save him in distress and give him glory.

With length of life I will content him;
I shall let him see my saving power.

Ant. Under the shadow of his wings,
  we shall not fear the night.

SUNDAYS II and IV

Psalm 4   **Night prayer of thanksgiving**

Fear not, little flock, for it is your Father's good pleasure to give you the kingdom (Luke 12:32)

Ant. Lift up the light of your face on us, O Lord.

When I call, answer me, O God of justice;
from anguish you released me, have mercy and hear me!

O men, how long will your hearts be closed,
will you love what is futile and seek what is false?

It is the Lord who grants favours to those whom he loves;
the Lord hears me whenever I call him.

Fear him; do not sin: ponder on your bed and be still.
Make justice your sacrifice and trust in the Lord.

'What can bring us happiness?' many say.
Lift up the light of your face on us, O Lord.

You have put into my heart a greater joy
than they have from abundance of corn and new wine.

I will lie down in peace and sleep comes at once
for you alone, Lord, make me dwell in safety.

Psalm 133   **Blessing for the night**

Jesus went out into the hills to pray; and all night he continued in prayer to God (Luke 6:12)

O come, bless the Lord,
all you who serve the Lord,
who stand in the house of the Lord,
in the courts of the house of our God.
Lift up your hands to the holy place
and bless the Lord through the night.

May the Lord bless you from Zion,
he who made both heaven and earth.

Ant. Lift up the light of your face on us, O Lord.

MONDAY

Blessed be God, who comforts us in all our afflictions
(2 Cor 1:3)

Ant. Have mercy on me, Lord,
    for I cry to you all the day long.

Turn your ear, O Lord, and give answer
for I am poor and needy.
Preserve my life, for I am faithful:
save the servant who trusts in you.

You are my God, have mercy on me, Lord,
for I cry to you all the day long.
Give joy to your servant, O Lord,
for to you I lift up my soul.

O Lord, you are good and forgiving,
full of love to all who call.
Give heed, O Lord, to my prayer
and attend to the sound of my voice.

In the day of distress I will call
and surely you will reply.
Among the gods there is none like you, O Lord;
nor work to compare with yours.

All the nations shall come to adore you
and glorify your name, O Lord:
for you are great and do marvellous deeds,
you who alone are God.

Show me, Lord, your way†
so that I may walk in your truth.
Guide my heart to fear your name.

I will praise you, Lord my God, with all my heart
and glorify your name for ever;
for your love to me has been great:
you have saved me from the depths of the grave.

The proud have risen against me;†
ruthless men seek my life:
to you they pay no heed.

But you, God of mercy and compassion,
slow to anger, O Lord,
abounding in love and truth,
turn and take pity on me.

O give your strength to your servant
and save your handmaid's son.
Show me a sign of your favour†
that my foes may see to their shame
that you console me and give me your help.

Ant. Have mercy on me, Lord,
for I cry to you all the day long.

TUESDAY

Psalm 142   **Prayer in desolation**

*A man is not justified by works of the law, but through faith
in Jesus Christ* (Gal 2:16)

Ant. Lord, do not call your servant to judgment.

Lord, listen to my prayer:†
turn your ear to my appeal.
You are faithful, you are just; give answer.
Do not call your servant to judgment
for no one is just in your sight.

The enemy pursues my soul;
he has crushed my life to the ground;
he has made me dwell in darkness
like the dead, long forgotten.
Therefore my spirit fails;
my heart is numb within me.

I remember the days that are past:
I ponder all your works.

I muse on what your hand has wrought†
and to you I stretch out my hands.
Like a parched land my soul thirsts for you.

Lord, make haste and give me answer;
for my spirit fails within me.
Do not hide your face
lest I become like those in the grave.

In the morning let me know your love
for I put my trust in you.
Make me know the way I should walk:
to you I lift up my soul.

Rescue me, Lord, from my enemies;
I have fled to you for refuge.
Teach me to do your will
for you, O Lord, are my God.
Let your good spirit guide me
in ways that are level and smooth.

For your name's sake, Lord, save my life;
in your justice save my soul from distress . . .

Ant. Lord, do not call your servant to judgment.

WEDNESDAY

Prayer 30   **Confident prayer in distress**

Father, into your hands I commit my spirit (Luke 23:46)

Ant. You, Lord, are my rock, my fortress.

In you, O Lord, I take refuge.
Let me never be put to shame.
In your justice, set me free,
hear me and speedily rescue me.

Be a rock of refuge for me,
a mighty stronghold to save me,
for you are my rock, my stronghold.
For your name's sake, lead me and guide me.

Release me from the snares they have hidden
for you are my refuge, Lord.
Into your hands I commend my spirit.
It is you who will redeem me, Lord . . .

Psalm 129   **Prayer of repentance and trust**

He will save his people from their sins (Matthew 1:22)

Out of the depths I cry to you, O Lord,
Lord, hear my voice!
O let your ears be attentive
to the voice of my pleading.

If you, O Lord, should mark our guilt,
Lord, who would survive?
But with you is found forgiveness:
for this we revere you.

My soul is waiting for the Lord,
I count on his word.
My soul is longing for the Lord
more than watchman for daybreak.
Let the watchman count on daybreak
and Israel on the Lord.

Because with the Lord there is mercy
and fulness of redemption,
Israel indeed he will redeem
from all its iniquity.

Ant. You, Lord, are my rock, my fortress.

THURSDAY

Psalm 15   **God, the source of true happiness**

*I go to prepare a place for you, that where I am you may
be also* (John 14:3)

Ant. Preserve me, God, my refuge is in you.

Preserve me, God, I take refuge in you.†
I say to the Lord: 'You are my God.
My happiness lies in you alone.'

He has put into my heart a marvellous love
for the faithful ones who dwell in his land.
Those who choose other gods increase their sorrows.†
Never will I offer their offerings of blood.
Never will I take their name upon my lips.

O Lord, it is you who are my portion and cup;
it is you yourself who are my prize.
The lot marked out for me is my delight:
welcome indeed the heritage that falls to me!

I will bless the Lord who gives me counsel,
who even at night directs my heart.
I keep the Lord ever in my sight:
since he is at my right hand, I shall stand firm.

And so my heart rejoices, my soul is glad;
even my body shall rest in safety.
For you will not leave my soul among the dead,
nor let your beloved know decay.

You will show me the path of life,†
the fulness of joy in your presence,
at your right hand happiness for ever.

Ant. Preserve me, God, my refuge is in you.

FRIDAY

Psalm 89   **God, man's refuge in the brevity of life**

*With the Lord, one day is as a thousand years, and a
thousand years as one day* (2 Pet 3:8)

Ant. Our days are passed in the radiance of your face.

O Lord, you have been our refuge
from one generation to the next.
Before the mountains were born†
or the earth or the world brought forth,
you are God, without beginning or end.

510

You turn men back into dust and say:
'Go back, sons of men.'
To your eyes a thousand years are like yesterday
   come and gone,
no more than a watch in the night.

You sweep men away like a dream,
like grass which springs up in the morning.
In the morning it springs up and flowers:
by evening it withers and fades.

So we are destroyed in your anger
struck with terror in your fury.
Our guilt lies open before you;
our secrets in the light of your face.

All our days pass away in your anger.
Our life is over like a sigh.
Our span is seventy years
or eighty for those who are strong.

And most of these are emptiness and pain.
They pass swiftly and we are gone.
Who understands the power of your anger
and fears the strength of your fury?

Make us know the shortness of our life
that we may gain wisdom of heart.
Lord, relent! Is your anger for ever?
Show pity to your servants.

In the morning, fill us with your love;
we shall exult and rejoice all our days.
Give us joy to balance our affliction
for the years when we knew misfortune.

Show forth your work to your servants;
let your glory shine on their children.
Let the favour of the Lord be upon us:†
give success to the work of our hands;
give success to the work of out hands.

Ant. Our days are passed in the radiance of your face.

SATURDAY

Blessed are those servants whom the master finds awake when he comes . . . . he will have them sit at table, and he will come and serve them (Luke 12:37)

Ant. My soul longs for you in the night.

To you have I lifted up my eyes,
you who dwell in the heavens:
my eyes, like the eyes of slaves
on the hand of their lords.

Like the eyes of a servant
on the hand of her mistress,
so our eyes are on the Lord our God
till he show us his mercy.

Have mercy on us, Lord, have mercy.
We are filled with contempt.
Indeed all too full is our soul with the scorn of the rich,
with the proud man's disdain.

Psalm 120 God the protector

They shall hunger no more, neither thirst any more (Rev 7:16)

I lift up my eyes to the mountains:
from where shall come my help?
My help shall come from the Lord
who made heaven and earth.

May he never allow you to stumble!
Let him sleep not, your guard.
No, he sleeps not nor slumbers,
Israel's guard.

The Lord is your guard and your shade;
at your right side he stands.
By day the sun shall not smite you
nor the moon in the night.

The Lord will guard you from evil,
he will guard your soul.
The Lord will guard your going and coming
both now and for ever.

Ant. My soul longs for you in the night.

The Word of God

1 Thess 5:9–10   Sunday

God has not destined us for wrath, but to obtain salvation
through our Lord Jesus Christ, who died for us so that
whether we wake or sleep we might live with him.

Deut 6:2, 7   Monday

You shall fear the Lord your God by keeping all his statutes
and his commandments all the days of your life; you shall
talk of them when you sit in your house, and when you
walk by the way, and when you lie down, and when you
rise.

Lam 2:19   Tuesday

Arise, cry out in the night,
at the beginning of the watches.
Pour out your heart like water
before the presence of the Lord!
Lift your hands to him.

Eph 4:26–27   Wednesday

Do not sin; do not let the sun go down on your anger, and
give no opportunity to the devil.

1 Pet 5:6–7   Thursday

Humble yourselves under the mighty hand of God,
that in due time he may exalt you. Cast all your anxieties on
him, for he cares about you.

Jer 14:9   Friday

You, O Lord, are in the midst of us,
and we are called by your name;
leave us not.

513

Is 30:15, 18

Thus said the Lord God,
'In returning and rest you shall be saved;
in quietness and in trust shall be your strength.'
The Lord waits to be gracious to you;
blessed are all those who wait for him.

Short Response

Into your hands, O Lord,
I commend my spirit.
V. It is you who will redeem me, Lord.
R. Into your hands, O Lord, I commend my spirit.
V. Glory be to the Father, and to the Son, and to the Holy
Spirit.
Into your hands, O Lord,
I commend my spirit.

Song of Simeon

Ant. Lord, save us while we are awake;
    protect us while we sleep:
    and Christ, with whom we keep our watch
    will guard our souls is peace.

At last, all-powerful Master,†
you give leave to your servant
to go in peace, according to your promise.
For my eyes have seen your salvation
which you have prepared for all nations,
the light to enlighten the Gentiles
and give glory to Israel, your people.

Ant. Lord, save us while we are awake;
    protect us while we sleep:
    and Christ, with whom we keep our watch
    will guard our souls in peace.

Prayers

Sundays I and III

O Lord, we entreat you to visit this house and drive far
away the snares of the enemy. May your holy angels dwell

here to keep us in peace, and may your blessing be always upon us. Through Christ our Lord.

Sundays II and IV

Lord God, we humbly pray you to grant that, as we have today celebrated the mystery of your resurrection, we may sleep free from fear in your peace and rise to praise you with joy. Through Christ our Lord.

Monday

Give our bodies health-giving rest, O Lord, and grant that what we have sown during the day by our labours may bring in a fruitful harvest. Through Christ our Lord.

Tuesday

O Lord, we pray that you will illumine this night, and grant that your servants may sleep in peace and wake in your name to greet the light of day in safety and joy. Through Christ our Lord.

Wednesday

Lord Jesus Christ, gentle and lowly of heart, who lay upon your followers an easy yoke and a light burden, receive our prayers and works of this day, and grant us sleep so that we may serve you with renewed fervour. Who live and reign.

Thursday

Lord, our God, we are weary with the labours of the day. Refresh us with quiet sleep, so that restored by your help we may serve you devotedly with both body and mind. Through Christ our Lord.

Friday

Almighty God, grant us such close union with your only-begotten Son, who went down into the grave for our sakes, that we may rise again with him in newness of life. Who lives and reigns.

Saturday

Be with us, O Lord, during this night, that rising at dawn, we may rejoice in the resurrection of Christ. Who lives and reigns.

Final antiphons to the Virgin Mary

One of the following may be chosen

Hail, holy queen, mother of mercy; hail, our life, our sweetness and our hope! To you do we cry, poor banished children of Eve; to you do we send up our sighs, mourning and weeping in this valley of tears. Turn then, most gracious advocate, your eyes of mercy towards us; and after this our exile show unto us the blessed fruit of your womb, Jesus. O clement, O Loving, O sweet Virgin Mary.

Salve Regína, mater misericórdiæ, vita, dulcédo et spes nostra, salve. Ad te clamámus, éxsules fílii Hevæ. Ad te suspirámus, geméntes et flentes in hac lacrimárum valle. Eia ergo, advocáta nostra, illos tuos misericórdes óculos ad nos convérte. Et Jesum, benedíctum fructum ventris tui, nobis post hoc exsílium osténde. O clemens, o pia, o dulcis Virgo María.

V. Pray for us, most holy mother of God.
R. That we may be made worthy of the promises of Christ.

All-powerful, eternal God, by the co-operation of the Holy Spirit you made ready the body and soul of the glorious Virgin Mother Mary to be a fit dwelling-place for your Son. As we celebrate her memory with joy, grant that through her motherly intercession we may be preserved from evil in this world and from eternal death. Through Christ our Lord. Amen.

or

Loving mother of the Redeemer, open door to heaven and star of the sea, come quickly to the aid of your people, fallen indeed but striving to stand again. To nature's astonishment you were the mother of your holy Creator without ceasing to be a virgin, and heard from Gabriel that greeting 'Hail'. Have pity on us sinners.

V. Blessed are you among women.
R. And blessed is the fruit of your womb, Jesus.

O God who through Mary's virginal motherhood held out to us new hope of life; grant that we may feel the power of her prayers, since she brought among us the author of life, our Lord Jesus Christ, your son. Amen.

or

V. The Angel of the Lord made the announcement to Mary.
R. And she conceived by the Holy Spirit.

Pour out your grace into our hearts, O Lord! By the voice of an angel we have learned of the incarnation of Christ, your Son; lead us by his passion and his cross, to the glory of the resurrection. Through Christ our Lord. Amen.

Hail, Queen of heaven; hail, mistress of the angels; hail, root of Jesse; hail, the gate through which the Light rose over the earth. Rejoice, Virgin most renowned and of unsurpassed beauty. Farewell, Lady most comely. Prevail upon Christ to pity us.

V. Let me praise you, most holy Virgin.
R. Give me strength against your enemies.

O God of mercy, be the support of our weakness, and we shall celebrate in a fitting manner the memory of the holy Mother of God; thus by her intercession may we rise from our sins. Through Christ our Lord. Amen.

In paschaltide

Queen of heaven, rejoice, alleluia. The Son whom it was your privilege to bear, alleluia, has risen as he said, alleluia. Pray God for us, alleluia.

V. Rejoice and be glad, Virgin Mary, alleluia!
R. For the Lord has truly risen, alleluia!

NIGHT PRAYER

O God, you were pleased to give joy to the world through the resurrection of your Son, our Lord Jesus Christ. Grant, we beseech you, that through the prayers of the Virgin Mary, his mother, we may come to possess the joys of life everlasting. Through Christ our Lord. Amen.

Readings

GENERAL RESPONSES

The following Responses may be used after the Readings at the office of Readings:

1.

O Lord God of heaven, great and terrible God, let your ear be attentive * to hear the prayer of your servant.

V. O Lord, let your ear be attentive. * To hear.

2.

The law of the Lord is perfect, it revives the soul; the rule of the Lord is to be trusted, it gives wisdom to the simple. * The precepts of the Lord are right, they gladden the heart; the command of the Lord is clear, it gives light to the eyes.

V. He who loves his neighbour has fulfilled the law: love is the fulfilling of the law. * The precepts.

3.

You will seek me and find me when you seek me with all your heart. * I will be found by you, says the Lord.

V. Seek, and you will find; knock, and it will be opened to you. * I will.

4.

You shall not forget the covenant that I have made with you. You shall not fear other gods. * You shall fear the Lord your God, and he will deliver you out of the hands of all your enemies.

V. Hear, O Israel: The Lord our God is one Lord. * You shall.

5.

All who keep his commandments abide in him, and he in them. * By this we know that he abides in us, because he has given us of his own Spirit.

V. The Lord himself created wisdom and poured her out upon all his works. * By this.

Table of Scripture Readings

CHRISTMASTIDE

Dec. 25   The Nativity of our Lord   Is 11:1–10
Sunday within the Octave of Christmas: Feast of the Holy
    Family   Eph 5:21–6:4

	Year 1	Year 2
Dec. 29	Col 1:1–14	S of S 1:1–8
Dec. 30	Col 1:15–2:3	S of S 1:9–2:7
Dec. 31	Col 2:4–15	S of S 2:8–3:5
Jan. 1	Solemnity of Mary Mother of God Heb 2:9–17	
Jan. 2	Col 2:16–3:4	S of S 4:1–5:1

*In places where the Epiphany is celebrated on the Sunday
occurring between 2–8 January, the readings given for 7–12
January are read after the Epiphany, the following being
omitted:*

Jan. 3	Col 3:5–16	S of S 5:2–6:2
Jan. 4	Col 3:17–4:1	S of S 6:3–7:10
Jan. 5	Col 4:2–18	S of S 7:11–8:7
Jan. 6	(*in places where the Epiphany is celebrated on Jan. 7 or 8*)	
	Is 42:1–8	Is 49:1–9
Jan. 7	(*in places where the Epiphany is celebrated on Jan. 7 or 8*)	
	Is 61:1–11	Is 54:1–17
Jan. 6	The Epiphany of our Lord Is 60:1–22	

*The readings assigned to 7–12 January are read on the days
which follow the solemnity of the Epiphany, even when this
is kept on the Sunday, until the following Saturday. From the
Monday after the Sunday on which the Baptism of our Lord
is celebrated, i.e. the Sunday occurring after 6 January, the
readings of the weeks of the year are begun, omitting any
which remain of those assigned to the ferias between 7–12
January.*

	Year 1	Year 2
Jan. 7 or Mon. after Epiphany	Is 61:1–11	Is 54:1–17
Jan. 8 or Tues. after Epiphany	Is 62:1–12	Is 55:1–13

	Year 1	Year 2
Jan. 9 *or Wed. after Epiphany*	Is 63:7–64:1	Is 56:1–8
Jan. 10 *or Thurs. after Epiphany*	Is 64:1–12	Is 59:15–21
Jan. 11 *or Fri. after Epiphany*	Is 65:13–25	Baruch 4:5–29
Jan. 12 *or Sat. after Epiphany*	Is 66:5–14a, 18–23	Baruch 4:30–5:9

Sunday occurring after Jan. 6: Feast of the Baptism of our Lord
Is 42:1–8; 49:1–9

LENT

Ash Wednesday Is 58:1–14

	Year 1	Year 2
Thursday	Deut 1:1, 6–18	Exod 1:1–22
Friday	Deut 4:1–8, 32–40	Exod 2:1–22
Saturday	Deut 5:1–22	Exod 3:1–20

Week I

	Year 1	Year 2
Sunday	Deut 6:4–25	Exod 5:1–6:1
Monday	Deut 7:6–14; 8:1–6	Exod 6:2–13
Tuesday	Deut 9:7–21, 25–29	Exod 6:29–7:24
Wednesday	Deut 10:12–11:7, 26–28	
		Exod 10:21–11:10
Thursday	Deut 12:1–14	Exod 12:1–20
Friday	Deut 15:1–18	Exod 12:21–36
Saturday	Deut 16:1–17	Exod 12:37–49; 13:11–16

Week II

	Year 1	Year 2
Sunday	Deut 18:1–22	Exod 13:17–14:9
Monday	Deut 24:1–25:4	Exod 14:10–31
Tuesday	Deut 26:1–19	Exod 16:1–18, 35
Wednesday	Deut 29:2–6, 10–29	Exod 17:1–16
Thursday	Deut 30:1–20	Exod 18:13–27
Friday	Deut 31:1–15, 23	Exod 19:1–19; 20:18–21
Saturday	Deut 32:48–52; 34:1–12	
		Exod 20:1–17

	Year 1	Year 2

Week III

Sunday	Heb 1:1–2:4	Exod 22:20–23:9
Monday	Heb 2:5–18	Exod 24:1–18
Tuesday	Heb 3:1–19	Exod 32:1–5, 15–34
Wednesday	Heb 4:1–13	Exod 33:7–11, 18–23;
		34:5–9, 29–35
Thursday	Heb 4:14–5:10	Exod 34:10–28
Friday	Heb 5:11–6:8	Exod 35:30–36:1; 37:1–9
Saturday	Heb 6:9–20	Exod 40:16–38

Week IV

Sunday	Heb 7:1–11	Lev 8:1–17; 9:22–24
Monday	Heb 7:11–28	Lev 16:2–27
Tuesday	Heb 8:1–13	Lev 19:1–18, 31–37
Wednesday	Heb 9:1–14	Lev 26:3–17, 38–46
Thursday	Heb 9:15–28	Num 3:1–13; 8:5–11
Friday	Heb 10:1–10	Num 9:15–10:10, 33–36
Saturday	Heb 10:11–25	Num 11:4–6, 10–33

Week V

Sunday	Heb 10:26–39	Num 12:1–15
Monday	Heb 11:1–19	Num 12:16–13:3, 17–33
Tuesday	Heb 11:20–31	Num 14:1–25
Wednesday	Heb 11:32–40	Num 16:1–35
Thursday	Heb 12:1–13	Num 20:1–13; 21:4–9
Friday	Heb 12:14–29	Num 22:1–8a, 20–35
Saturday	Heb 13:1–25	Num 24:1–19

Holy Week

Sunday	Is 50:4–51:3	Jer 22:1–8; 23:1–8
Monday	Is 52:13–53:12	Jer 26:1–15
Tuesday	Lam 1:1–12, 18–20	Jer 8:13–9:9
Wednesday	Lam 2:1–10	Jer 11:18–12:13
Thursday	Lam 2:11–22	Jer 15:10–21
Friday	Lam 3:1–33	Jer 16:1–15
Saturday	Lam 5:1–22	Jer 20:7–18

PASCHALTIDE

Easter Week

Easter Sunday: Any one of the Vigil readings may be used

	Year 1	Year 2
Monday	1 Pet 1:1–21	Acts 1:1–26
Tuesday	1 Pet 1:22–2:10	Acts 2:1–21
Wednesday	1 Pet 2:11–25	Acts 2:22–41
Thursday	1 Pet 3:1–17	Acts 2:42–3:11
Friday	1 Pet 3:18–4:11	Acts 3:12–4:4
Saturday	1 Pet 4:12–5:14	Acts 4:5–31

Year 1		Year 2
	Week II	
Sunday	Col 3:1–17	Col 3:1–17
Monday	Rev 1:1–20	Acts 4:32–5:16
Tuesday	Rev 2:1–11	Acts 5:17–42
Wednesday	Rev 2:12–29	Acts 6:1–15
Thursday	Rev 3:1–22	Acts 7:1–16
Friday	Rev 4:1–11	Acts 7:17–43
Saturday	Rev 5:1–14	Acts 7:44–8:3

Week III

Sunday	Rev 6:1–17	Acts 8:4–25
Monday	Rev 7:1–17	Acts 8:26–40
Tuesday	Rev 8:1–13	Acts 9:1–22
Wednesday	Rev 9:1–12	Acts 9:23–43
Thursday	Rev 9:13–21	Acts 10:1–33
Friday	Rev 10:1–11	Acts 10:34–11:4, 18
Saturday	Rev 11:1–19	Acts 11:19–30

Week IV

Sunday	Rev 12:1–17	Acts 12:1–23
Monday	Rev 13:1–18	Acts 12:24–13:14a
Tuesday	Rev 14:1–13	Acts 13:14b–43
Wednesday	Rev 14:14–15:4	Acts 13:44–14:7
Thursday	Rev 15:5–16:21	Acts 14:8–15:4
Friday	Rev 17:1–18	Acts 15:5–35
Saturday	Rev 18:1–20	Acts 15:36–16:15

	Year 1	Year 2

Week V

Sunday	Rev 18:21–19:10	Acts 16:16–40
Monday	Rev 19:11–21	Acts 17:1–18
Tuesday	Rev 20:1–15	Acts 17:19–34
Wednesday	Rev 21:1–8	Acts 18:1–28
Thursday	Rev 21:9–27	Acts 19:1–20
Friday	Rev 22:1–9	Acts 19:21–41
Saturday	Rev 22:10–21	Acts 20:1–16

Week VI

Sunday	1 Jn 1:1–10	Acts 20:17–38
Monday	1 Jn 2:1–11	Acts 21:1–26
Tuesday	1 Jn 2:12–17	Acts 21:27–39
Wednesday	1 Jn 2:18–29	Acts 21:40–22:21
Thursday	The ascension of our Lord Eph 4:1–24	
Friday	1 Jn 3:1–10	Acts 22:22–23:11
Saturday	1 Jn 3:11–17	Acts 23:12–35

Week VII

Sunday	1 Jn 3:18–24	Acts 24:1–27
Monday	1 Jn 4:1–10	Acts 25:1–27
Tuesday	1 Jn 4:11–21	Acts 26:1–32
Wednesday	1 Jn 5:1–12	Acts 27:1–20
Thursday	1 Jn 5:13–21	Acts 27:21–44
Friday	2 Jn	Acts 28:1–14
Saturday	3 Jn	Acts 28:15–31

Penetcost Sunday Rom 8:5–27

TIME THROUGHOUT THE YEAR

Week I

Monday	Rom 1:1–17	Gen 1:1–2:4a
Tuesday	Rom 1:18–32	Gen 2:4b–25
Wednesday	Rom 2:1–16	Gen 3:1–24
Thursday	Rom 2:17–29	Gen 4:1–24
Friday	Rom 3:1–20	Gen 6:5–22; 7:17–24
Saturday	Rom 3:21–31	Gen 8:1–22

525

	Year 1	**Year 2**

Week II

Sunday	Rom 4:1–25	Gen 9:1–17
Monday	Rom 5:1–11	Gen 11:1–26
Tuesday	Rom 5:12–21	Gen 12:1–9; 13:2–18
Wednesday	Rom 6:1–11	Gen 14:1–24
Thursday	Rom 6:12–23	Gen 15:1–21
Friday	Rom 7:1–13	Gen 16:1–16
Saturday	Rom 7:14–25	Gen 17:1–27

Week III

Sunday	Rom 8:1–17	Gen 18:1–33
Monday	Rom 8:18–39	Gen 19:1–17, 23–29
Tuesday	Rom 9:1–18	Gen 21:1–21
Wednesday	Rom 9:19–33	Gen 22:1–19
Thursday	Rom 10:1–21	Gen 24:1–27
Friday	Rom 11:1–12	Gen 24:33–41, 49–67
Saturday	Rom 11:13–24	Gen 25:7–11, 19–34

Week IV

Sunday	Rom 11:25–36	Gen 27:1–29
Monday	Rom 12:1–21	Gen 27:30–45
Tuesday	Rom 13:1–14	Gen 28:10–29:14
Wednesday	Rom 14:1–23	Gen 31:1–21
Thursday	Rom 15:1–13	Gen 32:3–30
Friday	Rom 15:14–33	Gen 35:1–29
Saturday	Rom 16:1–27	Gen 37:2–4, 12–36

Week V

Sunday	1 Cor 1:1–17	Gen 39:1–23
Monday	1 Cor 1:18–31	Gen 41:1–15, 25–43
Tuesday	1 Cor 2:1–16	Gen 41:55–42:26
Wednesday	1 Cor 3:1–23	Gen 43:1–17, 26–34
Thursday	1 Cor 4:1–21	Gen 44:1–20, 30–34
Friday	1 Cor 5:1–13	Gen 45:1–15, 21b–28;46:1–7
Saturday	1 Cor 6:1–11	Gen 49:1–28, 33

	Year 1	**Year 2**

Week VI

Sunday	1 Cor 6:12–20	1 Thess 1:1–2:12
Monday	1 Cor 7:1–24	1 Thess 2:13–3:13
Tuesday	1 Cor 7:25–40	1 Thess 4:1–18
Wednesday	1 Cor 8:1–13	1 Thess 5:1–28
Thursday	1 Cor 9:1–18	2 Thess 1:1–12
Friday	1 Cor 9:19–27	2 Thess 2:1–17
Saturday	1 Cor 10:1–14	2 Thess 3:1–18

Week VII

Sunday	1 Cor 10:14–11:1	2 Cor 1:1–14
Monday	1 Cor 11:2–16	2 Cor 1:15–2:11
Tuesday	1 Cor 11:17–34	2 Cor 2:12–3:6
Wednesday	1 Cor 12:1–11	2 Cor 3:7–4:4
Thursday	1 Cor 12:12–31	2 Cor 4:5–18
Friday	1 Cor 12:31–13:13	2 Cor 5:1–21
Saturday	1 Cor 14:1–19	2 Cor 6:1–7:1

Week VIII

Sunday	1 Cor 14:20–40	2 Cor 7:2–16
Monday	1 Cor 15:1–19	2 Cor 8:1–24
Tuesday	1 Cor 15:20–34	2 Cor 9:1–15
Wednesday	1 Cor 15:35–58	2 Cor 10:1–11:6
Thursday	1 Cor 16:1–24	2 Cor 11:7–29
Friday	Jas 1:1–18	2 Cor 11:30–12:13
Saturday	Jas 1:19–27	2 Cor 12:14–13:14

Week IX

Sunday	Jas 2:1–13	Gal 1:1–12
Monday	Jas 2:14–26	Gal 1:13–2:10
Tuesday	Jas 3:1–12	Gal 2:11–3:14
Wednesday	Jas 3:13–18	Gal 3:15–4:7
Thursday	Jas 4:1–12	Gal 4:8–5:1a
Friday	Jas 4:13–5:11	Gal 5:1b–25
Saturday	Jas 5:12–20	Gal 5:25–6:18

	Year 1	**Year 2**

Week X

Sunday	Sir 46:1–10	Phil 1:1–11
Monday	Josh 1:1–18	Phil 1:12–26
Tuesday	Josh 2:1–24	Phil 1:27–2:11
Wednesday	Josh 3:1–17; 4:14–19; 5:10–12	Phil 2:12–30
Thursday	Josh 5:13–6:21	Phil 3:1–16
Friday	Josh 7:4–26	Phil 3:17–4:9
Saturday	Josh 10:1–15	Phil 4:10–23

Week XI

Sunday	Josh 24:1–7, 13–28	Isa 44:12–45:3
Monday	Judg 2:6–3:4	Ezra 1:1–8; 2:68–3:8
Tuesday	Judg 4:1–24	Ezra 4:1–5, 24–5:5
Wednesday	Judg 6:1–6, 11–24	Hag 1:1–2:9
Thursday	Judg 7:1–8, 16–22a	Hag 2:10–23
Friday	Judg 8:22–32; 9:1–15	Zech 1:1–21
Saturday	Judg 11:1–9, 29–40	Zech 2:1–13

Week XII

Sunday	Judg 13:1–25	Zech 3:1–4:14
Monday	Judg 16:4–6, 16–31	Zech 8:1–17, 20–23
Tuesday	1 Sam 1:1–19	Ezra 6:1–5, 14–22
Wednesday	1 Sam 1:20–28; 2:11–21	Ezra 7:6–28
Thursday	1 Sam 2:22–36	Ezra 9:1–9, 15–10:5
Friday	1 Sam 3:1–21	Neh 1:1–2:8
Saturday	1 Sam 4: 1–18	Neh 2: 9–20

Week XIII

Sunday	1 Sam 5:1,6–6:4	Neh 4:1–23
Monday	1 Sam 7:15–8:22	Neh 5:1–19
Tuesday	1 Sam 9:1–6,14–10:1	Neh 7:73b–8:18
Wednesday	1 Sam 11:1–15	Neh 9:1–2, 5–21
Thursday	1 Sam 12:1–25	Neh 9:22–37
Friday	1 Sam 15:1–23	Neh 12:27–47
Saturday	1 Sam 16:1–13	Isa 59:1–14

	Year 1	Year 2

Week XIV

	Year 1	Year 2
Sunday	1 Sam 17:1–10, 23b–26, 40–51	Prov 1:1–7, 20–33
Monday	1 Sam 17:57–18:9, 20–30	Prov 3:1–20
Tuesday	1 Sam 19:8–10; 20:1–17	Prof 8:1–5, 12–36
Wednesday	1 Sam 21:1–9; 22:1–5	Prov 9:1–18
Thursday	1 Sam 25:14–24, 28–39	Prov 10:6–32
Friday	1 Sam 26:2–25	Prov 15:8–30; 16:1–9
Saturday	1 Sam 28:3–25	Prov 31:10–31

Week XV

	Year 1	Year 2
Sunday	1 Sam 31:1–4; 2 Sam 1:1–16	Job 1:1–22
Monday	2 Sam 2:1–11; 3:1–5	Job 2:1–13
Tuesday	2 Sam 4:2–5:7	Job 3:1–26
Wednesday	2 Sam 6:1–23	Job 4:1–21
Thursday	2 Sam 7:1–25	Job 5:1–27
Friday	2 Sam 11:1–17, 26-27	Job 6:1–30
Saturday	2 Sam 12:1–25	Job 7:1–21

Week XVI

	Year 1	Year 2
Sunday	2 Sam 15:7–14, 24–30; 16:5–13	Job 11:1–20
Monday	2 Sam 18:6–19:4	Job 12:1–25
Tuesday	2 Sam 24:1–25	Job 13:13–14:6
Wednesday	1 Chr 22:5–19	Job 18:1–21
Thursday	1 Kgs 1:11–35; 2:10–12	Job 19:1–29
Friday	1 Kgs 3:5–28	Job 22:1–30
Saturday	1 Kgs 8:1–21	Job 23:1–24:12

Week XVII

	Year 1	Year 2
Sunday	1 Kgs 8:22–34, 54–61	Job 28:1–28
Monday	1 Kgs 10:1–13	Job 29:1–10; 30:1, 9–23
Tuesday	1 Kgs 11:1–4, 26–43	Job 31:1–23, 35–37
Wednesday	1 Kgs 12:1–19	Job 32:1–6; 33:1–22
Thursday	1 Kgs 12:20–33	Job 38:1–30; 40:1–5
Friday	1 Kgs 16:29–17:16	Job 40:6–24; 42:1–6
Saturday	1 Kgs 18:16b–40	Job 42:7–17

	Year 1	**Year 2**

Week XVIII

	Year 1	**Year 2**
Sunday	1 Kgs 19:1–21	Obad 1–21
Monday	1 Kgs 21:1–21, 27–29	Joel 1:13–2:11
Tuesday	1 Kgs 22:1–9, 15–23, 29, 34–38	Joel 2:12–27
Wednesday	2 Chr 20:1–9, 13–24	Joel 2:28–3:8
Thursday	2 Kgs 2:1–15	Joel 3:9–21
Friday	2 Kgs 3:5–27	Mal 1:1–14; 2:13–16
Saturday	2 Kgs 4:8–37	Mal 3:1–4:6

Week XIX

Sunday	2 Kgs 4:38–44; 6:1–7	Jonah 1:1–17; 2:10
Monday	2 Kgs 5:1–19a	Jonah 3:1–4:11
Tuesday	2 Kgs 6:8–23	Zech 9:1–10:2
Wednesday	2 Kgs 6:24–25, 32–7:16	Zech 10:3–11:3
Thursday	2 Kgs 9:1–16, 22–27	Zech 11:4–12:8
Friday	2 Kgs 11:1–21	Zech 12:9–13:9
Saturday	2 Kgs 13:10–25	Zech 14:1–21

Week XX

Sunday	Eph 1:1–14	Eccles 1:1–18
Monday	Eph 1:15–23	Eccles 2:1–26
Tuesday	Eph 2:1–10	Eccles 3:1–22
Wednesday	Eph 2:11–22	Eccles 5:10–6:8
Thursday	Eph 3:1–13	Eccles 6:12–7:28
Friday	Eph 3:14–21	Eccles 8:5–9:10
Saturday	Eph 4:1–16	Eccles 11:7–12:14

Week XXI

Sunday	Eph 4:17–24	Tit 1:1–16
Monday	Eph 4:25–5:7	Tit 2:1–3:2
Tuesday	Eph 5:8–20	Tit 3:3–15
Wednesday	Eph 5:21–33	1 Tim 1:1–20
Thursday	Eph 6:1–9	1 Tim 2:1–15
Friday	Eph 6:10–24	1 Tim 3:1–16
Saturday	Philem 1–25	1 Tim 4:1–5:2

	Year 1	Year 2

Week XXII

Sunday	2 Kgs 14:1–27	1 Tim 5:3–25
Monday	Amos 1:1–2:3	1 Tim 6:1–10
Tuesday	Amos 2:4–16	1 Tim 6:11–21
Wednesday	Amos 3:1–15	2 Tim 1:1–18
Thursday	Amos 4:1–13	2 Tim 2:1–21
Friday	Amos 5:1–17	2 Tim 2:22–3:17
Saturday	Amos 5:18–6:14	2 Tim 4:1–22

Week XXIII

Sunday	Amos 7:1–17	2 Pet 1:1–11
Monday	Amos 8:1–14	2 Pet 1:12–21
Tuesday	Amos 9:1–15	2 Pet 2:1–8
Wednesday	Hos 1:1–9; 3:1–5	2 Pet 2:9–22
Thursday	Hos 2:2–23	2 Pet 3:1–10
Friday	Hos 4:1–10; 5:1–7	2 Pet 3:11–18
Saturday	Hos 5:15b–7:2	Jude 1–25

Week XXIV

Sunday	Hos 8:1–13	Esther 1:1–3, 9–16, 19; 2:5–10, 16–17
Monday	Hos 9:1–14	Esther 3:1–11
Tuesday	Hos 10:1–15	Esther 4:1–16
Wednesday	Hos 11:1–11	Esther 14:1–19
Thursday	Hos 13:1–16	Esther 5:1–14; 7:1–10
Friday	Hos 14:1–9	Baruch 1:14–2:5; 3:1–8
Saturday	2 Kgs 15:1–5, 32–35; 16:1–8	Baruch 3:9–15, 24–4:4

Week XXV

Sunday	Is 6:1–13	Tobit 1:1–22
Monday	Is 3:1–15	Tobit 2:1–3:6
Tuesday	Is 5:8–13, 17–24	Tobit 3:7–17
Wednesday	Is 7:1–17	Tobit 4:1–5, 19–21; 5:1–16
Thursday	Is 9:8–10:4	Tobit 6:1–17
Friday	Is 28:1–6, 14–22	Tobit 7:1, 8b–17; 8:5–13
Saturday	Mic 1:1–9; 2:1–11	Tobit 10:7c–11:15

	Year 1	Year 2

Week XXVI

Sunday	Mic 3:1–12	Judith 2:1–6; 3:6; 4:1–2, 9–15
Monday	Mic 6:1–15	Judith 5:1–21
Tuesday	2 Kgs 17:1–18	Judith 6:1–21; 7:1, 4–5
Wednesday	2 Kgs 17:24–41	Judith 8:1a, 10–14, 28–33; 9:1–14
Thursday	2 Chr 29:1–2; 30:1–16a	Judith 10:1–5, 11–17; 11:1–8, 20–23
Friday	Is 20:1–6	Judith 12:1–13:2
Saturday	2 Kgs 20:1–19	Judith 13:3–14:7

Week XXVII

Sunday	Is 22:1–14	Sir 1:1–20
Monday	Is 30:1–18	Sir 2:1–18
Tuesday	2 Kgs 18:17–36	Sir 3:1–16
Wednesday	2 Kgs 18:37–19:19, 35–37	Sir 3:17–4:10
Thursday	Is 37:21–35	Sir 5:1–6:4
Friday	2 Kgs 21:1–18, 23 –22:1	Sir 6:5–37
Saturday	Zeph 1:1–7, 14–2:3	Sir 7:22–36

Week XXVIII

Sunday	Zeph 3:8–20	Sir 10:6–18
Monday	Jer 1:1–19	Sir 11:11–28
Tuesday	Jer 2:1–13, 20–25	Sir 14:20–15:10
Wednesday	Jer 3:1–5, 19–4:4	Sir 15:11–20
Thursday	Jer 4:5–8, 13–28	Sir 16:24–17:14
Friday	Jer 7:1–20	Sir 17:15–32
Saturday	Jer 9:2–12, 17–22	Sir 24:1–22

Week XXIX

Sunday	2 Kgs 22:8, 10–23:4, 21–23	Sir 26:1–4, 9–18
Monday	Nahum 1:1–8; 3:1–7, 12–15a	Sir 27:22–28, 7
Tuesday	2 Chr 35:20–36:12	Sir 29:1–13; 31:1–4
Wednesday	Hab 1:1–2:4	Sir 35:1–17
Thursday	Hab 2:5–20	Sir 38:24–39:11
Friday	Jer 22:10–30	Sir 42:15–25; 43:27–33
Saturday	Jer 19:1–5, 10–20:6	Sir 51:1–12

	Year 1	**Year 2**

Week XXX

	Year 1	Year 2
Sunday	Jer 23:9–17, 21–29	Wisd 1:1–15
Monday	Jer 25:15–17, 27–38	Wisd 1:16–2:24
Tuesday	Jer 36:1–10, 21–32	Wis 3:1–19
Wednesday	Jer 24:1–10	Wis 4:1–20
Thursday	Jer 27:1–15	Wisd 5:1–23
Friday	Jer 28:1–17	Wid 6:1–25
Saturday	Jer 29:1–14	Wisd 7:15–30

Week XXXI

	Year 1	Year 2
Sunday	2 Kgs 24:20b–25:13, 18–21	Wisd 8:1–21
Monday	Jer 37:21; 38:14–28	Wisd 9:1–18
Tuesday	Jer 32:6–10, 26–40	Wisd 10:1–11:4
Wednesday	Jer 30:18–31:9	Wisd 11:20b–12:2, 11b–19
Thursday	Jer 31:15–22, 27–34	Wisd 13:1–10; 14:15–21; 15:1–6
Friday	Jer 42:1–16; 43:4–7	Wisd 15:18–16: 13, 20–25
Saturday	Ezek 1:3–14, 22–2:28	Wisd 18:1–15a; 19:4–9

Week XXXII

	Year 1	Year 2
Sunday	Ezek 2:8–3:11, 16–21	1 Macc 1:1–24
Monday	Ezek 5:1–17	1 Macc 1:41–64
Tuesday	Ezek 8:1–6a, 16–9:11	2 Macc 6:12–31
Wednesday	Ezek 10:18–22; 11:14–25	2 Macc 7:1–19
Thursday	Ezek 12:1–16	2 Macc 7:20–41
Friday	Ezek 13:1–16	1 Macc 2:1, 15–28, 42–50, 65–70
Saturday	Ezek 14:12–23	1 Macc 3:1–26

Week XXXIII

	Year 1	Year 2
Sunday	Ezek 16:3–19, 35–43, 59–63	1 Macc 4:36–59
Monday	Ezek 17:3–15, 19–24	2 Macc 12:36–45
Tuesday	Ezek 18:1–13, 20–32	1 Macc 6:1–17
Wednesday	Ezek 20:27–44	1 Macc 9:1–22
Thursday	Ezek 24:15–27	Dan 1:1–21
Friday	Ezek 28:1–19	Dan 2:1, 25–47
Saturday	Ezek 34:1–6, 11–16, 25–31	Dan 3:8–23, 24–30

	Year 1	Year 2

Week XXXIV

Sunday	Solemnity of Christ the King	Dan 7:1–27
Monday	Ezek 36:16–36	Dan 5:1–17, 23–31
Tuesday	Ezek 37:1–14	Dan 6:4–27
Wednesday	Ezek 37:15–28	Dan 8:1–26
Thursday	Ezek 38:14–39:10	Dan 9:1–4, 18–27
Friday	Ezek 40:1–4; 43:1–12; 44:6–9	Dan 10:1–21
Saturday	Ezek 47:1–12	Dan 12:1–13

Readings for Travellers

I

1 Thessalonians 4:1–18 **Exhortation to a saintly life; the resurrection of all at the Last Coming**

(For Advent and Saints)

We beseech and exhort you in the Lord Jesus, that as you learned from us how you ought to live and to please God, just as you are doing, you do so more and more. For you know what instructions we gave you through the Lord Jesus. For this is the will of God, your sanctification: that you abstain from immorality; that each one of you know how to control his own body in holiness and honour, not in the passion of lust like heathen who do not know God; that no man transgress, and wrong his brother in this matter, because the Lord is an avenger in all these things, as we solemnly forewarned you. For God has not called us for uncleanness, but in holiness. Therefore whoever disregards this, disregards not man but God, who gives his Holy Spirit to you.

But concerning love of the brethren you have no need to have any one write to you, for you yourselves have been taught by God to love one another; and indeed you do love all the brethren throughout Macedonia. But we exhort you, brethren, to do so more and more, to aspire to live quietly, to mind your own affairs, and to work with your hands, as we charged you; so that you may command the respect of outsiders, and be dependent on nobody.

But we would not have you ignorant, brethren, concerning those who are asleep, that you may not grieve as others do who have no hope. For since we believe that Jesus died and rose again, even so, through Jesus, God will bring with him those who have fallen asleep. For this we declare to you by the word of the Lord, that we who are alive, who are left until the coming of the Lord, shall not precede those who have fallen asleep. For the Lord himself will descend from heaven with a cry of command, with the archangel's call, and with the sound of the trumpet of God. And the dead in Christ will rise first; then we who are alive, who are left, shall be caught up together with them in the clouds to meet the Lord in the air; and so we shall always be with the Lord. Therefore comfort one another with these words.

Response

The Lord himself will descend from heaven with a cry of command, with the archangel's call, and with the sound of the trumpet of God. * And he will gather his elect from the four winds, from the ends of the earth to the ends of heaven.

V. When the Son of man has come, he will send out his angels with a loud trumpet call. * And he.

II

1 John 1:1–2:2   **The Word of God and the Light of God**
(*For Christmas and Epiphany*)

That which was from the beginning, which we have heard, which we have seen with our eyes, which we have looked upon and touched with our hands, concerning the word of life—the life was made manifest, and we saw it, and testify to it, and proclaim to you the eternal life which was with the Father and was made manifest to us—that which we have seen and heard we proclaim also to you, so that you may have fellowship with us; and our fellowship is with the Father and with his Son Jesus Christ. And we are writing this that our joy may be completed.

This is the message we have heard from him and proclaim to you, that God is light and in him is no darkness at all. If we say we have fellowship with him while we walk in darkness, we lie and do not live according to the truth; but if we walk in the light, as he is in the light, we have fellowship with one another, and the blood of Jesus his Son cleanses us from all sin. If we say we have no sin, we deceive ourselves, and the truth is not in us. If we confess our sins, he is faithful and just, and will forgive our sins and cleanse us from all unrighteousness. If we say we have not sinned, we make him a liar, and his word is not in us.

My little children, I am writing this to you so that you may not sin; but if any one does sin, we have an advocate with the Father, Jesus Christ the righteous; and he is the expiation for our sins, and not for ours only but also for the sins of the whole world.

Response

The life was made manifest, and we saw it, and testify to it, and proclaim to you the eternal life * which was with the Father and was made manifest to us.

V. We know that the Son of God has come. This is the true God and eternal life. * Which was.

III

1 John 4:7–5:2   Perfect love

(*For Christmas and Feasts*)

Beloved, let us love one another; for love is of God, and he who loves is born of God and knows God. He who does not love does not know God; for God is love. In this the love of God was made manifest among us, that God sent his only Son into the world, so that we might live through him. In this is love, not that we loved God but that he loved us and sent his Son to be the expiation for our sins. Beloved, if God so loved us, we also ought to love one another. No man has ever seen God; if we love one another, God abides in us and his love is perfected in us.

By this we know that we abide in him and he in us, because he has given us of his own Spirit. And we have seen and testify that the Father has sent his Son as the Saviour of the world. Whoever confesses that Jesus is the Son of God, God abides in him, and he in God. So we know and believe the love God has for us. God is love, and he who abides in love abides in God, and God abides in him. In this is love perfected with us, that we may have confidence for the day of judgment, because as he is so are we in this world. There is no fear in love, but perfect love casts out fear. For fear has to do with punishment, and he who fears is not perfected in love. We love, because he first loved us. If any one says, 'I love God,' and hates his brother, he is a liar; for he who does not love his brother whom he has seen, cannot love God whom he has not seen. And this commandment we have from him, that he who loves God should love his brother also.

Every one who believes that Jesus is the Christ is a child of God, and every one who loves the parent loves the child. By this we know that we love the children of God, when we love God and obey his commandments.

Response

God loved us and sent his Son to be the expiation for our sins. * So we know and believe the love God has for us. *V.* The Lord became our Saviour; in his love he redeemed us. *So we.

IV

Sirach 2:1–18   Patience in temptation
(For Lent, Memorials of Saints)

My son, if you come forward to serve the Lord,
prepare yourself for temptation.
Set your heart right and be steadfast,
and do not be hasty in time of calamity.
Cleave to him and do not depart,
that you may be honoured at the end of your life.
Accept whatever is brought upon you,
and in changes that humble you be patient.
For gold is tested in the fire,
and acceptable men in the furnace of humiliation.
Trust in him, and he will help you;
make your ways straight, and hope in him.

You who fear the Lord, wait for his mercy;
and turn not aside, lest you fall.
You who fear the Lord, trust in him, and your reward will
    not fail;
you who fear the Lord, hope for good things,
for everlasting joy and mercy.

538

Consider the ancient generations and see:
who ever trusted in the Lord and was put to shame?
Or who ever persevered in the fear of the Lord and was
  forsaken?
Or who ever called upon him and was overlooked?
For the Lord is compassionate and merciful;
he forgives sins and saves in time of affliction.

Woe to timid hearts and to slack hands,
and to the sinner who walks along two ways!
Woe to the faint heart, for it has no trust!
Therefore it will not be sheltered.
Woe to you who have lost your endurance!
What will you do when the Lord punishes you?
Those who fear the Lord will not disobey his words,
and those who love him will keep his ways.
Those who fear the Lord will seek his approval,
and those who love him will be filled with the law.
Those who fear the Lord will prepare their hearts,
and will humble themselves before him.
Let us fall into the hands of the Lord,
but not into the hands of men;
for as his majesty is, so also is his mercy.

Response

You who fear the Lord, hope for good things, for everlasting joy and mercy. Consider the ancient generations
and see: * Who ever trusted in the Lord and was put to
shame?

V. Look towards him and be radiant; let your faces not be
abashed. * Who ever.

V

Romans 6:1–11   **The baptized are likened to Christ**
(*For Eastertide*)

What shall we say then? Are we to continue in sin that grace
may abound? By no means! How can we who died to sin
still live in it? Do you not know that all of us who have

539

been baptized into Christ Jesus were baptized into his death? We were buried therefore with him by baptism into death, so that as Christ was raised from the dead by the glory of the Father, we too might walk in newness of life. For if we have been united with him in a death like his, we shall certainly be united with him in a resurrection like his. We know that our old self was crucified with him so that the sinful body might be destroyed, and we might no longer be enslaved to sin. For he who has died is free from sin. But if we have died with Christ, we believe that we shall also live with him. For we know that Christ being raised from the dead will never die again; death no longer has dominion over him. The death he died he died to sin, once for all, but the life he lives he lives to God. So you also must consider yourselves dead to sin and alive to God in Christ Jesus.

Response

We were buried with Christ by baptism into death, * so that as he was raised from the dead by the glory of the Father, we too might walk in newness of life. Alleluia, alleluia!

V. As many of you as were baptized into Christ have put on Christ. * So that.

VI

Revelation 12:1-17   **The great sign of the woman in heaven**
(For Easter and Feasts of the Blessed Virgin Mary)

And a great portent appeared in heaven, a woman clothed with the sun, with the moon under her feet, and on her head a crown of twelve stars; she was with child and she cried out in her pangs of birth, in anguish for delivery. And another portent appeared in heaven: behold, a great red dragon, with seven heads and ten horns, and seven diadems upon his heads. His tail swept down a third of the stars of heaven, and cast them to the earth. And the dragon stood before the woman who was about to bear a child, that he might devour her child when she brought it forth; she brought forth a male child, one who is to rule all the nations with a rod of iron, but her child was caught up to God and to his throne, and the woman fled into the wilderness, where she has a place prepared by God, in which to be nourished for one thousand two hundred and sixty days.

Now war arose in heaven, Michael and his angels fighting against the dragon; and the dragon and his angels fought, but they were defeated and there was no longer any place for them in heaven. And the great dragon was thrown down, that ancient serpent, who is called the Devil and Satan, the deceiver of the whole world—he was thrown down to the earth, and his angels were thrown down with him. And I heard a loud voice in heaven saying, 'Now the salvation and the power and the kingdom of our God and the authority of his Christ have come, for the accuser of our brethren has been thrown down, who accuses them day and night before our God. And they have conquered him by the blood of the Lamb and by the word of their testimony, for they loved not their lives even unto death. Rejoice then, O heaven and you that dwell therein! But woe to you, O earth and sea, for the devil has come down to you in great wrath, because he knows that his time is short!'

And when the dragon saw that he had been thrown down to the earth, he pursued the woman who had borne the male child. But the woman was given the two wings of the great eagle that she might fly from the serpent into the wilderness, to the place where she is to be nourished for a time, and times, and half a time. The serpent poured water like a river out of his mouth after the woman, to sweep her away with the flood. But the earth came to the help of the woman, and the earth opened its mouth and swallowed the river which the dragon had poured from his mouth. Then the dragon was angry with the woman, and went off to make war on the rest of her offspring, on those who keep the commandments of God and bear testimony to Jesus. And he stood on the sand of the sea.

541

Response

Blessed are you, holy Virgin Mary, and worthy of all praise,
* for Christ our Lord, the Sun of justice, was born of you.

Eastertide: Alleluia, alleluia!

V. Pray for our people, our priests and nuns. Come to the
help of all who keep your feast. * For Christ.

VII

Genesis 15:1–21   **God's covenant with Abraham**

(*Throughout the Year*)

After these things the word of the Lord came to Abram in a
vision, 'Fear not, Abram, I am your shield; your reward
shall be very great.' But Abram said, 'O Lord God, what
will you give me, for I continue childless, and the heir of
my house is Eliezer of Damascus?' And Abram said,
'Behold, you have given me no offspring; and a slave born
in my house will be my heir.' And behold, the word of the
Lord came to him, 'This man shall not be your heir; your
own son shall be your heir.' And he brought him outside
and said, 'Look toward heaven, and number the stars, if
you are able to number them.' Then he said to him, 'So
shall your descendants be.' And he believed the Lord; and
he reckoned it to him as righteousness.

And he said to him, 'I am the Lord who brought you from
Ur of the Chaldeans, to give you this land to possess.' But
he said, 'O Lord God, how am I to know that I shall possess
it?' He said to him, 'Bring me a heifer three years old, a
she-goat three years old, a ram three years old, a turtledove,
and a young pigeon.' And he brought him all these, cut
them in two, and laid each half over against the other; but
he did not cut the birds in two. And when birds of prey
came down upon the carcasses, Abram drove them away.
As the sun was going down, a deep sleep fell on Abram;
and lo, a dread and great darkness fell upon him. Then the
Lord said to Abram, 'Know of a surety that your descendants will be sojourners in a land that is not theirs, and
will be slaves there, and they will be oppressed for four

hundred years; but I will bring judgment on the nation which they serve, and afterwards they shall come out with great possessions. As for yourself, you shall go to your fathers in peace; you shall be buried in a good old age. And they shall come back here in the fourth generation; for the iniquity of the Amorites is not yet complete.'

When the sun had gone down and it was dark, behold, a smoking fire pot and a flaming torch passed between these pieces. On that day the Lord made a covenant with Abram, saying, 'To your descendants I give this land, from the river of Egypt to the great River, the river Euphrates, the land of the Kenites, the Kenizzites, the Kadmonites, the Hittites, the Perizzites, the Rephaim, the Amorites, the Canaanites, the Girgashites and the Jebusites.'

Response

Abraham believed God, and it was reckoned to him as righteousness; * and he was called the friend of God.

V. In hope he believed against hope, that he should become the father of many nations. * And he.

VIII

1 Corinthians 3:1–23   **Building up the kingdom of God; the rule of the apostles**

(*Throughout the year and for Apostles and Pastors*)

Brethren, I could not address you as spiritual men, but as men of the flesh, as babes in Christ. I fed you with milk, not solid food; for you were not ready for it; and even yet you are not ready, for you are still of the flesh. For while there is jealousy and strife among you, are you not of the flesh, and behaving like ordinary men? For when one says, 'I belong to Paul,' and another, 'I belong to Apollos,' are you not merely men?

What then is Apollos? What is Paul? Servants through whom you believed, as the Lord assigned to each. I planted, Apollos watered, but God gave the growth. So neither he who plants nor he who waters is anything, but only God who gives the growth. He who plants and he who waters are equal, and each shall receive his wages according to his labour. For we are God's fellow workers; you are God's field, God's building.

According to the commission of God given to me, like a skilled master builder I laid a foundation, and another man is building upon it. Let each man take care how he builds upon it. For no other foundation can any one lay than that which is laid, which is Jesus Christ.

Now if any one builds on the foundation with gold, silver, precious stones, wood, hay,s tubble—each man's work will become manifest; for the Day will disclose it, because it will be revealed with fire, and the fire will test what sort of work each one has done. If the work which any man has built on the foundation survives, he will receive a reward. If any man's work is burned up, he will suffer loss, though he himself will be saved, but only as through fire.

Do you not know that you are God's temple and that God's Spirit dwells in you? If any one destroys God's temple, God will destroy him. For God's temple is holy, and that temple you are.

Let no one deceive himself. If any one among you thinks that he is wise in this age, let him become a fool that he may become wise. For the wisdom of this world is folly with God. For it is written, 'He catches the wise in their craftiness,' and again, 'The Lord knows that the thoughts of the wise are futile.' So let no one boast of men. For all things are yours, whether Paul or Apollos or Cephas or the world or life or death or the present or the future, all are yours; and you are Christ's; and Christ is God's.

Response

You are fellow citizens with the saints and members of the household of God, built upon the foundation of the apostles, *Christ Jesus himself being the cornerstone.

V. God's spirit dwells in you: you are God's temple. *
Christ Jesus.

Common Offices

Dedication of a Church

EVENING PRAYER I

Hymn

Jerusalem, heavenly city, blest vision of peace!
Built from living stones,
you are raised on high to the heavens and attended, like a
    bride,
by countless thousands of angels.

How happy the bride of such a favoured destiny!
Your rich endowment is the Father's glory
and your comeliness is from the Bridegroom's grace—
queen most beautiful, bride of Christ the King,
radiant city of heaven.

In this city the gates of glittering pearls stand open for all
    to enter;
for every man that follows the path of virtue must come to
    those gates—
every man that endures sufferings here
for love of Christ.

It's stones are fashioned by many a stroke and blow
of the Saviour-mason's hammer and chisel.
Thus shaped they go to the making of this mighty structure,
each being fitly joined to each and finding its appointed place
in the whole building.

Let due glory be given to the Father most high,
to his only Son
and to the renowned Paraclete.
To God be praise, power and glory
through everlasting ages. Amen.

Psalmody

Psalm 146

Ant. In his temple they all cry: 'Glory!'

Praise the Lord for he is good;†
sing to our God for he is loving:
to him our praise is due.

The Lord builds up Jerusalem
and brings back Israel's exiles,
he heals the broken-hearted,
he binds up all their wounds.
He fixes the number of the stars;
he calls each one by its name.

Our Lord is great and almighty;
his wisdom can never be measured.
The Lord raises the lowly;
he humbles the wicked to the dust.
Sing to the Lord, giving thanks;
sing psalms to our God with the harp.

He covers the heavens with clouds;
he prepares the rain for the earth,
making mountains sprout with grass
and with plants to serve man's needs.
He provides the beasts with their food
and young ravens that call upon him.

His delight is not in horses
nor his pleasure in warrior's strength.
The Lord delights in those who revere him,
in those who wait for his love.

Ant. In his temple they all cry: 'Glory!'

Psalm 147

Ant. The Lord has blessed the children within you.

O praise the Lord, Jerusalem!
Zion, praise ryou God!

He has strengthened the bars of your gates,
he has blessed the children within you.

He established peace on your borders,
he feeds you with finest wheat.

He sends out his word to the earth
and swiftly runs his command.
He showers down snow white as wool,
he scatters hoar-frost like ashes.

He hurls down hailstones like crumbs.
The waters are frozen at his touch;
he sends forth his word and it melts them:
at the breath of his mouth the waters flow.

He makes his word known to Jacob,
to Israel his laws and decrees.
He has not dealt thus with other nations;
he has not taught them his decrees.

Ant. The Lord has blessed the children within you.

OUTSIDE LENT

Rev 19:1, 2, 5–8   **Wedding song of the Lamb**

Ant. The songs of the blessed fill the city of God, alleluia;
   angels sing without ceasing before his throne, alleluia!

R. Alleluia, alleluia!
Salvation and glory and power
belong to our God, alleluia!
His judgments are true
and just,
R. Alleluia, alleluia!

Praise our God,
all you his servants, alleluia!
You who fear him,
small and great.
R. Alleluia, alleluia!

The Lord our God,
the Almighty, reigns, alleluia!
Let us rejoice and exult
and give him the glory.
R. Alleluia, alleluia!

The marriage of the Lamb
has come, alleluia!
And his bride
has made herself ready.
R. Alleluia, alleluia!

It was granted her
to be clothed, alleluia!
with fine linen,
bright and pure.
R. Alleluia, alleluia!

Ant. The songs of the blessed fill the city of God, alleluia;
angels sing without ceasing before his throne, alleluia!

LENT

1 Pet 2:21–24   New Testament song of the suffering Servant

Ant. All the angels stood round the throne,
and they fell on their faces before the throne and worshipped God.

R. By his wounds you have been healed.

Christ suffered for you,†
leaving you an example
that you should follow in his steps. (R.)

He committed no sin;
no guile was found on his lips.
When he was reviled,
he did not revile in return.

When he suffered,
he did not threaten;
but he trusted to him
who judges justly. (R.)

549

He himself bore our sins
in his body on the tree,
that we might die to sin
and live to righteousness.
By his wounds you have been healed.†
For you were straying like sheep,
but have now returned to the Shepherd and Guardian of
    your souls. (*R*.)

Ant. All the angels stood round the throne, and they fell on
    their faces and worshipped God.

Word of God   Eph 2:19–22

You are no longer strangers and sojourners, but you are
fellow citizens with the saints and members of the household
of God, built upon the foundation of the apostles and
prophets, Christ Jesus himself being the cornerstone, in
whom the whole structure is joined together and grows into
a holy temple in the Lord; in whom you also are built into
it for a dwelling place of God in the Spirit.

Short Response

Holiness is fitting to your house, O Lord,
until the end of time.
V. They are happy who dwell in your house,
for ever singing your praise.
R. Until the end of time.
V. Glory be to the Father, and to the Son, and to the Holy
Spirit.
Holiness is fitting to your house, O Lord,
until the end of time.

Song of the Virgin Mary

Ant. Rejoice with Jerusalem for ever,
    and be glad for her, all you who love her.

Prayers

Let us pray to our Saviour, who laid down his life to gather into one the children of God who were scattered abroad; let us say to him:

R. Lord, remember your Church.

Or: My house shall be called a house of prayer for all the nations.

Lord Jesus, you built your Church on the rock of Peter;
—strengthen her in firm faith and confidence. (*R.*)

Lord Jesus, by the blood and water flowing from your side,
—re-create your Church by means of the sacraments of the new and everlasting covenant. (*R.*)

Lord Jesus, always present in the midst of those who gather together in your name,
—hear the united prayer of your Church. (*R.*)

Lord Jesus, together with the Father, you make your home with those who love you;
—may your Church be made perfect in divine love. (*R.*)
(*R.*)

Lord Jesus, you never cast out those who come to you;
—receive those who have died into your Father's house.
(*R.*)

Concluding prayer

On the anniversary of the dedication

O God, every year you renew the day of the consecration of this holy temple and continue to bring us safely to your holy mysteries. Graciously hear the prayers of your people. Grant that all who enter this temple to implore your blessings may rejoice in obtaining whatever they request. We make our prayer through our Lord.

On the day of dedication

O God, who invisibly sustain all things, and yet, for the salvation of mankind, show visibly the signs of your power, adorn this temple by the power of your indwelling presence, and grant that all who gather here to pray may obtain the blessings of your support, whatever their trials, when they call upon you. We make our prayer through our Lord.

OFFICE OF READINGS

Hymn *as at* Evening Prayer I, p. 546

Psalmody

Psalm 23

Ant. O gates, lift high your heads;
   grow higher ancient doors.

The Lord's is the earth and its fullness,
the world and all its peoples.
It is he who set it on the seas;
on the waters he made it firm.

Who shall climb the mountain of the Lord?
Who shall stand in his holy place?
The man with clean hands and pure heart,†
who desires not worthless things,
who has not sworn so as to deceive his neighbour.

He shall receive blessings from the Lord
and reward from the God who saves him.
Such are the men who seek him,
seek the face of the God of Jacob.

O gates, lift high your heads;†
grow higher, ancient doors.
Let him enter, the king of glory!

Who is the king of glory?
The Lord, the mighty, the valiant, the Lord, the valiant in
   war.

O gates, lift high your heads;†
grow higher, ancient doors.
Let him enter, the king of glory!

552

Who is he, the king of glory?
He, the Lord of armies, he is the king of glory.

Ant. O gates, lift high your heads;
grow higher ancient doors.

Psalm 83

Ant. How lovely is your dwelling place,
Lord, God of hosts!

How lovely is your dwelling place,
Lord, God of hosts.

My soul is longing and yearning,
is yearning for the courts of the Lord.
My heart and my soul ring out their joy
to God, the living God.

The sparrow herself finds a home
and the swallow a nest for her brood;
she lays her young by your altars,
Lord of hosts, my king and my God.

They are happy, who dwell in your house,
for ever singing your praise.
They are happy, whose strength is in you,
in whose hearts are the roads to Zion.

As they go through the Bitter Valley†
they make it a place of springs,
the autumn rain covers it with blessings.
They walk with ever growing strength,
they will see the God of gods in Zion.

O Lord God of hosts, hear my prayer,
give ear, O God of Jacob.
Turn your eyes, O God, our shield,
look on the face of your anointed.

One day within your courts
is better than a thousand elsewhere.
The threshold of the house of God
I prefer to the dwellings of the wicked.

For the Lord God is a rampart, a shield;
he will give us his favour and glory.
The Lord will not refuse any good
to those who walk without blame.

Lord, God of hosts,
happy the man who trusts in you!

Ant. How lovely is your dwelling place,
   Lord, God of hosts!

Psalm 86

Ant. Of you are told glorious things,
   O city of God!

On the holy mountain is his city
cherished by the Lord.
The Lord prefers the gates of Zion
to all Jacob's dwellings.
Of you are told glorious things,
O city of God!

'Babylon and Egypt I will count
among those who know me;
Philistia, Tyre, Ethiopia,
these will be her children
and Zion shall be called "Mother"
for all shall be her children.'

It is he, the Lord Most High,
who gives each his place.
In his register of peoples he writes:
'These are her children'
and while they dance they will sing:
'In you all find their home.'

Ant. Of you are told glorious things,
   O city of God!

V. I will adore before your holy temple.
R. Lord, I thank you for your faithfulness and love.

Readings

Advent   Rev 21:9–27

Response

Jerusalem will be built with sapphires and emeralds and her walls with precious stones. * All her lanes will cry 'Alleluia'! and will give praise:

V. Blessed is God who has exalted you for ever. * All her lanes.

Lent   1 Kings 8:1–4, 10–13, 22–30

Response

If two of you agree on earth about anything they ask, it will be done for them by my Father in heaven. * For where two or three are gathered in my name, there am I in the midst of them.

V. My eyes will be open and my ears attentive to the prayer that is made in this place. * For where.

Throughout the Year   1 Pet 2:1–17

Response

The foundations of the wall of the city were adorned with every jewel. * And the twelve gates were twelve pearls, each of the gates made of a single pearl.

V. The street of the city was pure gold, transparent as glass. * And the twelve.

Prayer *as at* Evening Prayer I, p. 551.

MORNING PRAYER

Psalm 94

Refrain: Holiness is fitting to the Church of God:
   Come, let us worship Christ her spouse.

Hymn

From the summit of the highest heaven came the sovereign
   Father's Son,
like the stone that was hewn from the mountain
and fell to the plains beneath.
He was the cornerstone where met the earthly house
and the heavenly one.

Now that heavenly one is always resounding with praises
and ever in unceasing song honouring the triune God.
And when we sing our hymns of praise,
we are one with heaven, our purpose the same
as that of holy Zion.

King of those that dwell in heaven,
fill this temple with your heavenly light.
Come down to it at our calling, there to receive your people's
    prayers,
and fill our hearts unceasingly
with heavenly grace.

Here may the prayers and entreaties of your suppliants
find their answer in graces from our home above
and may they find joy and comfort in graces received
until, being freed from the body, they take their place
among the blessed.
Let due glory be given to the Father most high,
to his only Son
and to the renowned Paraclete.
To God be praise, power and glory
through everlasting ages. Amen.

Psalmody

Psalm 62

Ant. My house shall be called a house of prayer.

O God, you are my God, for you I long;
for you my soul is thirsting.
My body pines for you
like a dry, weary land without water.
So I gaze on you in the sanctuary
to see your strength and your glory.

For your love is better than life,
my lips will speak your praise.
So I will bless you all my life,
in your name I will lift up my hands.

My soul shall be filled as with a banquet,
my mouth shall praise you with joy.

On my bed I remember you.
On you I muse through the night
for you have been my help;
in the shadow of your wings I rejoice.
My soul clings to you;
your right hand holds me fast.

Those who seek to destroy my life
shall go down to the depths of the earth.
They shall be put into the power of the sword
and left as the prey of the jackals.
But the king shall rejoice in God;†
all that swear by him shall be blessed,
for the mouth of liars shall be silenced.

Ant. My house shall be called a house of prayer.

Dan 3:57–88, 56   **Song of the universe**

Ant. Blessed are you, O Lord, in the temple of your glory.

O all you works of the Lord, O bless the Lord.
R. To him be highest glory and praise for ever.

And you, angels of the Lord, O bless the Lord.
R. To him be highest glory and praise for ever.

And you, the heavens of the Lord, O bless the Lord.
And you, clouds of the sky, O bless the Lord.
And you, all armies of the Lord, O bless the Lord.
R. To him be highest glory and praise for ever.

And you, sun and moon, O bless the Lord.
And you, the stars of the heav'ns, O bless the Lord.
And you, showers and rain, O bless the Lord.
R. To him be highest glory and praise for ever.

And you, all you breezes and winds, O bless the Lord.
And you, fire and heat, O bless the Lord.
And you, cold and heat, O bless the Lord.
R. To him be highest glory and praise for ever.

And you, showers and dew, O bless the Lord.
And you, frosts and cold, O bless the Lord.
And you, frost and snow, O bless the Lord.
R. To him be highest glory and praise for ever.

And you, night-time and day, O bless the Lord.
And you, darkness and light, O bless the Lord.
And you, lightning and clouds, O bless the Lord.
R. To him be highest glory and praise for ever.

O let the earth bless the Lord.
R. To him be highest glory and praise for ever.

And you, mountains and hills, O bless the Lord.
And you, all plants of the earth, O bless the Lord.
And you, fountains and springs, O bless the Lord.
R. To him be highest glory and praise for ever.

And you, rivers and seas, O bless the Lord.
And you, creatures of the sea, O bless the Lord.
And you, every bird in the sky, O bless the Lord.
And you, wild beasts and tame, O bless the Lord.
R. To him be highest glory and praise for ever.

And you, children of men, O bless the Lord.
R. To him be highest glory and praise for ever.

O Israel, bless the Lord, O bless the Lord.
And you, priests of the Lord, O bless the Lord.
And you, servants of the Lord, O bless the Lord.
R. To him be highest glory and praise for ever.

And you, spirits and souls of the just, O bless the Lord,
And you, holy and humble of heart, O bless the Lord.
Ananias, Azarias, Mizael, O bless the Lord.
R. To him be highest glory and praise for ever.

May you be blessed, O Lord, in the heavens.
R. To you be highest glory and praise for ever.

Ant. Blessed are you, O Lord, in the temple of your glory.

Psalm 149
Ant. Praise the Lord in the assembly of the faithful.

Sing a new song to the Lord,
his praise in the assembly of the faithful.
Let Israel rejoice in its Maker,
let Zion's sons exult in their king.
Let them praise his name with dancing
and make music with timbrel and harp.

For the Lord takes delight in his people.
He crowns the poor with salvation.
Let the faithful rejoice in their glory,
shout for joy and take their rest.
Let the praise of God be on their lips
and a two-edged sword in their hand,

to deal out vengeance to the nations
and punishment on all the peoples;
to bind their kings in chains
and their nobles in fetters of iron;
to carry out the sentence pre-ordained:
this honour is for all his faithful.

Ant. Praise the Lord in the assembly of the faithful.

Word of God   Is 56:7

I will bring them to my holy mountain,
and make them joyful in my house of prayer;
their burnt offerings and their sacrifices will be accepted on
    my altar;
for my house shall be called a house of prayer
for all peoples.

Short Response
The Lord is great
and worthy to be praised.
V. In the city of our God.
R. The Lord is great and worthy to be praised.
V. Glory be to the Father, and to the Son, and to the Holy
Spirit.
The Lord is great
and worthy to be praised.

Song of Zechariah

Ant. Zacchaeus, make haste and come down, for I must stay at your house today. So he made haste and came down, and received him joyfully—'Today salvation has come to this house' from God.

Prayers

We are living stones, built upon Christ, the chosen foundation stone; let us beseech the Almighty Father for the Church of his love; let us profess our sure trust in her, saying:

R. Truly this is the house of God, and the gate of heaven.

Or: Lord, how lovely is your dwelling place!

Father, you are the vinedresser; watch over your vine, prune it and give it increase;

—train its shoots until they fill the whole earth. (*R.*)

Eternal Shepherd, guard and extend your sheepfold;

—may all the sheep be united under the one Shepherd, your Son.(*R.*)

Almighty Sower, sow the field with your Word,

—that it may bear fruit a hundredfold in harvests of eternity. (*R.*)

Wisest of architects, make your house and family so holy,

—that all may recognize in them that heavenly city, the new Jerusalem, the glorious Bride. (*R.*)

Concluding prayer *as at* Evening Prayer I, p. 551

MIDDAY PRAYER

Psalmody

Ant. Holiness is fitting to your house, O Lord, until the end of time.

Psalm 117

I

Give thanks to the Lord for he is good, for his love has no end.

Let the sons of Israel say:
'His love has no end.'
Let the sons of Aaron say:
'His love has no end.'
Let those who fear the Lord say:
'His love has no end.'

I called to the Lord in my distress;
he answered and freed me.
The Lord is at my side; I do not fear.
What can a man do against me?
The Lord is at my side as my helper:
I shall look down on my foes.

It is better to take refuge in the Lord
than to trust in men:
it is better to take refuge in the Lord
than to trust in princes. . .
I was thrust, thrust down and falling
but the Lord was my helper.

II

The Lord is my strength and my song;
he was my saviour.
There are shouts of joy and victory
in the tents of the just.

The Lord's right hand has triumphed;
his right hand raised me up.
The Lord's right hand has triumphed;
I shall not die, I shall live and recount his deeds.
I was punished, I was punished by the Lord,
but not doomed to die.

III

Open to me the gates of holiness:
I will enter and give thanks.
This is the Lord's own gate

where the just may enter.
I will thank you for you have given answer
and you are my saviour.

The stone which the builders rejected
has become the corner stone.
This is the work of the Lord,
a marvel in our eyes.
This day was made by the Lord;
we rejoice and are glad.

O Lord, grant us salvation;
O Lord, grant success.
Blessed in the name of the Lord
is he who comes.
We bless you from the house of the Lord;
the Lord God is our light.

Go forward in procession with branches
even to the altar.
You are my God, I thank you.
My God, I praise you.
Give thanks to the Lord for he is good;
for his love has no end.

Ant. Holiness is fitting to your house, O Lord,
until the end of time.

Word of God
2 Cor 6:16

We are the temple of the living God; as God said,
'I will live in them and move among them,
and I will be their God,
and they shall be my people.'

V. For the peace of Jerusalem pray:
R. May peace reign in your walls!

Prayer *as at* Evening Prayer I, p. 551

EVENING PRAYER II

Hymn *as at* Evening Prayer I, p. 546

Psalmody

Psalm 45

Ant. The Lord dwells in this holy place:
  God is within, it cannot be shaken.

God is for us a refuge and strength,
a helper close at hand, in time of distress:
so we shall not fear though the earth should rock,
though the mountains fall into the depths of the sea,
even though its waters rage and foam,
even though the mountains be shaken by its waves.

R. The Lord of hosts is with us:
the God of Jacob is our stronghold.

The waters of a river give joy to God's city,
the holy place where the Most High dwells.
God is within, it cannot be shaken;
God will help it at the dawning of the day.
Nations are in tumult, kingdoms are shaken:
he lifts his voice, the earth shrinks away. (*R.*)

Come, consider the works of the Lord
the redoubtable deeds he has done on the earth.
He puts an end to wars all over the earth;†
the bow he breaks, the spear he snaps.
He burns the shields with fire.
'Be still and know that I am God,
supreme among the nations, supreme on the earth!' (*R.*)

Ant. The Lord dwells in this holy place:
  God is within, it cannot be shaken.

Psalm 121

Ant. Let us go to God's house, rejoicing.

I rejoiced when I heard them say:
'Let us go to God's house.'
And now our feet are standing
within your gates, O Jerusalem.

Jerusalem is built as a city
strongly compact.
It is there that the tribes go up,
the tribes of the Lord.

For Israel's law it is,
there to praise the Lord's name.
There were set the thrones of judgment
of the house of David.

For the peace of Jerusalem pray:
'Peace be to your homes!
May peace reign in your walls,
in your palaces, peace!'

For love of my brethren and friends
I say: 'Peace upon you!'
For love of the house of the Lord
I will ask for your good.

Ant. Let us go to God's house, rejoicing.

OUTSIDE LENT

Wedding song of the Lamb (Rev 19:1, 2, 5–8) *as at* Evening Prayer I,
p. 548, *with the following antiphon:*

Ant. Praise our God, all you his saints.

LENT

Rev 15:3–4   **Song of Moses and the Lamb**

Ant. Praise our God, all you his saints.

Great and wonderful are your deeds,
O Lord God, the Almighty!
Just and true are your ways,
O King of the ages!

Who shall not fear and glorify your name, O Lord?
For you alone are holy.

All nations shall come and worship you,
for you judgments have been revealed.

Ant. Praise our God, all you his saints.

Short Response
How lovely is your dwelling place,
Lord God of hosts!
V. They are happy who dwell in your house,
   for ever singing your praise.
R. Lord, God of hosts!
V. Glory be to the Father, and to the Son, and to the Holy
Spirit.

How lovely is your dwelling place,
Lord God of hosts!

Song of the Virgin Mary
Ant. The Lord dwells in this holy place: this is the house
of God where his name is invoked, the place of which it is
written, 'My name shall be there, says the Lord.'
Prayers *as at* Evening Prayer I, p. 551

Common of the Blessed Virgin Mary

EVENING PRAYER I

Hymn   Sir 24:3–12, 19–22

I came forth from the mouth of the Most High,
and covered the earth like a mist.
I dwelt in high places,
and my throne was in a pillar of cloud.

R. Mother of hope and everlasting love, pray for us.

Alone I made the circuit of heaven
and have walked in the depths of the abyss.
In the waves of the sea, in the whole earth,
and in every people and nation I have gotten a possession.
Among all these I sought a resting place;
I sought in whose territory I might lodge. (*R.*)

Then the Creator of all things gave me a commandment,
and the one who created me assigned a place for my tent:
'Make your dwelling in Jacob,
and in Israel receive your inheritance.' (*R.*)

From eternity, in the beginning, he created me,
and for eternity I shall not cease to exist.
In the holy tabernacle I ministered before him,
and so I was established in Zion. (*R.*)

In the beloved city he gave me a resting place,
and in Jerusalem was my dominion.
So I took root in an honoured people,
in the portion of the Lord, who is their inheritance. (*R.*)

Come to me, all you who desire me,
and eat your fill of my produce.
For the remembrance of me is sweeter than honey,
and my inheritance sweeter than the honeycomb. (*R.*)

Those who eat me will hunger for more,
and those who drink me will thirst for more.
Whoever obeys me will not be put to shame,
and those who work with my help will not sin. (R.)

Psalmody

Psalm 112

Ant. Hail, Mother of Christ, hail full of grace.

Praise, O servants of the Lord,
praise the name of the Lord!
May the name of the Lord be blessed
both now and for evermore!
From the rising of the sun to its setting
praised be the name of the Lord!

High above all nations is the Lord,
above the heavens his glory.
Who is like the Lord, our God,
who has risen on high to his throne
yet stoops from the heights to look down,
to look down upon heaven and earth?

From the dust he lifts up the lowly,
from the dungheap he raises the poor
to set him in the company of princes,
yes, with the princes of his people.
To the childless wife he gives a home
and gladdens her heart with children.

Ant. Hail, Mother of Christ, hail full of grace.

Psalm 147

Ant. You are the glory of Jerusalem, the joy of Israel!

O praise the Lord, Jerusalem!
Zion, praise your God!

He has strengthened the bars of your gates,
he has blessed the children within you.

He established peace on your borders,
he feeds you with finest wheat.

He sends out his word to the earth
and swiftly runs his command.
He showers down snow white as wool,
he scatters hoar-frost like ashes.

He hurls down hailstones like crumbs.
The waters are frozen at his touch;
he sends forth his word and it melts them:
at the breath of his mouth the waters flow.

He makes his word known to Jacob,
to Israel his laws and decrees.
He has not dealt thus with other nations;
he has not taught them his decrees.

Ant. You are the glory of Jerusalem, the joy of Israel!

Wedding song of the Lamb (Rev 19:1, 2, 5–8) *as for the* Dedication of a Church, p. 548, *with the following antiphon:*

Ant. A great portent appeared in heaven, a woman clothed with the sun, with the moon under her feet, and on her head a crown of twelve stars.

Word of God   Gal 4:4–5

When the time had fully come, God sent forth his Son, born of a woman, born under the law, to redeem those who were under the law, so that we might receive adoption as sons.

Short Response

In your splendour and state,
ride on in triumph, Virgin Mary.
V. Listen, O daughter, give ear to my words:
  the king desires your beauty.
R. Ride on in triumph, Virgin Mary.
V. Glory be to the Father, and to the Son, and to the Holy Spirit.
In your splendour and state,
ride on in triumph, Virgin Mary.

Song of the Virgin Mary

Ant. All ages will call me blessed,
   for God has looked on his servant in her nothingness.

Prayers

Let us pray to God the Almighty Father, and since it is his will that his Son's mother, Mary, should be venerated by all generations, let us say to him:

R. May the one you have so highly favoured intercede for us.

O God, you have raised the Immaculate Virgin, body and soul, to share in the heavenly glory of Christ;
—grant that we who are your children may ever aspire to the same glory. (*R.*)

Through the intercession of the blessed Virgin Mary heal the sick, comfort those who mourn, pardon sinners;
—give to all grace in good measure. (*R.*)

Lord, may your Church have but one heart and one soul, bound together in love;
—may all Christians persevere in prayer with Mary, the mother of Jesus. (*R.*)

O God, you have made Mary the mother of mercy,
—grant that all who turn to her in danger may experience her motherly love. (*R.*)

O God, who willed that Mary should fill the role of mother in the house of Jesus and Joseph,
—make all mothers of families holy and ardent in love. (*R.*)

O God, you have crowned Mary as Queen of heaven;
—may she open the gates of her kingdom to those who have died, that they may rejoice in the fellowship of saints. (*R.*)

Concluding prayer

Grant us, your servants, we pray you, Lord God, to enjoy perpetual health of mind and body. By the glorious intercession of blessed Mary ever Virgin, may we be delivered from present sorrows and enjoy everlasting happiness. We make our prayer through our Lord.

or

O God, through the fruitful virginity of the blessed Mary, you have given the treasure of salvation to mankind. Grant, we ask you, that we may be blessed by the prayers of her through whom it was possible for us to receive the source of life, our Lord Jesus Christ, your Son, who lives and reigns.

OFFICE OF READINGS

Hymn *as at* Evening Prayer I, p. 566

Psalmody

Psalm 23

Ant. Lord, such are the men who seek you.

The Lord's is the earth and its fullness,
the world and all its peoples.
It is he who set it on the seas;
on the waters he made it firm.

Who shall climb the mountain of the Lord?
Who shall stand in his holy place?
The man with clean hands and pure heart,†
who desires not worthless things,
who has not sworn so as to deceive his neighbour.

He shall receive blessings from the Lord
and reward from the God who saves him.
Such are the men who seek him,
seek the face of the God of Jacob.

O gates, lift high your heads;†
grow higher, ancient doors.
Let him enter, the king of glory!

Who is the king of glory?
The Lord, the mighty, the valiant, the Lord, the valiant in
     war.

O gates, lift high your heads;†
grow higher, ancient doors.
Let him enter, the king of glory!

Who is he, the king of glory?
He, the Lord of armies, he is the king of glory.

Ant. Lord, such are the men who seek you.

Psalm 45

Ant. The power of the Most High will overshadow you.

God is for us a refuge and strength,
a helper close at hand, in time of distress:
so we shall not fear though the earth should rock,
though the mountains fall into the depths of the sea,
even though its waters rage and foam,
even though the mountains be shaken by its waves.

R. The Lord of hosts is with us:
the God of Jacob is our stronghold.

The waters of a river give joy to God's city,
the holy place where the Most High dwells.
God is within, it cannot be shaken;
God will help it at the dawning of the day.
Nations are in tumult, kingdoms are shaken:
he lifts his voice, the earth shrinks away.

R. The Lord of hosts is with us:
the God of Jacob is our stronghold.

Come, consider the works of the Lord
the redoubtable deeds he has done on the earth.
He puts an end to wars over all the earth;
the bow he breaks, the spear he snaps.
He burns the shields with fire.
'Be still and know that I am God,
supreme among the nations, supreme on the earth!'

R. The Lord of hosts is with us:
the God of Jacob is our stronghold.

Ant. The power of the Most High will overshadow you.

Psalm 86

Ant. In you all find their home, holy Mother of God.

On the holy mountain is his city
cherished by the Lord.
The Lord prefers the gates of Zion
to all Jacob's dwellings.
Of you are told glorious things,
O city of God!

'Babylon and Egypt I will count
among those who know me;
Philistia, Tyre, Ethiopia,
these will be her children
and Zion shall be called "Mother"
for all shall be her children.'

It is he, the Lord Most High,
who gives each his place.
In his register of peoples he writes:
'These are her children'
and while they dance they will sing:
'In you all find their home.'

Ant. In you all find their home, holy Mother of God.

V. Mary kept all these things in her heart:

R. Blessed are those who hear the Word of God and keep it.

Readings *any one of the following:*

1 Chron 17:1–15	Sir 24:2–12, 16–22
S of S 2:8–14; 8:6–7	Rev 11:19–12:17

Responses *any one of the following:*

1.

Blessed are you, Virgin Mary! You bore in your womb the Lord, the Creator of the world. * You gave birth to him who made you, and you remain a virgin for ever.

V. Hail Mary, full of grace; the Lord is with you. * You gave birth.

2.

All ages will call me blessed. * The Almighty works marvels for me: holy his name!

V. His mercy is from age to age on those who fear him. * The Almighty.

3.

Rejoice with me, all you who love the Lord: in my lowliness I found favour with the Most High. * From my womb I brought forth him who is both God and man.

V. All ages will call me blessed, for God has looked on his servant in her nothingness. * From my womb.

Prayer *as at* Evening Prayer I, p. 569

MORNING PRAYER

Psalm 94

Refrain: Hail Mary, full of grace, the Lord is with you.

Hymn *as at* Evening Prayer I, p. 566

Psalmody

Psalms *as for* the Dedication of a Church, Morning Prayer, p. 556

Antiphons

1. Hail, Mother of Christ, hail full of grace.

2. You are the glory of Jerusalem, the joy of Israel!

3. A great portent appeared in heaven, a woman clothed with the sun, with the moon under her feet, and on her head a crown of twelve stars.

Word of God   Is 61:10

I will greatly rejoice in the Lord,
my soul shall exult in my God;
for he has clothed me with the garments of salvation,
he has covered me with the robe of righteousness,
as a bridegroom decks himself with a garland,
and as a bride adorns herself with her jewels.

Short Response *as at* Evening Prayer I, p. 568

Song of Zechariah

Ant. Blessed are you, holy Virgin Mary,
   for the sun of justice, Christ our God, was born of you.

Prayers

Let us pray to our Saviour, who willed to be born of the Virgin Mary; let us say to him:

R. Lord, may your mother intercede for us.

Most generous Jesus, who hanging on the cross, gave your own mother to John to be his mother,
—make us live as her true sons. (*R.*)

Christ our Saviour, your mother stood close to the cross;
—through her intercession may we rejoice to share in your sufferings. (*R.*)

Eternal Word, you chose the Virgin Mary to be your dwelling-place, as once you chose the ark of incorruptible wood;
—deliver us from all corruption of sin. (*R.*)

Sun of justice, grant that we may always recognize in the Immaculate Virgin the dawn of your rising;
—may we always walk in the light of your presence. (*R.*)

Lord, grant us to imitate Mary your mother, who chose the best part;
may we always seek the food which endures to eternal life. (*R.*)

King of kings, who willed to have your blessed mother with you, body and soul, in heaven,
—keep our thoughts fixed on heavenly realities. (*R.*)

Lord of heaven and earth, who placed Mary on your right hand as Queen,
—grant that we may share the same glory. (*R.*)

Saviour of the world, by virtue of your redeeming power you preserved your mother from all stain;
—keep sin far from us also. (*R.*)

Holy Redeemer, the immaculate Virgin Mary was the bridal chamber where you dwelt, and the sanctuary of the Holy Spirit;

—make us also the temple of the Holy Spirit. (*R.*)

Concluding prayer *as at* Evening Prayer I, p. 569

MIDDAY PRAYER

If a Solemnity, the psalms are as for the Dedication of a Church, Midday Prayer, p, 560, *with the following antiphon:*

Ant. Blessed is she who believed that there would be a fulfilment of what was spoken to her from the Lord.

If not a Solemnity, the antiphons and psalms are of the day, as in the psalter

Word of God   Zeph 3:14–15

Sing aloud, O daughter of Zion;
shout, O Israel!
Rejoice and exult with all your heart,
O daughter of Jerusalem!
The King of Israel, the Lord, is in your midst;
you shall fear evil no more.

V. Mary, his mother,

R. Kept all these things in her heart.

If a Solemnity which has no proper prayer, Prayer *as at* Evening Prayer I, p. 569. *Otherwise,* Prayer of the day.

EVENING PRAYER II

Hymn *as at* Evening Prayer I, p. 566

Psalmody

Psalm 109

Ant. Blessed are you among women,
and blessed is the fruit of your womb.

The Lord's revelation to my Master:†
'Sit on my right:
I will put your foes beneath your feet.'

The Lord will send from Zion your sceptre of power:
rule in the midst of all your foes.

575

A prince from the day of your birth on the holy mountains;
from the womb before the daybreak I begot you.

The Lord has sworn an oath he will not change.†
'You are a priest for ever,
a priest like Melchizedeck of old.'

The Master standing at your right hand
will shatter kings in the day of his great wrath . . .

He shall drink from the stream by the wayside
and therefore he shall lift up his head.

Ant. Blessed are you among women,
and blessed is the fruit of your womb.

Psalm 126

Ant. Behold, I am the handmaid of the Lord;
let it be to me according to your word.

If the Lord does not build the house,
in vain do its builders labour;
if the Lord does not watch over the city,
in vain does the watchman keep vigil.

In vain is your earlier rising,
your going later to rest,
you who toil for the bread you eat:
when he pours gifts on his beloved while they slumber.

Truly sons are a gift from the Lord,
a blessing, the fruit of the womb.
Indeed the sons of youth
are like arrows in the hand of a warrior.

O the happiness of the man
who has filled his quiver with these arrows!
He will have no cause for shame
when he disputes with his foes in the gateways.

Ant. Behold, I am the handmaid of the Lord;
let it be to me according to your word.

Eph 1:3–10   Song of thanks: election in Christ

R. Blessed are you, God our Father,
  who have blessed us in Christ.

Blessed be the God and Father
of our Lord Jesus Christ,
who has blessed us in Christ
with every spiritual blessing in the heavenly places. (*R.*)

He chose us in him
before the foundation of the world,
that we should be holy
and blameless before him. (*R.*)

He destined us in love
to be his sons through Jesus Christ,
according to the purpose of his will,†
to the praise of his glorious grace
which he freely bestowed on us in the Beloved. (*R.*)

In him we have redemption through his blood,
the forgiveness of our trespasses,
according to the riches of his grace
which he lavished upon us. (*R.*)

He has made known to us†
in all wisdom and insight
the mystery of his will,
according to his purpose
which he set forth in Christ. (*R.*)

His purpose he set forth in Christ
as a plan for the fulness of time,
to unite all things in him,
things in heaven and things on earth. (*R.*)

Word of God *and* Short Response *as at* Evening Prayer I, p. 568
Song of the Virgin Mary
Ant. Rejoice with me, you who love the Lord; in my
lowliness I found favour with the Most High, and from my
womb I brought forth him who is both God and man.
Prayers *as at* Evening Prayer I, p. 569

Common of Apostles

EVENING PRAYER I

Hymn

Let earth be glad and rejoice,
and heaven re-echo with praise.
Earth and heaven in unison
sing the Apostles' fame.

To you, judges of men
and true lights of the world,
we tell in prayer our heart's desires;
hear your suppliants' words.

You shut heaven's gates
and with a word undo their bolts;
give the word of command, we beg you,
for us sinners to be undone from our guilt.

As sickness and health
are instantly subject to your bidding,
heal the sickness of our souls
and enrich us with virtue,

That when Christ comes again at the end of time
to be man's judge,
he may graciously call us
to possess eternal joy.

To the Father and the Son together,
and to you, Holy Spirit,
may glory continue to be for all ages,
as it has been. Amen.

Psalmody

Psalm 116

Ant. Their span goes forth through all the earth,
their words to the utmost bounds of the world.

O praise the Lord, all you nations,
acclaim him all you peoples!

Strong is his love for us;
he is faithful for ever.

Ant. Their span goes forth through all the earth,
their words to the utmost bounds of the world.

Psalm 147

Ant. Blessed are the peacemakers,
blessed the pure in heart, for they shall see God.

O praise the Lord, Jerusalem!
Zion, praise your God!

He has strengthened the bars of your gates,
he has blessed the children within you.
He established peace on your borders,
he feeds you with finest wheat.

He sends out his word to the earth
and swiftly runs his command.
He showers down snow white as wool,
he scatters hoar-frost like ashes.

He hurls down hailstones like crumbs.
The waters are frozen at his touch;
he sends forth his word and it melts them:
at the breath of his mouth the waters flow.

He makes his word known to Jacob,
to Israel his laws and decrees.
He has not dealt thus with other nations;
he has not taught them his decrees.

Ant. Blessed are the peacemakers,
blessed the pure in heart, for they shall see God.

Song of thanks: election in Christ (Eph 1:3–10) *as for the* Common of
the Blessed Virgin Mary, p. 576, *with the following antiphon:*

Ant. Greater love has no man than this,
that a man lay down his life for his friends.

Word of God Acts 2:42–45

Those who received the word were baptized, and they devoted themselves to the apostles' teaching and fellowship, to the breaking of bread and the prayers.

And fear came upon every soul; and many wonders and signs were done through the apostles. And all who believed were together and had all things in common; and they sold their possessions and goods and distributed them to all, as any had need.

Short Response

Your Word, O Lord, for ever
stands firm in the heavens.
V. Your truth lasts from age to age.
R. It stands firm in the heavens.
V. Glory be to the Father, and to the Son, and to the Holy Spirit.
Your Word, O Lord, for ever
stands firm in the heavens.

Song of the Virgin Mary

Ant. You who have left everything and followed me
will receive a hundredfold and inherit eternal life.

Prayers

Since we hold our heavenly inheritance from the apostles, let us give thanks to our heavenly Father for all his benefits, saying:

R. The college of apostles praises you, Lord.

Praise to you, Lord, for the banquet of your Body and Blood, handed down to us through the apostles;
by it we are nourished and have life. (*R.*)

For the table of the Word, set out for us by the apostles
—where we are enlightened and refreshed. (*R.*)

For your holy Church, built on the apostolic foundation,
—into which we are incorporated as one. (*R.*)

For the cleansing rites of Baptism and Penance, first used
by the apostles,
—by which we are absolved from all sin. (*R.*)

Praise to you, Lord, for the eternal bliss which we hope
for from your mercy
—both for the living and the dead. (*R.*)

Concluding prayer   *as in the Proper of Saints*

OFFICE OF READINGS

Hymn
Let us joyfully sing songs of victory
and pay our tribute of praise in hymns
to commemorate Christ's eternal gifts,
the Apostles' glory.

Princes of the churches,
war-leaders that were honoured with a triumph,
picked soldiers of the heavenly court
and true lights of the world—

The devoted faith of these holy men,
the immovable hope that was theirs as believers
and their perfect love of Christ resulted in triumph
over the prince of this world.

In their persons the glory of the Father was enhanced,
the will of the Spirit was fulfilled
and the Son rejoiced;
all heaven was filled with joy.

To the Father and to the Son together,
and to you, Holy Spirit,

may glory continue to be for all ages,
as it has been. Amen.

Psalmody

Psalm 18

Ant. Their span goes forth through all the earth,
  their words to the utmost bounds of the world.

The heavens proclaim the glory of God
and the firmament shows forth the work of his hands.
Day unto day takes up the story
and night unto night makes known the message.

No speech, no word, no voice is heard†
yet their span goes forth through all the earth,
their words to the utmost bounds of the world.

There he has placed a tent for the sun;†
it comes forth like a bridegroom coming from his tent,
rejoices like a champion to run its course.

At the end of the sky is the rising of the sun;†
to the furthest end of the sky is its course.
There is nothing concealed from its burning heat.

The law of the Lord is perfect,
it revives the soul.
The rule of the Lord is to be trusted,
it gives wisdom to the simple.

The precepts of the Lord are right,
they gladden the heart.
The command of the Lord is clear,
it gives light to the eyes.

The fear of the Lord is holy,
abiding for ever.
The decrees of the Lord are truth
and all of them just.

They are more to be desired than gold,
than the purest of gold

and sweeter are they than honey,
than honey from the comb.

So in them your servant finds instruction;
great reward is in their keeping.
But who can detect all his errors?
From hidden faults acquit me.

From presumption restrain your servant
and let it not rule me.
Then shall I be blameless,
clean from grave sin.

May the spoken words of my mouth,
the thoughts of my heart,
win favour in your sight, O Lord,
my rescuer, my rock!

Ant. Their span goes forth through all the earth,
   their words to the utmost bounds of the world.

Psalm 63

Ant. Blessed are the peacemakers,
   blessed the pure in heart, for they shall see God.

Hear my voice, O God, as I complain,
guard my life from dread of the foe.
Hide me from the band of the wicked,
from the throng of those who do evil.

They sharpen their tongues like swords;
they aim bitter words like arrows
to shoot at the innocent from ambush,
shooting suddenly and recklessly.

They scheme their evil course;
they conspire to lay secret snares.
They say: 'Who will see us?
Who can search out our crimes?'

He will search who searches the mind
and knows the depths of the heart.

God has shot an arrow at them
and dealt them sudden wounds.
Their own tongue has brought them to ruin
and all who see them mock.

Then all men will fear;†
they will tell what God has done.
They will understand God's deeds.
The just will rejoice in the Lord†
and fly to him for refuge.
All the upright hearts will glory.

Ant. Blessed are the peacemakers,
blessed the pure in heart, for they shall see God.

Psalm 96

Ant. Greater love has no man than this,
that a man lay down his life for his friends.

The Lord is king, let earth rejoice,
the many coastlands be glad.
Cloud and darkness are his raiment;
his throne, justice and right.

A fire prepares his path;
it burns up his foes on every side.
His lightnings light up the world,
the earth trembles at the sight.

The mountains melt like wax
before the Lord of all the earth.
The skies proclaim his justice;
all peoples see his glory.

Let those who serve idols be ashamed,†
those who boast of their worthless gods.
All you spirits, worship him.

Zion hears and is glad;†
the people of Judah rejoice
because of your judgments O Lord.

For you indeed are the Lord†
most high above all the earth
exalted far above all spirits.

The Lord loves those who hate evil:†
he guards the souls of his saints;
he sets them free from the wicked.

Light shines forth for the just
and joy for the upright of heart.
Rejoice, you just, in the Lord;
give glory to his holy name.

Ant. Greater love has no man than this,
that a man lay down his life for his friends.

V. They proclaimed the works of God;
R. they understood what he had done.

Readings (*any of the following:*)
Acts 5:12–32   1 Cor 4:1–16
1 Cor 1:18–2:5   1 Cor 9:1–23
Eph 4:1–16 (For evangelists)

Responses

Outside Eastertide

No longer do I call you servants: I have called you friends,
* for all that I have heard from my Father I have made
known to you.
V. To you it has been given to know the secrets of the
kingdom of heaven: blessed are your eyes, for they see, and
your ears, for they hear. * For all.

In Eastertide

With great power the apostles gave their testimony to the
resurrection of the Lord Jesus; * and great grace was upon
them all, alleluia, alleluia!
V. They were all filled with the Holy Spirit and spoke the
word of God with boldness. * And great grace.

Prayer *as at* Evening Prayer I, p. 581

MORNING PRAYER

Psalm 94
Refrain: Come, let us worship the Lord, the King of apostles.

Hymn *as at* Evening Prayer I, p. 578

Psalmody
Psalms *as for the* Dedication of a Church, Morning Prayer, p. 556, *with the following antiphons:*

1. Their span goes forth through all the earth,
   their words to the utmost bounds of the world.
2. Blessed are the peacemakers,
   blessed the pure in heart, for they shall see God.
3. Greater love has no man than this,
   that a man lay down his life for his friends.

Word of God   Eph 2:19–21
You are no longer strangers and sojourners, but you are fellow citizens with the saints and members of the household of God, built upon the foundation of the apostles and prophets, Christ Jesus himself being the cornerstone, in whom the whole structure is joined together and grows into a holy temple in the Lord.

Short Response *as at* Evening Prayer I, p. 580

Song of the Virgin Mary
Ant. The apostles were filled with the Holy Spirit
   and spoke the Word of God with boldness.

Prayers
We are built upon the foundation of the apostles; let us pray the Father Almighty for his chosen people, saying:

R. I believe in the apostolic Church.
Or: Lord, remember your Church.

Father, who willed that the risen Christ should appear first to the apostles,
—make us his witnesses even to the ends of the earth. (*R.*)

Father, you sent your Son into the world to preach the Good News to the poor;

—grant that all men may have the Gospel preached to them. (*R.*)

Father, who sent your Son to sow the good seed of the Word,

—grant that those who now sow with great labour may reap with yet greater joy. (*R.*)

Father, you sent your Son to reconcile the world to yourself in his own blood;

—grant that we may all share in the ministry of reconciliation. (*R.*)

Concluding prayer *as in the Proper of Saints.*

MIDDAY PRAYER

If a Solemnity, the psalms are as for the Dedication of a Church, Midday Prayer, p. 560, *with the following antiphon:*

Ant. I chose you and appointed you that you should go and bear fruit and that your fruit should abide.

If not a Solemnity, the antiphons and psalms are of the day, as in the psalter.

Word of God   Acts 5:12, 14

Many signs and wonders were done among the people by the hands of the apostles. And more than ever believers were added to the Lord, multitudes both of men and women.

V. They proclaimed the works of God;
   they understood what he had done.

If a Solemnity, proper prayer. Otherwise, Prayer of the day

EVENING PRAYER II

Hymn *as at* Evening Prayer I, p. 578

Psalmody

Psalm 109

Ant. Their span goes forth through all the earth,
   their words to the utmost bounds of the world.

The Lord's revelation to my Master:†
'Sit on my right:
I will put your foes beneath your feet.'

The Lord will send from Zion your sceptre of power:
rule in the midst of all your foes.

A prince from the day of your birth on the holy mountains;
from the womb before the daybreak I begot you.

The Lord has sworn an oath he will not change.†
'You are a priest for ever,
a priest like Melchizedeck of old.'

The Master standing at your right hand
will shatter kings in the day of his great wrath...

He shall drink from the stream by the wayside
and therefore he shall lift up his head.

Ant. Their span goes forth through all the earth,
   their words to the utmost bounds of the world.

Psalm 125

Ant. Blessed are the peacemakers,
   blessed the pure in heart, for they shall see God.

When the Lord delivered Zion from bondage,
it seemed like a dream.
Then was our mouth filled with laughter,
on our lips there were songs.

The heathens themselves said: 'What marvels
the Lord worked for them!'
What marvels the Lord worked for us!
Indeed we were glad.

Deliver us, O Lord, from our bondage
as streams in dry land.
Those who are sowing in tears
will sing when they reap.

They go out, they go out, full of tears,
carrying seed for the sowing:
they come back, they come back, full of song,
carrying their sheaves.

Ant. Blessed are the peacemakers,
blessed the pure in heart, for they shall see God.

Song of thanks: election in Christ (Eph 1:3–10) *as for the* Common of
the Blessed Virgin Mary, p. 576, *with the following antiphon:*

Ant. Greater love has no man than this
that a man lay down his life for his friends.

Word of God   Eph 4:10–13

Christ ascended far above all the heavens, that he might fill
all things. And his gifts were that some should be apostles,
some prophets, some evangelists, some pastors and teachers,
for the equipment of the saints, for the work of ministry, for
building up the body of Christ, until we all attain to the
unity of the faith and of the knowledge of the Son of God,
to mature manhood, to the measure of the stature of the
fulness of Christ.

The rest is as at Evening Prayer I.

Common of Martyrs

EVENING PRAYER I

Hymn

Let us sing, fellow Christians, of the glorious joys
that the Saints gained through their merits,
let us sing of their heroic deeds.
Our soul is eager and ready to tell in song
the noble line of warriors.

These are the men that the world in its folly rejected.
But they were followers of you, Jesus,
kind King of those in heaven,
and therefore they despised a world that is barren of fruit
and blooms only to wither.

For your sake they triumphed over men's rage
and savage threats and cruel scourgings.
The hook that fiercely tore them to bits
effected nothing and left them
their spirit unconquered.

They are cut down by the sword as if animals for a sacrifice.
No sound, no complaint passes their lips.
Instead, their soul, dauntless and sure of its cause,
keeps their endurance
firm and unshaken.

What voice or what tongue can tell the rewards
that you prepare for your martyrs?
Red with the blood that is still flowing from their wounds,
they crown their heads with shining
laurel garlands.

We beseech you, mighty Godhead, one in essence,
to take away your servants' guilt;
remove all their sins and give them peace
that they may sing praise to you
for ever. Amen.

For a Virgin Martyr

Jesus, son of the Virgin and your Mother's Creator,
carried in the Virgin's womb and born of the Virgin,
we sing of the victory
won by a virgin saint's glorious death.

This saint was blessed with the grace of a twofold victory.
While it was her consuming wish
to master in her body its weakness in the face of sin,
she mastered in that same body her savage, murderous
    persecutor.

She feared neither death
nor the countless forms of torture which accompany it,
and the sacrifice of her life earned for her
entry into the peace of heaven.

By her intercession, forgive us, loving God,
the punishment that our sins deserve,
and so with hearts made pure we may sing to you
the song of our love.

Glory be to the Father and to the Son
and to the Spirit,
the co-equal power of Father and Son—one God,
for ever and ever. Amen.

Psalmody

Psalm 117

I

Ant. He who follows me will not walk in darkness,
    but will have the light of life.

Give thanks to the Lord for he is good,
for his love has no end.

Let the sons of Israel say:
'His love has no end.'
Let the sons of Aaron say:

'His love has no end.'
Let those who fear the Lord say:
'His love has no end.'

I called to the Lord in my distress;
he answered and freed me.
The Lord is at my side; I do not fear.
What can man do against me?
The Lord is at my side as my helper:
I shall look down on my foes.

It is better to take refuge in the Lord
than to trust in men:
it is better to take refuge in the Lord
than to trust in princes . . .

I was thrust, thrust down and falling
but the Lord was my helper.
The Lord is my strength and my song;
he was my saviour.
There are shouts of joy and victory
in the tents of the just.

The Lord's right hand has triumphed;
his right hand raised me up.
The Lord's right hand has triumphed;
I shall not die, I shall live and recount his deeds.
I was punished, I was punished by the Lord,
but not doomed to die.

Ant. He who follows me will not walk in darkness,
   but will have the light of life.

II

Ant. God tries his elect like gold in the furnace.

Open to me the gates of holiness:
I will enter and give thanks.
This is the Lord's own gate
where the just may enter.
I will thank you for you have given answer
and you are my saviour.

The stone which the builders rejected
has become the corner stone.
This is the work of the Lord,
a marvel in our eyes.
This day was made by the Lord;
we rejoice and are glad.

O Lord, grant us salvation;
O Lord, grant success.
Blessed in the name of the Lord
is he who comes.
We bless you from the house of the Lord;
the Lord God is our light.

Go forward in procession with branches
even to the altar.
You are my God, I thank you.
My God, I praise you
Give thanks to the Lord for he is good;
for his love has no end.

Ant. God tries his elect like gold in the furnace.

New Testament song of the suffering Servant (1 Pet 2:21–24) *as for the* Dedication of a Church, Evening Prayer I, p. 549, *with the following antiphon:*

Ant. Everlasting light will shine upon your saints, O Lord.

Word of God

Eastertide   **Rev 3:10–12**

Because you have kept my word of patient endurance, I will keep you from the hour of trial which is coming on the whole world, to try those who dwell upon the earth. I am coming soon; hold fast what you have, so that no one may seize your crown. He who conquers, I will make him a pillar in the temple of my God; never shall he go out of it, and I will write on him the name of my God, and the name of the city of my God, the new Jerusalem which comes down from my God out of heaven, and my own new name.

Outside Eastertide   Rom 8:35, 37–39

Who shall separate us from the love of Christ? Shall tribulation, or distress, or persecution, or famine, or nakedness, or peril, or sword?

No, in all these things we are more than conquerors through him who loved us. For I am sure that neither death, nor life, nor angels, nor principalities, nor things present, nor things to come, nor powers, nor height, nor depth, nor anything else in all creation, will be able to separate us from the love of God in Christ Jesus our Lord.

Short Response

He who looks towards God shall be radiant,
his face shall not be abashed.

V. He is happy who takes refuge in him.

R. His face shall not be abashed.

V. Glory be to the Father, and to the Son, and to the Holy Spirit.

He who looks towards God shall be radiant,
his face shall not be abashed.

or

Rejoice, rejoice in the Lord,
exult, you just!

V. O come, ring out your joy,
all you upright of heart.

R. Exult, you just!

V. Glory be to the Father, and to the Son, and to the Holy Spirit.

Rejoice, rejoice in the Lord,
exult, you just!

Song of the Virgin Mary

Ant. Blessed are those who are persecuted for righteousness' sake,
for theirs is the kingdom of heaven.

Prayers

This is the time of day when the King of martyrs offered up his life in the supper-room, and was immolated on the cross; let us give him thanks and say:

R. We praise you, O Lord.

All martyrdom has its source and exemplar in yours, our Saviour, because you loved us to the end. (*R.*)

Because you have called all sinners to the reward of eternal life. (*R.*)

Because we have today offered up the blood of the new and everlasting covenant, shed for the remission of sins. (*R.*)

Because by your grace, we have persevered in the faith until this day. (*R.*)

Because today you have granted a share in your death to many of our brothers. (*R.*)

Concluding prayer

Grant, we pray you, Almighty God, that through the prayers of blessed N., your martyr(s), we may be delivered from all adversities in body, and purified from all evil thoughts in mind. We make our prayer through our Lord.

For a martyr bishop

1.

Be mindful of our weakness, Almighty God, and since the burden of our deeds is grievous to us, grant that the glorious prayers of blessed N., your martyr and bishop, may protect us. We make our prayer through our Lord.

2.

O God, you gladden us by the yearly celebration of blessed N., your martyr and bishop. Mercifully grant that we may rejoice in the protection of him whose heavenly birthday we celebrate. We make our prayer through our Lord.

3.

O Lord, we ask that the festival of your holy martyr(s) and bishop(s) N. (and N.) may bring us safety. May his (their) worthy prayers win us favour. We make our prayer through our Lord.

For a martyr not a bishop

1.

Almighty God, we pray you to grant that we who celebrate the heavenly birthday of blessed N., your martyr, may by his prayers be strengthened in the love of your name. We make our prayer through our Lord.

2.

O God, you grant us to celebrate the heavenly birthday of your holy martyr(s) N. (and N.). Grant us to enjoy his (their) fellowship in everlasting happiness. We make our prayer through our Lord.

3.

O God, year by year you gladden us by the solemnity of your holy martyr(s) N. (and N.). Mercifully grant that we, who rejoice in his (their) merits, may be inspired by his (their) example. We make our prayer through our Lord.

For a woman martyr

1.

O God, among the wonders of your power you have granted to women the triumph of martyrdom. Mercifully grant that we who celebrate the heavenly birthday of blessed

N., your (virgin and) martyr, may through her example come nearer to you. We make our prayer through our Lord.

2.

May blessed N., your virgin and martyr, we pray you, Lord, implore for us your forgiveness. For she was ever pleasing to you both by the merit of her chastity, and by her confession of your power. We make our prayer through our Lord.

3.

Grant us, we pray you, O Lord our God, to revere with unceasing devotion the victories of your holy martyr(s) N. (and N.). May we at least approach with lowly homage her (those) whom we cannot fittingly celebrate. We make our prayer through our Lord.

OFFICE OF READINGS

Hymn

Let us honour in joyous hymns
the Martyrs' blood shed for Christ,
their victories and their triumph
that won them heaven.

They overcame the fear of the world,
despised all tortures inflicted on them
and by the short cut of a holy death
entered into the light of bliss.

We now ask you, our Redeemer,
to unite us, your servants and suppliants,
to the company of the martyrs
for all eternity. Amen.

Psalmody

Psalm 2

Ant. He who follows me will not walk in darkness,
but will have the light of life.

Why this tumult among nations,
among peoples this useless murmuring?
They arise, the kings of the earth,
princes plot against the Lord and his Anointed.
'Come, let us break their fetters,
come, let us cast off their yoke.'

He who sits in the heavens laughs;
the Lord is laughing them to scorn.
Then he will speak in his anger,
his rage will strike them with terror.
'It is I who have set up my king
on Zion, my holy mountain.'

I will announce the decree of the Lord:†
The Lord said to me: 'You are my Son.
It is I who have begotten you this day.
Ask and I shall bequeath you the nations,
put the ends of the earth in your possession.
With a rod of iron you will break them,
shatter them like a potter's jar.'

Now, O kings, understand,
take warning, rulers of the earth;
serve the Lord with awe
and trembling, pay him your homage
lest he be angry and you perish;
for suddenly his anger will blaze.

All: Blessed are they who put their trust in God.

Ant. He who follows me will not walk in darkness,
but will have the light of life.

Psalm 10

Ant. God tries his elect like gold in the furnace.

In the Lord I have taken my refuge.†
How can you say to my soul:
'Fly like a bird to its mountain.

See the wicked bracing their bow;†
they are fixing their arrows on the string
to shoot upright men in the dark.
Foundations once destroyed,
what can the just do?'

The Lord is in his holy temple,
the Lord, whose throne is in heaven.
His eyes look down on the world;
his gaze tests mortal men.

The Lord tests the just and the wicked:
the lover of violence he hates.
He sends fire and brimstone on the wicked;
he sends a scorching wind as their lot.

The Lord is just and loves justice:
the upright shall see his face.

Ant. God tries his elect like gold in the furnace.

Psalm 16

Ant. Everlasting light will shine upon your saints, O Lord.

Lord, hear a cause that is just,
pay heed to my cry.
Turn your ear to my prayer:
no deceit is on my lips.
From you may my judgment come forth.
Your eyes discern the truth.

You search my heart, you visit me by night.†
You test me and you find in me no wrong.
My words are not sinful as are men's words.

I kept from violence because of your word,†
I kept my feet firmly in your paths;
there was no faltering in my steps.

I am here and I call, you will hear me, O God.
Turn your ear to me; hear my words.
Display your great love,†

you whose right hand saves your friends
from those who rebel against them.

Guard me as the apple of your eye.†
Hide me in the shadow of your wings
from the violent attack of the wicked.

My foes encircle me with deadly intent.†
Their hearts tight shut, their mouths speak proudly.
They advance against me, and now they surround me.

Their eyes are watching to strike me to the ground†
as though they were lions ready to claw
or like some young lion crouched in hiding.

Lord, arise, confront them, strike them down!
Let your sword rescue my soul from the wicked;
let your hand, O Lord, rescue me from men,
from men whose reward is in this present life . . .

As for me, in my justice I shall see your face
and be filled, when I awake, with the sight of your glory.

Ant. Everlasting light will shine upon your saints, O Lord.

The following two sections of Psalm 32 *may be substituted for Psalms*
10 *and* 16:

Psalm 32

I

Ant. God tries his elect like gold in the furnace.

Ring out your joy to the Lord, O you just;
for praise is fitting for loyal hearts.

Give thanks to the Lord upon the harp,
with a ten-stringed lute sing him songs.
O sing him a song that is new,
play loudly, with all your skill.

For the word of the Lord is faithful
and all his works to be trusted.
The Lord loves justice and right
and fills the earth with his love.

By his word the heavens were made,
by the breath of his mouth all the stars.
He collects the waves of the ocean;
he stores up the depths of the sea.

Let all the earth fear the Lord,
all who live in the world revere him.
He spoke; and it came to be.
He commanded; it sprang into being.

He frustrates the designs of the nations,
he defeats the plans of the peoples.
His own designs shall stand for ever,
the plans of his heart from age to age.

Ant. God tries his elect like gold in the furnace.

II

Ant. Everlasting light will shine upon your saints, O Lord.

They are happy, whose God is the Lord,
the people he has chosen as his own.
From the heavens the Lord looks forth,
he sees all the children of men.

From the place where he dwells he gazes
on all the dwellers on the earth,
he who shapes the hearts of them all
and considers all their deeds.

A king is not saved by his army,
nor a warrior preserved by his strength.
A vain hope for safety is the horse;
despite its power it cannot save.

The Lord looks on those who revere him,
on those who hope in his love,
to rescue their souls from death,
to keep them alive in famine.

Our soul is waiting for the Lord.
The Lord is our help and our shield.

In him do our hearts find joy.
We trust in his holy name.

May your love be upon us, O Lord,
as we place all our hope in you.

Ant. Everlasting light will shine upon your saints, O Lord.

V. Our soul is waiting for the Lord.
R. He is our help and our shield.

Readings

Eastertide

Rev 7:9–17

Response

Daughters of Jerusalem, come and see the martyrs with the crowns with which the Lord crowned them * on the day of solemn rejoicing, alleluia, alleluia!

V. He has strengthened the bars of your gates, he has blessed the children within you. * On the day.

For one martyr, a man

Wis 4:7–17

Response

This holy man was not afraid of the threats of godless men, but upheld the law of God to his last breath: * for he was founded upon solid rock.

V. He hated his life in this world and achieved an everlasting kingdom. * For he was.

For a woman martyr

Sir 51:1–12

Response

I give thanks to your name, O Lord, * for you have been my protector and helper.

V. Let me be glad and rejoice in your love. * For you.

For several martyrs

Wis 3:1–19
Rom 8:12–39

Response

These holy men shed their blood for the Lord: they loved
Christ during their life, they followed his example in death.
* And so they earned crowns of victory.
V. One spirit and one faith was theirs. * And so.

Prayer *as at* Evening Prayer I, p. 595

MORNING PRAYER

Psalm 94
Refrain: Come, let us worship the Lord, the King of martyrs.

Hymn

Glorious King of martyrs,
crown of them that confess you
and leader to heaven
of all that despise worldly pleasures.

Give a ready and gracious hearing
to our hymn;
our theme is the martyrs' holy triumph,
our plea is for pardon for our sins.

Your might is displayed in the martyrs,
and your mercy in those that confess you.
Exert your mighty power over our sins
and pour out your mercy on us.

To God the Father be glory,
and to his only Son,
with the Spirit, the Paraclete,
now and for ever. Amen.

Psalmody

Psalms *as for the* Dedication of a Church, Morning Prayer, p. 556, *with the following antiphons:*

1. He who follows me will not walk in darkness,
   but will have the light of life.
2. God tries his elect like gold in the furnace.
3. Everlasting light will shine upon your saints, O Lord.

Word of God

Eastertide   1 John 5:3–5

This is the love of God, that we keep his commandments. And his commandments are not burdensome. For whatever is born of God overcomes the world; and this is the victory that overcomes the world, our faith. Who is it that overcomes the world but he who believes that Jesus is the Son of God?

Outside Eastertide   2 Cor 1:3–7

Blessed be the God and Father of our Lord Jesus Christ, the Father of mercies and God of all comfort, who comforts us in all our affliction, so that we may be able to comfort those who are in any affliction, with the comfort with which we ourselves are comforted by God. For as we share abundantly in Christ's sufferings, so through Christ we share abundantly in comfort too. If we are afflicted, it is for your comfort and salvation; and if we are comforted, it is for your comfort, which you experience when you patiently endure the same sufferings that we suffer. Our hope for you is unshaken; for we know that as you share in our sufferings, you will also share in our comfort.

Short Response *as at* Evening Prayer I, p. 594

Song of Zechariah

Ant. Blessed are those who are persecuted for righteousness' sake,

   for theirs is the kingdom of heaven.

Prayers

Let us pray to our Saviour, the faithful witness, through the martyrs who have sacrificed their lives in defence of God's truth; let us say to him:

R. By your blood you ransomed us for God.

Through the merits of your martyrs, who freely laid down their lives to bear witness to the true faith,
—give us, Lord, true liberty of spirit. (R.)

Through your martyrs who professed the true faith even at the cost of their lives,
—give us faith, Lord, integral and unwavering. (R.)

Through your martyrs who have followed in your footsteps carrying the cross,
—give us magnanimity in facing the trials of life. (R.)

Through your martyrs who have washed their robes in the blood of the Lamb,
—help us, Lord, to overcome all bodily and worldly hindrances. (R.)

Concluding prayer *as at* Evening Prayer I, p. 595.

MIDDAY PRAYER

If a Solemnity, the psalms are as for the Dedication of a Church, Midday Prayer, p. 560, *with the following antiphon:*

Ant. Unless a grain of wheat falls into the earth and dies, it remains alone; but if it dies, it bears much fruit.

If not a Solemnity, the antiphons and psalms are of the day, as in the psalter

Word of God

Eastertide   Rev 3:21

He who conquers, I will grant him to sit with me on my throne, as I myself conquered and sat down with my Father on his throne.

Outside Eastertide   Jas 1:12

Blessed is the man who endures trial, for when he has stood the test he will receive the crown of life which God has promised to those who love him.

V. Our soul is waiting for the Lord.
R. He is our help and our shield.

If a Solemnity which has no proper prayer, Prayer *as at* Evening Prayer I, *Otherwise,* Prayer of the day.

EVENING PRAYER II

Hymn *as at* Evening Prayer I, p. 590

Psalmody

Psalm 109

Ant. He who follows me will not walk in darkness,
    but will have the light of life.

The Lord's revelation to my Master:†
'Sit on my right:
I will put your foes beneath your feet.'

The Lord will send from Zion your sceptre of power:
rule in the midst of all your foes.

A prince from the day of your birth on the holy mountains;
from the womb before the daybreak I begot you.

The Lord has sworn an oath he will not change.†
'You are a priest for ever,
a priest like Melchizedeck of old.'

The Master standing at your right hand
will shatter kings in the day of his great wrath . . .

He shall drink from the stream by the wayside
and therefore he shall lift up his head.

Ant. He who follows me will not walk in darkness,
    but will have the light of life.

Psalm 115

Ant. God tries his elect like gold in the furnace.

I trusted, even when I said:
'I am sorely afflicted,'
and when I said in my alarm:
'No man can be trusted.'

How can I repay the Lord
for his goodness to me?
The cup of salvation I will raise;
I will call on the Lord's name.

My vows to the Lord I will fulfil
before all his people.
O precious in the eyes of the Lord
is the death of his faithful.

Your servant, Lord, your servant am I;
you have loosened my bonds.
A thanksgiving sacrifice I make:
I will call on the Lord's name.

My vows to the Lord I will fulfil
before all his people,
in the courts of the house of the Lord,
in your midst, O Jerusalem.

Ant. God tries his elect like gold in the furnace.

Rev 4:11; 5:9, 10, 12   **Song to the victorious Lamb**

Ant. Everlasting light will shine upon your saints, O Lord.

Worthy are you, our Lord and God,
to receive glory and honour and power.

R. To the Lamb be glory, honour and power!

For you created all things,
and by your will they existed and were created. (*R.*)

Worthy are you, O Lord, to take the scroll
and to open its seals. (*R.*)

607

For you were slain,†
and by your blood you ransomed men for God
from every tribe and tongue and people and nation. (*R.*)

You have made us a kingdom and priests to our God,
and we shall reign on earth. (*R.*)

Worthy is the Lamb who was slain
to receive power and wealth
and wisdom and might
and honour and glory and blessing. (*R.*)

Ant. Everlasting light will shine upon your saints, O Lord.

Word of God

Eastertide   **Rev 7:14–17**

These are they who have come out of the great tribulation;
they have washed their robes and made them white in the
blood of the Lamb.

Therefore are they before the throne of God,
and serve him day and night within his temple;
and he who sits upon the throne will shelter them with his
presence.

They shall hunger no more, neither thirst any more;
the sun shall not strike them, nor any sorching heat.

For the Lamb in the midst of the throne will be their
shepherd,
and he will guide them to springs of living water;
and God will wipe away every tear from their eyes.

Outside Eastertide   **1 Pet 4:13–14**

Rejoice in so far as you share Christ's sufferings, that you
may also rejoice and be glad when his glory is revealed. If
you are reproached for the name of Christ, you are blessed,
because the spirit of glory and of God rests upon you.

The rest is as at Evening Prayer I, pp. 594 ff.

Common of Holy Men and Women

EVENING PRAYER I

Hymn

For pastors and holy men

This Confessor of the Lord,
honoured and lovingly praised by the peoples of the world,
on this day merited to receive with joy
the highest honour and praise.

He was holy, discreet,
humble and chaste;
and as long as the breath of life was in him,
he led a mortified and blameless life.

Because of his outstanding holiness
many sick people from different places
were freed of the malady that afflicted them
and restored to health.

For this reason we as a choir sing his praise
and celebrate his renowned victories,
so that he may help us now and always
by his prayers.

Salvation, glory and power be to him
that sits in dazzling splendour on the heavenly throne
and guides creation on its ordered course,
God, three and one. Amen.

For virgins

Jesus, the virgins' crown,
born of that Mother who alone gave birth to a child
and yet remained a virgin,
graciously receive these prayers.

You walk among the lilies,
surrounded by choirs of virgins—

a bridegroom beautiful with glory
and giving rewards to his brides.

Wherever you go virgins follow,
hastening after you with songs of praise
and making heaven resound
with melodious hymns.

We ask and beg you
to give us this grace in our life of thoughts—
not to have any knowledge of anything
that may wound or corrupt our virtue.

Strength, honour, praise and glory
be to God the Father,
together with the Son and the Paraclete,
for ever and ever. Amen.

For other holy women

By her intercession, forgive us, loving God,
the punishment that our sins deserve,
and so with hearts made pure
we may sing to you the song of our love.

Glory be to the Father and to the Son
and to the Spirit,
the co-equal power of Father and Son—
one God, for ever and ever. Amen.

Psalmody

Psalm 112

Ant. Lord, you have delivered to me five talents;
here I have made five talents more.

Praise, O servants of the Lord,
praise the name of the Lord!
May the name of the Lord be blessed
both now and for evermore!
From the rising of the sun to its setting
praised be the name of the Lord!

High above all nations is the Lord,
above the heavens his glory.
Who is like the Lord, our God,
who has risen on high to his throne
yet stoops from the heights to look down,
to look down upon heaven and earth?

From the dust he lifts up the lowly,
from the dungheap he raises the poor
to set him in the company of princes,
yes, with the princes of his people.
To the childless wife he gives a home
and gladdens her heart with children.

Ant. Lord, you have delivered to me five talents;
here I have made five talents more.

Psalm 145

Ant. Well done! You have been faithful over a little, I will
set you over much. Enter into the joy of your master.

My soul, give praise to the Lord;†
I will praise the Lord all my days,
make music to my God while I live.

Put no trust in princes,
in mortal men in whom there is no help.
Take their breath, they return to clay
and their plans that day come to nothing.

He is happy who is helped by Jacob's God,
whose hope is in the Lord his God,
who alone made heaven and earth,
the seas and all they contain.

It is he who keeps faith for ever,
who is just to those who are oppressed.
It is he who gives bread to the hungry,
the Lord, who sets prisoners free,

the Lord who gives sight to the blind,
who raises up those who are bowed down,

the Lord, who protects the stranger
and upholds the widow and orphan.

It is the Lord who loves the just
but thwarts the path of the wicked.
The Lord will reign for ever,
Zion's God, from age to age.

Ant. Well done! You have been faithful over a little, I will
set you over much. Enter into the joy of your master.

Song of thanks: election in Christ (Eph 1:3–10) *as for the* Common of
the Blessed Virgin Mary, p. 577, *with the following antiphon:*

Ant. Bless the Lord, you priests of God;
    sing a hymn to God, you servants of the Lord.

Word of God

For pastors   1 Pet 5:1–4

I exhort the elders among you, as a fellow elder and a witness
of the sufferings of Christ as well as a partaker in the glory
that is to be revealed. Tend the flock of God that is your
charge, not by constraint but willingly, not for shameful
gain but eagerly, not as domineering over those in your
charge but being examples to the flock. And when the chief
Shepherd is manifested you will obtain the unfading crown
of glory.

For doctors   Jas 3:17–18

The wisdom from above is first pure, then peaceable, gentle,
open to reason, full of mercy and good fruits, without
uncertainty or insincerity. And the harvest of righteousness
is sown in peace by those who make peace.

For virgins   1 Cor 7:32–34

I want you to be free from anxieties. The unmarried man is
anxious about the affairs of the Lord, how to please the
Lord; but the married man is anxious about worldly affairs,
how to please his wife, and his interests are divided. And
the unmarried woman or girl is anxious about the affairs of
the Lord, how to be holy in body and spirit; but the married

woman is anxious about worldly affairs, how to please her husband.

Common 1
Phil 3:7–8

Whatever gain I had, I counted as loss for the sake of Christ. Indeed I count everything as loss because of the surpassing worth of knowing Christ Jesus my Lord.

Common 2
Rom 8:28–30

We know that in everything God works for good with those who love him, who are called according to his purpose. For those whom he foreknew he also predestined to be conformed to the image of his Son, in order that he might be the first-born among many brethren. And those whom he predestined he also called; and those whom he called he also justified; and those whom he justified he also glorified.

Short Response
The just man will never waver:
he will be remembered for ever.
V. Happy the man who fears the Lord.
R. He will be remembered for ever.
V. Glory be to the Father, and to the Son, and to the Holy Spirit.
The just man will never waver:
he will be remembered for ever.

Song of the Virgin Mary
Ant. He who endures to the end will be saved.

Prayers

For holy men

Let us implore the Father, source of all sanctity, to guide us to holiness through the example and intercession of the saints; let us say to him:

R. You shall be holy, for I am holy.
Or: Lord, graciously hear us.

Holy Father, you want us to be your sons, and to be known as such;
—may your Church proclaim you throughout the world. (R.)

Holy Father, it is your will that we should lead lives worthy of you and fully pleasing to you;
—grant that we may bear fruit in every good work. (R.)

Holy Father, you have reconciled us to yourself in Christ;
—keep us in your name, that we may be one. (R.)

Holy Father, you have called us to a heavenly banquet;
—increase our charity through the Bread which has come down from heaven. (R.)

Holy Father, remit the debt of all sinners;
—receive the departed into the light of your glory. (R.)

For holy women

Let us beseech the Lord through the women saints, all in various ways types of the Church, and let us say:

R. Holy Church, Mother of the living!
Or: Lord, graciously hear us!
Or: Lord, remember your Church!

Through the merits of all virgins who have vowed their lives to Christ alone,
—give to your Church, O Lord, integral and persevering faith. (R.)

Through all the martrys in whom the gift of fortitude triumphed over bodily death,
—strengthen your Church, O Lord, in the hour of trial. (R.)

Through all the devoted wives who have grown in holiness in the married state,
—make the apostolate of the Church fruitful, O Lord. (R.)

Through all widows who have overcome their loneliness by prayer and hospitality.

—grant that the world may recognize in your Church a supernatural love. (*R.*)

Through all mothers who brought forth children not only to natural but also to supernatural life,

—receive your Church into heaven, Lord, with all her children. (*R.*)

Concluding prayer

For popes

Eternal Shepherd, look graciously on your flock, and through blessed N., your (martyr and) chief bishop, whom you appointed Pastor of the whole Church, keep it in your constant care. We make our prayer through our Lord.

For pastors

1.

Grant, we pray you, Almighty God, that the holy feast of blessed N., your bishop, may increase our devotion and promote our salvation. We make our prayer through our Lord.

2.

Graciously hear, we pray you, Lord, the prayers which we offer you on the feast of blessed N., your bishop. By the merits and entreaty of him who so worthily served you, absolve us from all our sins. We make our prayer through our Lord.

3.

O Lord, we ask that the festival of your holy martyrs and bishops N. and N. may bring us safety. May their worthy prayers win us favour. We make our prayer through our Lord.

For doctors

O God, you gave your people blessed N. to be a minister of eternal salvation. Grant, we pray you, that we may be worthy to have as a petitioner in heaven him (her) whom we have had as teacher of life on earth. We make our prayer through our Lord.

For a holy man

O Lord, hear the prayers which we offer you on the feast of blessed N., your faithful servant. May we who trust not in our own righteousness be helped by the prayers of him who served you well. We make our prayer through our Lord.

For a holy woman

O God our Redeemer, graciously hear us. While we rejoice in the feast of blessed N., may we learn to serve you with love. We make our prayer through our Lord.

OFFICE OF READINGS

Hymn

For pastors and holy men, *as at* Evening Prayer I, p. 609

For a virgin

Jesus, Son of the Virgin and your Mother's Creator,
carried in the Virgin's womb and born of the Virgin,
we sing of the feast of a blessed virgin.
Receive our prayer.

By her intercession, forgive us, loving God,
the punishment that our sins deserve,
and so with hearts made pure we may sing to you
the song of our love.

Glory be to the Father and to the Son
and to the Spirit,
the co-equal power of Father and Son—one God
for ever and ever. Amen.

For other holy women, *as at* Evening Prayer I, p. 610

Psalmody

Psalm 20

Ant. Lord, you have delivered to me five talents;
here I have made five talents more.

O Lord, your strength gives joy to the king;
how your saving help makes him glad!
You have granted him his heart's desire;
you have not refused the prayer of his lips.

You came to meet him with the blessings of success,
you have set on his head a crown of pure gold.
He asked you for life and this you have given,
days that will last from age to age.

Your saving help has given him glory.
You have laid upon him majesty and splendour,
you have granted your blessings to him for ever.
You have made him rejoice with the joy of your presence.

The king has put his trust in the Lord:
through the mercy of the Most High he shall stand firm.
His hand will seek and find all his foes,
his right hand find out those that hate him.

You will burn them like a blazing furnace
on the day when you appear.
And the Lord shall destroy them in his anger;
fire will swallow them up.

You will wipe out their race from the earth
and their children from the sons of men.
Though they plan evil against you,
though they plot, they shall not prevail.

For you will force them to retreat;
at them you will aim with your bow.
O Lord, arise in your strength;
we shall sing and praise your power.

Ant. Lord, you have delivered to me five talents;
here I have made five talents more.

Psalm 91

Ant. Well done! You have been faithful over a little, I will
set you over much. Enter into the joy of your master.

It is good to give thanks to the Lord
to make music to your name, O Most High,
to proclaim your love in the morning
and your truth in the watches of the night,
on the ten-stringed lyre and the lute
with the murmuring sound of the harp.

Your deeds, O Lord, have made me glad;
for the work of your hands I shout with joy.
O Lord, how great are your works!
How deep are your designs!
The foolish man cannot know this
and the fool cannot understand.

Though the wicked spring up like grass
and all who do evil thrive,
they are doomed to be eternally destroyed;
but you, Lord, are eternally on high.
See how your enemies perish;
all doers of evil are scattered.

To me you give the wild-ox's strength;
you anoint me with the purest oil.
My eyes looked in triumph on my foes;
my ears heard gladly of their fall.
The just will flourish like the palm-tree
and grow like a Lebanon cedar.

Planted in the house of the Lord
they will flourish in the courts of our God,
still bearing fruit when they are old,
still full of sap, still green,
to proclaim that the Lord is just.
in him, my rock, there is no wrong.

Ant. Well done! You have been faithful over a little,
I will set you over much. Enter into the joy of
your master.

V. The Lord guides the righteous man on straight paths.
R. He shows him the kingdom of God.

Readings

For pastors

Acts 6:1–6; 8:1, 4–8 (For deacons)

Acts 20:17–36	1 Tim 3:1–7; 4:12–16
2 Cor 4:1–18	1 Tim 5:17–22; 6:10–14
Col 1:21–2:3	Titus 1:7–11; 2:1–8
1 Thess 2:1–13, 19–20	1 Pet 5:1–11

Response

I became a minister of the Church * according to the divine office which was given to me for you, to make the word of God fully known.

V. I stood between the Lord and you, to declare to you the word of the Lord. * According.

For doctors

Wis 7:7–16, 22b–30	1 Cor 2:1–16
Sir 39:1–10	2 Tim 2:1–7, 15–26

Response

The Lord opened his mouth in the midst of the assembly, * and he filled him with the spirit of wisdom and understanding.

V. The Lord gave him gladness and a crown of rejoicing. * And he filled.

For virgins

1 Cor 7:25–35

Response

The King has desired the beauty which he himself has made: he is your God and your King. * He is your King and your husband.

V. You are wedded to your God and King, by whom you are endowed, adorned, redeemed and made holy. * He is your King.

For holy men and women

Eastertide

Rev 14:1–5; 19:5–9

Outside Eastertide

Prov 31:10–31 (For a holy woman)	1 Cor 13:1–13
	Eph 4:1–24
Wis 5:1–16	Eph 5:21–33
Wis 8:2–13	Phil 1:29–2:16
Sir 11:11–27	Phil 3:8b–4:1, 4–9
Rom 12:1–21	

Col 3:1–17
1 Pet 3:7–17 (For a holy
   man)

1 Pet 3:1–6, 8–17
   (For a holy woman)
1 John 4:7–21

Responses

For a holy man

1.

This is the love of God, that we keep his commandments.
* And his commandments are not burdensome.
V. There is nothing sweeter than to heed the commandments
of the Lord. * And his commandments.

2.

Gird up your minds, be sober. * As he who called you is
holy, be holy yourselves in all your conduct.
V. I am the Lord your God; be holy for I am holy. * As
he who called you.

For a holy woman

Charm is deceitful, and beauty is vain. * The woman who
fears the Lord is to be praised.
V. Give her of the fruit of her hands, and let her works
praise her in the gates. * The woman.

Prayer *as at* Evening Prayer, I, p. 615

MORNING PRAYER

Psalm 94

Refrain: Come, let us worship the Lord Jesus,
   the faithful witness.

For virgins: R. Come, let us worship the Lord, the King of
virgins.

Hymn

For pastors

Jesus, Redeemer of the world
and eternal crown of bishops,
show yourself today
even more gracious and kindly disposed to our prayers.

For on this day the loving Confessor of your holy name
first shone with heavenly glory;
and your devoted people today
are keeping his yearly feast.

He rightly disdained
the fleeting joys of this world
and so obtained an imperishable reward
among the angels in heaven.

Graciously grant us
to follow in his footsteps
and through his intercession
forgive us our sinful guilt.

O Christ, most loving King,
glory be to you and to the Father,
with the Spirit, the Paraclete,
now and for all ages. Amen.

For a holy man

Jesus, crown most glorious
and truth most sublime,
you gave an eternal reward
to your humble confessor.

He was renowned for his virtue and faith,
and steadfast in confessing you;
he lived his earthly life in fasting
and now shares in the feasts of heaven.

Therefore, we your suppliants
together ask you, most loving God,
to remit, as a favour to your saint,
the punishment that our sins deserve.

Unending glory be to the Father
and to the Father's only Son
and to the holy Paraclete,
always, for all ages. Amen.

For virgins *as at* Evening Prayer I, p. 609

Psalmody

Psalms as at the Dedication of a Church, Morning Prayer, p. 556,
with the following antiphons:

Antiphons

1. Lord, you have delivered to me five talents;
   here I have made five talents more.

2. Bless the Lord, you priests of God;
   sing a hymn to God, you servants of the Lord.

3. Well done! You have been faithful over a little, I will set
you over much. Enter into the joy of your Master.

Word of God

For pastors   **Heb 13:7–9**

Remember your leaders, those who spoke to you the word
of God; consider the outcome of their life, and imitate their
faith. Jesus Christ is the same yesterday and today and for
ever. Do not be led away by diverse and strange teachings.

For doctors   **Wis 7:13–14**

I learned without guile and I impart without grudging;
I do not hide her wealth,
for it is an unfailing treasure for men;
those who get it obtain friendship with God,
commended for the gifts that come from instruction.

For virgins   **S. of S. 8:7**

Many waters cannot quench love,
neither can floods drown it.
If a man offered for love
all the wealth of his house,
it would be utterly scorned.

623

Common   Rom 12:1–2

I appeal to you therefore, brethren, by the mercies of God, to present your bodies as a living sacrifice, holy and acceptable to God, which is your spiritual worship. Do not be conformed to this world but be transformed by the renewal of your mind, that you may prove what is the will of God, what is good and acceptable and perfect.

Short Response

The just man will never waver:
he will be remembered for ever.
V. Happy the man who fears the Lord.
R. He will be remembered for ever.
V. Glory be to the Father, and to the Son, and to the Holy Spirit.
The just man will never waver:
he will be remembered for ever.

Song of Zechariah

Ant. Whoever does the will of my Father in heaven
is my brother, and sister, and mother.

Prayers

For holy men

Let us pray to the all-holy God that we may serve him in holiness and justice all the days of our life in his presence; let us say to him:

R. Lord, you alone are holy.

You willed to endure all the trials we have to bear, yet without sinning;
—Lord Jesus, have mercy on us. (*R.*)

You have called us all to become perfect in love,
—Lord Jesus, make us holy. (*R.*)

You have commanded us to be the salt of the earth and the light of the world:
—let your light shine through us, Lord Jesus. (*R.*)

You chose to serve, not to be served:
—make our service of you and your members like your own in humility. (*R.*)

You are the radiant light of God's glory and the perfect image of his nature;
—Lord Jesus, grant that we may look upon your face in the glory of eternal life. (*R.*)

For holy women

Let us listen to our Saviour's word in imitation of all saintly women; let us praise him and say:

R. Come, Lord Jesus!

Lord Jesus, you forgave the sinner her many sins because she loved so much;
—forgive us our many sins. (*R.*)

Lord Jesus, devoted women ministered to you on your journeys;
—enable us to follow in your footsteps. (*R.*)

Jesus, Lord and Master, Mary listened to your word while Martha served;
—may we serve you in living faith and love. (*R.*)

Jesus, Lord and Bridegroom, as the wise virgins waited for your coming,
—make us constant in our vigil of hope until you come. (*R.*)

Concluding prayers *as at* Evening Prayer I, p. 615

MIDDAY PRAYER

If a Solemnity, the psalms are as for the Dedication of a Church, Midday Prayer, p. 560, *with the following antiphon:*

Ant. You are the salt of the earth; you are the light of the world.

If not a Solemnity, the antiphons and psalms are of the day, as in the psalter

Word of God

For pastors 1 Tim 4:6–7

If you put these instructions before the brethren, you will be a good minister of Christ Jesus, nourished on the words of the faith and of the good doctrine which you have followed. Have nothing to do with godless and silly myths. Train yourself in godliness.

For doctors, virgins, or common use 1 Cor 9:26–27

I do not run aimlessly, I do not box as one beating the air, but I pommel my body and subdue it, lest after preaching to others I myself should be disqualified.

V. He who loves his life loses it;

R. He who hates his life in this world will keep it for eternal life.

If a Solemnity which has no proper prayer, Prayer *as at* Evening Prayer I, p. 615. *Otherwise,* Prayer of the day.

EVENING PRAYER II
Hymn *as at* Evening Prayer I, p. 690

Psalmody
Psalm 109

Ant. Lord, you have delivered to me five talents; here I have made five talents more.

The Lord's revelation to my Master:†
'Sit on my right:
I will put your foes beneath your feet.'

The Lord will send from Zion your sceptre of power:
rule in the midst of all your foes.

A prince from the day of your birth on the holy mountains;
from the womb before the daybreak I begot you.

The Lord has sworn an oath he will not change,†
'You are a priest for ever,
a priest like Melchizedeck of old.'

The Master standing at your right hand
will shatter kings in the day of his great wrath . . .

He shall drink from the stream by the wayside
and therefore he shall lift up his head.

Ant. Lord, you have delivered to me five talents;
here I have made five talents more.

Psalm 111

Ant. Well done! You have been faithful over a little,
I will set you over much. Enter into the joy of your Master.

Happy the man who fears the Lord,
who takes delight in his commands.
His sons will be powerful on earth;
the children of the upright are blessed.

Riches and wealth are in his house;
his justice stands firm for ever.
He is a light in the darkness for the upright:
he is generous, merciful and just.

The good man takes pity and lends,
he conducts his affairs with honour.
The just man will never waver:
he will be remembered for ever.

He has no fear of evil news;
with a firm heart he trusts in the Lord.
With a steadfast heart he will not fear;
he will see the downfall of his foes.

Open-handed, he gives to the poor;†
his justice stands firm for ever.
His head will be raised in glory.

The wicked man sees and is angry,†
gnashes his teeth and pines away;
the desire of the wicked leads to doom.

Ant. Well done! You have been faithful over a little,
I will set you over much. Enter into the joy of your Master.

Song of Moses and the Lamb (Rev 15:3–4) *as for the* Dedication of a
Church, Evening Prayer II, p. 564, *with the following antiphon:*

Ant. Bless the Lord, you priests of God;
sing a hymn to God, you servants of the Lord.

All the rest as at Evening Prayer I, p. 612

Prayer for the Dead

OFFICE OF READINGS

Hymn

Remember those, O Lord,
Who in your peace have died,
Yet may not gain love's high reward
Till love is purified.

With you they faced death's night,
Sealed with your victory sign,
Soon may the splendour of your light
On them for ever shine.

Sweet is their pain, yet deep,
Till perfect love is born;
Their lone night-watch they gladly keep
Before your radiant morn.

Your love is their great joy;
Your will their one desire;
As finest gold without alloy
Refine them in love's fire.

For them we humbly pray;
Perfect them in your love.
O may we share eternal day
With them in heaven above.

Psalmody

Psalm 39

I

Ant. You formed me of clay and clothed me with flesh;
  called me back to life on the last day,
  my Lord and my Redeemer.

I waited, I waited for the Lord†
and he stooped down to me;
he heard my cry.

He drew me from the deadly pit,
from the miry clay.
He set my feet upon a rock
and made my footsteps firm.

He put a new song into my mouth,
praise of our God.
Many shall see and fear
and shall trust in the Lord.

Happy the man who has placed
his trust in the Lord
and has not gone over to the rebels
who follow false gods.

How many, O Lord my God, are the wonders and designs†
that you have worked for us;
you have no equal.
Should I proclaim and speak of them,
they are more than I can tell!

You do not ask for sacrifice and offerings,
but an open ear.
You do not ask for holocaust and victim.
Instead, here am I.

In the scroll of the book it stands written
that I should do your will.
My God, I delight in your law
in the depth of my heart.

Ant. You formed me of clay and clothed me with flesh;
called me back to life on the last day,
my Lord and my Redeemer.

II

Ant. O Lord, come to my rescue,
Lord, come to my aid.

Your justice I have proclaimed
in the great assembly.

My lips I have not sealed;
you know it, O Lord.

I have not hidden your justice in my heart
but declared your faithful help.
I have not hidden your love and your truth
from the great assembly.

O Lord, you will not withhold
your compassion from me.
Your merciful love and your truth
will always guard me.

For I am beset with evils
too many to be counted.
My sins have fallen upon me
and my sight fails me.
They are more than the hairs of my head
and my heart sinks.

O Lord, come to my rescue,
Lord, come to my aid . . .

O let there be rejoicing and gladness
for all who seek you.
Let them ever say: 'The Lord is great',
who love your saving help.

As for me, wretched and poor,
the Lord thinks of me.
You are my rescuer, my help,
O God, do not delay.

Ant. O Lord, come to my rescue,
    Lord, come to my aid.

Psalm 41

Ant. My soul is thirsting for God;
    when shall I see him face to face,
    the God of my life?

Like the deer that yearns
for running streams,

630

so my soul is yearning
for you, my God.

My soul is thirsting for God,
the God of my life;
when can I enter and see
the face of God?

My tears have become my bread,
by night, by day,
as I hear it said all the day long:
'Where is your God?'

These things will I remember
as I pour out my soul:
how I would lead the rejoicing crowd
into the house of God,
amid cries of gladness and thanksgiving,
the throng wild with joy.

Why are you cast down, my soul,
why groan within me?
Hope in God; I will praise him still,
my saviour and my God.

My soul is cast down within me
as I think of you,
from the country of Jordan and Mount Hermon,
from the Hill of Mizar.

Deep is calling on deep,
in the roar of waters:
your torrents and all your waves
swept over me.

By day the Lord will send
his loving kindness;
by night I will sing to him,
praise the God of my life.

I will say to God, my rock:
'Why have you forgotten me?

Why do I go mourning
oppressed by the foe?'

With cries that pierce me to the heart,
my enemies revile me,
saying to me all the day long:
'Where is your God?'

Why are you cast down, my soul,
why groan within me?
Hope in God; I will praise him still,
my saviour and my God.

Ant. My soul is thirsting for God;
when shall I see him face to face,
the God of my life?

V. Numberless, Lord, are your mercies;
R. With your decrees give me life.

Reading   1 Cor 15:12–28, 35–37

If Christ is preached as raised from the dead, how can some
of you say that there is no resurrection of the dead? But if
there is no resurrection of the dead, then Christ has not
been raised; if Christ has not been raised, then our preaching is in vain and your faith is in vain. We are even found
to be misrepresenting God, because we testified of God that
he raised Christ, whom he did not raise if it is true that the
dead are not raised. For if the dead are not raised, then
Christ has not been raised. If Christ has not been raised,
your faith is futile and you are still in your sins. Then those
also who have fallen asleep in Christ have perished. If for
this life only we have hoped in Christ, we are of all men most
to be pitied.

But in fact Christ has been raised from the dead, the first
fruits of those who have fallen asleep. For as by a man
came death, by a man has come also the resurrection of the
dead. For as in Adam all die, so also in Christ shall all be
made alive. But each in his own order: Christ the first fruits,

then at his coming those who belong to Christ. Then comes the end, when he delivers the kingdom to God the Father after destroying every rule and every authority and power. For he must reign until he has put all his enemies under his feet. The last enemy to be destroyed is death. 'For God has put all things in subjection under his feet.' But when it says, 'All things are put in subjection under him,' it is plain that he is excepted who put all things under him. When all things are subjected to him, then the Son himself will also be subjected to him who put all things under him, that God may be everything to every one.

But some one will ask, 'How are the dead raised? With what kind of body do they come?' You foolish man! What you sow does not come to life unless it dies. And what you sow is not the body which is to be, but a bare kernel, perhaps of wheat or of some other grain. But God gives it a body as he has chosen, and to each kind of seed its own body. For not all flesh is alike, but there is one kind for men, another for animals, another for birds, and another for fish. There are celestial bodies and there are terrestrial bodies; but the glory of the celestial is one, and the glory of the terrestrial is another.

There is one glory of the sun, and another glory of the moon, and another glory of the stars; for star differs from star in glory.

So it is with the resurrection of the dead. What is sown is perishable, what is raised is imperishable. It is sown in dishonour, it is raised in glory. It is sown in weakness, it is raised in power. It is sown a physical body, it is raised a spiritual body. If there is a physical body, there is also a spiritual body. Thus it is written, 'The first man Adam became a living being'; the last Adam became a life-giving spirit. But it is not the spiritual which is first but the physical and then the spiritual. The first man was from the earth, a man of dust; the second man is from heaven. As was the man of dust, so are those who are of the dust; and as is the man of heaven, so are those who are of heaven. Just as we have borne the image of the man of dust, we shall also bear the image of the man of heaven. I tell you this, brethren: flesh and blood cannot inherit the kingdom of God, nor does the perishable inherit the imperishable.

Lo! I tell you a mystery. We shall not all sleep, but we shall all be changed, in a moment, in the twinkling of an eye, at the last trumpet. For the trumpet will sound, and the dead will be raised imperishable, and we shall be changed. For this perishable nature must put on the imperishable, and this mortal nature must put on immortality. When the perishable puts on the imperishable, and the mortal puts on immortality, then shall come to pass the saying that is written:

'Death is swallowed up in victory.'

'O death, where is your victory?

O death, where is your sting?'

The sting of death is sin, and the power of sin is the law. But thanks be to God, who gives us the victory through our Lord Jesus Christ.

Response

He must reign until he has put all his enemies under his feet. The last enemy to be destroyed is death, * for he has put all things in subjection under his feet.

V. The sea gave up the dead in it, Death and Hades gave up the dead in them, and all were judged by what they had done. Then Death and Hades were thrown into the fire. * For he.

Prayer

Nov 2

O God, to whose bounty and love man owes his pardon and salvation, we beg of your mercy that the intercession of blessed Mary, ever-virgin, and of all your saints, may win for your servants who have gone from this world entrance into a fellowship of eternal bliss. We make our prayer through our Lord.

On the day of death or burial

O God, to whom it belongs to have mercy and to spare, we humbly entreat you for the soul of your servant (handmaid) N., whom you have summoned today from this world. Do not deliver him (her) into the hands of the enemy, nor forget him (her) for ever, but bid your holy angels receive him (her) and bear him (her) to our home in paradise. Since he (she) believed and hoped in you, may he (she) not undergo the pains of hell but possess eternal joys. We make our prayer through our Lord.

For a deceased priest

O Lord, grant that the soul of N., your priest, whom you honoured with sacred office during his earthly life, may find joy for ever in the glories of heaven. We make our prayer through our Lord.

For general use

O God, to whose bounty and love man owes his pardon and salvation, we beg of your mercy that through the intercession of the blessed, ever-virgin Mary and of all your saints, the souls of our brethren, kinsmen and benefactors who have departed from this life may be admitted into the fellowship of everlasting bliss. We make our prayer through our Lord.

MORNING PRAYER

Psalm 94

Refrain: Come let us worship our King,
    for whom all live.

Hymn *as at* Office of Readings, p. 628

Psalmody

Psalm 50

Ant. The bones you have crushed, Lord, will thrill.

PRAYER FOR THE DEAD MORNING

Have mercy on me, God, in your kindness.
In your compassion blot out my offence.
O wash me more and more from my guilt
and cleanse me from my sin.

My offences truly I know them;
my sin is always before me.
Against you, you alone, have I sinned;
what is evil in your sight I have done.

That you may be justified when you give sentence
and be without reproach when you judge,
O see, in guilt I was born,
a sinner was I conceived.

Indeed you love truth in the heart;
then in the secret of my heart teach me wisdom.
O purify me, then I shall be clean;
O wash me, I shall be whiter than snow.

Make me hear rejoicing and gladness,
that the bones you have crushed may thrill.
From my sins turn away your face
and blot out all my guilt.

A pure heart create for me, O God,
put a steadfast spirit within me.
Do not cast me away from your presence,
nor deprive me of your holy spirit.

Give me again the joy of your help;
with a spirit of fervour sustain me,
that I may teach transgressors your ways
and sinners may return to you.

O rescue me, God, my helper,
and my tongue shall ring out your goodness.
O Lord, open my lips
and my mouth shall declare your praise.

For in sacrifice you take no delight,
burnt offering from me you would refuse,

my sacrifice, a contrite spirit.
A humbled, contrite heart you will not spurn.

In your goodness, show favour to Zion:
rebuild the walls of Jerusalem.
Then you will be pleased with lawful sacrifice,†
burnt offerings wholly consumed,
then you will be offered young bulls on your altar.

Ant. The bones you have crushed, Lord, will thrill.

Is 38:10–14, 17–20　　　　　　　　**Song of Hezekiah**

Ant. Hold back my life, O Lord.
　from the pit of doom.

I said, 'So I must go away,
my life half spent,
assigned to the world below
for the rest of my years.'

I said, 'No more shall I see the Lord
in the land of the living,
no more shall I look upon men
within this world.

My home is pulled up and removed
like a shepherd's tent.
Like a weaver you have rolled up my life,
you cut it from the loom.

Between evening and morning you finish it.
I cry for help until dawn.
I suffer as though a lion
were breaking my bones.

I cry out in grief like a swallow,
I mourn like a dove.
My eyes look wearily to heaven.
Take care of me, Lord!' . . .

You have held back my life
from the pit of doom.

637

You have cast far from your sight
every one of my sins.

For the world below cannot thank you,
nor death give you praise.
Those who go down to the grave
cannot hope for your mercy.

The living, the living man thanks you
as I do this day;
the father shall tell his children
of your faithful mercy.

O Lord, come to our rescue
and we shall sing psalms
all the days of our life
in the house of the Lord.

Ant. Hold back my life, O Lord,
  from the pit of doom.

Psalm 145

Ant. I will praise my God all my days.

My soul, give praise to the Lord;†
I will praise the Lord all my days,
make music to my God while I live.

Put no trust in princes,
in mortal men in whom there is no help.
Take their breath, they return to clay
and their plans that day come to nothing.

He is happy who is helped by Jacob's God,
whose hope is in the Lord his God,
who alone made heaven and earth,
the seas and all they contain.

It is he who keeps faith for ever,
who is just to those who are oppressed.
It is he who gives bread to the hungry,
the Lord, who sets prisoners free,

the Lord who gives sight to the blind,
who raises up those who are bowed down,
the Lord, who protects the stranger
and upholds the widow and orphan.

It is the Lord who loves the just
but thwarts the path of the wicked.
The Lord will reign for ever,
Zion's God, from age to age.

Ant. I will praise my God all my days.

Word of God   1 Thess 4:14

Since we believe that Jesus died and rose again, even so,
through Jesus, God will bring with him those who have
fallen asleep.

Short Response

I will praise you, Lord,
you have rescued me.
V. You have changed my mourning into dancing.
R. You have rescued me.
V. Glory be to the Father, and to the Son, and to the Holy
Spirit.
I will praise you, Lord,
you have rescued me.

Song of Zechariah

Ant. I am the resurrection and the life; he who believes in
me, though he die, yet shall he live, and whoever lives and
believes in me shall never die.

Prayers

Let us pray to God, the omnipotent Father, who raised
Jesus Christ from the dead, and who will give life to our
mortal bodies also:

R. Lord, bring us to life in Christ.

Heavenly Father, we were buried with your Son by baptism into death and raised up with him in his resurrection;
—grant us so to walk in newness of life, that after our death, we may be with Christ for ever. (R.)

Grant us always to receive with so much reverence the Bread of angels, living Bread come down from heaven,
—that we may have eternal life and be raised up on the last day. (R.)

God of all joy, while we are in the body we walk by faith, but separated from you,
—in the hour of death may we be happy to leave our body, so that we may enjoy your presence for ever. (R.)

Lord, when your Son was in agony you sent an angel to comfort him;
—at the hour of our death, strengthen us with a peaceful confidence. (R.)

God of the living and the dead, who raised up Jesus from the tomb,
—give life to the dead, and unite us with them in glory. (R.)

Prayer *as at* Office of Readings, p. 365

MIDDAY PRAYER

Hymn *of the day, as in the psalter*

Psalmody

Psalm 69

Ant. Revive us now, God, our helper!

O God, make haste to my rescue,
Lord, come to my aid!
Let there be shame and confusion
on those who seek my life.

O let them turn back in confusion,
who delight in my harm,
let them retreat, covered with shame,
who jeer at my lot.

Let there be rejoicing and gladness
for all who seek you.
Let them say for ever: 'God is great,'
who love your saving help.

As for me, wretched and poor,
come to me, O God.
You are my rescuer, my help,
O Lord, do not delay.

Psalm 84

O Lord, you once favoured your land
and revived the fortunes of Jacob,
you forgave the guilt of your people
and covered all their sins.
You averted all your rage,
you calmed the heat of your anger.

Revive us now, God, our helper!
Put an end to your grievance against us.
Will you be angry with us for ever,
will your anger never cease?

Will you not restore again our life
that your people may rejoice in you?

Let us see, O Lord, your mercy
and give us you saving help.

I will hear what the Lord God has to say,
a voice that speaks of peace,
peace for his people and his friends
and those who turn to him in their hearts.
His help is near for those who fear him
and his glory will dwell in our land.

Mercy and faithfulness have met;
justice and peace have embraced.
Faithfulness shall spring from the earth
and justice look down from heaven.

The Lord will make us prosper
and our earth shall yield its fruit.
Justice shall march before him
and peace shall follow his steps.

Ant. Revive us now, God, our helper!

Word of God   Job 19:25,26

I know that my Redeemer lives, and at last he will stand
upon the earth; then from my flesh I shall see God.

V. If I should walk in the valley of darkness,
R. No evil would I fear, for you are there.

Prayer *as at* Office of Readings, p. 635

EVENING PRAYER

Hymn *as at* Office of Readings, p. 628

Psalmody

Psalm 120

Ant. The Lord will guard you from evil,
  he will guard your soul.

I lift up my eyes to the mountains:
from where shall come my help?
My help shall come from the Lord
who made heaven and earth.

May he never allow you to stumble!
Let him sleep not, your guard.
No, he sleeps not nor slumbers,
Israel's guard.

The Lord is your guard and your shade;
at your right side he stands.
By day the sun shall not smite you
nor the moon in the night.

The Lord will guard you from evil,
he will guard your soul.
The Lord will guard your going and coming
both now and for ever.

Ant. The Lord will guard you from evil,
  he will guard your soul.

Psalm 129

Ant. If you, O Lord, should mark our guilt,
  Lord, who would survive?

Out of the depths I cry to you, O Lord,
Lord, hear my voice!
O let your ears be attentive
to the voice of my pleading.

If you, O Lord, should mark our guilt,
Lord, who would survive?
But with you is found forgiveness:
for this we revere you.

My soul is waiting for the Lord,
I count on his word.
My soul is longing for the Lord
more than watchman for daybreak.
Let the watchman count on daybreak
and Israel on the Lord.

Because with the Lord there is mercy
and fulness of redemption,

Israel indeed he will redeem
from all its iniquity.

Ant. If you, O Lord, should mark our guilt,
Lord, who would survive?

Phil 2:6–11   **Song of Christ's exaltation**

Ant. As the Father raises the dead and gives them life,
so also the Son gives life to whom he will.

Though he was in the form of God,
Jesus did not count equality with God a thing to be grasped.

R. Jesus Christ is Lord
to the glory of God the Father!

He emptied himself,†
taking the form of a servant,
being born in the likeness of men. (*R.*)

And being found in human form,†
he humbled himself and became obedient unto death,
even death on a cross. (*R.*)

Therefore God has highly exalted him
and bestowed on him the name which is above every
name, (*R.*)

That at the name of Jesus every knee should bow,
in heaven and on earth and under the earth. (*R.*)

And every tongue confess that Jesus is Lord,
to the glory of God the Father. (*R.*)

Ant. As the Father raises the dead and gives them life,
so also the Son gives life to whom he will.

Word of God   **1 Cor 15:55–57**

O death, where is your victory?
O death, where is your sting?
The sting of death is sin, and the power of sin is the law.
But thanks be to God, who gives us the victory through our
Lord Jesus Christ.

Short Response

In you, O Lord, I take refuge.

Let me never be put to shame.

V. Let me be glad and rejoice in your love.

R. Let me never be put to shame.

V. Glory be to the Father, and to the Son, and to the Holy Spirit.

In you, O Lord, I take refuge.

Let me never be put to shame.

Song of the Virgin Mary

Ant. All that the Father gives me will come to me; and him who comes to me I will not cast out.

Prayers

Let us pray to Christ our Lord, trusting that he will conform our lowly body to his own glorious body; let us say to him:

R. Lord, you are our life and resurrection.

Christ, Son of the living God, who raised your friend Lazarus from the tomb,

—awake to the life of glory those whom you have redeemed with your precious blood. (*R.*)

Christ, Consoler of the afflicted, you were deeply moved by the death of Lazarus, of the youth of Naim, and the daughter of Jairus, and you lovingly turned the grief of the mourners into joy;

—console all who are mourning for their departed. (*R.*)

Christ, always living to intercede for us and for everyone,

—teach us always to offer the sacrifice of praise for the dead, so that they may be loosed from their sins. (*R.*)

Christ our Saviour, destroy in our mortal body the reign of sin through which we merit death;

—grant that, by the grace of God, we may attain eternal life in you. (*R.*)

Lord, we implore your pity for all who are enemies of your cross, and for those who have no hope.
—give them faith in the resurrection and the life of the world to come. (*R.*)

As ordained in your immemorial plan, this earthly dwelling place of ours will eventually fall into ruin;
—give us, in heaven, an eternal home not made by human hands. (*R.*)

Concluding prayer *as at* Office of Readings, p. 635
Night Prayer *of the day, as in the psalter*

Suggestions for Hymns for Singing*

This brief list contains hymns for the various hours of the day, readily available in existing hymnals, and suitable for singing. Other hymns may also be chosen.

Office of Readings

Before all creation the Word had been born (John 1:1–5, 9–14)	New Hymns 58
Christ be beside me (*St Patrick's Breastplate*)	New Hymns 36
From all that dwells below the skies	BBC 5; Songs of Praise 408
I believe in God the Father	New Hymns 8
O Lord, our God, arise	BBC 25
Teach me my God and King	English 485; Songs of Praise 652
Word of God come down on earth	New Hymns 10

Morning Prayer

Come, praise the Lord, the Almighty, the King of all nations (Psalm 116)	New Hymns 6
Forth in the peace of Christ we go	New Hymns 38
Morning has broken	Songs of Praise 30
Sing all creation, sing to God in gladness (Psalm 99)	New Hymns 5
This day God gives me (*St Patrick's Breastplate*)	New Hymns 7
To God in gladness sing (Psalm 94:1–7)	New Hymns 4

Midday Prayer

God is love, his the care	Songs of Praise 502; Praise the Lord 142
How full of kindness is the Lord (Psalm 114–5)	New Hymns 45
How deep the riches of our God (Rom 11:33–36)	New Hymns 52
I call, O Lord, on you (Psalm 140)	New Hymns 46

*Abbreviations:
  English: The English Hymnal (OUP)
  BBC: The BBC Hymnal (OUP)
  New Hymns: New Hymns for All Seasons, by James Quinn, S.J. (Geoffrey Chapman)

Love is long-suff'ring, love is kind (1 Cor 13:4–7)	New Hymns 53
Let all be one in mind and heart (Phil 2:5–11)	New Hymns 54
King of glory, king of peace	Songs of praise 553; Praise the Lord 145

Evening Prayer

As now the sun's declining rays	English 265; BBC 411
Creator of the earth and sky	Songs of Praise 44
Day is done, but Love unfailing	New Hymns 39
God, that madest earth and heaven	BBC 415; BBC 46; English 268
Now it is evening; time to cease from labour	BBC 418
Peace with the Father, peace with Christ his Son	New Hymns 15

Night Prayer

Glory to thee my God this night	BBC 414; Songs of Praise 45; English 267
Hail, gladdening light, of his pure glory poured	BBC 416
Hail our Queen and Mother blest (*Salve Regina*)	New Hymns 79
Joy fill your heart, O Queen most high (*Regina Caeli*)	New Hymns 72
Now with the fast-departing light	Praise the Lord 136

Saints

Translations of the Latin hymns of the Breviary for the Common and Proper of Saints, including hymns for Our Lady, will be found in *The English Hymnal*.

I saw the new city, Jerusalem (for *Dedication of Church*)	Biblical Hymns and Psalms
Joseph, wise ruler of God's earthly household	New Hymns 86
Mother of holy hope and of love everlasting	Biblical Hymns and Psalms

Index

Index of Psalms

Index of Canticles used in Psalmody

Index of Canticles used as Hymns